CONFEDERATE GEORGIA

www.ingramcontent.com/pod-product-compliance
Lightning Source LLC
Chambersburg PA
CBHW030129240426
43672CB00005B/77

CONFEDERATE GEORGIA

by

T. CONN BRYAN

THE UNIVERSITY OF GEORGIA PRESS

ATHENS

Paperback edition, 2009
© 1953 by the University of Georgia Press
Athens, Georgia 30602
www.ugapress.org
All rights reserved
Printed digitally in the United States of America

The Library of Congress has cataloged the hardcover edition of this book as follows:
Library of Congress Cataloging-in-Publication Data

Bryan, Thomas Conn.
Confederate Georgia.
x, 299 p. 25 cm.
An outgrowth of the author's thesis, Duke University.
Bibliography: p. 275–290.
1. Georgia—History—Civil War, 1861–1865. I. Title.
E559 .B89
973.7458   53-7145

Paperback ISBN-13: 978-0-8203-3499-8
ISBN-10: 0-8203-3499-5

Cover design based on original by Vincent Dieball and Frank Skinner

To my father and mother
SOLON H. BRYAN AND MARY CONN BRYAN

CONTENTS

	Preface	ix
I	SECESSION	1
II	PREPARATIONS FOR WAR	18
III	POLITICAL CONTROVERSIES AND MEASURES	34
IV	WARTIME FINANCE	48
V	MILITARY AND NAVAL OPERATIONS, 1861-1863	66
VI	RELATIONS WITH THE CONFEDERACY	80
VII	INDUSTRY AND TRANSPORTATION	101
VIII	PLANTER AND SLAVE	118
IX	DISLOYALTY AND DESERTION	137
X	THE SHERMAN INVASION	156
XI	WOMEN'S WARTIME ACTIVITIES	174
XII	SOCIAL LIFE AND DIVERSIONS	188
XIII	THE PRESS AND LITERARY PURSUITS	201
XIV	EDUCATION	216
XV	THE CHURCHES DURING THE WAR	230
	Notes	247
	Bibliography	275
	Index	291

PREFACE

Georgia was the heart of the cotton-growing ante-bellum South. During the years immediately preceding the War Between the States the outstanding prosperity of the lower South existed there, and the state was noted for her railroads and industries as well as for her agriculture. She led the South in textile manufacturing; her railroad mileage exceeded that of any other Southern State except Virginia, and her comparatively small public debt was being rapidly diminished. Georgia's geographic location and economic security gave her a position of leadership in the South.

The period from 1830 to 1860 was Georgia's "Golden Age," the era of her relatively greatest wealth and importance in the Union. The basis of the state's wealth was the plantation economy, which reached its highest development just prior to the war. Plantations and slaves signified not only a source of income but also a way of life. The War Between the States altered Georgia's fabric of society and revolutionized her basic political and economic institutions.

Many monographs have been written concerning particular events which occurred in Georgia during the War Between the States, but this study presents in one book the principal phases of Georgia's history during the war. The political, military, economic, and social factors of Confederate Georgia have been narrated and explained. Although the relation of Georgia to the Confederacy has been emphasized, my primary purpose has been to depict as completely as possible the scene within the state.

Confederate Georgia began as a dissertation suggested and directed by Dr. Robert H. Woody of Duke University. Whatever merit it has is due largely to his expert guidance and sympathetic criticisms. Helpful encouragement was given to me by other members of the faculty in the Department of History at Duke University, primarily Dr. W. T. Laprade and Dr. Charles S. Sydnor. From Dr. E. Merton Coulter of the University of Georgia and Dr.

PREFACE..

Wendell H. Stephenson of Tulane University I received valid suggestions.

I am grateful to the curators of manuscript collections and other personnel at the Library of Congress, the National Archives, Emory University, the University of Georgia, Duke University, and the University of North Carolina for furnishing me with much useful material. Especially do I thank the staff of the Georgia Department of Archives and History for their co-operation in making available to me many public archival materials and manuscripts. Newspaper files and many printed sources were made accessible to me by the librarians of the Georgia State Library, the Georgia State College for Women, the Columbia Theological Seminary in Decatur, Georgia, the Atlanta Historical Society, and the Washington Memorial Library of Macon, Georgia. Further assistance was given to me by the library staffs of the University of Kentucky and the University of Tennessee. To all others whose friendly interest made this book possible I express my sincere appreciation.

T. CONN BRYAN

CHAPTER I

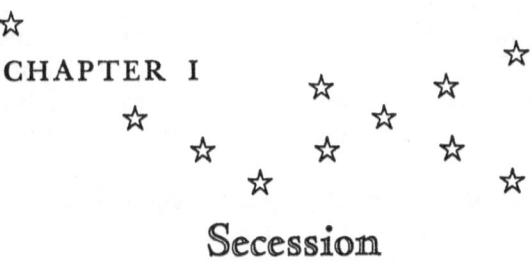

Secession

THE GEORGIA LEGISLATURE CONVENED for its annual session on November 6, 1860, the day of Lincoln's election, and on the following day Governor Joseph E. Brown delivered a special message to the general assembly. The result of the presidential election was as yet unknown, but many Georgians believed that the election of Lincoln was a foregone conclusion. The Governor's message laid before the legislature an invitation of South Carolina to a convention of Southern states "to concert measures for united action." Governor Brown opposed South Carolina's proposal, but in doing so he did "not wish to be understood as expressing a willingness to acquiesce in the repeated aggressions of the non-slave-holding states."[1]

Justifying secession upon the concept of the Union as a business partnership, Governor Brown said that whether the will of the people of the South should be ascertained by a general convention of the Southern states, or whether each state should decide for herself, was an unsettled question, but that for himself, he had "no doubt of the right of each state to decide and act for herself." He recommended in the event of the election of the Republicans that a state convention be summoned; and for the purpose of defense and to prepare for an emergency, he asked for an appropriation of a million dollars as a military fund.

The Governor further suggested to the legislature that laws be passed giving him the authority to seize the property in Georgia of any citizen of the offending Northern states. He urged also that laws be enacted that would drive Northern manufactured articles from the markets of Georgia; and he declared that, if necessary, "all . . . laws of this State which protect the lives, liberties, and property of the citizens of other states while in this State" should be repealed.[2]

The effect of Governor Brown's message, reaching the public along with the news of Lincoln's election, was astonishing. Public meetings were held throughout the state, and resolutions poured in upon the legislature. A majority of these memorials consisted of references to "Southern rights" and condemnations of "Republican fanaticism." A few of the memorials, however, were deprecatory of secession and urged the prudent co-operation of all the Southern states, and in many counties large anti-secession groups existed. Even Robert Toombs at first advised delay "to test Republican willingness to do the South justice."[3]

The excitement in Milledgeville, the capital, was bewildering. Nearly all of the leaders who had favored John C. Breckinridge for President were there, demanding immediate secession. When the legislature first assembled after the Governor's message, the members were wavering and without a plan. Herschel V. Johnson, the preceding governor, who was in Milledgeville at the time, says in his *Autobiography* that if the legislature had been left to itself, it would have inclined to a conservative course, but many distinguished men urged the legislature to take Georgia out of the Union.[4] Thomas R. R. Cobb influenced the general assembly with his secession oratory; and Robert Toombs, "the Mirabeau of the Revolution," shouted for secession. Edmund Ruffin of Virginia, Robert Barnwell Rhett of South Carolina, and Judge W. L. Harris of Mississippi, who were given seats in the legislature as official delegates from their respective states, urged Georgia to act.[5] Howell Cobb on December 6th issued a pamphlet in which he warned the people of Georgia of the dangers of delay, and then resigned his office of Secretary of the Treasury to return to Georgia and advocate the state's leaving the Union.[6]

Georgia had three prominent statesmen, however, who, while admitting the theoretical "right" of a state to secede, opposed immediate secession. These men were Alexander H. Stephens, Benjamin H. Hill, and Herschel V. Johnson. Amid the clamor for secession, Stephens on November 14th begged the legislature not to stampede the state out of the Union. He favored exhausting "all that patriotism demanded before taking the last step" of secession and urged that a convention be held to reaffirm the Georgia platform,[7] with an additional plank in it that the Northern states would repeal their obnoxious laws as the condition of Georgia's remaining in the Union.[8] Hill also urged Georgia not to secede and stated his belief that all of the South's grievances could be

..SECESSION

remedied within the Union. Believing that the election of Lincoln was not a sufficient cause to justify secession, Johnson urged both an appeal to the non-slave-holding states and a consultation with other Southern states in place of independent secession.

Events leading Georgia toward secession then occurred quickly. Acting according to the recommendations of Governor Brown, the legislature on November 16th appropriated $1,000,000 for military purposes. Won over by the secessionists, the legislature on the following day rejected the plan of an all-Southern convention and by a unanimous vote issued a call for a state convention. Four days later Governor Brown signed a bill which provided that the people on January 2nd would be given the opportunity of voting for delegates who should, two weeks later, assemble in Milledgeville as a sovereign convention to consider all grievances affecting the rights of the state and to determine the future course Georgia would take. On the same day he issued a proclamation calling for the convention. The Governor on December 7th in an open letter advocated immediate secession, whereupon the legislature, in response to his earlier recommendations, created the office of adjutant and inspector general, incorporated volunteer companies, and authorized the Governor to accept ten thousand troops.[9] On the following day he warned that "the present aspect of our political affairs makes it the duty of the legislative authority of the State to provide . . . for direct and speedy communication with Europe."[10] In another speech to the legislature, Governor Brown stated that immediate secession before Lincoln's inauguration might lead to Northern concessions and reunion, and that disunion would very probably not result in war.

The attitude of Georgians concerning the national issues during the weeks following the election of Lincoln is reflected, to some extent, in the state's newspaper editorials. The Carrollton *Advocate,* predicting that South Carolina would secede, praised the determination of the Palmetto state.[11] The Milledgeville *Federal Union* asserted that "the best thing we could do would be to quietly secede, . . . and if the General Government attempts to coerce us (which I have no idea it will) then fight. . . ."[12] The more conservative LaGrange *Reporter* said that it did not condemn the South for resenting the wrongs heaped upon her by the North, but that it did condemn "that imprudence which would wildly precipitate us out of the Union without making the last effort to maintain our rights and honor in it."[13] Another paper advocated

CONFEDERATE GEORGIA..

"immediate secession from a Union which has only proved itself a burden and expense to us."[14] Urging Georgia to secede, the Rome *Semi-Weekly True Flag* saw no reason why the Union should be saved, for to do so would be like saving "a vessel whose timbers are so *rotten* it cannot hold itself together."[15] An Augusta paper declared that "we must have equality . . . in the Union, or we shall, however reluctantly, be forced . . . to conquer peace and independence."[16]

In the midst of the campaign for the election of delegates to attend the convention which was scheduled to meet in Milledgeville on January 16th, South Carolina seceded. The action of South Carolina produced excitement throughout Georgia and aided the secession movement. In Atlanta cannons were fired, and there were a balloon ascension and a torchlight procession. Similar festivities occurred elsewhere in Georgia as news was received of the secession of Mississippi, Florida, and Alabama, on January 9th, 10th, and 11th, respectively. Exulting because of the secession of Alabama, the Savannah *Daily Morning News* predicted that Georgia would be the next state to leave the Union, and exclaimed, "The Rubicon is passed—a new nation is born!"[17] Toombs on December 24th sent his well-known telegram from Washington urging Georgia to secede.

The co-operationists, however, deplored the precipitate action of the seceding states and desired that should the Georgia convention pass an ordinance of secession, it be submitted to the people.[18] Herschel V. Johnson, speaking against secession in his home county, Jefferson, said that the South's duty was to seek for justice in the Union, but that if all efforts failed, the safety of Georgia required co-operation with the other Southern states in seceding rather than acting as a separate state. Benjamin H. Hill wrote to Johnson that he had received letters from various portions of the state approving the plan of seeking a settlement of the slavery disputes without resorting to secession.[19] Other men tried to prevent disunion. Garnett Andrews, a judge of the Northern Circuit of Georgia, did his best to hold Georgia in the Union, but his daughter said that "he might as well have tried to tie up the northwest wind in the corner of a pocket handkerchief."[20]

In the election of delegates to attend the Milledgeville convention, each county which had two members in the state legislature elected three delegates, while counties which had only one member in the legislature, elected two delegates each. A majority of the delegates favored secession, but the voting indicated that much Union sentiment still remained within the state. In electing the delegates, there were 50,243 members of the electorate who voted for the immediate action candidates and 37,123 who voted against such delegates, leaving a majority of only 13,120 votes favoring disunion.[21]

Several factors brought about victory for the secessionists in the election of the delegates and their subsequent success in the Georgia convention. Since November, 1860, many members of the planter and commercial classes had joined the ranks of the secessionists. Failure to secure compromise was a strong force for immediate action, and many planters felt that there was danger of losing their slaves and thus becoming impoverished. Another explanation for the increase in the number of Georgians who supported secession is the probability that many of those who voted for disunion delegates expected an ultimate reunion of the Federal government under conditions guaranteeing the security of Southern institutions. To these men, secession was expected to be only temporary, for as soon as more favorable terms were secured, union would be re-established. Thomas R. R. Cobb used this argument, and Stephens after the war declared that the idea motivated a large majority of those persons who supported disunion.

Many former Douglas supporters, moreover, joined the secessionists rather than to be suspected of holding free soil principles. The change to support of immediate secession on the part of a Democratic paper is indicated in the following editorial: "We supported Douglas and . . . Johnson from a sense of . . . party obligation . . . never endorsed the territorial views of Douglas, or doubted the right of secession. . . . Why should not the Southern rights men of 1850 and the Douglas men of 1860 rally now to this movement, which looks to independence out of the Union?"[22]

The plan of a confederacy, proposed by South Carolina, caused many co-operationists to move into the secession ranks, for they feared the danger of a disintegration of the South. The failure of Congress to sanction guarantees to protect Southern institutions also converted many co-operationists who had previously favored delay. Other factors gave an advantage to the immediate secessionists. In the matter of leadership they were in a stronger position than the co-operationists. The Governor of the state, two of the three members of the Georgia Supreme Court, the Federal

Circuit judge, the former Secretary of the Treasury, both Georgia senators, and six of the eight representatives in Congress favored immediate secession. Four of the five former governors of Georgia alive in 1860 favored secession.[23]

In newspaper propaganda the secessionists also had an advantage. Although in 1850 the Constitutional Union papers had a larger circulation than the "Southern rights" publications, by 1860 the total circulation of the Democratic papers, most of which favored secession, was about twenty thousand copies in excess of the opposition press.

When the news reached Georgia in late December, 1860, that the Federal garrison at Fort Moultrie, near Charleston, South Carolina, had removed to nearby Fort Sumter, Governor Brown decided to seize the chief fortification on the Georgia coast, Fort Pulaski, at the mouth of the Savannah River, before the Federal authorities had time to strengthen it. He realized that in the event of war Fort Pulaski would be a military necessity to the state. Proceeding to Savannah, Governor Brown on January 2, 1861, gave secret orders to the First Regiment of Georgia Volunteers, under Colonel Alexander R. Lawton, to seize the fort, which was to be held until the state convention should decide whether Georgia would separate from the Union. The seizure was made on January 3rd without any casualties, and the fort was rapidly put in order to protect the river in case of invasion. Savannah approved of the Governor's action, and the state convention which met soon afterward in Milledgeville passed a resolution in favor of what he had done.[24]

In response to Governor Brown's call for a convention, 297 delegates assembled at the capital on January 16th. As in 1850, Georgia to some extent held the key to the secession situation, for, although four states already had seceded, her action would decidedly influence the other states of the South which had not withdrawn from the Union. The delegates consisted of Georgia's ablest and most representative men. Included within its membership was nearly every important public man in the state and the leaders of all parties and shades of political opinion. George W. Crawford, a delegate from Richmond County and a former governor of Georgia, was elected permanent president of the convention; and Albert R. Lamar, of Muscogee County, a journalist of repute, was chosen secretary.

Other leaders in the convention were Toombs, the two Stephens

..SECESSION

brothers, Alexander and Linton, ex-Governor Herschel V. Johnson, Eugenius A. Nisbet, Benjamin H. Hill, and Thomas R. R. Cobb. Not all of the delegates were professional politicians, for among those present was Dr. Joseph P. Logan, an eminent physician. In addition to the regularly elected delegates, Governor Brown, Howell Cobb, and the judges of the State Supreme and Superior Courts were given seats on the floor. Two unexpected workers for secession were Judge Nisbet and Thomas R. R. Cobb. The former had always been a very conservative man, and the latter prior to 1860 had never taken any part in political life, but both men now became unwearied champions of secession. Robert Barnwell Rhett was present from South Carolina and William L. Yancey from Alabama, and these and other commissioners brought pressure to bear in order to cause Georgia to throw her great weight into the movement for separation.[25] The historian Avery says that conservative men were powerless in the heated temper of the era. A visitor to Milledgeville while the convention was in session, Martha Low Fort, later wrote in her *Memoirs* that "the air seemed filled with the gravity of the hour, the old capitol trembled under the burning eloquence of these great statesmen, it was a battle of giants."[26]

Realizing the gravity of the occasion, the convention on the first day of its session passed a resolution excluding all persons who were not members of the convention from its sessions, suppressing all noisy proceedings, and opening the session with prayer. The rules adopted forbade the members from interrupting anyone who was speaking and required that votes must be taken by roll call. With the exception of Alexander H. Stephens' address, the speeches were not recorded; but Stephens in later years referred to an excellent address delivered by Thomas R. R. Cobb.[27]

James L. Orr, a commissioner from South Carolina, addressed the convention after it assembled. He urged the acceptance of Alabama's invitation to a convention at Montgomery, and recommended the Constitution of the United States as a basis for the formation of a provisional government. A commissioner from Alabama, John G. Shorter, also urged that Georgia join the proposed Confederacy.

Judge Nisbet on January 18th introduced two resolutions, the first one declaring that Georgia had a right to secede and should secede, and the second authorizing the appointment of a committee to report an ordinance to that effect. Herschel V. Johnson, acting in concert with Alexander H. Stephens, then offered a substitute resolution. His motion recited Georgia's attachment to the Union and the peril that threatened the South from a hostile majority, and stated that while Georgia could not abide permanently in the Union without ample constitutional guarantee, she was not disposed to withdraw hastily. Johnson proposed also that the Southern and border states send delegates to a congress to be held in Atlanta on February 16th to consider the situation, and that after every possible means of friendly adjustment in the Union had been exhausted, Georgia would help form a Southern confederacy.[28]

A long discussion of the Nisbet and Johnson resolutions ensued, with Nisbet, Toombs, Thomas R. R. Cobb, Augustus Reese, and Francis S. Bartow championing the cause of secession, and Johnson, Stephens, Hill, and Alexander Means favoring a further attempt at a friendly settlement of the difficulties. The keynote of the secessionists was, as condensed by Cobb, "We can make better terms out of the Union than in it!" The vote on the resolutions would serve as a preliminary test of secession sentiment; but a direct vote on the Johnson resolution was prevented by a demand for the previous question, and the resolution offered by Nisbet was adopted by a vote of 166 to 130. A committee of seventeen was then appointed to draw up a secession ordinance.[29]

After the vote on the Nisbet resolution had been taken, a communication from Governor Edwin D. Morgan of New York to Governor Brown was presented to the convention. It contained resolutions passed by the New York legislature which denounced as treason the action of South Carolina in firing upon the *Star of the West*, and tendered men and money to the President of the United States to be used in upholding the authority of the Federal government. Toombs promptly had the convention adopt a resolution endorsing Governor Brown's action in seizing Fort Pulaski, and the legislature ordered that a copy of the resolution be forwarded to Governor Morgan. The incident served to stimulate the secession sentiment in the convention.[30]

On January 19th, Nisbet, as chairman of the Committee of Seventeen, offered the Ordinance of Secession. Immediately upon the submission of the ordinance, Benjamin H. Hill renewed the motion that the convention adopt, in lieu of the proposed measure, the substitute resolution offered the preceding day by Johnson. Hill's object was to get a test vote, for it was still a

..SECESSION

matter of uncertainty how the majority stood. The vote on Hill's motion was 164 nays to 133 yeas, showing by inference a majority of thirty-one in favor of the ordinance for immediate secession. Immediately afterwards, the vote on the passage of the ordinance was taken, and the ordinance was adopted by a vote of 208 to 89.[31] Among those voting for secession were forty-four co-operationists, including Hill, who had changed sides after the test votes had already determined the eventual outcome.[32] Johnson and Hill had fought energetically for co-operation, but the tide against them was too strong. After the ordinance was adopted, an amendment was offered that the ordinance not go into effect until March 3, 1861, but this effort at delay was also defeated by an overwhelming vote.

The large number of delegates who opposed secession was disturbing to the secessionists, who were anxious to give the impression that the action of the convention was endorsed by all the members. A resolution was passed, therefore, that all members of the convention, even those who voted against the ordinance, sign it as a pledge that they would defend the state regardless of approval or disapproval. This was done, but the attitude of the eighty-nine delegates who voted against the ordinance was clearly expressed by six of them who formally drafted the following resolution:

We, the undersigned delegates . . . , while we . . . protest against the action of the majority in adopting an Ordinance for the immediate . . . secession of this State, and would have preferred the policy of cooperation with our Southern sister States, yet, as good citizens, we yield to the will of a majority . . . , and we hereby pledge "our lives, our fortunes, and our sacred honor" to the defense of Georgia, if necessary, against hostile invasion. . . .[33]

After the ordinance had been adopted, William Martin, a delegate from north Georgia, offered a resolution to submit the ordinance to the people, the question on the ballot to read "secession or no secession," but this resolution was crushed by an avalanche of votes. Toombs was authorized to prepare an address to the people of Georgia to accompany and justify the secession ordinance, and ten thousand copies of his address were printed for distribution.[34]

An analysis of the vote of the eighty-nine delegates who opposed immediate secession even after the two test votes had indicated that their efforts would be futile reveals more than forty votes against the ordinance from among the hill counties of north Georgia. In the pine barrens of south Georgia objection was apparent, and most of the delegates from the "old cotton lands" in central Georgia favored co-operation. In the rich coastal lands, where Negroes composed an extremely large portion of the population, the secession sentiment was very pronounced, and a majority of the delegates from the newer cotton lands voted for secession. Among the towns and cities of Georgia the desire for secession was overwhelming. There was a general, though by no means universal, tendency in favor of secession among delegates from the counties where slaves were numerous, and an opposite, but no more universal, tendency from the sections in which the whites were in a majority. Phillips in his *Georgia and State Rights* attributes importance to the personal influence of Governor Brown, Toombs, Stephens, Johnson, Hill, the Cobb brothers, and other leaders in causing their respective sections to vote either for secession or for co-operation; but Irons in "The Secession Movement in Georgia" contends that in most cases Georgia's statesmen were simply giving expression to local sentiments already formed by social and economic factors. Governor Brown doubtless did have considerable influence in determining the attitude of the non-slave-holding Georgians; and he sought to frighten them into secession by declaring that if the slaves should be freed, the United States government would be forced to raise more than two billion dollars by taxation with which to pay for them, and that the former slaveholders would receive the money and with it buy up all the land and make tenants of the small farmers.

The action of the Secession Convention was acclaimed by general jubilation and celebration. There were bonfires, barbecues, and mass meetings to proclaim the advent of better days. Milledgeville was literally alive with joyous excitement. Cannons were fired and the flag of independence was waved from the capitol amid the blazing of skyrockets, music, and other demonstrations. In Savannah a salute of one hundred guns was fired by the Chatham Artillery, and in Athens a similar salute was fired by the Troup Artillery. Newnan was brilliantly illuminated, and the "Newnan Guards" were out in full uniform and kept up a continuous firing until late at night.

The Milledgeville *Federal Union* rejoiced that Georgia was "a free and independent Republic," while its rival, the Milledgeville *Southern Recorder,* which previously had opposed secession, an-

..SECESSION

nounced that it would no longer resist the movement. The latter paper said that had "the North manifested a kindly feeling toward the South, . . . there would have been no rupture of commercial or political ties. . . ."[35] The *Southern Field and Fireside* of Augusta declared that the action of the five states which had seceded "affords the strongest assurance of the efficiency of republican government. . . ."[36] The Carrollton *Advocate* asserted that "the Delegates, in voting for . . . secession, did just what we would have had them do."[37] The Sandersville *Central Georgian* remarked that "Outside of the Southern Confederacy . . . there is great ignorance of the secession movement. Instead of looking upon it as an . . . irresistible . . . march of the enlightened millions of the slave States, . . . some regard it as a slight disaffection of a few citizens or communities. . . ."[38]

Thousands of Georgians, however, looked to the future with great apprehension. Amid the rejoicing and bonfires that illuminated Milledgeville, Benjamin H. Hill retired into his rooms, and "grieved for the Union he had loved and labored so earnestly to maintain."[39] "I never felt so sad before," recorded Herschel V. Johnson, in his *Autobiography*. "The clustering glories of the past thronged my memory, but they were darkened by the gathering gloom of the lowering future."[40] The Augusta *Daily Chronicle and Sentinel* deplored the decision of the convention, but pledged its loyalty to the new republic. In her *War-Time Journal*, Eliza Frances Andrews noted that her father, Judge Garnett Andrews, was greatly agitated when he learned that Georgia had seceded. She said that "while the people of the village were celebrating the event," he remained at home, and "Every now and then, when the noise of the shouting and ringing of bells would penetrate the closed doors and windows, he would . . . exclaim: 'Poor fools! They may ring their bells now, but they will wring their hands — yes, and their hearts, too — before they are done with it.' "[41]

The task of providing the machinery of government for the "independent" state of Georgia occupied the greater part of the ten remaining days of the first session of the convention. All ties with the Federal government were severed. The convention voted to continue, until changed, all Federal laws except those which the convention specified. The foreign slave trade was made punishable by imprisonment for a period of from five to twenty years. Provisions were made for trade and commerce, and all citizens connected with the customs under the United States government were to retain the same position and pay. The revenue collection and navigation laws of the United States were as far as possible temporarily adopted, and all taxes collected would go into the state treasury. Georgia, moreover, was to take jurisdiction over all places within the state formerly held by the United States, but was to provide just compensation for all such property taken. The convention adjourned on January 29th to meet again at Savannah on March 7th.[42]

Public opinion in Georgia was favorable to Governor Brown in a controversy which he had with the state of New York during the time of Georgia's withdrawal from the Union. A shipment of guns, purchased by a Georgia firm and by the state of Georgia, was seized by the New York police on January 22nd in New York harbor and placed in a state arsenal. When the New York governor refused to release the arms, Governor Brown ordered all vessels in Savannah harbor belonging to New York citizens to be seized and sold, and the proceeds used to indemnify the owners of the arms. A few days before the date advertised for the sale, the arms were released and Governor Brown rescinded his order.[43]

With characteristic promptness, Governor Brown on January 23rd seized the Federal arsenal at Augusta, which was commanded by Captain Arnold Elzey with a force of eighty soldiers. The Governor went to Augusta and ordered Captain Elzey to surrender his post to the state authorities. Eight hundred troops assembled for the purpose of seizing the arsenal. Captain Elzey, whose force was too weak to defend the place, agreed to surrender, and Governor Brown gave him a receipt for the material in the arsenal so that a fair settlement later might be made.[44]

The six states which had seceded — South Carolina, Mississippi, Florida, Alabama, Georgia, and Louisiana — sent delegates to a convention at Montgomery, Alabama, on February 4th to form a provisional government. Georgia's delegation, which had been elected by the Milledgeville convention, consisted of Robert Toombs and Howell Cobb, representing the state at large, and eight district delegates: Francis S. Bartow, Martin J. Crawford, Eugenius A. Nisbet, Benjamin H. Hill, Augustus R. Wright, Thomas R. R. Cobb, Augustus H. Kenan, and Alexander H. Stephens. By a unanimous vote of the delegates attending the convention, the Constitution of the Confederate States of America was adopted. Toombs and Thomas R. R. Cobb served on one of the committees to prepare the Constitution, and Toombs, Stephens, and Howell Cobb supported the provision for the Cabinet to have seats in the Confederate Congress.[45]

Although Howell Cobb had been elected president of the convention, this fact did not prevent his being considered for the presidency of the Confederacy. A majority of the Georgia delegation, however, preferred Toombs and only a minority favored Cobb. Stephens proposed the nomination of Toombs for the office, and Toombs was surprised when members of the Georgia delegation told him that the delegates from four of the six states had decided to elect Jefferson Davis. The Georgia delegation thereupon did not present a candidate for the presidency, but proposed Stephens for the vice-presidency; and on February 9th Davis and Stephens were unanimously elected by the Provisional Confederate Congress. Toombs reluctantly accepted the position of Secretary of State, for he preferred the Treasury post.

The Confederate Constitution was not submitted to the people of Georgia for ratification, but the Georgia convention, which resumed its sessions at Savannah on March 7th, ratified it on March 16th. Georgia thus became a state in the Confederate States of America, after existing as an independent *de facto* republic for approximately two months. The following statement from a Georgia newspaper probably is representative of Georgians' opinions of the Confederate Constitution: "The Constitution of the Confederate States has, we believe, given very general satisfaction .... It is in substance what the people of the South in most respects have always interpreted the Constitution of the United States to be."[46]

A committee headed by Thomas R. R. Cobb had been appointed by the Milledgeville convention with instructions to revise the existing state constitution in conformity with changed conditions. This committee submitted its report to the Savannah convention on March 23rd. The new document resembled the Constitution of 1798 in many essential features. Both the old and the new constitutions provided for a bicameral legislature, but the new document called for forty-four state senators instead of forty-seven and for annual meetings of the legislature instead of the previous biennial meetings. The chief executive continued to be the governor, elected for a term of two years; but instead of having been a citizen of the United States for twelve years prior to his election, the new constitution required that the governor must have been a citizen within the Confederacy for twelve years.

CONFEDERATE GEORGIA..

The judiciary department continued to consist of a supreme court, superior and inferior courts, and various minor courts. The new constitution could be amended only by a convention of the people called for that purpose, whereas the old constitution had been amended by a two-thirds vote of each branch of the legislature.

Like the old constitution, the new one prohibited the importation of Negroes from foreign countries; and while the legislature might forbid their importation from other states, it could not prevent immigrants from bringing their slaves with them. Both constitutions stipulated that slaves could not be emancipated by the legislature without the consent of their owners.[47]

The new constitution was ratified by the people of Georgia on the first Tuesday in July, 1861. Comparatively little interest was manifested in the ratification and the voting was comparatively light, because of the fact that no major issue was involved and the people were already absorbed in the war. A total of 11,499 votes were cast for the constitution and 10,704 against it, a majority of only 795 favoring its adoption.[48] As the new constitution was made by the secessionists, the opposition vote may have been cast largely by the opponents of secession. The Savannah *Daily Morning News* said that "Those who were induced to believe the Constitution was a fraud, were at the polls to defeat it, while the majority of our citizens, believing the opposition would be small, did not take the trouble to vote."[49] Another factor which may have caused the large opposition vote was that the new constitution failed to state definitely what was meant by "representative population," whereas the Constitution of 1798 had defined representative population as "all free white persons and three-fifths of all persons of color."

During the weeks immediately following secession, Georgians were full of enthusiasm and feverish excitement. Except among a small minority, there was unbounded confidence in the future, and the masses exaggerated the ease with which the South could defeat the North in case of war. When Jefferson Davis passed through Georgia on his way to Montgomery to be inaugurated as President of the Confederacy, his trip was a continuous ovation.

The inauguration of Abraham Lincoln as President of the United States naturally was not looked upon with enthusiasm by Georgians. Several weeks prior to the inauguration, one of Georgia's leading newspapers stated that "Gen. Scott is about to inaugurate a Military Despotism at Washington. . . . He has ordered troops . . . to protect Abe Lincoln at his inauguration. . . . Have we not fallen upon evil times when it requires an army . . . to protect the American President?"[50]

The declaration by Lincoln in his inaugural that the Union must be preserved and the laws enforced in the seceded states caused pronounced condemnations in Georgia. The Sandersville *Central Georgian* stated that "Whenever Mr. Lincoln attempts to carry out the policy shadowed forth in his inaugural, he will find that Southern men are not to be ruled by Northern bayonets. . . ."[51] Soon after the inauguration, Howell Cobb addressed a letter to ex-President James Buchanan, in which he wrote:

As you know, I have never doubted the result of Lincoln's election. My opinion was and is that it would and ought to dissolve the Union. Whilst with the good and true men of the north we could have happily . . . lived as brethren, there is between us and the northern abolitionists an intense mutual hatred which was irreconcilable. Separation was a necessity which could not be avoided and reunion an impossibility which will never be realized.[52]

In the meantime, although the hope still persisted that secession would not mean war, preparations were being made for the defense of the state. The Milledgeville convention, as a provisional measure of public safety, had authorized the Governor to raise and equip two regiments, to purchase vessels for the defense of Georgia's coast, and to commission into the army and navy of Georgia, officers who should resign their appointments in the United States army and navy and tender their services to the state. The first Georgia company was tendered to the Confederate service on March 5th, and in connection with this event, the flag of the Confederacy was first raised in Georgia. The Savannah convention on March 20th and 23rd adopted ordinances transferring to the Confederate government all military operations in Georgia, the arms and munitions acquired from the seizure of Federal forts and arsenals, all vessels and steamers, and the use and occupancy of the forts, arsenals, navy yards, custom houses, and other public sites within the state. The ships were placed under the command of Commodore Josiah Tattnall, and all of the land and naval forces of the state were put under the command of Henry R. Jackson, whom the Governor had appointed brigadier general, and who held the command until the transfer of the forces to the Confederate government.[53]

The policies pursued by Lincoln during the first few weeks of his administration were neither understood nor appreciated by many Georgians. Commenting upon the actions of the Federal government, one Georgia newspaper stated:

> The conduct of the Lincoln Administration is a mystery and a riddle to every one, both friend and foe. They profess to be desirous of avoiding civil war, and yet talk as coolly of collecting the revenue in the seceded States as if they believed there would be no resistance to such a measure. They have promised . . . to withdraw the troops from Fort Sumter, but they still remain there. . . . What are we to think of this shuffling policy between peace and war? It shows clearly that Mr. Lincoln and his party have the inclination . . . to ruin the Southern States by war if they would; but as they have not got the power to carry their wishes into effect, they seem disposed to do us all the injury they can by keeping up the appearance of war.[54]

Another paper remarked that "great preparations are being made by Lincoln to carry on war in some quarter. Lincoln seems to have been goaded to desperation by . . . his Northern friends, and is determined to do something. If he wants war, he will doubtless have it."[55]

Until the actual beginning of military operations, many Georgians, probably a majority, believed that there would be no war. Toombs, in fact, was reported to have said that he would drink all of the blood shed in a war for Southern independence. "We, in the South, honestly believed we could engineer a peaceable separation," a writer of Georgia history has recorded.[56] When General Beauregard on April 12th, however, bombarded Fort Sumter, and Lincoln called for volunteers, Georgians became convinced of the futility of further efforts to preserve peace.

An extra edition of the Macon *Daily Telegraph* announced the action of the Federal government: "In a word, the North . . . is bent upon fighting out the quarrel to the death — determined that the South shall feel the weight of as heavy a blow as she can inflict. Such is the response to the first gun from the South in defence of our right to govern ourselves. . . ."[57] The Milledgeville *Southern Recorder* maintained that Lincoln's administration had "acted with duplicity toward the Confederate States, and that bloodshed could have been honorably avoided, had his mind or his will been capacious enough to perform the duties of his position."[58] In a series of effective editorials, the Milledgeville *Federal Union* condemned Lincoln's actions and placed the entire responsibility for the war upon the abolitionists. The editor regretted

..SECESSION

that "many of our former friends at the North appear . . . mortified" that the South had started the war. "How can they say we commenced the war?" he inquired. "When the robber points a pistol at the head of a traveller and says, your money or your life, if the traveller knocks him down, is he the aggressor?"[59]

CHAPTER II

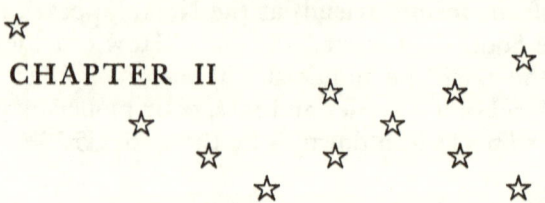

Preparations for War

"LINCOLN CALLS ON THE NIGGER STEALING States of the North for seventy-five thousand troops to invade our soil. Let them come — they will find our June and July suns quite as fatal to their souls as our balls and bayonets," an editorial in the Milledgeville *Federal Union* announced.[1] Determined not to rely too strongly upon the warm Southern sun to defeat the Yankees, Georgians began military preparations in earnest. The first problem was to secure soldiers and to organize them into troops. Prior to the beginning of hostilities, recruiting stations had been established at strategic points throughout Georgia, and military officers had been enlisting men into the service of the Confederacy, but volunteering became a mania after April 18th when Governor Brown issued a call for volunteers. Students left college, clerks resigned their positions, merchants closed their stores, and farmers left their crops in order to volunteer. A nineteen-year-old Stewart County youth walked thirty-six miles to join a company. Believing that the sword was mightier than the pen, the editor of the Sandersville *Central Georgian* left with his corps for Pensacola. Captain Richard Hughs, aged seventy-two years, who had fought in the War of 1812 and for many years had been the tax collector of Clarke County, left with the Athens Guards for Virginia. In Augusta Colonel A. F. Rudler, recently returned from captivity in Honduras, recruited a company of eighty men.[2] Newspapers and churches were used to inflame the war spirit, and "stump" speakers made the flamboyant declaration that one "Reb" could whip ten "Yanks."

Scores of organized companies promptly tendered their services to the Governor. Newton County, which had been a Union stronghold, organized five companies within a few days, and the city of Macon quickly furnished five hundred men. The war spirit was equally as strong in other counties and cities. Local military units,

..PREPARATIONS FOR WAR

such as the "Baldwin Blues" and "University Guards," paraded through the streets of various communities, and many merchants closed their stores early in the afternoons in order that their clerks might drill with their companies. Many of the companies had bizarre names, such as the "Mountain Tigers," "Cherokee Lincoln Killers," and "Salacoa Silver Grays." Men of property and influence seemed especially eager to enlist. Unable to resist the war impulse, Howell Cobb accepted the tender of a regiment in June, 1861, and was followed quickly by Thomas R. R. Cobb and Robert Toombs, each of whom became a brigadier-general.

Peterson Thweatt, the Comptroller-General of Georgia, expressed to Vice-President Stephens the feeling of enthusiasm which prevailed in the state during the first months of the war:

The War spirit is pretty high in Georgia at this time. Captains and others are coming every day offering their services. There are about fifty companies now who have complied with all requisitions, and *waiting for orders* to be *sent any where,* and they *beg* and *plead* to be put in first, &c.

Last Friday the "Baldwin Blues" left for Richmond, and the scene at parting with families and friends was very affecting. Our preacher, Mr. Flynn, is full of the war spirit. He leaves in the morning for Richmond to join the Baldwin Blues as Chaplain and Soldier.[3]

Another friend of Stephens, Richard Malcolm Johnston, wrote to the Vice-President that "It is a sad sight to see our young men go away to war, and to hear the lamentations of mothers, wives and sisters. I have seen three companies go away already. . . ."[4] Johnston wrote Linton Stephens that the Georgia volunteers "will be hard to conquer. If we are conquered it will be after the bloodiest war that modern times have seen."[5]

During the first months of the war, Vice-President Stephens received numerous letters from Georgians asking his aid in securing authority from the Secretary of War to organize companies and regiments for service. James A. Nisbet who lived in Lookout Valley, wrote Stephens that his son Cooper "tenders a very massive Company of men to our Service. They are hardy, and athletic. . . . I ask your influence for prompt orders to him with the War Department. He will carry old *Rifles* and Bowie Knives and his men will know how to use them."[6] Nisbet said that the men were "accustomed to the maul and the axe . . . and by their habits of life particularly well suited for Scouts and sharp shooters."[7] Captain Isaac W. Avery of Varnells Station told Stephens that he had "offered for service to the Secretary for three years, or for the war, a fine cavalry corps of seventy (70) hardy Georgia mountain boys. Over two thirds have fine horses...." He requested Stephens to use his influence in getting the corps armed, equipped, and accepted.[8]

Stephens was also deluged with requests from men who solicited his help in securing positions in the military or civil departments of the Confederacy. A prominent citizen of Milledgeville, A. H. Kenan, asked Stephens to see that his nephew was appointed to a lieutenancy in a Georgia regiment. Stephen Elliott, Jr., son of the distinguished Episcopal bishop of Savannah, notified Stephens that he had "long wished to follow the army as a profession," and inquired if the Vice-President could procure for him a commission. A citizen of Cedartown wrote: "Our information here is that President Davis will take the field in person.... I desire to enter the Military Service and would be delighted with an appointment on his Staff."[9] An Atlanta man told Stephens that he was willing to enter the Federal camp as a spy. "I have been raised in Philadelphia and Delaware state, am known in both states and have several friends in Washington and am confident of going there with but little risk," he declared.[10]

Numerous other Georgians wrote Stephens that they were eager to serve the cause. A man in Warrenton said that he "was too old to serve as a soldier, but if nurses were needed at the hospital in Va., I would like to serve the Confederacy in that capacity."[11] Physicians who desired commissions as army doctors and surgeons, lawyers who wished to be appointed to political positions in Richmond, and men who were eager to obtain employment as quartermasters, tax collectors, assayers, cotton agents, industrial engineers, deputies, post office clerks, and purchasers of army provisions were among the scores of office seekers who urged Stephens to lend them his assistance.

Governor Brown was likewise the recipient of many requests for civil and military appointments. "Allow me to recommend my friend James B. Stafford . . . ," a Barnesville man wrote to the Governor. "Mr. Stafford wants to do any service in his power for the States."[12] "Mr. William G. Brown of this place wishes to get the appointment as Commissary [sic] for some of the Regiments in this state," a man in Sandersville told Brown.[13] A physician in Terrell County urged the Governor to appoint him "as Surgeon . . . on our Coast or such other point as you may think best to send . . . me."[14]

..PREPARATIONS FOR WAR

Other Georgians in seeking positions solicited the aid of Howell Cobb. "I have applied to Hon. Jefferson Davis for an appointment in the Southern army and I wish you would . . . use your influence for me," a man in Augusta requested of Cobb.[15] Another Georgian asked Cobb's aid in securing the office of "purser in the Navy" for a friend. An Albany man told Cobb that he would "be very glad to have the position of aide-de-camp to the Commander-in-Chief."[16] "I have not received my commission from the P. O. Dept. I have written to Richmond but have received no answer yet. Please stir them up," was the request made to Cobb by a citizen of Athens.[17] Another man wrote Cobb that "If you will see the Secretary of War, Mr. Walker, and relieve myself and Henry Allan from the [Banks County] Guards we will . . . make up a company to join your regiment."[18]

Numerous Georgians applied to other Confederate leaders for positions for themselves or their friends. For example, Martin J. Crawford of Columbus informed Acting Secretary of War Benjamin that "Mr. Zannington . . . would be pleased to fill some place in the War Office at Richmond."[19]

Among the companies of volunteers organized during the early months of the war were those drawn from various nationality groups. While on a visit to Savannah in the spring of 1861, an English traveller, William Howard Russell, said that there was "a considerable population of Irish and Germans in Savannah, who to a man are in favor of the Confederacy, and will fight to support it."[20] The first company which may be designated as foreign was a German artillery company, known as the German Volunteers, which constituted one of the companies of the First Volunteer Regiment of Georgia. Numbering more than sixty men, the German Volunteers were mustered into service at Savannah in August, 1861, and later were engaged in the defense of Fort Pulaski. A second unit of Germans, an infantry company, was organized in Atlanta, and a third German company was an infantry organization from Savannah. At least four Irish units were organized: the Irish Volunteers, a company from Augusta; two companies calling themselves the Irish Jasper Greens, from Savannah; and the Jackson Guards, Company B, all of whom were said to be Irish.[21]

The Confederate government in July, 1861, requested that Governor Brown provide two camps for military instructions where men might be drilled and disciplined. These camps were to be under the control of the Confederate War Department, and President Davis planned to organize the companies into battalions or regiments, himself appointing field officers and staff. Three such camps were established early in 1862: Camp McDonald, near Marietta; Camp Stephens, at Griffin; and Camp Davis, thirty miles from Savannah.

By May 4, 1861, Governor Brown had organized six regiments and two battalions. Three days later the Milledgeville *Southern Recorder* announced that 263 volunteer Georgia companies were "ready for the field — a force of not less than 18,000 vigorous men." In a letter to Vice-President Stephens, written on June 25th, Brown said that "The regiment to Rendezvous on Monday will be the 10th and besides this we have two Battalions in service equivalent to a Regt and the enlist Rgt. making 12. These have all been fully armed and accoutred and equipped *by the State*."[22] By July Georgia had sent off fourteen thousand soldiers in addition to the regulars, and on October 1, 1861, approximately twenty-five thousand Georgia troops were in the Confederate service. The Comptroller-General's report in November stated that Georgia had furnished to the Confederacy forty regiments and three battalions, of which twenty-one regiments and the battalions had been armed, accoutred, and equipped by the state. The battalions and thirty regiments had gone into service in response to the Governor's request; the remaining ten regiments had been raised independently of state authority. Of these, twenty-three regiments, two legions,[23] and three battalions were enlisted for the war. The remainder were twelve-months men. A year later the state had seventy-five thousand men in the field.[24]

As thousands of men rushed to volunteer, the state was confronted with the problem of equipping them with weapons, for many companies were organized before the state was ready to issue arms. Georgia was unprepared for war, and the Governor was pressed even to annoyance with demands for arms and equipment. He told Secretary of War L. P. Walker that he was doing all in his power to get heavy guns and munitions to Fort Pulaski, but that the guns were being mounted very slowly, "for . . . we lack scientific officers who understand the business."[25] Because they were improperly armed, many Georgia companies were not accepted immediately by the Confederate government. An Augusta man in May, 1861, wrote Stephens that the "Letcher Guards" were ready to be tendered to the Confederacy, but that the com-

..PREPARATIONS FOR WAR

pany was improperly armed. A month later Secretary Walker notified Stephens that the War Department could not accept the "Wilkie Rangers" because they were unarmed. "Brown has placed me so that I can get only 300 carbines from him," Thomas R. R. Cobb told Howell Cobb in June, 1861. "My idea *now* is for a legion, 300 horse, 600 foot and 100 Artillery. I hope to get arms for all from Brown."[26] The mayor of Augusta notified the Governor that the Augusta "Home Guards" had scarcely enough arms to defend the city.[27]

Governor Brown had supplemented the state's supply of arms by taking some guns from the Augusta arsenal before turning it over to the Confederacy, and at the beginning of the war the state had a total of 22,714 arms captured from the Federal forts and arsenals in Georgia. These arms were given to the Confederate government, and within a short time a serious shortage of arms and equipment existed in Georgia. The supply of arms from the iron works in Richmond was uncertain, and inasmuch as arms were contraband, they could not definitely be depended upon from Europe. Consequently, the state continued assembling all available arms within Georgia and commenced making her own weapons, not only by means of private endeavor but also as a state project. "This is no time to be idle!" warned the Milledgeville *Federal Union*. "Many things are to be supplied for which we were formerly dependent on the North. . . ."[28]

Heeding such admonitions, men and women began inventing and manufacturing arms. A man in Savannah invented a breech-loading rifle-cannon, and five women in the same city made four thousand cartridges within five days. Two brothers in Columbus invented a sword bayonet which could be attached to double-barreled guns, and in Athens a man invented a "six-shooter revolver rifle," said to be an improvement upon the Colt revolver. A Marietta inventor wrote Alexander H. Stephens that he had worked out an "idea of wadds with the Minie principle so attached that Canister Solid and red hot shot might be thrown with twice or thrice the range as heretofore." He claimed that his discovery would destroy windage, and by "Securing the . . . revolving motion of the ball in its passage through the air . . . attain much greater range and precision. . . ."[29]

A Macon company in the spring of 1861 was manufacturing percussion caps for muskets which were believed to "compare favorably with those of the best Northern manufactories." The

Macon *Daily Telegraph* said that "the Messrs. Nobles, of Rome, are now busily engaged in manufacturing Rifled Cannon, from Round Mountain ore, for the Confederate States. The Confederate Government have contracted with them for 27 field pieces, and a 'Minnie Rifle Bullet Press' which will turn out 70 balls per minute."[30] Adjutant-General Wayne in March, 1862, sent the following notice to Captain R. M. Cuyler, of the Confederate Ordnance Office in Savannah:

Hodgkins and Co of Macon, and Moses and Hall of Columbus are the only reliable men with machinery I know of who have undertaken to manufacture rifles or muskets.

Johnston & Co of Macon, DeWitt & Co of Columbus, make Swords. Watkins of Monroe is now making rifles for me, by hand, . . . to be in all respects like the Harper's Ferry Rifle.[31]

The Confederate Arsenal at Augusta reported in September, 1861, that within three months preparations would be completed for "the complete manufacture of everything connected with artillery but the guns themselves."[32] By 1862 the Confederate Arsenal in Atlanta was busily engaged in purchasing and repairing guns, cannons, swords, and other munitions. Ordnance supplies were brought to the Atlanta Arsenal from Nashville, Tennessee, and an ordnance officer at the arsenal explained that workmen were "busy putting in operation our Manufactories, at present however we are entirely out of everything most needed." Friction primers were being manufactured at the arsenal, but the work was delayed "owing to the interruptions to our workmen occasioned by rough accomodations [*sic*],"[33] the officer disclosed. In the spring of 1862 the Atlanta Arsenal contracted with a firm in Coweta County for the manufacture of one thousand canteens made of maple wood and requested a Columbus factory to submit terms for the manufacture of cavalry sabers. A few months later the commander of the Atlanta Arsenal remarked that he had "been working hard for near Six weeks to get off about 4 Batteries — repairing them &c" and that he was "compelled to *omit* many of the Smaller items required for an outfit proper."[34]

Determined to retain all of the military supplies in the state, Governor Brown in May, 1861, announced that any officer who permitted his men to carry arms out of Georgia would be punished; and he even tried unsuccessfully to get the Confederacy to allow cargoes of arms which landed at Georgia ports while en route to the Confederate government to remain in the state.[35]

..PREPARATIONS FOR WAR

His policy of forbidding arms to leave the state caused the Atlanta *Daily Intelligencer* to say that "Virginia sends fifty thousand armed men in the field, and spends her dollars freely in the cause; other States follow her example, but Georgia's Governor cannot afford to arm her gallant sons, though gladly they rush to meet the foe."[36] The Governor on June 25th announced that all the arms in the State Arsenal were exhausted, and in July he appealed to the citizens to lend their rifles to the state, promising to return or pay for them at the end of the war.

Although by July, 1861, the state was able to arm and equip seventeen thousand troops, the supply of arms that remained was sufficient for only two or three additional regiments. Forty thousand country rifles and twenty-five thousand double-barreled shot guns served as a temporary source of supply. Gunsmiths and manufacturers of small arms were requested by Henry C. Wayne, Georgia's Adjutant- and Inspector-General, to meet with him and Brown in Atlanta on August 29th for the purpose of "repairing . . . the old muskets, rifles and guns in the State, and establishing uniform prices therefor; and, also, to compare notes as to our resources for the manufacture of small arms. . . ."[37] The Governor on September 18th notified General Albert Sidney Johnston that Georgia had no arms to furnish for the defense of the state's northern border. "Georgia has now to look to the shot guns and rifles in the hands of her people for coast defense and to guns which her gunsmiths are slowly developing," Brown stated.[38] Two days later he announced that all persons engaged as operatives in the manufacture of arms, powder, machinery, and cotton or woolen products were exempt from militia duty until further notice. He recommended to the legislature on November 16th that a state foundry be established or that a guarantee be offered by the state to any private company willing to manufacture arms. The state offered a bonus of $10,000 to anyone who would erect a cannon factory, and in December, 1861, the legislature appropriated $350,000 for the manufacture and purchase of arms. In 1862 the penitentiary in Milledgeville was converted into a state armory and soon was producing 125 rifles a month.[39]

The problem of arms continued acute, however, and when Major Lachlan H. McIntosh, of the Milledgeville Ordnance Bureau, shipped a quantity of ammunition to the Savannah Arsenal, he notified General Henry R. Jackson that "this was all that could be done at present."[40] Adjutant-General Wayne informed Jackson that there were no facilities in Milledgeville for casting shot and shell and that all field pieces should be made in Savannah. "My impression is that we have not more than 100 first-class Guns in the Brigade," General F. W. Capers, commanding the second brigade of state troops at Savannah, wrote to General Jackson in January, 1862.[41] A few weeks later Governor Brown sent nineteen "sharps carbines" from Milledgeville to Savannah, with a notice that they were positively the last that he could secure. Writing disconsolately to Alexander H. Stephens, Peterson Thweatt said, "If we only had arms, I should not fear anything, but I fear we have not the arms to arm what volunteers we now have."[42] In March Major McIntosh told General Jackson: "We are driving ahead as fast as possible in the repair of guns, and I hope in a few days, to have one hundred and fifty good . . . muskets . . . , beside a number of shot guns."[43]

The difficulty in securing arms to protect Savannah caused Governor Brown to propose raising a battalion armed with pikes. He asked mechanics to lay aside other work and manufacture the pikes, known as "Joe Brown Pikes." Between March and September of 1862 more than twelve thousand of these pikes were received at the State Arsenal and were distributed to Augusta, Savannah, and to the Confederate Quartermaster in Chattanooga.[44]

In addition to the problem of arms, the state had to solve the question of securing clothing for the troops. Prior to the establishment of the Confederacy's Quartermaster Department, volunteers were required to furnish their own clothing.[45] At first some of the companies were resplendently clothed, but soon many volunteers were unable to purchase uniforms. In order to assist the soldiers, many counties levied extra taxes, issued bonds, or solicited subscriptions for the purpose of purchasing clothing and other supplies for the volunteers. A group of Bibb County citizens met in June, 1861, and adopted measures to have the volunteers from Macon and Bibb County supplied with clothes and other articles necessary for their comfort. The Macon City Council was requested to levy an extra tax or loan, if necessary, in order to obtain the supplies, and was requested to confer with the Inferior Court concerning the problem. The Cass County Inferior Court instructed the county treasurer to issue $20,000 worth of bonds and "negotiate said bonds at par"; and the Clay County Inferior Court ordered "that so much of the funds now in the hands of

..PREPARATIONS FOR WAR

the County Treasurer, as may be necessary for the purposes" of supporting volunteers and needy families "be . . . appropriated to the support of the . . . aforesaid."[46] In LaGrange the county's Inferior Court and City Council authorized the LaGrange and West Point Light Guards to draw on the city and county treasury "for whatever . . . money they may need . . . for their personal . . . conveniences while in service."[47]

In all parts of the state women were busy knitting socks and making uniforms. On hundreds of plantations and in numerous villages and towns the spinning-wheel was humming and looms were rattling. Many planters manufactured shoes with wooden soles, and an Augusta paper said that they were "better than the brogans we once got from the North." "After the commencement of the war I did all I could to feed and clothe the soldiers," said Joseph Addison Turner of Eatonton. ". . . I organized a hat factory on my plantation . . . , and never turned off any one, especially a soldier, hatless."[48] Factories in north Georgia were running day and night, turning out "butternut jeans" from which women throughout the state were fashioning uniforms. At Savannah seventy-five women were busily engaged in the industry of Lathrop & Company, at work on a variety of garments, mostly for soldiers' wear. Soldiers' water-proof oilcloth overcoats, capes, and leggings were being manufactured by a firm in Washington, Georgia. A shoe factory was established in Marietta, and the Masonic Hall in Augusta was converted into a clothing establishment where the soldiers could secure garments. Substitutes for wool were used by many people, some of them making cloth of cow hair so that the wool could be used by the soldiers. The penitentiary at Milledgeville contained a card factory, which, despite the difficulty of securing wire, turned out hundreds of cotton and woolen cards. Two Milledgeville citizens made woolen cloth for the army from raw wool, and the Milledgeville *Federal Union* said that "Messrs. Cyphers and Kidd of this city are in the daily receipt of orders for their oil cloth garments for the soldiers. They have made a large number of coats, blankets, etc., which, . . . have given entire satisfaction."[49] The proprietors of an Augusta dry goods company announced that they were going to Europe in order to purchase blankets and heavy clothing for the army.

Governor Brown was active in securing clothing and blankets for the troops. In a message "to the people of Georgia," delivered on September 4, 1861, he said that he wished to purchase thirty thousand pairs of shoes and enough woolen cloth to make thirty thousand suits of clothing, "together with all the good blankets that can be found in the market." He requested all manufacturers of shoes or woolen cloth, and persons having blankets for sale to inform him of the supply which they could furnish.[50] The problem of obtaining army clothing was temporarily relieved in the fall of 1861 when the Confederacy established quartermaster's depots under military supervision. Garment shops were established by the Confederacy in Augusta, Atlanta, and Columbus, and shoe shops were built in Atlanta and Columbus. Georgia companies campaigning in Virginia sent men to Georgia to collect clothing and blankets for the soldiers. Adjutant-General Wayne instructed Colonel Ira R. Foster, Quartermaster-General at Milledgeville, to "proceed personally, or by duly accredited agents, into all parts of the State, and buy 25,000 suits of clothes and 25,000 pairs of shoes for destitute Ga. troops in the Confederate service."[51]

As the Federal blockade became effective, however, the necessity for domestic industries increased. The legislature in December, 1862, appropriated $1,500,000 to procure clothing and blankets for the soldiers and authorized Brown to seize factories and manufactured articles in order to secure clothing. The Governor executed the order but authorized Colonel Foster to reimburse those selling goods with ten per cent of the cost, and those manufacturing them with twenty-five per cent. Foster appealed to the people's "love of liberty" to meet the demands that might be made on them.[52]

Correspondence between Georgians and their relatives who were in the army indicates how critical was the clothing problem during the first months of the war. Writing to her uncle, a soldier in Virginia, a Georgia girl said:

... Uncle Moses ... has been trying to get you a pair of boots ..., but the stock ... has been so picked over that he can find none to suit — he will therefore have you a pair put up to order, ... we sent you the other day by Lieut Hawkins your over-coat-pants, and one pair of woolen socks we have nother pair now ready — but we learn that Lieut Powell will take nothing but letters, so we must wait another opportunity to send them.[53]

From his son, who likewise was in Virginia, Irby H. Scott of Eatonton received the following information: "I was very proud of my vest, which Mrs. Boswell presented me with. . . . I know from experience that it is warm.

..PREPARATIONS FOR WAR

"... do not send me any more clothes untill [sic] I write for them, except what I wrote you for, a hot pair of pants and those boots you had made for me."⁵⁴ Writing from Fort Pulaski early in 1862, Lieutenant Theodorick W. Montfort, of Macon County, informed his wife of his clothing predicament:

> I am getting quite short of pants only three pr & I have worn them regularly & daily for the last six months — they are my black cloth gray & red domestic pants. they all have rents in them I am darning & patching them the best I can, yet I shall have none soon with all the care I can bestow on them — I have plenty of all other kinds of apparel — if I get no assistance from home untill [sic] compelled to surrender from hunger, I think the Yankees will turn us loose for pity sake as we shall be entirely naked.⁵⁵

Another Confederate officer, writing from Camp Bartow to his father, acknowledged "the receipt of the blankets sent to Ed for me and also for James. . . ." Two months later he expressed appreciation for "the pair of gloves from Miss Elisa B . . . and the box of Shoes. . . ."⁵⁶

In caring for the sick and wounded, as in the matter of clothing for the troops, Georgia at first was compelled to look after her own soldiers. Relief work was actively conducted by the Georgia Relief and Hospital Association, a great state-wide organization which collected funds and provided medical attention and transportation facilities for the sick and wounded. The association cooperated with the Georgia Hospital Association which was established at Richmond in September, 1861, and through a central committee in Augusta received contributions of money, clothing, and medicine to relieve the sick and disabled soldiers from Georgia.⁵⁷ The first general agent of the association was a Baptist minister and professor at Mercer University, the Reverend Henry H. Tucker. Writing to Governor Brown in September, 1861, the Reverend Tucker explained the work which the association was accomplishing:

> I have just seen your Excellency's proclamation stating that you have placed at the disposal of our Association in Richmond, funds sufficient for the establishment of a Hospital there for the benefit of our sick and wounded.
> Your Excellency may not be aware that the "Georgia Hospital and Relief Association" whose chief Bureau is at Augusta, who inaugurated this hospital movement, and with whom the gentlemen in Richmond

are cooperating, is now sending agents to every county in the State to solicit funds and other supplies in aid of this enterprise. I am one of the agents and in five days have collected subscriptions to the amount of Nine Thousand Dollars. We have some six or eight other agents who may have been equally or more successful. We are expecting to raise by voluntary contribution a sum not less than One Hundred Thousand Dollars, which we are sure will be none too much.[58]

The Georgia Relief and Hospital Association was a voluntary organization until December, 1861, when the state appropriated $200,000 for its use. In 1862, $400,000 was granted, while in 1863 and 1864, $500,000 was appropriated annually. Shipments of hospital stores were sent by the Association from Augusta to the Georgia regiments and battalions in Virginia and other states. The association maintained hospitals in Georgia at Camp Harrison in Brunswick, and at Savannah, Augusta, Macon, Guyton, Springfield, Genesis Point, Atlanta, Jekyll Island, St. Simons, and Camp Davis.[59] Four hospitals were maintained in Richmond by the association. In a letter to the *Southern Christian Advocate,* the chaplain in charge of religious work at the Georgia hospitals in Richmond described the situation there:

We are using as hospitals, three tobacco factories, . . . affording very good accommodations for hospital purposes. Coverlets and quilts are from Georgia homes. I have visited many hospitals in Richmond, but have found none so well arranged, and so well managed as the Georgia Hospitals. . . . The hospitals are visited by our Representatives in Congress, especially Vice-Pres. Stephens who is a constant visitor. Mrs. General Toombs, Mr. J. A. Jones of Columbus and Mrs. Captain Harris of Marietta visit and comfort. . . .[60]

The Association supported several "wayside homes" in Georgia for the relief of sick and wounded soldiers. These homes were located at railroad terminals. Members of the association met the soldiers upon their arrival at the railroad stations, took them to the wayside homes, and furnished the men with food, lodging, clothing, and medical care.

As the war progressed, the Confederacy began establishing hospitals for the soldiers in Georgia. Beginning in February, 1862, the Confederate army constructed seven hospitals in Atlanta, making the city one of the principal centers of the medical department of the army. Georgians contributed liberally to the hospitals in money and supplies, and the contributions were distributed by such organizations as the "Ladies' Soldiers Relief Society" and

..PREPARATIONS FOR WAR

the "St. Philip's Hospital Society," working in conjunction with the Georgia Relief and Hospital Association.

Local associations for relief were sponsored by women, who made thousands of garments, socks, and bandages for the soldiers. Many women raffled jewelry, tapestries, and other treasures in order to secure funds for the sick and wounded men, and supplied them with sheets, blankets, and miscellaneous articles. Business firms and wealthy citizens liberally donated money, food, and clothing to the numerous "ladies relief societies," which often worked in conjunction with the local churches. In April, 1862, the Georgia Relief and Hospital Association acknowledged the receipt of "Ten dollars from a Lady; seven dozen Eggs, a can of Butter and a package of Tea, from the Belle Point Society, Tebeauville." The Pulaski House in Savannah contributed all of the carpets in the hotel to the army, enough carpets to furnish five hundred blankets. The manager of an Augusta hotel refused to receive pay from wounded soldiers who registered at his hotel.

Concerts, tableaux, and plays were given in order to secure funds. "We school girls are preparing for a Tableau for the benefit of the soldiers. I hope we will succeed with it," a Milledgeville girl recorded in her diary.[61] The proceeds of an entertainment given by the "Johnson's Minstrels" in Savannah netted $128 for the benefit of the sick men, while a series of concerts offered by the "Atlanta Amateurs" netted substantial profit for the same cause. A Negro musical prodigy of Columbus, known as "Blind Tom," presented piano concerts in numerous communities, and many other entertainments of both a professional and an amateur character were held in order to raise money for the convalescent troops.

Home guards were organized by many Georgia cities for the protection of the communities in case of invasion. Composing the guards were men too old or disabled and boys too young to enroll in the army or state militia. Approximately seventy-five men in Columbus organized themselves into a military company with the title of "Columbus Volunteers." The company was not designed entirely as a home guard, for the men wished to be prepared to render effective service wherever they were needed. In Americus young boys organized into the "Dixie Guards" for the purpose of drilling in order that when they became old enough they would be ready for combat. The mayor of Augusta notified Governor Brown that the entire volunteer force of the city had been called into the service of the Confederacy. He said that "they were in the habit of Guarding by turns the Magazine which is located outside the Corporate limits of the City. Under these Circumstances I have deemed it proper to employ a force of ten men as guards who will be at their Post day and night."[62]

Thus by 1862 Georgia was geared to a high level of military preparations for a war which she confidently believed would be of short duration. "I dont think that a Yankee is the man to persist in fighting when the chances are at all favorable to his being whipped," declared Richard Malcolm Johnston.[63] Despite the intense feeling of optimism which prevailed, Georgians were ready to sacrifice their entire resources in order to achieve victory. The attitude of the majority was expressed in the following statement, "Our people now have something presented to them of higher importance than the acquisition of wealth — that is the achievement of independence, to accomplish which they are willing, not only to give the last dime, but life itself."[64]

CHAPTER III

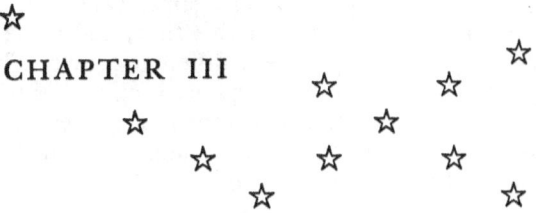

Political Controversies and Measures

WHILE THE PEOPLE OF THE STATE were busily engaged in military preparations, the time was approaching for another gubernatorial election. No governor of Georgia had within fifty years been elected for a third term, but as early as February, 1861, the Milledgeville *Federal Union* asserted that there was no more danger in electing a governor for three terms than in allowing a United States senator, representative, or judge to serve three times. "If the citizens of Georgia are wise . . . , they will not exchange a good man that has been tried, for one that has not been tried," this newspaper averred.[1] An article entitled "The Man for *The Times*," published in the *Georgia Forester* in March, also urged the re-election of Governor Brown.[2] Many Georgians believed, however, that Brown[3] would not attempt to be re-elected; and others felt that the candidate should be selected, regardless of party considerations, who would best unify the people. Brown realized, moreover, that the long-established custom regarding a third term would arouse opposition. He was aware also that he could not be nominated in a convention; and on August 13th, in reply to a letter from Jared I. Whitaker,[4] the owner of the Atlanta *Intelligencer*, he expressed the opinion that it was "impolitic and unwise to . . . hold either Gubernatorial or Congressional Conventions, while our people remain united and party spirit is dormant." In this letter he consented to serve for a third term "if the masses of the people, without regard to old party lines, were . . . to demand my services. . . ."[5]

A few days following Brown's announcement that he would run for a third term, Peterson Thweatt, the state's Comptroller-General and an intimate friend of the Governor, wrote to Alexander H. Stephens, saying:

33..

As I consider the current very strong against Gov B at this time, I advised him not to consent to run at this time, and to be cautious, &c. He has thought proper to pursue a different course. The opposition to him may not be able to unite against him, and if not I think he stands a pretty fair chance of re-election. But, if they do unite my present impression is, he will be badly beaten. . . . I reckon I shall vote for him, and "take the consequences."[6]

The Atlanta *Intelligencer* and the Milledgeville *Federal Union*, the only important newspapers to support the Governor in the campaign, praised his management of the state under difficult war conditions and urged his re-election;[7] but the Savannah *Republican* and Cassville *Standard* started a campaign for Judge Eugenius A. Nisbet. The former newspaper said that except for "two newspapers in the bounty of the present administration, we have no indication of a popular desire for the re-election of the present Executive," and declared that Brown was the only governor of a Confederate state who had been unable to act in perfect accord with Jefferson Davis.[8]

Despite Governor Brown's request that no conventions be held, an assembly of his opponents, composed of delegates from fifty-eight of the state's 132 counties, met in Milledgeville on September 11th and nominated Judge Nisbet for governor. David Irwin of Cobb County and Thomas E. Lloyd of Chatham County were nominated by the convention for Confederate presidential electors of the state at large. District electors also were named. Commenting upon the work of the convention, the Atlanta *Weekly Intelligencer* said that "It is a strange *misnomer* . . . to apply the term 'State Convention' to it. With some exceptions, it was nothing more nor less than a gathering together of old political opponents of Governor Brown."[9]

Writing to his brother, a private in Virginia, Moses W. Davis of Oak Hill made these interesting reflections concerning the approaching political campaign:

Joe Brown is a candidate a convention has been held in Milledgeville and nominated Judge Nesbet they say there was only fifty two counties represented the opposers of Brown plead the precedent, well I think Joe's economy will over balance the pleadings of the opposition their will be wonderful splitting among the old parties in this county [DeKalb] a greate many of Browns old friends are hot againts him.[10]

The nomination of Judge Nisbet was a very strong one, for he had been the leader of the secession convention and was extremely popular.[11] The press of the state, with few exceptions, supported Nisbet, with the Savannah *Republican* and the Augusta papers taking the lead in his behalf. Brown's refusal to abide by the action of the convention caused bitter criticism; and most of the press berated him for his "arbitrary, unconstitutional acts" and accused him of being "greedy of power, inflated, and vain." Widespread opposition to a third term was expressed, the controversies which Brown had had with the Confederacy concerning troops and arms were emphasized, and he was even accused of speculating in munitions.[12]

The Columbus *Daily Sun* opposed a third term for any governor, irrespective of its preference for candidates, and said that "a provision should exist in the Constitution prohibiting the re-election to a second or third term of the same Governor without an interval of four years."[13] Favoring Nisbet for governor, the Milledgeville *Southern Recorder* said that no evil would result from changing executives during the war, and called attention to the fact that in 1813 "we were in the midst of a war with Great Britain and the Indians, and yet Georgia suffered no inconvenience by the retirement of Governor Mitchell at the end of his second term, and the induction of Governor Early. . . ."[14] The Louisville *Gazette* stated that "For the sake of precedent we hope Nisbet may be elected, and thus forever put a veto upon future *third term* men."[15] The Marietta *Advocate* declared that "while some twenty presses of the State . . . supported Judge Nisbet and only four or five, supported the Governor's re-election — he persists in dividing the people of the State by an unprecedented candidacy."[16] Unrelenting in its attacks upon Brown, the Savannah *Republican* believed that "Georgia never had a Governor who managed her affairs with less ability, and . . . who made us oftener the laughing stock of the whole intelligent public."[17]

The Milledgeville *Federal Union* and the Atlanta *Intelligencer* remained loyal to the Governor. The latter paper said that in the North Brown was regarded as "the official . . . head of secession in Georgia," and that if he were defeated for re-election, "the belief will be induced in the North . . . that the Union still has a majority of friends in Georgia." "His administration has been wise, patriotic, successful . . ." asserted the *Intelligencer,* and "the honest farmers and working men will support Brown, who has stood by them, in every contest where the 'privileged class' and 'aristocratic snobs' have attempted to ride rough shod over their rights."[18] Brown received the praise of this newspaper for sending five thousand dollars from the state treasury to the Georgia Relief and Hospital Association in Richmond, and for making a personal donation of one thousand dollars to the same cause.

Brown refused to canvass. In August he wrote Alexander H. Stephens that while the "press and the politicians" were against him, he was confident that the people would sustain him; but a few weeks later he wrote Stephens, "Had I known the opposition . . . would have been so bitter, . . . I should not have consented to the use of my name. . . ."[19] In his only published address during the campaign, delivered on September 19th, he pointed out that the Milledgeville convention, which had failed to condemn his administration, was simply a caucus of politicians rekindling party strife when the people should be united; and he emphasized the value of his executive experience to the state.[20] Although the attacks of the press were savage, and a correspondent to the Savannah *Republican* predicted a few days before the election that Nisbet would receive a majority of eight thousand votes in the counties north of the Chattahoochee River alone, Brown had no cause for worry. When the election took place on the first Wednesday in October, he received 46,493 votes to 32,802 for Nisbet.[21] Judge Thomas W. Thomas, a friend of Stephens, declared that the election was a "triumph of the people over the newspapers."[22] A "Nisbet legislature" was elected, however, which many Georgians expected would give Brown "the devil."

Dressed in a suit of Georgia-made jeans, Brown was inaugurated on November 8th and delivered his annual message to the legislature. Besides condemning the acts of the Confederate Congress, which authorized the President to accept state troops without reference to state authority and gave to the President the appointment of the field officers, he urged an appropriation of $3,500,000 for the military needs of 1862, the passage of a stay law, the legalization of further bank suspension, and other war measures. Again, on December 5th, Brown spoke to the legislature, condemning a proposed measure to transfer to the Confederacy the Georgia troops called out by the Governor for six months' service on the coast. He asserted that the legislature had no right to transfer the troops without their consent. The Governor's message was referred to a committee, which on December 13th presented a report charging the Governor with an unwarrantable interference in the business of the House. Brown pro-

..POLITICAL CONTROVERSIES AND MEASURES

tested the report, the legislature divided hopelessly on the issue, and finally resolutions were passed which provided for the transfer of state troops only with their consent.[23]

Resenting the fact that Robert Toombs strongly disagreed with many Confederate policies, the legislature on November 19th elected Benjamin H. Hill for the full term in the Confederate Senate by a vote of 127 to 68. After five ballots were taken to fill the short term, with no one of the candidates receiving a majority, former United States Senator Alfred Iverson, Toombs' nearest competitor, withdrew his name, and on the sixth ballot Toombs was elected. Humiliated by the apparent reluctance of the legislature to elect him, Toombs refused to serve, preferring to remain in the army. Governor Brown then appointed Dr. John W. Lewis, a personal friend, to the position.[24]

Writing to Vice-President Stephens a short time after the adjournment of the legislature, Peterson Thweatt expressed his opinion of the Senatorial election:

In relation to the Senators election, had Mr. Toombs suffered his name to be used in the nature of a candidate, he would have been elected by a handsome majority from the start — but, as it was doubtful until a day or two before the election whether or not he would let his name be used, Judge Iverson came near being reelected. Had both Senators been elected *together* or on the *same vote*, I think Iverson would most surely have been elected — as he was here and had fixed up things to that point. He calculated upon 128 votes on the 1st vote. The *separation* of him and Hill killed him.[25]

Although the Governor quarreled often with the Confederate administration, he continued to direct the affairs of Georgia boldly and effectively. He devoted untiring energy to such matters as aid to soldiers' families, the supplying of troops with clothing, the curbing of the distillation of whiskey in order to conserve food, and relief of the salt famine. As the needs of the soldiers' families increased, Brown requested the legislature to enact measures to meet their demands. In November, 1862, he recommended a bounty of $100 to the family of each soldier whose property was less than $1,000, the funds to be raised from the net proceeds of the state-owned railroad and from freight rates increased by 25 per cent, together with a tax of 33 1/3 per cent upon the net incomes of speculators. The legislature appropriated $2,500,000 for the purpose.[26] A year later the legislature, acting in accordance with the Governor's recommendations, appropriated $5,000,000 for needy families; and in 1864 and 1865 each, an appropriation of $6,000,000 was made. Brown also urged the legislature to appropriate funds with which to purchase clothing and shoes for the soldiers. The assembly responded with an appropriation of $1,500,000 in 1862 and $2,500,000 in 1863.[27] The Governor notified General Henry R. Jackson, commanding the state troops at Savannah, that "If the officers certify to you that clothing is necessary for a Company or individually it will be furnished at once in place of money. If the supply of clothing there should be exhausted your qu master will make requisition on the Quarter Master Genl. for more."[28]

Late in 1863 the Governor informed General William J. Hardee, who was commanding the Department of Tennessee, that "Having learned that the Georgia troops in your Command, are in great need of Blankets, . . . I have instructed my Aid-de-Camp, Col Aaron Wilbur to go abroad at once, and try to get and import a lot of blankets for the troops."[29] Blankets were secured from England via Nassau. George O. Johnson of the firm of Johnson and Brothers at Nassau wrote Wilbur, "We shall ship you in a few days one Bale Blankets per Sch Sophia, and shall also ship you per Steamer to Wilmington as per your order."[30] In another letter Johnson and Brothers said that some of the blankets had been sent and that "we shall continue to ship the balance per steamers."[31] In order to negotiate with agents of an English firm concerning the purchase of blankets for the state, Henry Lathrop was sent by Wilbur to Halifax, Nova Scotia, and to England.

Brown was keenly interested also in seeing that the salaries of Confederate soldiers were increased. In April, 1863, and again in November of that year, he requested the legislature to enact a resolution instructing the Confederate Congress to pass an act "to allow all commissioned officers in the Confederate service an increase of twenty-five per cent upon their pay . . . and to increase the compensation of private soldiers to twenty-two dollars per month, and of non-commissioned officers in like proportion."[32] Commenting upon Brown's recommendation, the Savannah *Republican* on April 30, 1863, accused the Governor of "attempting to get up a war of classes" and said that he "slanders the rich for the simple reason that the poor have more votes."

The distillation of liquor needed to be curbed, for the practice consumed grain required for food, and the copper in the distilleries was necessary for munitions. By a proclamation issued on

..POLITICAL CONTROVERSIES AND MEASURES

February 29, 1862, Brown commanded that all distilleries, except those having contracts with the Confederate Government, be closed until the next meeting of the legislature. Railroads were ordered not to transport liquor.[33] Urging the public to aid in enforcing the order, the Atlanta *Southern Confederacy* on March 4, 1862, stated that the Governor's proclamation was "wise, just, and legal." Carrying out the Governor's orders, Adjutant-General Wayne seized numerous distilleries. For instance, in October, 1862, he captured distilleries near Thomaston and in Heard and Pike counties. When the legislature met in November, it enacted a law forbidding the manufacture of liquor except for medicinal and chemical purposes, with heavy penalties for disobedience, and making illegal the exportation of grains for distillation. A few weeks later the legislature provided compensation for the stills seized by the Governor.[34]

Brown insisted that any Confederate officials in Georgia who wished to manufacture liquor for military purposes should be licensed by him. H. H. Waters of the state executive department in Milledgeville expressed in a letter to the superintendent of the Confederate laboratories in Macon the Governor's determination to control the distillation of liquor: ". . . parties will be licensed by the Governor to make alcohol required from Ga. for the Ordnance Dept. of the Confederate Govt. Licenses will be issued on the same terms upon which they are issued to make whisky for medical dept."[35]

Apparently Brown had expected that greater opposition would be manifested to his proclamation forbidding the distillation of liquor than developed, for in a letter to Stephens, he said that he had been "agreeably disappointed in the reception which my proclamation on . . . distilleries has met in the State. Few even of the distillers themselves have ventured to condemn it. A few have disregarded the proclamation. . . . In every such case . . . I have issued orders for the immediate seizure of the Still."[36]

With liquor selling at thirty and forty dollars a gallon in Confederate currency, many people were tempted to evade the law. Especially in the mountains of north Georgia whiskey continued to be made. Moreover, potatoes, molasses, fruits, and other products were used as substitutes for grains. The legislature in the spring of 1863 enacted a measure which outlawed the use of all foodstuffs for the distillation of liquor. In the following November and in March, 1864, Brown asked the legislature for more stringent regulations, and in 1865 he vetoed a bill to permit heads of families to distill liquor.[37]

As in the other Confederate states, the problem of obtaining salt for both civilians and soldiers was a matter of great portent. Because of inadequate refrigeration, salt was in great demand, but the South had been accustomed to importing most of its salt requirements. When the packing season approached in 1861, salt prices soared and profiteers speculated. In November the Macon *Daily Telegraph* said that the price of salt was rising at the rate of about one dollar per day, and that a Macon firm, to prevent speculation, "positively refuses to sell more than five sacks to one man, and he must be a planter."[38] Governor Brown on November 20th ordered the state Commissary-General to seize for the use of the Georgia troops all salt in Atlanta, Macon, and Columbus offered for sale at more than five dollars a sack, which amount the officer was told to pay to the owners as just compensation.[39] One thousand sacks of salt in the possession of A. K. Seago of Atlanta were confiscated under orders of the Governor, causing the editor of the Atlanta *Southern Confederacy* to write a protesting statement to Vice-President Stephens: "Gov. Brown has, I think, put his foot into it, in seizing the Salt. It has certainly operated very disastrously for the Country. I look upon it as entirely un-necessary and un-authorized. . . ."[40]

After the Governor had seized the salt, the Savannah *Republican* stated that the price of salt still ranged from twenty to twenty-five dollars per sack. "Verily the planters and house-keepers of Georgia should hold a convention and give the Governor a vote of thanks for his marvellous '*reduction*' scheme! *vive la Humbug!*" the *Republican* exclaimed.[41]

Brown ordered the principal railroads of the state to detain all salt unless shipped under affidavit that it was for personal use, justifying his action upon a constitutional clause which provided for seizure of private property for public use with just compensation. The refusal of the Central of Georgia Railroad to ship salt from Savannah caused a clamor which obliged the Governor to modify his order slightly: any quantity of salt might be shipped to any point in the state for Georgia citizens. When the legislature met in November, 1861, Brown recommended a law authorizing him to seize any supplies necessary for the troops in return for just compensation to be fixed by competent agents. Although the legislature did not pass such a law, it did enact a measure to aid

..POLITICAL CONTROVERSIES AND MEASURES

in prosecuting extortioners and speculators and appropriated $50,000 to aid private concerns in establishing salt works. The legislature also appointed a "joint committee on salt supply," which requested Governor Brown to encourage salt-making on the coast by directing the state railroad to afford special facilities for transportation of salt.[42] The Atlanta *Southern Confederacy* was skeptical as to the Governor's ability to secure salt and urged every family to procure salt by any means it could.

The 1863 session of the legislature made a much larger appropriation for salt, $500,000, in the use of which the Governor might purchase or make salt, or advance it to individuals or associations for the purchase, manufacture, or transportation of salt. Brown contracted with two Georgia companies at Saltville, Virginia, to furnish salt on state account, and contracted with another Georgia company to import salt from New Iberia, Louisiana. He arranged a plan of distribution whereby one-half bushel was donated to widows of soldiers and to those who had lost a son in service, and one-half bushel could be sold for one dollar to each family of a soldier. After these persons were supplied, heads of families could each purchase a bushel for $4.50.[43] Due to numerous circumstances, including the inability of the Virginia works to supply the needs, there was never enough salt to carry out the Governor's plans, and the salt famine continued throughout the war.

Brown's leadership and achievements in time of war were a strong inducement to the citizens of Georgia to continue the aggressive governor in office for a fourth term, despite his opposition to various Confederate measures. Brown had the advantage of being already in office and, furthermore, had the prestige associated with his power of appointment. Other factors in Brown's favor were his ability in political strategy, his popularity with the masses, and the fact that he had the support of Stephens and Toombs. Peterson Thweatt in January, 1863, wrote Alexander H. Stephens that he did not believe that Brown would run again for governor. "He [Brown] says he prefers your brother Linton to any other — but thinks if *W*. [A. R. Wright] is run that perhaps Mr. Toombs would make the best race. . . . I am under the impression that Gen. Toombs would be very much pleased to be Governor," Thweatt wrote.[44] Almost nine months prior to the biennial election, Brown wrote Alexander Stephens that he did not intend to be a candidate and suggested Linton Stephens for the position. Alexander Stephens apparently urged Brown to stand for re-election, for on February 16, 1863, Brown wrote Stephens, "I have not said publicly that I will not . . . be a candidate for another term . . . but I do not think there is any state of facts likely to . . . induce me to change my purpose." He said that if Linton Stephens refused to be a candidate, he favored Toombs.[45] A month later Brown regretted that Linton Stephens had declined to make the race and feared that Toombs' cotton crop of the previous year had jeopardized his chances.[46]

As early as March, 1863, the Savannah *Republican* expressed fear that Brown would be a candidate for re-election, and said that the one thousand dollars which Brown had donated for the relief of the soldiers' families and the corn which he had dispensed from his farm for charity were political gestures. Two months later Thweatt had changed his mind concerning Brown's political ambitions and wrote Alexander Stephens that he was inclined to think that the Governor would attempt to be re-elected. ". . . I think his friends have shaken him pretty considerably, and rather than see those who have heretofore been trying to put him down, get the Gubernatorial office, I think will try again, especially if you and two or three others insist."[47]

The majority of the state's newspapers sought, as in 1861, to prevent Brown's nomination;[48] but the Atlanta *Intelligencer* and Milledgeville *Federal Union* again supported him, and the Augusta *Daily Constitutionalist,* which had been bitterly hostile in the previous election, called for his re-election.[49] Letters from all parts of the state urged him to continue as governor, and Brown became convinced that he should run for re-election. His political strategy was a repetition of that of 1861: nomination by a few friends, early announcement of his candidacy, and emphasis upon his support of the Confederate administration. Following a prearranged plan, James Gardner, the owner of the Augusta *Constitutionalist,* and three other citizens of Augusta sent a letter to Brown on May 16th asking him to serve for another term. The Governor replied on May 21st that he felt his duty required him to contribute his knowledge and experience to the state during the gigantic war in which it was engaged.[50]

As in 1861, Brown's candidacy aroused a storm of opposition. The Milledgeville *Southern Recorder* pointed out that to vote for him would be to endorse his opposition to conscription, his "foolhardy correspondence with the President," and his "unjust protection of militia officers."[51] The Atlanta *Commonwealth* insinuated that he was being nominated and supported by "bank influence," but the Savannah *Daily Morning News* said that the witnesses against Brown "are in exactly the same predicament as those who testified . . . before Pontius Pilate, more than eighteen centuries ago."[52]

Joshua Hill, who had been a member of the United States Congress from 1857 to 1861, was the choice of the Union men in north Georgia, and his candidacy was announced in August by the Rome *Southerner* and the Atlanta *Gazette*. Urging the election of Hill, the Athens *Watchman* said: "We are learning from experience that hot spurs and demagogues are unfit to govern a country. They brought us into trouble and are incapable of taking us out."[53] Hill's name aroused almost as much opposition as that of Brown, however, for Hill had been a Whig Unionist in 1860-61 and had condemned Brown's seizure of Fort Pulaski. Hill was accused of favoring a "reconstruction of the Union," but he denied the accusation. In early September he published an open letter to his political friends, George W. Adair, J. J. Thrasher, and James M. Calhoun, of Atlanta, in which he explained his attitude in the race for the governorship. He did not refuse to allow his name on the ballot, but he said that he had "never felt the desire to occupy the executive office, even in ordinary times," and that "now, with its vast responsibilities . . . , it is surely not a place to be coveted by any modest conscientious man." He frankly admitted that he had often expressed his "conviction that the idea of dissolving the Union, with the hope of reconstructing it, on a basis more . . . protective . . . of the slave states, was fallacious and absurd," but that "the war had eradicated all idea of reconstruction." He added that if the North should win, the Union would then exist only in name and would not be "the free government of our fathers." "I want no such union as that and will not accept it," he declared.[54]

The candidacy of a third man, Captain Timothy M. Furlow of Americus, was announced and advocated by the Milledgeville *Southern Recorder* on September 15, 1863. Furlow, a wealthy planter, was relatively inexperienced in public affairs, but he strongly supported the policies of the Confederate administration. He represented the normal opposition to Brown's war policies on the part of the Davis administration forces. In announcing his candidacy, Furlow stated:

My official support should upon every call be given to the Government, when not clearly unconstitutional. This is no time for factious opposition or grudging support to the Administration. . . . If elected Governor, I shall throw no official protection around any citizen, within the embrace of the Conscript Law, and in my appointments my policy shall be to give . . . assistance . . . to those who have been disabled in the service of the Country. . . .[55]

With Hill representing the conservative element and Furlow the ardent secessionists, Brown's opponents hoped that the election would be thrown into the legislature, where Brown's defeat was practically assured, for it was believed that the Governor would not secure a majority over both of his competitors.

The campaign was not particularly lively, for people were too concerned with the war to take an intense interest in politics. Hill announced no platform, and all three candidates refused to electioneer, depending primarily upon published letters and editorials. Brown was too astute to make his opposition to the Confederate administration an issue in his election, and he even emphasized his close accord with the President. The Milledgeville *Southern Recorder* accused the Governor of being "a swift historian when he himself is the hero. He has disgusted the public mind with his self-praise."[56] Hill maintained that while he did not approve of every act of President Davis' administration, he did not know of another man "more capable of serving the Confederacy," and that he "sympathized with no factions in opposition to the Davis administration."[57] "What can be more ridiculous than to hear advocates of Joshua Hill who never entertained a political opinion in common with President Davis, denouncing such men as Gov. Brown as hostile to the Confederate Government?" asked the Savannah *Daily Morning News*. The *News* also stated that "not a paper in the State advocates . . . Hill . . . which proves that in Georgia a suspicion of disloyalty to the Confederate cause is fatal to the prospects of any aspirant for office."[58] The Savannah *Republican* ironically commented near the close of the campaign that the friends of each candidate had vied with each other in putting their candidate in "as close co-operation . . . with the Confederate administration as possible."[59] In a letter to Alexander H. Stephens, Brown accused Hill of having resigned his position in the Lincoln Congress long after the state had seceded and of denying that the Ordinance of Secession took the state out of the Union. "I suppose Mr. Hill relies upon the failure of our own government and disaster of our armies for success," the letter stated.[60]

The total vote cast was smaller than in previous elections, probably because of the difficulty of taking the soldier vote. Of the 64,804 votes polled, Brown received 36,558; Hill, 18,222; and Furlow, 10,024, with Brown securing more votes than the combined votes of his opponents. As was to be expected, Brown carried the army vote by a large majority, receiving 10,012 votes to 3,324 and 1,889 for Hill and Furlow, respectively. Hill received a clear majority in twenty-one counties, and these counties with a few exceptions were in the upper piedmont and mountain region. Brown's large majority was due largely to the heavy vote he received in the cities and in the army.[61]

At the time of Brown's re-election, Toombs was a candidate for the Senate. He spoke before the legislature on November 13th, denouncing Confederate war measures. A man who was in Milledgeville during the senatorial race commented to Howell Cobb regarding the contest:

We are having an exciting canvass here for Senator. I am satisfied neither Mr. Toombs or Mr. Johnson can be elected. Mr. Johnson will receive a good many votes from his friends on the first ballot, but they have no hope of electing him and they do not desire to go to Mr. Toombs. They desire some one more friendly to the administration. Your name has been suggested in private circles for the place.[62]

Because of Toombs' hostility toward President Davis, the legislature hesitated to elect him and instead chose Herschel V. Johnson for the position.[63]

Brown's fourth term was as vigorously conducted and equally as turbulent as his preceding administrations. His annual message to the legislature, delivered on November 5, 1863, urged the adopting of a resolution requesting Congress to repeal that part of the Conscript Act which authorized the employment of substitutes. He asked that authority be granted to civil officers to arrest absentees from the army, again advocated the right of state troops to elect their own officers, and strongly denounced impressment. The legislature passed a measure calling for the enrollment into the state militia of all men between sixteen and sixty who were not in the Confederate army and empowered the Governor to conscript them if necessary.[64]

A few months later, March 10, 1864, the legislature met in a special session and again listened to an address by the Governor.

After dealing with the problems of relief for soldiers' families, cotton planting, illegal distilleries, and the currency, Brown devoted the remainder of his message to the new conscript law, the suspension of the writ of habeas corpus, causes of the war, and how peace should be sought. Supported by the Stephens brothers, he urged the legislature to vote against turning the militia over to the Confederacy; but despite the wrath of the Governor, the legislature relinquished the state troops. Brown also pronounced the Confederacy's suspension of the writ of habeas corpus as a blow against liberty. Linton Stephens, assisted by his brother, formulated denunciatory resolutions which were adopted by the legislature in opposition to the suspension of habeas corpus.[65] So determined was Brown that his political views should be widely known that he had copies of his legislative address distributed to the army and sent to newspapers in the North and in Europe.[66]

Until the end of the war, Brown towered over the legislature and dominated the state almost as though he were the sovereign of an independent republic. Although the press and the aristocratic element in general opposed him, he retained his power from the support of the "common people." He continued his denunciation of the Confederate authorities; and his arbitrary, cantankerous attitude aroused increasing opposition within the state and caused many Georgians to regard him as being little less than a provincial demagogue. One of Howell Cobb's sons in June, 1864, expressed a hope that the Governor would die. In writing to his wife, he said, "Joe Brown is in Atlanta with his pets the militia officers and says he will lead them in the fight when the time comes. I hope the time will soon come, and that his time may come at the same time. I think his death would be a blessing to the country."[67] "There is this difference between Gov. Brown and Nebuchadnezzar," a newspaper remarked a few weeks before the war ceased. "The one required all men to worship an image he had raised, whilst the other would have all men bow down and worship him."[68] The Chattanooga *Rebel* declared that "Joe Brown is on a rampage again. Nothing suits him."[69] "The Governor must be of the pachydermatous order, else he would have been stung to death long ago," said the Savannah *Daily Herald*.[70]

A movement was begun, however, to elect Brown for a fifth term. The Milledgeville *Confederate Union* said that a majority of the people wanted his services continued; and on May 3, 1865, the Augusta *Weekly Chronicle and Sentinel* approved him for

..POLITICAL CONTROVERSIES AND MEASURES

another term. Opposition to continuing the Governor in office was expressed by several papers, including the Columbus *Weekly Times,* the Savannah *Daily Herald,* and the Milledgeville *Southern Recorder.* The latter paper on March 21, 1865, gave three reasons why it would oppose the re-election of Brown: first, his acts toward the Confederate administration; second, the need for an executive who would investigate the state's financial accounts; and third, the desirability of having a governor who would ascertain how many men were exempt from military duty by holding offices under state authority. While another gubernatorial campaign was thus in the offing, the armies of the Confederacy surrendered. Brown's final proclamation was issued on May 3, 1865, convening the legislature in extra session "to consider the existing state of things," and led to his arrest in Milledgeville six days later by United States authorities.[71] Thus ended the gubernatorial career of one of the most extraordinary and unparalleled characters in Georgia history.

President Andrew Johnson on June 27th appointed James Johnson of Columbus as provisional governor of Georgia. When President Johnson's reconstruction program permitted the election of a governor in November,[72] Judge Charles J. Jenkins was unanimously elected.[73] In this election Brown refused to be a candidate. The legislature met for the first time after the war in December, 1865.

CHAPTER IV

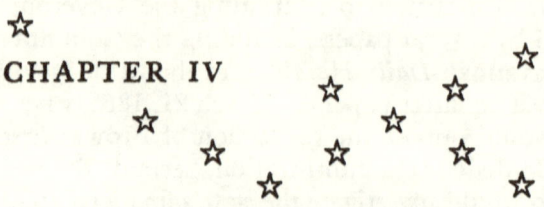

Wartime Finance

GEORGIA ENTERED THE WAR IN A sound financial condition. The assessed taxable property of the state in 1860 was $686,326,086, an increase of more than ninety-two per cent in ten years. The state owned the Western and Atlantic Railroad, valued at nearly $8,000,000, and she held bonds in various banks and railroads amounting to $2,670,750. Miscellaneous assets amounted to nearly another $1,000,000. The total bonded indebtedness of the state was the $2,670,750 invested in banks and railroads. At the close of the fiscal year of 1860 the state treasury had a cash balance of $33,092.64.[1]

Under normal conditions the state government derived its income from an *ad valorem* tax of 6½ cents per $100 on general property and 39½ cents per $100 on corporation stocks owned by individuals, and from the revenues derived from state-owned properties, including the Western and Atlantic Railroad. In 1860 the state secured $429,349 from the *ad valorem* tax and $486,429 from the state properties.[2] Georgia, like other states and like the Confederate government, showed an unwillingness during the first two years of the war to meet the demands of war by increasing taxes, preferring the indirect method of bonds and paper currency. Before the war ended, however, the state not only resorted to issuing bonds, treasury notes, certificates of deposit, and change bills, but also increased existing tax levies and devised new ones, and authorized the county and municipal governments to make new bond issues and tax levies.

The first method used by the state to perform its share in the war was the sale of bonds. The $1,000,000 appropriation of November, 1860, directed the Governor to obtain the funds for this initial call on the treasury by offering 20-year six per cent bonds. Hardly had these state bonds been placed on the market when

..WARTIME FINANCE

the Confederate Congress in February, 1861, issued $15,000,000 in 10-year eight per cent bonds secured by a tax on cotton exports. Although Georgians were buying the state "sixes" above par,[3] and also began purchasing the Confederate bonds, Governor Brown believed that the latter bonds were an imposition upon the state, for "persons having money to invest preferred these bonds to the six per cent bonds." Consequently, the Governor discontinued the sale of the Georgia "sixes" and entered into "executive contracts" with Georgia banks for loans at seven per cent interest, thus causing the legislature in November, 1861, to repay the banks by issuing new 20-year seven per cent bonds. Fifty million dollars' worth of state bonds were issued in 1861.[4]

Although the Confederate government was reluctant to levy taxes, the Confederate Congress in August, 1861, issued $100,000,000 of Confederate treasury notes, funded by 20-year eight per cent bonds. The bonds were to be secured by a tax levy on one-half of one per cent of all property except money on hand and Confederate bonds. The tax was due by May 1, 1862, but at any time prior to April 1, 1862, it might be assumed by the state at a ten per cent rebate. Each state was allowed to raise the tax by its own devices, and states that secured the money were promised immunity from Confederate tax collectors. Brown favored securing the ten per cent discount and was opposed to "intervention" by Confederate tax agents.[5] In order to raise Georgia's quota of $2,441,000, the legislature on December 11, 1861, authorized the sale of 20-year eight per cent bonds. Two million dollars' worth of the bonds were quickly subscribed to by banks in Savannah, Augusta, and Columbus, and by one South Carolina bank. The remaining sum of $441,000 was purchased by individuals. Brown had the money on deposit in Georgia banks a month before it was due the Confederacy.[6]

Peterson Thweatt told Vice-President Stephens in the winter of 1862 that both the seven and the eight per cent state bonds were selling rapidly:

> We find a great demand for Georgia 7 and 8 per cent Bonds. The Governor has determined only to issue the amount in bonds to pay the Banks for the $842,000 loaned us last year. At present, such is the favorable appearance for Georgia, that the Governor *does not contemplate issuing any thing but 7 per cent Bonds, ... payable Ten years after date.* . . . The Governor thinks he will not be able to supply the demand for bonds — as except for the proposed above

stated, he will issue Treasury notes redeemable in Eight per cent Bonds, or Specie, six months after Peace.[7]

Two months later Thweatt was even more optimistic, for the demand for the seven per cent bonds had far exceeded the supply.

Meanwhile, the Confederate Congress had provided for the first Confederate produce loan. Acts passed in May and August, 1861, authorized loans of $100,000,000, half of which might be subscribed to by planters who wished to pledge their produce, such as cotton, tobacco, stock, and other agricultural products, to the government in return for 20-year eight per cent bonds.[8] These bonds were intended as a means by which the government might secure supplies without having to advance money for them. Although the loan promised to be very helpful to Confederate finance, what the planter needed for his cotton were not bonds but treasury notes, which he might use as a medium of exchange. Agents were appointed by Congress to sell the bonds in every Congressional district of Georgia, and Alexander H. Stephens and Benjamin H. Hill delivered addresses in Georgia in behalf of the loan. Subscriptions came in very slowly, however, for many planters were reluctant to part with their cotton for government bonds. By January, 1862, only seventy-five thousand bales of cotton and 150,000 bushels of rice had been sold by Georgians to the government.[9]

During the summer and fall of 1861, Georgians deluged Vice-President Stephens and other officials of the Confederate administration with letters explaining their financial predicament, caused primarily by their inability to sell cotton for cash, and calling upon the government for aid. Because of their need for a market for their cotton a majority of the planters urged the government to establish a currency based upon cotton. For instance, a man at Madison said:

> The question has become a grave one with our people, "how shall I pay my taxes?" The planters are the men principally looked to for the tax in this part of the country. The expectation of the ports being opened this winter has pretty well been given up. All the money in the country except that in the hands of Shylocks has gone in equipping soldiers and furnishing hospitals.

He suggested that the government should buy the entire cotton crop with treasury notes.[10] J. Henly Smith, editor of the Atlanta *Southern Confederacy*, told Stephens that "The Government will

..WARTIME FINANCE

have to buy our Cotton, Tobacco, Sugar and Rice and pay for it in notes — have to — no other chance; and when the notes begin to depreciate from being too plentiful, fund them. We must have money to pay the taxes levied on us, and that must come out of our crops."[11] Another Georgian declared that "Cotton producers are scotched" and "Unless Congress will agree to take the whole crop, at a fixed price, payable in Treasury notes we shall be undone."[12] A planter wrote Stephens that "unless the cotton and other produce can be sold and shipped, money which is now very scarce, will be still more so. . . . Issue treasury notes as a circulating medium, and Bonds as many as can be disposed of, raising money in any way, rather than to a direct tax."[13] Another planter said that the people were finding it difficult "to keep their heads above the flood of destruction caused by numerous taxes and high prices" and that "if we cant get some means of relief we are gone. . . ."[14]

Similar letters were sent by the planters to Howell Cobb. A man in Cedartown made some suggestions regarding the financing of cotton:

> If our Government can arrange it, to advance on Cotton *in case of need* say 7 cts a pound to the planter in Bonds or Treasury notes, and stipulate at the same time the amount the planter will leave in the hands of the authorities, as his quota, in support to carry on the war, these notes would give a circulating medium equal to our present Bank Bills, as their solvency and redemption is secured by the Cotton the Government holds till it can be realised to advantage, and would besides establish the value of cotton at a minimum price below which it could not go.[15]

J. J. Hussey of Meriwether County informed Cobb that he preferred for the government to purchase the cotton directly from the planter. Such a policy, he said, "would not change the liability of the Government or effect [sic] the interest of the planter, for if he sells the Cotton himself . . . he will turn over the proceeds to the Government and for the amount receive Confederate bonds."[16] Another Georgian notified Cobb: "I make no Cotton to Subscribe for Southern Bonds, but I will Sell what little *all* I have and the S. C. S. Bonds for it I will take as Cash."[17]

A committee of three men, acting "in behalf of the people of Washington County," submitted to Stephens a plan whereby, they believed, planters could realize money on cotton: "Let the Government condemn for its own use the entire cotton crop, paying the planter a fair price, say ten cents per pound, ¼ now in Treasury notes, ¼ in January, also in Treasury notes for the remaining half issue Confederate bonds as proposed in the produce Loan."[18] Such proposals caused Judge Martin J. Crawford of Columbus to assert that the planters were "mad upon the subject of the governments buying the cotton crop, . . . It convinces me . . . that our people are not prepared to pay the purchase price for freedom if the planters demand that a poor government, . . . shall pay them 2 or 3 cts a pound more for their cotton than the markets afford."[19]

Many leaders of the Confederacy, however, did not believe that it was feasible for the government to buy the cotton. Secretary of the Treasury C. G. Memminger in October, 1861, expressed disapproval of such a policy. He said that the Confederate Constitution did not grant the power "to any department to lend money for the relief of any interest" and that "If the Government should undertake, for the sake of private interests, so large an increase of issues, it may hazard its entire credit and stability."[20] Commenting upon the reluctance of the government to purchase the cotton, an Augusta newspaper expressed doubt that the Confederacy had either the constitutional authority or the financial ability to make the transaction.[21]

A resolution was offered to the Confederate Congress in November, 1861, requesting that a committee be appointed to consider the "expediency . . . of the Government making advances in Treasury notes or Confederate bonds on cotton, tobacco, and other products."[22] When the resolution failed to be adopted, the Columbus *Weekly Times* said that "a majority of voters in the 3rd Congressional District of Georgia" were bitterly disappointed, but that it was glad "Congress has extinguished this *ignis fatuus*."[23]

The Confederate produce loan was modified on April 21, 1862, in order to enable planters who had obtained advances in bonds on their agricultural products to redeem their produce in depreciated treasury notes. Until redemption, or until called for by the government, the cotton and other produce were to be kept in storage on the plantations, with the planter being allowed the privilege, if the price rose, of recovering his produce and selling it at a profit. Under this new system, however, subscriptions continued to come in very slowly, and by January 9, 1863, only 6,281 bales of cotton costing $499,172.88 had been purchased in Georgia since the act of April 21, 1862, had been put into effect.[24]

Vice-President Stephens regretted that the government had not purchased the cotton. In an address at Crawfordville in November, 1862, he said that he "was in favor, . . . of the Government taking all the cotton that would be subscribed for 8 per cent bonds at a rate or price as high as ten cents a pound." Stephens believed that cotton was "an element of power such as no other people ever had," and that it might be used not only for breaking the blockade but also in supplying the treasury with specie to pay interest on government bonds, "thus giving us a credit that no Government ever had before."[25]

Secretary Memminger in January, 1863, presented a report to Congress recommending that Confederate bonds be guaranteed by all of the Confederate states. The Secretary's plan was designed to enable the Confederacy to fund its debt by finding a market for the bonds in Europe. To accomplish this purpose a heavy war tax and a loan to be guaranteed by the states were recommended. The proposed measure, adopted by Congress on March 23, 1863, authorized the Secretary to sell $200,000,000 worth of 30-year, six per cent bonds, guaranteed by the states, for treasury notes which were not to be reissued.[26] Two days after Congress passed the law, Governor Brown told the Georgia legislature that the measure was unwise, for "it would level the credit of all the states to an equality and injure the credit of those states who have managed their financial affairs better than others."[27] A bill in the lower house to authorize the Governor to endorse Georgia's quota of $50,000,000 passed by a small majority, but the state senate voted to postpone the matter indefinitely.[28] Secretary Memminger blamed Brown for the failure of the states to endorse the plan. Stephens also opposed state endorsement, but Toombs favored the measure.

The Confederate Congress enacted a more comprehensive tax law on April 24, 1863, combining in one measure the features of an income levy, a license tax, and a general internal revenue measure. By April, 1864, Georgia had contributed more than $21,000,000 by this tax. One of the most distasteful features of this Confederate tax was a direct "tax in kind" which amounted to approximately one-tenth of the produce of the farmers for the year 1863. Instead of money, a tithe of actual crops was paid by the farmer to the government collector. Because the tax was an additional burden upon the agricultural classes it proved exceedingly unpopular and at times was not collected. Writing to Howell Cobb from Athens in January, 1865, General A. W. Reynolds said that "Owing to the negligence of the officers charged with the collection of the tax in kind, I have found in the District a greater quantity of forage and provisions than I expected."[29]

By 1864 the Confederate currency had become so depreciated in value that the Confederate Congress on February 17th adopted a law for the compulsory reduction of the currency. This funding act provided for a 33 1/3 per cent discount upon all treasury notes of five dollars or more. ". . . the *currency bill* . . . is creating considerable excitement through the Country," a Georgia girl wrote to her uncle. "It is really amusing to see how puzzled some men are to know what to do with their money. If they were in the army where they ought to be, they wouldn't have so much money to bother them."[30] The Americus *Sumter Republican* commented: "We are no financier but it does seem to us that the passage of just such a bill at this time is what the country needed. . . . There is no real cause for alarm. The bonds of the Government are certainly good if the South gets her independence. . . ."[31] The funding act was opposed, however, by Governor Brown. He told a special session of the legislature in March, 1864, that the measure had "seriously embarrassed the financial system of this State, and has shaken the confidence of our people . . . in the justice of . . . Congress or its competency to manage our financial affairs."[32]

A majority of the state's newspapers condemned Brown for his opposition to the funding bill. The Columbus *Weekly Times* called Brown's message "factious and slanderous" and said that the funding bill "strikes down speculation" and was "essential to arrest that downward . . . career to worthlessness which would have resulted in wholesale repudiation."[33] The Savannah *Republican* declared that Brown talked about "repudiation" without "show of reason" and that "Congress had to choose between what it has done and a state of things far more disastrous. . . . It may be that Governor Brown has a personal feeling of hardship that renders him particularly susceptible to drafts upon his purse."[34] No less critical of the Governor was the Marietta *Rebel*, which on March 29, 1864, said that Brown harped upon every objectionable feature of the funding act and ignored every justification for the measure. Alexander H. Stephens believed, however, that the Confederacy's financial acts had caused confidence in the government to disappear.

Governor Brown also objected to the Confederacy's policy of paying debts due the states with bonds rather than with the treas-

..WARTIME FINANCE

ury notes. In 1862 he asked Secretary Memminger to use treasury notes in paying a debt due the state-owned Western and Atlantic Railroad, but Memminger said that the government was not able to do so:

> The desire you express to have the amount due . . . Georgia paid in Treasury Notes would have been a sufficient inducement to make the payment, had it been in my power. Unless you can make use of the Bonds, the payment of the Rail Road account is necessarily deferred for two sufficient reasons; one is that we cannot get a sufficient supply of Notes from the printers; the other is that the issue is so near the amount authorized by Congress, that we must wait for an extension of the authority to issue Currency Notes. We have sufficient authority to issue Interest Notes or Bonds.[35]

The war had not progressed very far before Governor Brown became convinced that state treasury notes, issued in the form of money to circulate as currency, were preferable to bonds as a means of meeting Georgia's financial obligations. In his annual message to the legislature in November, 1861, he said that the state might find it difficult to meet its expenses by the sale of bonds and requested the legislators to authorize the issuance of treasury notes, similar to those issued by the Confederate government, and to make them "receivable in the payment of taxes or any other debt due the State."[36] After hearing the Governor's message, the legislature authorized him to meet the military appropriations of 1862 by issuing 30-year eight per cent bonds, or treasury notes, as he should decide. As the Governor preferred the treasury notes, no further bonds were issued, and the seven per cent and eight per cent Confederate War Tax bonds, both of which had been issued in 1861, constituted the war's bonded indebtedness in Georgia.[37]

Again in November, 1862, Brown adverted to the desirability of the treasury notes, explaining that the sale of state bonds would cause the state to pay interest on the bonds whereas the treasury notes were negotiable. Beginning in November, 1862, the legislature voted in favor of treasury notes rather than bonds for meeting appropriations. The initial issues of treasury notes were to be funded in quantities of $500 or more by bonds or by specie six months after the declaration of peace. The legislature of 1863 provided for the refunding of the notes in quantities of $5,000 or more in treasury certificates of deposit, and the certificates of deposit were redeemable in six per cent bonds or in specie six months after peace. Between 1861 and 1865 a total of $13,739,500 of the treasury notes and certificates of deposit were issued, and these treasury obligations constituted the heaviest indebtedness of the state at the close of the war.[38]

In order to raise $600,000 for the support of the state government during 1861, the Georgia legislature in December, 1860, levied an *ad valorem* tax at the rate of 10½ cents on every $100 worth of taxable property, which included "all real and personal property . . . whether owned by individuals or corporations."[39] Peterson Thweatt told Stephens in August, 1861, that the decrease in the returns of property evaluations was not as large as he had expected:

. . . I am happy to inform you that the falling off, in returns, of value of property in the State is not as great as I anticipated. I don't think it will exceed $26,000,000 which will not be *four per cent* from our last year. This will show that this *war* has not *alarmed* our people *very much*. Last year, we were required to raise $400,000 . . . which we got at 6½ on our $100. This year we nett [*sic*] $600,000 at 10½ cents on our $100. This is a pretty small tax for "war times."[40]

Direct taxes, as a means of supporting the greater demands of war, were not increased until the end of 1862, when the legislature widened the scope of the general property tax, declaring cotton, grain, or other produce held for barter or sale on April 1st of each year, not belonging to the original producer, to be merchandise, and hence subject to taxation as other property. There was an estimated levy of $1,000,000 for 1862, and the rate of taxation was 18½ cents per $100. The levy was increased to $1,500,000 for 1863, but on account of the evaluations being given in inflated Confederate currency, the rate was reduced to seventeen cents. The legislature in December, 1863, stipulated that the general property tax for 1864 was not to exceed one per cent for all taxable property as estimated in Confederate treasury notes, and the rate for 1864 was twenty-five cents.[41]

Persons who failed to pay their property taxes were fined, but the legislature in December, 1861, extended the time allowed for the payment of taxes. In December, 1863, the legislature enacted a law exempting soldiers, and the widows and orphans of deceased soldiers, from paying taxes upon property of less than $2,000 in value. Free Negroes and slaves hiring their time were taxed $25 a year, and slave owners were required to pay a tax of from two to six dollars for each slave they owned.[42]

..WARTIME FINANCE

In response to recommendations from Governor Brown, the legislature in April, 1863, enacted Georgia's first profit and income tax. This tax provided for a graduated tax on the net income or profit of twenty per cent or more of "all persons and bodies corporate in this State engaged in the sale of goods, wares and merchandise, groceries and provisions; in the manufacture and sale of cotton and woolen goods; in the tanning and sale of leather, and in the manufacture and sale of any articles made thereof, and in the distillation and sale of spirituous liquors. . . ." When the net profits of an individual or corporation amounted to less than twenty per cent of the capital or credit invested, no tax was charged; but if the income was twenty per cent, the tax was fifty cents on every one hundred dollars. The graduation of rates and profits above twenty per cent was as follows: two per cent on profits of twenty to thirty per cent of capital or credit involved; two and one-half per cent of profits from thirty to forty per cent; three per cent on profits from forty to fifty per cent; and so on in the same ratio *ad infinitum*. The revenue was to be prorated among the counties according to the populations of 1860 and distributed to the families of indigent soldiers. A supplementary act of December 14, 1863, lowered the minimum taxable profits from twenty per cent to eight per cent and added other classes of business. A final measure of March 11, 1865, raised the profit exemption from eight to ten per cent and made further classifications, but the schedule of rates remained as in the act of December, 1863.[43]

The income and profit tax was aimed primarily at speculation and excessive profits, but it was poorly administered and generally evaded. Comptroller-General Thweatt estimated the returns as only one-fifth of the legitimate number. Only $683,235.29 was collected from the tax in 1863 from the profits of $15,737,479 which were reported, and in the following year only $767,839.44 was collected. In his annual report for 1863, the Comptroller-General commented pessimistically concerning the tax:

. . . many persons have failed to make their returns in accordance with the requirements of the Act. Instead of returning only the original capital according to their returns made on the 1st of April, 1862, and paying tax on their profit, according to the per cent made on the same; as they would make profits during the year from this original capital, they would re-invest it and make further profits, and then when called upon to make their return for the Income Tax they in-

CONFEDERATE GEORGIA..

clude all these investments and *re-investments of profits* during the year, *as Capital* — thereby whittling down the tax to a comparatively small sum.⁴⁴

Thweatt in 1864 wrote Stephens that "The State Income Tax Act for this year bids fair to give me as much trouble as our Act for last year. Innumerable questions are arising under it. . . ."⁴⁵

Georgia had twenty-five banks in 1860 with a total authorized capital of $17,000,000. Nine banks having a total capital of $10,000,000 were located in Savannah, six banks with a capital of $3,400,000 were in Augusta, two banks were in each of the towns of Macon and Dalton, while Columbus, Rome, LaGrange, Athens, Atlanta, and Ringgold had one bank each. These twenty-five banks employed only $9,028,078 of their capital stock in 1860 and paid state taxes totalling $33,085.29 on their stock.⁴⁶

When the legislature in November, 1860, authorized the Governor to obtain funds for the $1,000,000 military appropriation by offering for sale 20-year six per cent bonds, most of the banks purchased the bonds, but a few did not, thus causing Governor Brown to send a threatening note to the president of the Merchants and Planters Bank of Savannah:

> I shall in my next message to the General Assembly state the names of the Banks which have assisted the State by taking part of this loan and of those which have refused, should there be any such. The Bank over which you preside will be expected to take $30,000 of these Bonds at present, and $20,000 more during the Summer, should it become necessary for the State to raise a larger sum than is now needed.⁴⁷

Brown's letter caused Hiram Roberts, the president of the bank, to make a vehement reply:

> In this hour of danger wedded to your low designs, you make an application for money not as the Act requires to protect . . . the liberties of . . . Georgia but under cover of a *threat*. . . .
>
> While I feel that I speak the entire sentiments of the entire Board of Directors of The Merchants and Planters Bank when I say that each . . . one of them would put forward the last cent they own . . . to protect the rights . . . of Georgia — Yet they are not disposed to obey your *threat*. I am authorized to say that with an application under the spirit of the Act raising the fund to be expended by the Governor, That fifty thousand dollars will be most cheerfully loaned at Seven per cent Interest and an additional fifty thousand and more if it be necessary for the defence of Georgia.⁴⁸

..WARTIME FINANCE

As the war progressed, the liabilities of the banks increased from $51,438,264 in 1862 to $70,713,048 in 1863. The Confederacy's currency and tax measures of 1864 further reduced the profits of the banks by increasing the taxes, causing the presidents of five Savannah banks (Bank of Commerce, Bank of the State of Georgia, Farmers and Mechanics Bank, Marine Bank of Georgia, and the Merchants and Planters Bank) to send to the Confederate Congress a *Memorial* in which they urged that their currency and foreign exchange be relieved from the heavy taxation.[49]

The legislature of 1861 authorized all chartered banks in Georgia to suspend specie payments and to issue upon their assets "change bills" in denominations running from five cents to one dollar.[50] The purpose of the change bills was to afford a small medium of exchange, and the banks were allowed to issue them up to one per cent of their capital stock. The bills were redeemable in quantities of five dollars or more in bank notes and Confederate treasury notes. The legislature of 1862 required the banks to issue change bills up to five per cent of their capital and authorized the state treasury department to issue $100,000 worth of change bills from five cents to four dollars to be used as legal tender for all state debts. There is no record of how many such bills were issued by the banks, but the state issued $473,660 of change bills in 1863 and $937,782 in 1864, and there were $997,775 of them outstanding at the end of the war.[51]

Although it was illegal for private corporations or individuals to issue change bills, there was an epidemic in 1862 of shinplasters, as small bills issued privately were called. The prevalence of the shinplasters caused the Atlanta *Southern Confederacy* to announce that it would not accept them in payment for subscriptions or advertisements. By 1864 many Georgians would not accept even the legal change bills at par value. For instance, five-dollar change bills were accepted by several of the Georgia railroads at a valuation of only $3.25, and an Augusta newspaper announced that it would take them only at a discount of 33 1/3 per cent.

Counterfeiters, both Southern and Federal, helped to undermine the currency. When two men in Columbus were arrested in 1862 for buying cotton with counterfeit Confederate notes, the Columbus *Daily Sun* remarked, "This is no doubt an extensive plot. . . . There has been a constant underground line of communication going on between Nashville and . . . East Tennessee and Georgia, . . . for nearly four months. . . . The Yankees have resorted to this last cowardly method to ruin us. . . ."⁵² Several men were arrested in Atlanta under suspicion of circulating counterfeit Confederate notes, and a man was apprehended in Thomasville for having in his possession $200,000 worth of spurious bank bills. Members of a photographer's firm in Macon were arrested in 1863 for receiving counterfeit Confederate notes through the mail. The Atlanta *Southern Confederacy* warned that counterfeiters were changing the five and ten cent shinplasters to fifty cents. In 1864 a detective in Atlanta wrote Secretary Memminger that he was convinced "efforts will be made to bring out a new counterfeit at Columbia, S. C., as soon as the new issue of Treasury notes are put in circulation."⁵³

Early in the war speculators and profiteers made their appearance. A planter in Jones County wrote Stephens in 1861 that "the common farmers" are having difficulty "to keep our heads above the flood of destruction" caused by numerous taxes, "but the worst of all is the money thieves, those Speculators the merchants. They have put Salt to ten Dollars per Sack, Coffee from Thirty-Seven to fifty cents per pound, in fact Every thing the farmer is oblige to have . . . is held by the merchant at three and four prices."⁵⁴ The Savannah *Republican* on December 18, 1861, remarked that "One speculator can do the Southern cause more injury in one week than a dozen Yankees could in a month." The legislature in December of that year passed an act forbidding "Speculation in Breadstuffs and other articles of general use and consumption, and to make such acts criminal . . . ." The penalty for falsely representing that one was purchasing articles for the army was one to three years in the penitentiary, and the penalty for monopolizing vital articles was a fine of not less than $500 or more than $5,000.⁵⁵

Although many Georgia newspapers had condemned speculators and extortioners, some of the editors and contributors opposed the punitive laws as futile and even tending to make prices still higher. An Atlanta citizen, for instance, pointed out that merchants were compelled to pay high prices for their goods and could not sell unless at a profit. The *Southern Confederacy* said that "Commerce should be untrammeled and protected by law, the same as agriculture, the mechanic arts or labor. Where this is the case, competition soon regulates temporary extortions much more effectually than laws. . . ."⁵⁶ Governor Brown admitted in September, 1862, that the law to suppress monopolies and specu-

..WARTIME FINANCE

lation had been a "dead letter" in Georgia. Writing to Governor Zebulon B. Vance of North Carolina, he said that the act passed by the legislature to suppress extortion had not met expectations, and that speculators and extortioners "have been the greatest enemy to our cause."[57]

The Milledgeville *Federal Union* complained that "people with abundance of provisions are not selling them. They keep them back to make the scarcity greater, in hope of getting more money."[58] "A few sordid spirits are open in their complaints against taxation," stated the Augusta *Daily Constitutionalist*. "These grumblers... have made fortunes out of speculations..., and it annoys them to part with even a modicum of their gains for the common good."[59]

In addition to the widespread speculation, inflation was an inevitable consequence of the Confederacy's failure to achieve financial stability. Prior to the war salt sold in Georgia for two dollars a sack, but in September, 1862, it was bringing eighty dollars. The price of sugar advanced from eight cents a pound at the beginning of the war to about ninety cents in September, 1862, and to anywhere from seven to ten dollars a pound near the close of the war. Butter that sold for twelve cents a pound in 1861 commanded a price of seventy-five cents in April, 1863, and five dollars or more in February, 1865. Corn advanced from approximately two dollars a bushel in 1863 to seven dollars in 1864 and fourteen dollars in February, 1865. The prices of other commodities increased in a similar ratio. The Atlanta *Southern Confederacy* in 1863 said that "Anything will bring any price demanded for it."

The wave of speculation and extortionary prices victimized the public until the end of the war. "... it is the hardest times in olde Cobb I ever saw. Lyeing, swindling and a specalation is all that is goinge on here now.... There is a heape of Yankies here as well as in north and Some as mean men...," a man wrote to his brother.[60] "The World is full of Speculators at this time," another man wrote. "I give them a turn once in a while. I have made four hundred dollars Since Christmas and only went on a Small Scale. I sold two gallons of brandy for fifty dollars...."[61] A Columbus newspaper in 1863 remarked: "We have no doubt ... that there was never before half the amount of corn stored away in Columbus as at the present time,... It has been bought for speculation, and the speculators are still buying...."[62]

Real estate in Atlanta reached "palace figures," and a newspaper stated that "If an owner does not like his neighbor, he has nothing to do but 'price his property.' "⁶³ In 1864 a Columbus woman was renting a small one-story house at $800 a year, but the owner notified her that the rent would be $3,000 for the year 1865. An Augusta paper complained that wood dealers were charging fifty dollars a load for wood and were taking advantage of the "necessitous in our cities." The Savannah *Republican* said that a Negro drayman who charged "six dollars for hauling a gentleman's trunk from the Railroad depot to his residence . . . was fined . . . six dollars, which it is hoped will have a good effect upon his extortionate propensities hereafter."⁶⁴ An officer in Savannah commented regarding the class of *nouveau riche* in that city:

The social changes that progress with the revolution are many . . . ; the rich are ruined, the poor grow rich; some of the best property in this City . . . has been purchased by German Jews, who were lately the poorest of the poor. Any one who is willing to buy, keep, and re-sell at a profit can grow rich; the recipe is simple — the practice successfull [*sic*], vide the Israelites.⁶⁵

Near the end of the war an Augusta correspondent to the Columbus *Daily Times* said that "A few more days and a man cannot live unless he is a Jew, a speculator, a quartermaster or a commissary."⁶⁶

During the war the legislature appropriated large sums of money for purposes other than the usual state expenses. Among these numerous appropriations were $45,000 to obstruct navigable rivers; $400,000 for clothing for the troops; $500,000 for salt; $100,000 for wool and cotton cards; $100,000 to reimburse the Western and Atlantic Railroad; $30,000 to remove indigent noncombatants from areas threatened by the enemy; and $18,846 to combat an epidemic of smallpox. The greatest financial problem and expense during the war, however, besides the military appropriations, was the care of the indigent soldiers and their families. The legislature appropriated for this purpose $2,500,000 in 1861, $2,500,000 in 1862; $5,000,000 in 1863, and $6,000,000 in both 1864 and 1865. An act passed on December 13, 1862, required the justices of the inferior courts in each county to make a report, under oath, to the Comptroller-General of the number of persons in his county who needed to be beneficiaries of the funds and the amount and nature of the property held by each beneficiary. The

..WARTIME FINANCE

funds were then distributed among the counties in proportion to the number of beneficiaries, ranging in 1861 from $74,448 for Gwinnett County to $4,798 for Glascock. The justices of the inferior courts disbursed the funds, which were in the form of Confederate and state treasury notes.[67] In 1863 there were 83,628 eligible beneficiaries of the state relief fund, and the increasing number of dead and disabled soldiers brought the number to 117,889 in 1864. Indigent soldiers and their families received from the state a dole totalling $5,968,359, not counting large sums appropriated for the same purpose by the various counties.[68]

No estimate of the amount of money raised by local taxation is available, but one writer has said that "such agencies probably expended as much as did the state government."[69] The legislature in 1861 received several petitions from counties requesting the authority to vote special taxes and bonds with which to support their volunteers and the indigent families of volunteers. In compliance with these requests, the legislature in November, 1861, passed two acts which laid the bases for a potentially greater county revenue. The first act authorized the counties to issue bonds and borrow money to equip their troops and to support their needy families, while the second measure allowed counties to levy "military" taxes for similar purposes. The military tax was to be paid in currency or in commodities as each county should determine.[70]

Many counties soon began levying extra taxes. Coweta County voted a military tax of one dollar per hundred dollar valuation as based upon the state assessment. Stewart County trebled the state assessment and exempted from the tax all, or in part, people who had donated a minimum of fifteen dollars in cash or twenty dollars in clothing to soldiers. The Upson County tax law allowed "relief reimbursements or credits to persons who have made voluntary contributions to the objects . . . for which said extra tax was levied."[71] A citizen of Quitman informed one of his friends that "Under the Tax Law of last Session of our Legislature, we have levied a Tax sufficient to raise $4000 for the families of our men in service, payable in provisions . . . or . . . in money as the Taxpayer prefers."[72] The Americus *Sumter Republican* announced on August 8, 1862, that it had been "requested by the Inferior Court of this county, to state that the Funds for the relief of the families of our soldiers will have been exhausted by the next pay day, . . . and to urge the Tax Payers . . . to . . . pay, in advance, a portion of their Relief Tax for next year."[73]

CONFEDERATE GEORGIA..

Although the state paid $700,000 on her public debt in 1861, she was unable to prevent the debt from increasing, and in November, 1862, the debt had grown to $8,417,750. State expenditures of $7,640,117 in 1863 and $13,288,435 in 1864 caused the public debt to rise to $14,747,270 at the end of the 1864 fiscal year. The total debt in 1864 consisted of a bonded indebtedness of $6,086,250, treasury notes of $6,993,000, and certificates of deposit of $1,395,000. Included in the bonded debt was the $2,670,750 which had been incurred before the war in constructing the Western and Atlantic Railroad and in purchasing stock in the Atlantic and Gulf Railroad. Brown told the legislature in November, 1864, that to meet her liabilities the state had public property consisting of the Western and Atlantic Railroad, bank stock, and railroad stock, valued before the depreciation of the currency at $8,840,124.68, and that the total taxable property of the state was worth more than $700,000,000 upon a specie basis. The Western and Atlantic Railroad paid into the state treasury $438,000 in 1861, $440,000 in 1862, $1,650,000 in 1863, and $1,117,522.48 in 1864. Despite the mounting public debt, Comptroller-General Thweatt was able to report a cash balance of $2,099,603.44 in the state treasury at the close of the 1863 fiscal year, and a balance of $2,146,087.62 a year later.[74]

After Sherman's march through the state, the capital in Georgia's banks shrank from $70,713,048 to $44,816,979; and the Comptroller-General's report for 1865 stated that "there have been no Bank Dividends this year. . . ."[75] Taxes became almost impossible to collect. For instance, a group of Newton County citizens in February, 1865, asked Governor Brown to allow the tax collector an extension of the time necessary for him to do his work. "Owing to the disturbed state of the country, it was late before the Tax Collector . . . was able to commence business," they said, "and on account of the loss of horses . . . it was impossible for many taxpayers to meet him at his appointments."[76] During the winter of 1865 many people, in order to have their taxes reduced, made affidavits of property destroyed by Sherman or taken by Confederate troops. These affidavits listed such items as slaves, horses and mules, cattle, wagons, buggies, and carriages. One tax collector wrote Brown that on account of the work arising from the necessity of having affidavits written by persons who had lost their property he would need two additional months in which to complete his work.

..WARTIME FINANCE

Any statement of the total cost of the war to Georgia must necessarily be a general one. Besides the money and supplies expended by all agencies of the state during the war, it has been estimated that Georgia lost three-fourths of her wealth. Land values decreased by one-fourth, and the slaves, valued at $454,042,282 in 1860, were a total loss. The public debt was increased to $20,-811,525.85, including a war debt of $18,035,775, of which $3,308,-500 was in bonds and the remainder in treasury notes, treasury certificates, and change bills. The Comptroller-General's report of October, 1865, said that there was a cash balance in the treasury of $5,201,086.18, but only $44,750 was in United States currency and a few thousand dollars was in state treasury notes and state change bills, while the remainder was in Confederate treasury notes, which were worthless. The bonded debt had been increased by back interest due on bonds amounting to $1,047,000.[77]

In 1866, after the repudiation of the Confederate debt, Georgia still had a public debt of $5,706,500, whereas in 1860 the debt had been only $2,670,750. The debt of $5,706,500 was in five, six, and seven per cent bonds which were obligated to be paid between the years 1868 and 1886. The increased debt was due to the state's issuing, according to an act of March 12, 1866, $3,030,000 worth of seven per cent mortgage bonds which were to be due in 1886, and were to be used in funding the six and seven per cent bonds which were past due but had not been funded. Although encumbered with a relatively large debt, the state in October, 1866, had a cash balance in the treasury of $71,752.05, possessed bank and railroad stock valued at $1,126,900.00, and still owned the Western and Atlantic Railroad. In his annual report to the Governor, made on October 16, 1866, the Comptroller-General announced that "It is a cheering fact to know, that in the face of repudiation by the Convention of a large part of the State's indebtedness, that her credit is almost unimpaired, and her new bonds, which only a few months since were selling at ninety cents, are now bringing ninety-seven and a half, and will doubtless be at par in a short time."[78]

CHAPTER V

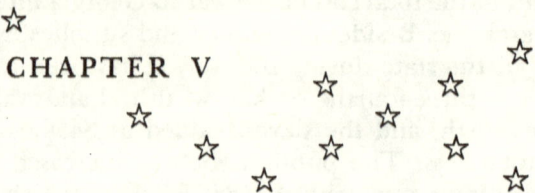

Military and Naval Operations, 1861-1863

"YOU NEED NOT FEAR OUR COAST IN Georgia for old man Colen and myself will meet the Yankees if they come their [sic]," wrote Moses W. Davis, of Oak Hill, to his brother, a private in Virginia, in September, 1861.[1] Georgians living along the coast were apprehensive of impending danger, however, and many of them began sending their slaves and valuable personal property into the interior of the state. Governor Brown in January, 1861, had ordered an artillery company from Macon to St. Simons Island to guard Brunswick Harbor, and in April he notified Secretary of War Walker that he had "ordered one company of artillery with the regiment now on its way to Savannah."[2] In a letter to Vice-President Stephens, Brown said that the people living near the coast felt so great a sense of insecurity "that I cannot too strongly urge upon you the importance of this question" of strengthening the coastal defenses. The Governor asked Stephens to urge Secretary Walker to distribute along the coast one of the Confederate regiments stationed at Savannah, and promised to fill the place of that regiment by ordering out the Savannah regiment of state volunteers.[3]

The coastal defenses continued to be inadequate, however,[4] and Hiram Roberts, the president of the Merchants and Planters Bank in Savannah, accused Brown of failing to take proper steps to defend the coast:

> With one Million of treasure five months what progress have you made towards defending . . . Georgia from the Enemy. You have collected a number of worthy men together and placed them in Fort Pulaski and Fort Jackson to be preyed upon by an enemy, if they so determine, for want of proper Arms — You have refused to Arm the citizen soldiery along the coast. . . . You hold arms . . . at Milledgeville instead of having distributed them where they might be used. . . .[5]

..MILITARY AND NAVAL OPERATIONS, 1861-1863

In a letter to the Savannah *Daily Morning News,* "Themistocles" warned: "Upon the sea the enemy is . . . superior to us . . . and our coasts will be ravaged. We should have a double line of batteries . . . connected by small vessels of war, and by transports prepared for the purpose at any cost."[6] A soldier at Camp Lawton, near Savannah, asserted that "The city of Savannah if tomorrow the test that was applied to Sodom and Gomorrah was forced upon her would barely escape the fate of those cities."[7]

During the summer of 1861 Commodore Josiah Tattnall organized a "Mosquito Fleet," composed of a river steamer and four tugs mounted with such guns as could be procured. The vessels were called the *Savannah, Lady Davis, Resolute,* and *Sampson.* This semblance of a navy plied the waters from Port Royal, South Carolina, southward, aiding vessels coming from England with war supplies.[8] "Contempt for Lincoln's blockade must prevail even at Timbucktoo!" exclaimed the Atlanta *Daily Intelligencer.*[9] During the first week in November, however, a Federal naval expedition, consisting of forty-one vessels, captured Port Royal and Hilton Head, off the South Carolina coast, and threatened the Georgia seaboard. Commodore Tattnall, with his little flotilla of four vessels, attacked the Federal fleet at the entrance to Port Royal Sound, but the Confederates were forced to retire. "The next demonstration will probably be upon our own State," admonished the Sandersville *Central Georgian* on November 13, 1861. "Shall one of Lincoln's vandals set foot upon Georgia's soil? Let it not be so."

The legislature was in session, and Governor Brown on November 6th warned the assembly that the number of Confederate troops upon the coast was insufficient and that ten thousand additional state troops were needed. Repeatedly urging the legislature to lay aside all differences of opinion and to take further defensive measures, the Governor asked for an appropriation of "at least five million dollars," but the assembly hesitated, feeling that the state's defense should be accomplished by the Confederate government. Brown shared in this feeling, but he realized "that it is not now the time to stop to count the cost."[10]

Commodore Tattnall's boats attacked a Federal fleet of six vessels in Cockspur Road, at the mouth of the Savannah River, on November 26th, but finding it impossible to draw the enemy into range of the guns of Fort Pulaski, the Confederates retired.[11] After three Federal vessels had shelled Tybee Island, near Fort

Pulaski, to ascertain whether any masked batteries might render an invasion hazardous, several hundred Federal troops occupied the island on November 24th, forcing the Confederates to withdraw. By early December from five hundred to two thousand Federal troops were encamped at Tybee and they began erecting batteries upon the island, working mostly at night.[12]

Soon after the Federal forces had occupied Port Royal and Hilton Head, Union gunboats entered Ossabaw, Warsaw, St. Helena, and Cumberland sounds, along the Georgia coast, going as far south as Fernandina, Florida. "The enemy's gun-boats have entered Warsaw sound, accompanied by a number of transports — . . . have run up Wilmington River, and are now within long range of Savannah River," General Alexander R. Lawton, commanding the Confederate forces at Savannah, warned General Henry R. Jackson.[13] The fear of attack caused the evacuation of St. Simons Island by the planters in December, 1861, the families retreating to their inland plantations or to Savannah. The island was left deserted except for fifteen hundred Georgia troops stationed there under the command of Colonel Carey M. Stiles.[14]

Increasing efforts were made to defend the Georgia coast, especially the principal port, Savannah. General Jackson concentrated his forces closer to Savannah, directing General William H. T. Walker, commanding the third brigade of state troops, to remove his brigade to the immediate vicinity of the city. "Here his [Walker's] command will be in the vicinity of the only town of the seaboard, against which any attack of the enemy, at all formidable . . . , must be directed," Jackson notified Adjutant-General Wayne.[15] Jackson co-operated closely with General Lawton in strengthening the coastal defenses; and from November, 1861, until the following February, General Robert E. Lee directed the entire defense of the coast from South Carolina to Florida. Writing from his headquarters at Coosawhatchie, South Carolina, General Lee sent the following dispatch to General Jackson:

> I . . . am much gratified to learn that the Division under your command, is ready for the defence of . . . Georgia, and is placed at my disposal for that purpose. The troops in the Confederate service under Gen. Lawton have already been distributed with a view to the protection of the most exposed points, and particularly to guard the approaches to Savannah. There is no point at which reinforcements may not be required, and I will direct Genl Lawton to indicate to you where your troops can be of most service, and to designate

..MILITARY AND NAVAL OPERATIONS, 1861-1863

such points as you may take under your exclusive charge. At present ... I beg that you will see the preparation of your command ... be perfected as far as possible.[16]

In another letter to Jackson, General Lee requested a detail of mechanics to assist the Confederates in constructing ships for coastal defense:

> You have been kind enough to offer to furnish mechanics, to aid in building some boats, that we may be able to employ the troops on the water when necessary; and Genl Walker informed me a few days since, that there were skillful carpenters in his Brigade, that he would recommend for such service. I have therefore the honor to apply for a detail of 35 mechanics acquainted with boat building, to report tomorrow morning at "Harding's Ship Yard" near Miller's Foundry. . . .[17]

Working feverishly, the state troops placed obstructions in the Savannah River, erected batteries to command the obstructions, and built fortifications around Savannah. "I am willing that the State troops in common with such Conf. troops as are near the city and not engaged in fortifying at other points, proceed with fortifications, but think it should be done by fatigue parties," Governor Brown informed General Jackson on February 5, 1862.[18] A few days later Adjutant-General Wayne told Jackson that ". . . the Governor empowers you to do whatever . . . necessary for the Safety of the City. . . . It is only by Strict discipline and harmonious Subordination that we can look for Success against the powerful forces now threatening us by land and by water."[19] A soldier at Camp Wilson, three miles from Savannah, described some of the measures being taken for the defense of the city:

> ... we are ... now engaged in throwing up Batteries at different points and in cutting down trees on all the roads leading from the Coast to Savannah, that is not across them but every tree on each side of the Road to the swamp — the object of this is to prevent the Yankees from flanking us on either side with their artillery or cavalry, but compell them to keep the road, by this means they can bring but few men into action at any one time and with our Batteries we can sweep the roads — the cause of this unusual excitement is daily increase of the Yankee Fleet on our Coast.[20]

Several weeks later Jackson received a letter from General Lawton concerning the obstructions which were being placed in the Savannah River:

As you have kindly consented to take entire charge of the making, filling, and mooring, of the "cribs" to be used as obstructions in the Savannah River, I beg to State, that in a conference to-day with General Pemberton, it was decided that we must use the stones in the streets as ballast. . . . It is important that a large force be at work to-morrow in taking up these stones. . . .[21]

Governor Brown recommended that Jackson build bomb proof casemates — "and use Six, Twelve, or Eighteen pounder field pieces to cooperate with your rifles — upon their Barges."[22] With Savannah in danger of capture, the police force of the city was received into the service of the state as an organized military company and was detailed by Jackson for duty in defending the city. In order to have more troops and guns available for the defense of Savannah, General Lee in February, 1862, ordered the military evacuation of St. Simons Island. Withdrawal of Confederate forces from all of the islands along the Georgia coast occurred within a month, and by March, 1862, Union forces were in control of practically the entire Georgia coast with the exception of the Savannah area. Writing to Governor Brown, a woman made the unique suggestion that the Federal fleet near Savannah might be destroyed if five hundred or a thousand barrels of turpentine were poured into the Savannah River at night within a mile of the fleet. ". . . having allowed the proper time to elapse . . . then set fire to the Turpentine . . . and it will do them much damage if not entirely rout them," the letter stated.[23]

The next objective of the Federal troops after their occupation of Tybee Island was the capture of Fort Pulaski, an irregular pentagon surrounded by a moat, situated on Cockspur Island at the mouth of the Savannah River, about seventeen miles below the city of Savannah. After the fort had been occupied by Georgia troops in January, 1861, Governor Brown had expended about $80,000 from the state treasury for heavy guns and other necessary equipment for the fort. Brown had called several times upon the Confederacy for more troops to defend the fort, and on November 17, 1861, he had asked for two long-range guns.[24] The garrison in the fort consisted of 365 men and twenty-four officers, under the command of Colonel Charles H. Olmstead, and it was supplied with provisions by Commodore Tattnall, in spite of attacks from Federal gunboats. The armament of the fort was rather obsolete. There were ten or more heavy ten-inch and eight-inch Columbiads in the casemates, three or four forty-two pounders on the barbette,

MILITARY AND NAVAL OPERATIONS, 1861-1863

and several ten-inch mortars near the south wharf. The total number of guns was forty-eight.[25]

Although the Confederates had driven piles into the channels which opened into the Savannah River below the fort, the Federals on February 22, 1862, succeeded in isolating the fort by removing the obstructions in an artificial channel called "Wall's Cut," and entering the river in the rear of the fortifications.[26] The fort thus was cut off from communication with Savannah.

One of the officers defending the fort sent the following information to his wife:

We are entirely cut off, the Yankees . . . are daily increasing their force, both in men and ships. . . . We are endeavoring to employ a man . . . who is acquainted with all the Inlets from here to Savannah to run the Blockade to carry and bring us our mail once or twice a week.

I am now virtually a prisoner, the Yankees are on evry [sic] side of us. . . . We have full 12 months provisions on hand. . . . I think however a desperate fight will soon come of [sic], here. . . .[27]

A few weeks later the same officer said, "I am beginning to think we shall never be rescued or relieved and that we shall eventually be perished out and compelled to surrender. . . . The excitement of firing at each other keeps us alive and in good spirits — I dont mean (Whiskey spirits) for that kind we have long since lost sight of."[28] Writing three weeks later to a man in Columbus, the officer at Pulaski said that the Federal forces had "several Batteries on Tybee, one opposite the Fort across the South Channel about nineteen hundred yards from the Fort. This is a very formidable Battery some ½ mile long. . . . Their ships and gun boats are around us in evry [sic] direction ready to take a hand."[29]

After the siege had lasted for several weeks, General David Hunter, commanding the Federal forces, on the morning of April 10th demanded the surrender of the fort. Colonel Olmstead replied that he was there to defend, not to surrender, the fort. The Federals then began a two-day bombardment from eleven batteries which they had erected on Tybee Island, hurling a thousand large shells into the fort.[30]

In reporting the bombardment, the Atlanta *Southern Confederacy* on April 12, 1862, commented that "The fire upon Fort Pulaski was kept up throughout the night at intervals of a half hour, for the purpose . . . as is supposed, of keeping our troops from sleeping. After daylight a general cannonade was renewed with terrific violence. The reports shook the windows in the city [Savannah] like an earthquake."[31] A vivid description of the bombardment was given by an eyewitness, a young Georgia captain who at the time was stationed at nearby Skidaway Island:

> We were six miles off, but we could distinctly see the heavy columns of white smoke shooting up from the mortars on Tybee, and then see the immense shells bursting over the Fort. The enemy fired four and five times every minute, while the Fort replied slowly and coolly. The flag staff was shot away about noon. At night the sight was grand. The tongue of flame was seen to leap from the mortars and then the flash of the bursting shell appeared just above the Fort.

The Savannah *Daily Morning News* said that "The heavy Parrot guns of the enemy, with conical and steel pointed shot, bored into and shivered the masonry at every discharge."[32] Several breaches were made in the walls, the magazine was in danger of exploding, most of the guns on the side of the fort facing the enemy were dismounted, and retreat was impossible. Among the last guns fired from the fort were those on the parapet, the Confederates standing there exposed to a storm of iron and hail. Entirely cut off from any chance of reinforcement, the garrison was forced to surrender. In the afternoon of April 11th, the terms of capitulation whereby the Confederates were made prisoners of war were arranged. One Confederate was killed during the bombardment and eighteen were wounded, and one Federal soldier lost his life.[33]

The loss of Fort Pulaski stimulated the preparations for the defense of Georgia, and Governor Brown issued a proclamation for the complete organization of the state militia, warning that "those who fail to volunteer may be drafted."[34] Adjutant-General Wayne ordered "State troops who have been discharged by reason of expiration of Service . . . to report forthwith to your respective Colonels and to aid in defending Savannah."[35] The legislature appropriated $45,000 to obstruct the channels of the Apalachicola, Chattahoochee, and Flint rivers, and a short time later authorized the expenditure of $500,000 for the same purpose. Governor Brown was urged to construct iron-clad boats and place them in the Savannah, Altamaha, and Chattahoochee rivers; and the city council of Columbus appropriated $3,000 to aid in obstructing the Chattahoochee River. Attention was called to the defenseless position of Augusta, and the possibility of obstructing the entire channel of the Savannah River from Savannah to Augusta was considered.

The fall of Fort Pulaski caused great alarm in Savannah, but the Federals did not attack the city, for the Confederate forces stationed along the coast were able to offer considerable resistance. Consequently, the Federals contented themselves with raiding the sea island and coastal plantations and seizing supplies. The Savannah newspapers rejoiced when General Lawton, commanding the district at Savannah, instituted immediate measures to strengthen the city's defenses and announced that he would protect the city at all hazards, but the Sandersville *Central Georgian* caustically remarked:

Well, if Gen. Lawton has been at Savannah with an army for more than a year, and has just discovered that he was sent there to defend the city, we are at a loss to know the ground of rejoicing, unless, indeed, it be because this long delayed and remote spark of intelligence has at last, after a tediously tortuous journey, arrived at headquarters.[36]

Uncertainty concerning the fate of Savannah continued. The legislature in a resolution declared that Savannah must never be surrendered, but, if necessary, should be defended house by house and street by street. By August, 1862, approximately twelve hundred Negroes were laboring on the Savannah fortifications, in addition to the free Negroes of Savannah, who were impressed into service by General Hugh W. Mercer, successor to General Lawton. Most of the Negroes were furnished by planters in the middle Georgia counties. When in November General Mercer reported that the Confederacy was withdrawing Negroes from their work upon the Savannah fortifications, Brown called upon one-tenth of the working hands in the surrounding district to work on the fortifications for thirty days. As only a few slaves were sent, he threatened to impress them. Three months later, when the Federals were believed to be planning an attack upon Port Royal, Charleston, and Savannah, General Mercer requested the use of 2,500 Negroes for sixty days in order to strengthen the fortifications. Brown called for 1,500 hands and urged all Georgians to rally to the cause with whatever weapons they could secure. The Negroes were sent, but north Georgia failed to send its full quota.[37]

Several minor skirmishes occurred along the Georgia coast during 1862 and 1863. In April, 1862, a skirmish on Whitemarsh

CONFEDERATE GEORGIA..

Island took place between some companies of the Thirteenth Georgia Regiment and a Federal regiment from Michigan, and on May 1st a skirmish occurred in Liberty County between Confederate and Federal gunboats. In June of the following year Union raiders in gunboats ascended Turtle River near Brunswick and burned a bridge on the Brunswick and Albany Railroad. Federal troops in July, 1863, burned the town of Darien after the Confederates, under the command of General Mercer, found it impossible to concentrate a force sufficient to oppose a landing.[38] The Federals were unsuccessful, however, in their repeated attacks upon Fort McAllister, a simple earthwork with stone parapets at the mouth of the Ogeechee River. A Federal fleet in March, 1863, attacked the fort, but the ships were forced to retreat, badly crippled, after the garrison, commanded by Captain George W. Anderson, had resisted an eight-hour bombardment.[39] An interesting account of the battle was given by Captain George A. Mercer of Savannah in a letter to his sister:

We are greatly encouraged by the repulse of the Iron Clads by Fort McAllister on 3rd inst. The Battery was subjected to a terrible storm of shot and shell for eight hours, but Geo. Wayne, Commanding, Geo. Nicoll, and their brave officers and men, were undaunted, and drove back the invader; wonderful to say there were only two men slightly wounded, though the narrow escapes were numerous and miraculous; one Surgeon had a pipe knocked from his mouth. The moral effect of this engagement has been very wholesome; iron-clad gun boats have lost their terrors for us![40]

During the early summer of 1863 Captain T. S. Hopkins of the Twenty-fourth Battalion of Georgia Cavalry, accompanied by six men, made a reconnaissance of Ossabaw Island. After secreting their boat, they advanced toward the northern end of the island, and upon discovering no signs of the enemy at two plantations, they became careless. At a third plantation a sergeant went to the dwelling house and opened the front door; he saw a Yankee officer sitting down cleaning a pistol. The officer, without looking up, said, "Come in." The sergeant, with great presence of mind, replied, "In a minute, sir," and descended the steps to communicate with his party. In his "Diary" Captain Mercer described what happened:

In the mean while Capt. H. imprudently ordered his men to seize two negro women who were crossing the yard; these screamed, and instantly, from every building, Yankee soldiers rushed out; the few

..MILITARY AND NAVAL OPERATIONS, 1861-1863

Confederates would have been captured, had not the Yankees been so completely astounded; their confusion was increased by the order from one of our men, in a loud tone, to fall back and call up the reserves; in the midst of it our men beat a hasty retreat and escaped from the island. One company of Yankee Artillery was ascertained to be at the plantation.[41]

One purpose of the Federal navy during the war was to gather slaves from abandoned coastal plantations and to locate them in colonies in order to "protect" them. In March, 1862, Commander S. W. Godon established a colony of forty Negro contrabands on St. Simons Island, housing them on the plantation of T. Butler King. In compliance with a request for military aid, the first company of the first Negro regiment in the war, composed mostly of South Carolina ex-slaves, was ordered from Beaufort, South Carolina, to St. Simons in August, 1862. Severe depredations were committed on the island during its occupation by the Negro troops. They raided the plantations, stole, and destroyed property. In November, 1862, the troops were sent back to South Carolina and the contraband colony was disbanded. Two months later a Federal expedition under the command of Colonel Thomas Wentworth Higginson occupied the island.[42]

In addition to these coastal operations, Georgia experienced two raids into the state prior to Sherman's invasion in 1864. Both raids were for the purpose of cutting the Western and Atlantic Railroad, which connected Atlanta with Chattanooga. The first attempt was made in April, 1862, when a group of twenty Federals selected from three Ohio regiments, under the command of "Captain" James J. Andrews, entered the state with the object of destroying thirteen bridges on the Western and Atlantic Railroad and thus cutting off communications between the Confederate troops and their source of supply. General O. M. Mitchell, commanding a division of Buell's army near Shelbyville, Tennessee, gave permission to Andrews, who was a Union spy and contraband merchant, to make the venture. Dressed in civilian clothes, Andrews and his men went down the Western and Atlantic Railroad, boarded a train at Marietta, and at Big Shanty, seven miles north of Marietta, uncoupled an engine, the "General," and three box cars from the passenger coach while the crew and passengers were eating breakfast at the Big Shanty Hotel. They then headed for Chattanooga, leaving the conductor, engineer, passengers, and spectators lost in amazement.[43]

William A. Fuller, the conductor of the passenger coach, Jeff Cain, the engineer, and Anthony Murphy, the foreman of machine and motive power of the railroad shop, started in pursuit of the raiders, first on foot and then in a hand car. At Acworth the fleeing Federals blocked the track with cross-ties and tore down the telegraph wire, but the pursuers removed the obstructions and continued the chase. When the Southerners reached Etowah Station, they obtained an engine, the "Yonah," and dashed on toward Kingston.[44] A short distance south of Kingston the pursuers found the track blocked by three freight trains; but they secured another engine, the "William R. Smith," which stood on a "Y" where the Rome branch of the railroad joined the main line north of where the freight trains were standing. Between Kingston and Adairsville the pursuers were compelled to abandon the "William R. Smith," for the fleeing Federals had torn up the track. Continuing on foot, the Southerners soon signaled and stopped a south bound freight train, the "Texas," detached the cars, and resumed the chase by running the "Texas" in reverse. Although the fugitives continued dropping coaches and cross-ties and destroying the tracks in order to hinder the pursuit, they finally were captured near Ringgold when their fuel supply became exhausted. They were court-martialed, and Andrews and seven of the men were hanged as spies during the summer of 1862. Military events delayed further trials, and on October 16, 1862, the rest of the party escaped from jail, eight of them reaching the Union lines. The other six were exchanged in March, 1863.[45] The raid by Andrews caused tremendous excitement in Georgia; and the Milledgeville *Southern Federal Union* declared that martial law should be established not only in Atlanta but all along the Western and Atlantic Railroad, and that independent guerrilla companies should be formed to defend the state.

The second attempt to disrupt traffic on the Western and Atlantic Railroad occurred in the spring of 1863 when Colonel Abel D. Streight of the Fifty-first Indiana Volunteers was sent by General W. S. Rosecrans to dissever the line south of Dalton. Success of the plan would result in preventing troops and supplies from being sent to General Braxton Bragg at Tullahoma, Tennessee, via the railroad. With approximately sixteen hundred cavalrymen, Colonel Streight in April, 1863, advanced southward from Nashville, Tennessee, into northern Alabama. Leaving Tuscumbia, Alabama, on April 26th, Streight's force moved eastward across Alabama, entered Georgia, and began marching up the Coosa River toward Rome. "The Yankees are coming!" was the dreadful cry heard throughout the alarmed Georgia city. There was no organized home guard in Rome, but convalescent soldiers turned out from the military hospitals, and citizens armed with shotguns and rifles were mustered quickly into service. When Captain M. H. Russell was sent by Streight with a select band of men to seize the bridge at Rome and hold it until the main body of troops arrived, Rome made such a show of resistance that Russell was led to believe that the defenses were quite formidable. He retreated without attempting to take the bridge.

In the meantime, General Nathan Bedford Forrest had been sent by General Bragg to intercept the Federal troops. Leaving Spring Hill, Tennessee, on April 24th, and pressing into service all of the citizens whom he could reach while marching, General Forrest pursued Colonel Streight with about six hundred men. At certain points the Federals stopped to give battle for a few hours and at other times they engaged their pursuers in a running fight. After five days and nights of marching and fighting through a rugged country filled with Union sympathizers, General Forrest came upon Colonel Streight's troops near Cedar Bluff, Alabama, between Gadsden and Rome. Pretending to communicate with unseen military forces, General Forrest deceived Colonel Streight as to the strength of the Confederate army, and on May 3rd his opponent surrendered his entire force of about sixteen hundred men and a large quantity of supplies.[46] A few days later citizens of Floyd and surrounding counties met in Rome and formed a "military organization for repelling the thieving, house burning, and vandal foe that may venture upon our soil."[47]

During the same year that Colonel Streight made his unsuccessful invasion, the bloodiest battle ever fought in Georgia occurred near Chickamauga Creek, in the northwestern corner of the state about twelve miles south of Chattanooga. Maneuvered out of Chattanooga by General William S. Rosecrans' Army of the Cumberland, General Bragg moved the Army of Tennessee to Lafayette, Georgia, in order to await reinforcements from Virginia and to protect the Western and Atlantic Railroad, upon which his army's communications depended. He soon perceived, however, that Rosecrans, in hastily moving his army to the rear of Chattanooga, had dangerously divided his own troops, and that the Confederate army might defeat separately each of the three Union corps.

CONFEDERATE GEORGIA..

The Confederate attack was delayed, however, and several days elapsed during which Bragg lost his chance to strike the Union army before it was fully concentrated. On September 17, 1863, the two armies were aligned along Chickamauga Creek, with the Confederates on the east bank and the Union forces on the west. In this position Bragg determined to attack with his entire army, without waiting longer for the reinforcements from Virginia. Bragg expected to envelop one corps of the enemy's army, commanded by General Thomas L. Crittenden, and to drive Rosecrans' entire army back upon Lookout Mountain. His plan was defeated, however, when Rosecrans, during the night of September 18th, moved General George H. Thomas' corps to the extreme left in order to secure his line of retreat to Chattanooga. On the following morning the battle began when Thomas, sending a division on a reconnaissance towards Chickamauga Creek, encountered dismounted Confederate cavalry. Both sides rapidly brought up reinforcements until almost all of Rosecrans' and most of Bragg's forces were engaged. Thick forests concealed the movements of both armies, and the fighting consisted of a series of independent engagements, with alternate success and repulse for each side. The general result of the struggle on September 19th was favorable to Rosecrans.[48]

During the night Bragg reorganized his army into two wings, the right one under General Leonidas Polk and the left one under General James Longstreet, who had just arrived from Virginia. The battle was resumed on the following morning when the right wing of the Confederate army attacked the left flank of the Union army, commanded by General Thomas. The fighting was proceeding with varying fortune, when, in pursuance of a misinterpreted order from Rosecrans, four divisions, instead of only three, were withdrawn from the Federal right wing to assist Thomas on the left, thus leaving a gap in the Federal line. Through this gap poured General Longstreet's troops, routing the Federal right and center, commanded by Generals Alexander M. McCook and Thomas L. Crittenden, respectively. The right and center corps of the Union army broke in flight for Chattanooga, carrying with them General Rosecrans and the Assistant Secretary of War, Charles A. Dana, who had been sent by Secretary Stanton to observe the battle. The entire Confederate army was then massed against the Federal left, but Thomas, who had stood firm against heavy odds throughout the day, saved the Federals from an over-

..MILITARY AND NAVAL OPERATIONS, 1861-1863

whelming defeat and withdrew his corps in an orderly retreat through McFarland's Gap to Chattanooga.[49] After the two days of fighting in which each side suffered casualties exceeding sixteen thousand, the Confederates were in possession of the field but were too exhausted to pursue the enemy. The battle had resulted in an indecisive victory for the Army of Tennessee;[50] and although Rosecrans retained possession of Chattanooga, his troops were almost starved into surrender before General U. S. Grant arrived in October and soon defeated the Confederates at Lookout Mountain and Missionary Ridge.

Among the many Georgians who fought at Chickamauga was Lieutenant A. J. Neal of Zebulon, who immediately after the battle wrote to his father regarding the engagement:

> We have had a terrible fight. . . . Day before yesterday we were held in reserve and kept under heavy fire but we had few casualties in the Battalion. Yesterday we were in all day but did not get a fair showing till near sundown when the whole battalion were brought into action at once. It was for half an hour the most terrible bombardment I ever witnessed. Our fire was so demoralizing on the enemy that they broke in utter rout. . . .[51]

Following the Chickamauga campaign, fighting in north Georgia was desultory prior to the invasion of Sherman. In the early winter of 1863-64 a force of approximately two thousand Federal troops advanced from Murphy, North Carolina, into northern Georgia, while attempting to capture a number of wagons which General Joseph Wheeler was sending from East Tennessee to Dahlonega, Georgia, for safekeeping. After advancing to the vicinity of Brasstown Bald, the Federal troops retreated from the state upon hearing of the safe arrival of the wagons in Dahlonega. The Quartermaster Department of the Confederacy at Atlanta issued an appeal to the people of Georgia to furnish artillery horses and transportation mules for the Army of Tennessee, stationed in northwest Georgia. The demand for the animals was great and the Confederacy was unable to furnish them. When General Joseph E. Johnston assumed from General Bragg the command of the Army of Tennessee on December 27th near Dalton, Georgia, he found an alarming deficiency in arms, supplies, and cavalry. He immediately began reorganizing and equipping the army in order to be prepared to defend the state from the threat of an invasion of major proportions. How well justified he was in his apprehension was borne out by subsequent events

79

CHAPTER VI

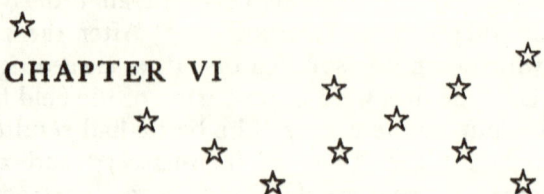

Relations with the Confederacy

ALTHOUGH CONSIDERABLE CO-OPERA-
tion prevailed between the Confederate and Georgia administrations, inevitable conflicts arose when the central government attempted to subordinate the rights of the state to the national welfare. Several unpopular policies adopted by the Confederate government, principally the conscription acts, the laws impressing supplies, unfortunate financial measures, and the suspension of the writ of habeas corpus, led to clashes between the two administrations.

The undisputed leader of the opposition to the Confederate policies in Georgia was Governor Brown, who was aided by Alexander H. Stephens and his half-brother, Linton, by Robert Toombs, and to some extent by Herschel V. Johnson. The supporters of the Confederate administration were led by Benjamin H. Hill and Howell Cobb, but since Hill was in the Senate much of the time and Cobb was in the army, their attempts to aid President Davis did not balance the criticisms of the state rights group. Brown fought the President on numerous issues, at times giving the impression that he considered the Confederate administration a hostile power, but his opposition to conscription was more pronounced than was his dislike for other Confederate measures. Alexander H. Stephens opposed the President on practically every important issue, but he and his brother sincerely believed that the suspension of habeas corpus was the most tyrannical of the Confederate acts. Toombs was vociferous in trying to protect property rights. Although Herschel V. Johnson opposed many administrative policies, he generally disapproved of the activities of Brown, the Stephenses, and Toombs.

Brown's disputes with the Confederate administration began in March, 1861, when Secretary of War L. P. Walker requested that he send volunteers to Fort Pulaski and Pensacola. Brown con-

..RELATIONS WITH THE CONFEDERACY

tended that the troops should be sent as fully organized regiments in order that he might commission the officers before the troops left the state, for if the men were sent as companies, the President would organize them into regiments and appoint the officers. Although Walker had urged haste, Brown did not send the volunteers until after the firing upon Fort Sumter. "I shall insist on Georgia having her rights and wishes respected," the Governor asserted. When Brown in the following month called for volunteers in order to send two regiments to Virginia, he notified Walker that the companies should be mustered into the Confederate service at Augusta, and that upon their arrival at Richmond, they should form a regiment and elect their own officers. The Confederacy wanted to organize the troops into regiments, but Brown was determined to organize them himself. The Secretary acquiesced "for the sake of harmony" and agreed to allow Brown to muster the troops into service at such places as he might designate.[1]

In a letter to his brother, Linton Stephens commented disparagingly concerning Secretary Walker's behavior:

The Secretary of War seems to be a fool. The substance of his letter was that he understood Brown's position to be that no more arms should go out of this State for the Confederate army [Brown never took such a position] and suggested as an "overture" . . . that he [the secretary] should accept all the Regiments which Brown would arm, for 12 months, but that he greatly preferred them for the war. I can't understand how he imagined himself to be offering an "overture" . . . in offering to accept troops for 12 months instead of for the war. Brown had never made any point on the term of service. . . .[2]

Brown's attitude toward the Confederacy's policy of mustering troops is revealed in a letter which he addressed jointly to Alexander H. Stephens and Thomas R. R. Cobb. He stated that the officers of the Fourth Brigade at Camp McDonald were unanimously requesting President Davis that the brigade as a whole be recruited into the service of the Confederacy and that Davis not select the officers. "I do not feel it my duty to disband the Brigade I have armed and equipped and trained," Brown declared. "I shall continue to hold the Brigade subject to the order of the President as a Brigade. . . . If they are not accepted . . . the fault will not be mine. . . ." In order to present the matter to the President, Brown sent Colonel William T. Wofford and Lieutenant Colonel Seaborn Jones to Richmond.[3] Comptroller-General Peterson Thweatt informed Vice-President Stephens that he did not agree with Brown's attitude in regard to mustering the troops:

> This idea of keeping men in camp and drilling them . . . and keeping the arms in the state, when men and arms are now waiting and anxious to go, for want of arms, or because not ordered I say, that, this expensive . . . *useless* expenditure of money . . . *I do not like at all,* even though done by my friend, Gov. Brown. I wish you and others with him would advise him to quit his foolishness.[4]

As the fear of invasion increased, Brown in September issued a proclamation calling for volunteers to serve along the coast for six or twelve months "as the exigencies may require" and took steps for the more thorough organization of the state militia. He said that he desired "to act in perfect harmony with the Confederate authorities," but that the "imminent danger" of invasion might soon justify him constitutionally in calling the state troops into actual service. Conceiving the idea of directing the whole coastal defense himself, Brown demanded that the Confederate government move no more native troops from the state, and he began organizing the coastal defense without reference to Confederate plans.[5]

In his annual message to the legislature in November, 1861, Brown attacked the constitutionality of the President's appointment of company officers, although he admitted that Davis could appoint all field and staff commanders. He questioned also the constitutionality of the Confederate Act of May 11, 1861, which authorized the President to receive into service companies, battalions, or regiments without calling upon the respective states for them. A month later, in a special message to the legislature, Brown again protested against the transfer of the state troops to the Confederacy, saying that they were not "cattle to be bought and sold in the market." He said that the law authorized the President to accept the troops by companies, battalions, or regiments but gave him no authority to accept a brigade or division. "The adoption of any policy looking to a transfer of the state troops, which may result in their disorganization, . . . would be . . . suicidal," the Governor asserted.[6]

After a struggle with the legislature in which Brown attempted to retain the state troops, he finally assented to a resolution of the assembly transferring the volunteer forces into the service of the Confederacy, provided the troops were used for the defense of Georgia and were not transferred to the Confederate service

..RELATIONS WITH THE CONFEDERACY

without their consent. Many of the state volunteers favored Brown in the controversy, and a regiment at Camp Harrison adopted resolutions in protest against the transfer of the troops.[7] The Savannah *Daily Morning News* thought "it would have been better for the service and for the credit of the State if the Legislature had not meddled with the matter at all."[8]

Not only did Governor Brown attempt to retain his state troops and to commission the officers, but he proposed also to keep the supply of arms within the state and to secure additional arms from the Confederate government. In May, 1861, he issued a proclamation that any officer who allowed his men to take arms out of Georgia which had been furnished to them by the state would be held responsible before the proper military tribunal for violating his order. Upon learning that volunteers from Newton County intended to carry out of Georgia the guns which they had received from the state arsenal at Augusta, he ordered Major General Josiah A. Clark of the Georgia militia to go to Covington and demand that the arms be surrendered "unless said officers will sign . . . a . . . pledge . . . that said guns shall not be carried beyond . . . this state without the consent of the Commander-in-Chief. . . ."[9] Brown's determination to retain the arms caused Secretary Walker to write him that "Every effort of State as well as Confederate authority is demanded for the maintenance of our Independence . . . and yet, Companies in Georgia armed for the desperate Struggle are disarmed by your Excellency."[10]

Brown also claimed that twenty-nine thousand pounds of powder stored in the Confederate arsenal at Augusta belonged to Georgia; and when the Confederate authorities delayed in releasing the powder, he ordered the state arsenal at Savannah closed to Confederate officials. He reminded Secretary Walker that the Savannah arsenal and its contents "are the property of the state" and that no Confederate officer had any rights there unless agreed to by the state government.[11] Brown's opinion was echoed by Major Lachlan H. McIntosh, Chief of Ordnance at Milledgeville, in a letter to General Henry R. Jackson, in command of the state troops at Savannah:

> The Confederacy . . . were supplied with powder by . . . Georgia. The State has now run short, and is in need. It does seem to me that if this is a joint affair in which we are engaged, viz, the defence of Savannah, . . . that we should have a proper proportion of the article necessary to that defence, especially when it originally came from us.[12]

CONFEDERATE GEORGIA..

In April, 1862, Brown requested that the Confederacy return to Georgia all of the rifles in the hands of the twelve months' troops whose term was soon to expire, for "The arms in their possession are the property of the State"; but Secretary of War Randolph informed him that the act retaining the state arms within the control of the President must be obeyed. Not content with trying to retain all arms within the state, Brown induced General Alexander H. Lawton to seize a cargo of arms which landed at Savannah while en route to Virginia and to use them in defending the state. Secretary of War Benjamin ordered Lawton to recover immediately all of the arms except "1,000 rifles and 1 rifle cannon, which the Department has appropriated for the use of your command," and remarked that if the seizure of Confederate property continued, "it would be better to abandon at once all attempts to conduct the defense of the country on an organized system." Not deterred by Benjamin's remarks, the Governor tried to capture the next cargo of arms that landed in Georgia.[13]

Despite the Governor's acrimonious quarrels with the Confederacy, there were times when he created the impression that he was eager to co-operate. Letters from Adjutant-General Henry C. Wayne to General Henry R. Jackson reveal an inner desire on the part of Brown that harmonious relations might exist between Confederate and state authorities. Wayne wrote Jackson that "The Governor directs, in order that there may be no conflict between . . . Georgia and the Confederate Government, that no movement of State Troops be made except upon consultation with Brigadier General Lawton . . . or under the Orders of General Lee." Wayne added, however, that in all matters of military administration other than the movement of troops, "the Governor directs that you receive orders only from himself directly. . . ."[14] A few days later Wayne again corresponded with Jackson, informing him that the Governor expressed "his unfeigned pleasure at the harmonious agreement between the state and Confederate forces." Wayne even agreed that although some of the guns used by Lawton's forces were the property of the state, "if the need for them in Virginia is greater than in Georgia we must patriotically yield them up."[15]

Correspondence between the Confederate and state military authorities indicates that a spirit of mutual respect and co-operation existed between them in their work of coastal defense in 1861 and early 1862. General Lawton accepted General Jackson's offer

..RELATIONS WITH THE CONFEDERACY

to take charge of erecting defensive earthworks around Savannah and told Jackson that he would furnish him three hundred men a day to construct the earthworks.[16] When Jackson needed a steamboat to assist in completing the building of rafts, Lawton informed him where a steamer might be secured and suggested that he have "a perfect understanding with General Lee" concerning where the rafts should be moored.[17] Jackson placed a company of state troops at Lawton's disposal for the reinforcement of Fort Jackson, and Lawton directed that no men who already were on duty in the state service should be recruited into his Confederate forces. With Savannah in danger of attack, Lawton told Jackson, "I shall be pleased to have your co-operation . . . in this emergency."[18]

Brown continued to express a desire for harmony. Writing to General Jackson and to Thomas Purse, the mayor of Savannah, he expressed approval of military plans for the defense of the city, and said:

> I am prepared to do all in my power without usurping the proper prerogatives of Genl Lee. . . . My greatest regret is my inability to furnish a single gun. Eighty thousand dollars of the guns and ammunition now on . . . the coast, are the property of the State, but they have been turned over to Confederate offices, and I cannot now take possession of them without destroying the harmony necessary between the State and Confederate forces.[19]

Acting under instructions from Governor Brown, Adjutant-General Wayne on February 12, 1862, issued an order temporarily ending the recruiting of men into the state service "in order that there may be no interference with the requisition from the Confederate . . . government."[20] With the passage of the first conscription act on April 16, 1862, Brown disbanded his state troops "in order to avoid confusion . . . at a time when harmony is of vital importance."[21]

The first conscription act declared subject to Confederate service every white man between the ages of eighteen and thirty-five. From the beginning, serious opposition to the act was manifested in Georgia, and in some of the northern counties it was not executed. Herschel V. Johnson denounced conscription as "odious" because it "*compelled* men to fight for liberty" and "enslaved them under the pretext of making them free."[22] Robert Toombs said that "When we began to hunt up men with dogs like Mexicans, they necessarily became as worthless as Mexicans. . . ."[23] Alexander

H. Stephens stated that the measure was unconstitutional. The undisputed leader of the opposition to conscription, however, was Governor Brown, who apparently was the only governor who refused to aid the conscription officers. He opposed conscription as unconstitutional and likely to destroy state sovereignty, and he claimed that it was a scheme of the President to create a military despotism. From April through July, 1862, Brown corresponded with Davis concerning conscription, denying the necessity for the law.[24]

Brown soon made it known that he would not permit the conscription of any military officers whom he considered necessary to the state. To avoid conflict, Secretary Randolph agreed not to enroll state officers. The agents conscripted some of the militia officers, however, causing Brown to inform Randolph that if necessary he would "order the arrest of each officer who arrests a state officer."[25] In his reply Randolph said significantly, "I think we might as well drive out our common enemy before we make war on each other."[26] Using his right to exempt all civil and military officers and clerks necessary for the administration of state affairs, Brown included judges, sheriffs, deputy clerks, reporters, ordinaries, tax-collectors, treasurers, surveyors, mayors, employees of the state railroad, financial agents, and numerous other state employees. Persons not in sympathy with the Governor referred to the exempted officers as "Joe Brown's Pets," and the Atlanta *Southern Confederacy* remarked on June 20, 1862, that officers had been "retained to enroll the militia with no militia left to train." J. Henly Smith, the editor of the *Southern Confederacy*, expressed to Vice-President Stephens his opinion of Brown's contentious activities:

> I may do Gov. Brown an injustice; but I think he is a very cranky and a very unsafe man — governed as much by . . . bad impulses as by patriotism; . . . and the outrage of exempting *officers* and not *men* I think deserves something severe. . . . I can't understand what the man means unless it is to be *contrary*. He certainly can't be playing the demagogue in this — though his triumph over the Confederate government may give him more *eclat* than I suppose. It seems impossible that he is aiming to defend State Rights; it is too circumscribed in its effects.[27]

Although the Augusta *Constitutionalist* was uncompromising in its opposition to conscription, a majority of the Georgia papers favored the measure. The Milledgeville *Southern Recorder* con-

..RELATIONS WITH THE CONFEDERACY

sidered it a military necessity, the Columbus *Sun* said that it was needed, and the Atlanta *Southern Confederacy* stated that it was the only just method of maintaining an army. The Sandersville *Central Georgian* asserted that "the course pursued by Gov. Brown has had a tendency to produce discontent among the people."[28] The Savannah *Republican* declared that Brown's "heart is fixed upon himself" while the soul of President Davis "pants for the deliverance of his country."[29]

After much protest, Brown submitted to the first conscription act, but when the second one was passed on September 27, 1862, extending the age limit of conscripts up to forty-five years, he became defiant. He refused to allow the new act to be enforced in Georgia until the legislature had deliberated upon it. Most of the Georgia papers again ridiculed Brown's position. The Savannah *Daily Morning News* regretted the conflict between the Confederate and state authorities, and the Atlanta *Southern Confederacy* thought "the government should conscribe every man able to bear arms, unless his services at home should . . . be worth more to the country's cause . . . than in the army."[30] The Georgia State Supreme Court on November 11th rendered a decision (unanimously) in favor of conscription; and influential administration friends, such as Senator Hill, committed the state to the policy despite the opposition of Brown and the Stephens brothers.[31] The legislature did pass, however, a resolution of protest against the principle of conscription and authorized the Governor to raise two regiments of militia from men not actually in the Confederate service. Writing to Howell Cobb from Richmond in January, 1863, Colonel William M. Browne, commandant of conscripts in Georgia, said that the conscription law had "almost failed in Georgia, owing in a great measure to the utter imbecility of those appointed to administer it. . . . Bad designing men . . . are doing all they can to bring Joe Brown into open rebellion; we therefore need . . . men like yourself to counteract their efforts. . . ."[32]

Although Brown had disbanded his state militia in April, 1862, following the passage of the first conscription act, he soon organized another militia composed of men who were more than thirty-five years of age, the upper limit set by the Confederate law. Hardly had he succeeded in organizing this new militia when the second conscription act extended the age limit to forty-five, thus taking away more of the state troops. Soon after the passage of the second conscription act, Brown influenced the legislature to enact a law providing for a state force to be composed of any men not in actual Confederate service. By early 1863 he had salvaged two regiments of state troops from exempted men and was calling out for state defense all men between eighteen and forty-five not in the Confederate service. He continued refusing to let his militia officers be enrolled as conscripts, the State Supreme Court having held that they were not subject; but in February, 1863, he surprised the state by ordering all of the militia officers into service at Savannah to aid General Beauregard in defending the coast. The officers obeyed, but the emergency soon passed and they were sent back home.[33] A young Sparta woman, in writing to her "soldier friend," remarked concerning Brown's strange behavior:

> Our community is now in general commotion from Gov. Brown's last order. He has called for all of his *pet* militia officers to go to Savannah and there be formed into companies . . . etc., the Major-General commanding the companies formed of officers of the lower ranks. If these men do not respond to the call, those under (45) forty five are to be immediately conscripted, those above he will have tried by a court-martial. I hope Joe Brown's thirst for "military glory" will be somewhat satisfied and I am glad that he has called out many who have hitherto sheltered themselves from conscription beneath their state office. . . .[34]

Such activities on the part of Brown are difficult to interpret, especially when he continued to profess admiration for President Davis. Writing to the President on April 4, 1863, the Governor said:

> I have differed from you upon the Constitutionality of the Conscript law . . . but in the main, I have cordially approved of your official course, and have always accorded to you, high Administrative ability, and the most lofty patriotism. I trust . . . I am incapable of factious opposition to the head of an able and vigorous administration, on account of difference of opinion on a few points.[35]

Using a law which allowed non-conscripts to be called out as Confederate reserves, or home guards, the Confederate government in September, 1863, took eight thousand men from Brown's militia and appointed Brown's enemy, Howell Cobb, to command them. In corresponding with his wife, General Cobb stated that the appointment was very distasteful to him:

> . . . I have just received a dispatch from . . . Richmond, ordering me to . . . take command of the State troops raised by Gov. Brown. If the President had done his very best to place me in the most unpleasant position possible, he could not have succeeded better than

..RELATIONS WITH THE CONFEDERACY

by this order. I am placed under Gen. Bragg, for whom I have no respect, and have to cooperate with Joe Brown about whom you know my opinions too well to repeat them. My duty requires me to submit without murmur or complaint, and I shall do it.[36]

A few days later, however, Cobb notified Adjutant- and Inspector-General S. Cooper that he had had an interview with Governor Brown and that the Governor had "manifested every disposition in his power to aid me in the business and I have no doubt there will be cordial cooperation between the State and Confederate Authorities."[37] Brown claimed the right to appoint the officers of the Confederate reserves, and General Cobb, in order to preserve harmony, advised the War Department to yield to him. Secretary of War James A. Seddon declined, however, to allow Brown to appoint the officers, but he did aver that the President would give consideration to any recommendations which Brown might make. Despite the apparent efforts of Brown and Cobb to co-operate, they soon were engaged in a bitter quarrel concerning conscription and the Governor's exemption from the draft of thousands of men who he claimed were necessary for running the state government.[38]

Brown had just succeeded in again reorganizing his militia when the Confederacy on February 17, 1864, lowered the conscription age limit to seventeen and raised it to fifty. Aside from Brown's opposition to the policy of conscription, he objected to the new law because it would disrupt his militia, which then included all men between sixteen and sixty years of age not in Confederate service. Brown declared that the new conscription act proposed to take from the state her entire military force, which was unconstitutional. He asked the legislature to say whether the "necessities of the State" do not forbid the militia organization from being broken up. The legislature resisted the Governor's recommendations, however, and voted to turn the militia over to the Confederacy.[39] Brown succeeded in organizing another militia, composed largely of old men and boys, and by June, 1864, he had a state force composed of five regiments and two battalions.

Although Brown exempted thousands of Georgians from military service, he vigorously objected to Davis' recommendations to Congress that the Confederate laws regarding exemptions be strengthened. The law exempting entire classes worked poorly, and the President several times recommended its repeal and the enrollment of all men within conscription ages, with military details for industrial and agricultural purposes. In a message devoted to the subject, Brown on November 17, 1864, when Sherman was almost literally within sight of the capital of Georgia, protested against the proposal. He said that the effect of the policy would be to invest the President with such power that no man could cultivate his fields or run his factory without "a *detail* from the President."[40]

The final conflict between Brown and the Confederate authorities regarding conscription developed in the fall of 1864 when Sherman was advancing across Georgia. Secretary of War Seddon requested Brown to have the state militia report to General Hood, but Brown sarcastically replied, "In common with the people of Georgia, I have abundant reason to regret, that the President has been so late in making this discovery" of Georgia's danger.[41] Brown set about to raise another militia force, taking men without much regard to their status, and when Seddon notified him that men in the Confederate service could not be forced to serve in the militia, Brown defied him. He ordered the militia which he had furloughed on September 10th to bring back with it all persons who remained at home under Confederate exemption. Davis then made a requisition on Georgia for Brown's ten thousand militiamen, but the Governor refused to surrender what he considered "the last vestige of the sovereignty of the state." A caustic correspondence ensued between Brown and the Secretary of War. The conflict continued, and on February 24, 1865, Brown told General Beauregard that he was withdrawing his militia from the General's command in order that they might attend to agricultural work. A month later he still was defying the Confederacy, this time refusing to allow the agricultural details then in the militia to be conscripted.[42]

Resistance to conscription made enforcement almost impossible. It was reported that conditions in the mountain section of Georgia and the neighboring states due to conscript evaders menaced the Confederacy "as fatally as . . . the armies of the United States." Howell Cobb declared in December, 1864, that if the same conditions existed throughout the Confederacy as in Georgia, Alabama, and Tennessee, it would require the whole army to enforce the conscript law.

The Confederate policy of impressing supplies as a measure necessary for the subsistence of the army aroused opposition in Georgia from its inception in 1861; and, after March, 1863, when it became necessary to regulate the practice by law and arrange for a system of price fixing, cries of protest came from all parts of the state. The depreciation of the currency, the subsequent rise of

..RELATIONS WITH THE CONFEDERACY

prices, the operations of speculators, and the reluctance of planters to sell their produce caused the government to adopt impressment, hateful though it was. Immediately after the first impressment law was passed, protests from farmers and state authorities were sent to Richmond.[43] The practice of seizing articles at a valuation far below market price was a chief cause of complaint. A planter in Marion County complained that he had lost a thousand dollars when Confederate agents seized his bacon at a valuation of thirty-five cents a pound, while the state authorities allowed fifty. Planters of corn believed it unfair that they were allowed only a dollar a bushel by impressing agents when the market price was nearly three dollars. When horses in Atlanta were impressed for government use, there was grumbling, and tricky attempts were made to have the horses released, although the government paid "fair prices" for the horses taken. A Savannah paper stated that "The Government allows $45 per barrel for flour, which is less than half the market price."[44]

In 1863 impressment commissioners seized most of the sugar in Atlanta for the use of the government and allowed seventy-five cents a pound for it, but owners of the sugar refused to accept the amount offered and instituted legal action against Major J. F. Cummings, who had authorized the impressment. The case was argued in Atlanta before a court of equity, and the judge sustained the constitutionality of the law but gave his unofficial opinion that the sugar was worth more than the government had paid. When the case was taken to the Georgia Supreme Court, the judges avoided giving any opinion on the constitutionality of the act but did reverse the judgment of the lower court "upon the ground that the . . . schedule of prices . . . did not secure the holder of the property seized by the Government just compensation. . . ."[45]

Brown, Toombs, and Johnson were leaders in protesting impressment. Brown said that the system of "inadequate compensation" imposed the burden of supplying the army upon the producing classes alone. Although the Milledgeville *Southern Recorder* predicted that impressment would cause a decrease in the price of necessities, Toombs said that price-fixing had prevented free bargaining between producer and consumer, and that thus the very object of impressment had been defeated. Johnson believed that the scale of prices was so low that citizens would not voluntarily sell to the government.[46]

Brown's prophecy that the farmers would be alienated from the cause was soon fulfilled, and when he and President Davis appealed to the farmers to plant corn, many refused to respond. Toombs frequently declared that he would plant as much cotton as he pleased regardless of law.[47] Brown complained not only that the impressment agents were taking too many supplies from some communities and none from others, but also that many unauthorized persons had resorted to impressment as a convenient method of stealing. He told the people to resist unless the officer could show a proper certificate. In the fall of 1863 the Governor urged the adoption of a law to make impressment by unauthorized persons a felony punishable with ten years of imprisonment and thirty-nine lashes on the bare back. Although the legislature did not comply with the Governor's request, it did resolve that all impressment officers in Georgia subject to conscription should be removed by the Secretary of War and that citizens not subject to conscription be appointed.[48] The Georgia Supreme Court declared one principle of impressment illegal on the grounds that the value at the time of impressment could not be determined by rates fixed at a previous time. The court's opinion was that the value should be determined at the time of impressment, and that "just compensation" meant whatever the local appraisers decided upon, which practically meant that the government must pay the market price.[49]

Until 1863 there was no law that regulated impressment, and the Confederate authorities were compelled to act upon custom and general principle. When the Confederate Congress on March 26, 1863, passed a law regulating the manner in which impressments should be made and appeals heard, it was hoped that opposition to impressment would cease, but resistance to the policy continued in Georgia. The legislature on December 14, 1863, passed an act to prevent illegal impressment. Simultaneously, the War Department began allowing a local appraisement in all cases of impressment, and a Congressional act of February 16, 1864, made slight amendments in the act of March, 1863. Opposition in Georgia increased, however, and there were men who questioned even the necessity of impressment. Among these was Stephens, who declared that "The Tithe ought to feed the army without the expenditure of a dollar by way of purchase."[50] *The Countryman,* published in Eatonton by Joseph Addison Turner, said on June 7, 1864, "Three times . . . the agent for impressing horses has been among us, and . . . a different agent has been sent every time, and has, every time, . . . made a call upon the same individual. We are willing that the

..RELATIONS WITH THE CONFEDERACY

government shall have our last horse.... But let an equal distribution ... be made among the different ... citizens." Herschel V. Johnson in August, 1864, wrote Secretary of the Treasury George A. Trenholme that the impressment law, as it was being enforced, was violating the Constitution. He admitted that the government had the power to impress property, but he declared that the "power of impressment does not carry with it the power to regulate prices" and that the impressing agents "must give just compensation." A few weeks later he wrote to Secretary of War Seddon, expressing the same objections. He warned Seddon that the limit had been reached in Georgia, and that impressment could no longer be enforced.[51] Brown notified Seddon that "The houses, lands and effects of the people of Georgia are ... seized ... to the use of the Government ... without the shadow of law...."[52]

Brown tried to prevent Confederate details from delivering their provisions to the government. He told the legislature in November, 1864, that the men who had been detailed to impress the supplies had been exempted from military service "on condition that they sell to the Confederate Government all their surplus at schedule prices, which are now [so] far below market value as to afford not even the appearance of just compensation." He said that in this way "the Confederate Government prohibits citizens of Georgia from selling ... to their own State, when the State needs these productions and is ready to pay just compensation for them." He urged the legislature to enact a law authorizing the impressment of such supplies. When the legislature postponed action, Brown returned to the subject three months later, and this time the general assembly complied with the Governor's wishes.[53]

Discontent in Georgia grew also out of the disastrous financial policy of the Confederate government, for the government depended for its support chiefly on the issue of paper money and bonds. The levy of an adequate tax was difficult, since the Constitution required that direct taxes should be apportioned, and war conditions made a census impracticable. In 1863 Toombs analyzed the weaknesses of the financial policy when he declared that "The first great error was in attempting to carry on a ... war solely on credit—without taxation. The second error ... consummated the destruction of public credit. It is a ... sound principle ... that a nation ... cannot add to the value of ... currency by any further addition to its quantity."[54]

The tax-in-kind law, which was passed by Congress on April 24,

1863, took a tenth of the farmers' produce and was denounced for much the same reasons as impressment. In some cases the law was abused and the tithe was collected by unauthorized persons. The tax became especially burdensome when it operated simultaneously with impressment. "There are hundreds of families that have not one ear of corn left," wrote an indigent citizen who had been visited by impressing agents, "and now we are notified that our tithing must be paid."[55] Toombs declared that the execution of the law was "productive of much fraud." Stephens favored the tax but complained that it was mismanaged. Brown recommended to the legislature that the law be repealed; and the legislature itself on November 18, 1863, requested the Governor to use his exertions with the Confederate government to have the collection of the tax-in-kind suspended in cases where the citizens' crops, out of which their tax was to be paid, had been taken by the enemy or by the Confederate army.[56]

Brown quarrelled also with Davis over space on the blockade-runners, which the President was trying to appropriate to the Confederacy. The Confederacy's regulations, issued on March 5, 1864, required that vessels exporting certain enumerated articles must carry one-half their tonnage on outbound and homeward voyages for the government at fixed rates and bring back at least one-half the proceeds of the owner's cargo in goods not prohibited by Confederate law. Vessels owned by states and employed for exclusive use of states were not subject to the regulations.[57]

Immediately prior to the announcement of the Confederacy's regulations, Governor Brown had chartered four vessels for the state of Georgia and prepared to engage in a more extensive shipping business. After the regulations were published, Brown had the *Little Ada* loaded with cotton and telegraphed for clearance. As the vessel was not owned by the state and did not offer one-half its tonnage to the Confederate government, his request was refused. Brown reported to the legislature his difficulties, declaring that the Confederacy's policy was an utter disregard of every principle of state sovereignty. In a letter to Colonel Aaron Wilbur, his foreign agent for Georgia, Brown said, "I regret that we cannot still get out the small vessels. The folly of Government in this matter is very painful. I trust when Congress assembles we may get Mr. Memminger's decision reversed."[58] The movement for repeal continued until March, 1865, when Congress passed a bill removing all the restrictions.

..RELATIONS WITH THE CONFEDERACY

The seizure of the state railroad by General Bragg in 1863 was another incident which caused Brown to remonstrate with President Davis. The Governor considered the road "as absolutely the property of the State as is the State House," and he threatened to stop all operations on the road until Bragg's orders were revoked. There was further friction in 1864 when General Johnston complained to Davis that "The railroad from Atlanta does not supply our wants . . . because of negligence in the management of the trains. . . ."[59] When Davis asked Brown for his prompt attention to the matter, the latter characterized Johnston's complaint as "without foundation." Brown did make improvements upon the road, however, causing Johnston to thank him; but he never permitted the government to take over the road as a part of a unified transportation system.

The three acts of the Confederate Congress suspending the writ of habeas corpus lasted over the period from February 27, 1862, to August 1, 1864, and were condemned in Georgia as unnecessary, as fostering despotism, and as subordinating civil rights to military power.[60] At first the "military despotism" was not widely complained of, but soon Vice-President Stephens became the leader in Georgia in opposing the acts. In August, 1862, when General Bragg placed Atlanta under martial law, Stephens informed Mayor James Calhoun, the new civil governor, "that General Bragg had no more authority for appointing you civil governor of Atlanta than I had."[61] Brown openly asked for resistance, saying that acquiescence would "tend to the subversion of the . . . sovereignty of the state. . . ."[62] Toombs, too, objected to Bragg's order. So great was the opposition that the War Department repudiated Bragg's action and issued instructions forbidding military officers from proclaiming martial law or suspending the writ without authority from the President.

Despite the furor which had been caused, Congress renewed, on October 13, 1862, the privilege of the President to suspend the writ; and again on February 15, 1864, Congress allowed the writ to be suspended during the Federal invasion until August 1, 1864. In Georgia the feeling against the last act was particularly bitter. The legislature unanimously passed a resolution which provided that a justice of any court refusing to grant a writ of habeas corpus should forfeit $2,500 to the aggrieved party. Alexander H. Stephens on March 12, 1864, wrote Herschel V. Johnson that ". . . when the Gov't undertakes to close the courts . . . they virtually declare war

95..

against the people as signally as Charles I of England did against his people when he erected the Royal Standard at Nottingham."[63] Stephens was unsuccessful in winning the support of Senator Johnson, for the latter wrote to him, "I will not participate in denouncing Congress and the President.... If the war cannot be conducted on my plan ... I will fight the war according to the President's plan...."[64] Benjamin H. Hill also supported Davis and said that the suspension of the writ did not annul a citizen's constitutional rights. Howell Cobb, A. H. Kenan, and Lucius Q. C. Lamar, who were in Georgia encouraging the people in support of the war, likewise defended the administration.

When a special session of the legislature met on March 10, 1864, Brown condemned the Confederacy's suspension of the writ, but deprecated a conflict between the state and Confederate authorities. The power to suspend the writ was an implied power and as such "must ... yield to the restrictions found in the Bill of Rights," he declared.[65] Linton Stephens then introduced resolutions, prepared in conjunction with his brother, condemning the suspension of the writ and calling for its abandonment. A few days later Alexander Stephens by invitation addressed the legislature in support of Linton's resolutions. He said that the suspension of the writ was not only unconstitutional but also dangerous to public safety.

As a result of the speeches by Brown and Alexander H. Stephens and the resolution introduced by Linton Stephens, the legislature adopted a resolution condemning the suspension of the writ and declaring it void. At the same time that this resolution was passed, the legislature adopted a vote of confidence in the integrity and patriotism of Jefferson Davis.[66] Governor Brown continued to condemn the President, however, and during the last session of the Confederate Congress, beginning November 7, 1864, he again protested against any increase of powers being granted to Davis.

Another purpose of convening the legislature in March, 1864, was to afford the Brown-Stephens coalition an opportunity to clarify their views concerning the possibility of peace. Signs of war weariness in Georgia had become evident soon after the Confederate defeats of Vicksburg and Gettysburg, and by the early part of 1864 a conviction was growing that Davis was determined to have peace his own way or not at all. For several weeks before the legislature met Brown and the Stephens brothers discussed peace resolutions which should be introduced into the legislature by Linton Stephens. In his address condemning the suspension of

..RELATIONS WITH THE CONFEDERACY

habeas corpus, Brown said that the war could not be terminated by force of arms, but must be brought to an end through negotiation. He thought the Confederate government should tell the world that the South was willing to make peace whenever the enemy was ready to recognize "the principles of the Declaration of Independence. . . ." Included in Linton Stephens' resolutions concerning the habeas corpus were statements regarding peace. Extremely vague, the peace resolutions breathed the Declaration of Independence and state rights, and asked Davis to make after each Confederate victory an offer of peace on the "principles of 1776."[67]

Soon after Sherman's peace proposal for Georgia had been rejected by Brown and Stephens,[68] the legislature assembled in November, 1864, and Brown advocated a convention of all the Confederate states to formulate a peace program and force Davis to accept it. Linton Stephens introduced resolutions calling for a state convention to consider peace negotiations, but the supporters of the Confederate administration countered with resolutions pledging anew the fidelity of the state to the Confederacy. Members of the legislature asked Davis for his opinion and were told that the only agency to treat for peace was the Confederate government. The resolutions calling for a convention did not pass.[69] Not satisfied, Brown in February, 1865, asked the legislature to call for a convention of Southern states for the purpose of deposing Davis. When the vote was taken, there were only two affirmative votes in the lower house, and the senate passed a resolution for a vigorous prosecution of the war.[70]

The press was divided concerning the quarrel over habeas corpus and peace, but the majority of the newspapers attacked Brown and the Stephenses for criticizing the acts of Congress. The Savannah *Republican* said that if the people were "ready to support Brown and Stephens . . . they have made up their minds to an act of suicide. . . ."[71] The Savannah *Daily Morning News* pointed out the absurdity of the legislature in passing a vote of confidence in Jefferson Davis after it had "just solemnly charged him with a betrayal of his trust. . . ."[72] The Macon *Daily Telegraph* facetiously declared that the legislature's action in regard to Davis was similar to that of an individual who caught a thief robbing his hen house and then praised the thief's honesty. The *Telegraph* said: "Oh my fine fellow, I have caught you robbing my hen-roost—your pockets full of eggs and your hands full of chickens. I find you guilty of . . . theft . . . but you are an honest chap and I have undiminished confidence in your integrity!"[73] A paper published in another state, the Richmond *Examiner,* said that "Governor Brown is what the French call *mauvais coucheur.* There are men ... to whom ... common sense ... is odious; ... and we fear that Governor Brown is one of that kind."[74] On the other hand, the Augusta *Chronicle and Sentinel* on March 13, 1864, said that the legislature should "sustain the Governor in the bold ... position he has taken. ..." The Atlanta *Daily Intelligencer* asserted that in the legislature's action on habeas corpus it had maintained a principle "inestimable to freemen."[75]

Although a majority of the newspapers condemned Brown and the Stephenses for their opposition to suspending the writ, many prominent men approved of what they had done. Henry Watterson, who then was in Atlanta editing the Chattanooga *Rebel* and the Atlanta *Southern Confederacy,* wrote Alexander Stephens that he endorsed his legislative speech and that he also approved of Brown's address. "Not a third of the men who denounce the message of Governor Brown have the slightest notion of its real contents," Watterson claimed.[76] Ira R. Foster, Quartermaster-General of the Georgia militia, wrote Stephens: "Your name, Brown's, and others may be cast out *as evil* by those in power but in coming time, they will shine forth with the brightness of the diamond."[77] In a letter to Stephens, Judge Thomas W. Thomas of Elberton approved of the addresses by Alexander and Linton Stephens: "I can say truthfully it is one of the best ... speeches I ever read—it is in fact apples of gold in pictures of silver. I am delighted to see Linton's resolutions. They are master pieces ... and he has risen a whole man's length in the last 30 days."[78] Peterson Thweatt said that many Georgians did not deny the correctness of Brown's views, but objected to the time and circumstances. "They seem to think every man unsound or traitorous that did not ... *trust all to Jeff Davis.* There is a great deal more of this slavish feeling ... than I like to see. ..."[79]

While many Georgians believed that Brown and the Stephenses were attempting to overthrow the Confederate administration, Alexander H. Stephens, in a letter to Herschel V. Johnson, assured the latter that he had no such intention:

> I assure you I have no *antipathy* to Mr. Davis nor am I *hostile* to him — and if there is an object ... to organize a party in opposition to the administration I know nothing of it. As to the ... action of Georgia upon the subject of Habeas Corpus and ... Peace ... I

..RELATIONS WITH THE CONFEDERACY

think I know as much as any body else. . . . It is true that these Resolutions were not drawn up by me but they were prepared by Linton after full consultation — and as for Mr. Davis or his administration they had but little to do with it — nothing . . . except in so far as they fall within the scope of the principles stated.

Stephens said that while he had never regarded Davis as a great man, he had considered the President to be "a man of good intentions." He added:

I am now beginning to doubt his good intentions. . . . Since his first elevation to power he has changed many of his former States Rights principles. . . . You may have heard me . . . speak of his weakness and imbecility but certainly with no bitterness of feeling. . . . I had no more feelings of resentment towards him . . . than I had towards the defects . . . of my poor old . . . dog.[80]

A few weeks later Henry Cleveland, the editor of the Augusta *Constitutionalist,* resigned his position when the stockholders and proprietor of the paper told him that he must support the Confederate administration. Writing to Alexander H. Stephens, Cleveland said that he had opposed the peace resolutions of Linton Stephens for the following reasons:

First, because no proposition yet made, goes far enough to have the slightest effect upon the North. . . . Second, because no human power can change Mr. Davis, and consequently, no human power can save the Confederacy from . . . ruin. I am satisfied that the immediate secession of . . . Georgia from the Confederate States would be the best thing we could do, and am equally satisfied that nine tenths of the people will follow the lead of the Administration, untill [sic] our Cause is beyond the hand of resurrection.[81]

The agitation for peace as encouraged by Brown and the Stephenses left the Confederacy appreciably weaker. In suggesting to the North a peace plan, even though extremely vague, Brown and the Stephenses apparently were preparing the way for a peace without victory and very probably for a reunion with the North, with as much state sovereignty as they could wring from the Lincoln government.

Toward the end of the war the Georgia newspapers expressed a growing dissatisfaction with the obstructionist activities of the Brown-Stephens-Toombs coalition, especially with those of Governor Brown. The Columbus *Times* of January 12, 1865, said that the hatred existing between Brown and Davis had "never resulted in any good to the country; and like all other quarrels, both sides at times doubtless have been wrong." The Milledgeville *Southern Recorder* blamed Brown for the conflict, and said that "Brown seems never to think for a second, that he has had as much, if not more to do with the disaffection of thousands in Georgia, than all that has ever been done by the President or Congress."[82] The Milledgeville *Southern Federal Union,* on the other hand, was "glad that, in Governor Brown, we still have one man who adheres to ... *State Rights.*"[83] The editor of *The Countryman* accused the Augusta *Chronicle and Sentinel* of "so hating Jeff. Davis and idolizing Joe Brown as to become the ... tool of the Yankees. ..."[84] A correspondent to the Columbus *Sun* said that Toombs had delivered an address in Augusta and that his motto was "onward with the revolution," but that his croaking and complaining had not encouraged the people but had increased their dissatisfaction.[85]

John A. Campbell, Assistant Secretary of War, on March 5, 1865, said that Georgia was in a condition which he would call "insurrectionary" against the Confederate leaders. He found that this situation had cast reproach upon the Confederate authorities and had made the execution of the laws almost impossible. Jefferson Davis probably was thinking of Brown, Stephens, and Toombs, when, near the close of the war, he wrote to the wife of Howell Cobb:

Faction has done much to cloud our prospects and impair my power to serve the country. That such was not their purpose I am well assured and if we may be permitted to hope that when they see the indulgence of evil passion against myself injured not the individual only but the cause also of which I am a zealous though feeble representative; the discovery will lead to a change of conduct and ... it may in the end be well for us.[86]

CHAPTER VII

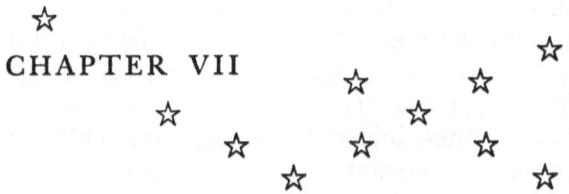

Industry and Transportation

GEORGIA IN 1860 WAS FAR FROM BEING dependent upon a purely agrarian economy. With the exception of Virginia and Tennessee, she led all other Confederate states in the amount of capital invested in manufacturing and in the annual value of industrial products. The decade prior to 1860 was an era of rapid industrial expansion in Georgia. Between 1850 and 1860 the number of industrial establishments had increased from 1,522 to 1,890, the capital invested from $5,456,483 to $10,890,875, the cost of raw materials used from $3,404,917 to $9,986,532, the number of employees from 8,368 to 11,581, and the value of the yearly product from $7,082,075 to $16,925,564. During the same decade her railroad mileage had expanded from 643 to 1,404 miles, and the cost of railroads that had been constructed in the state had increased from $13,272,540 to $29,057,742. Georgia's railroad mileage was greater than that of any other Southern state except Virginia.[1]

The largest single Georgia industry in the value of its product was the grain milling business, which in 1860 employed 620 persons in 378 establishments and produced $4,550,007 worth of flour and meal. Next in importance in the value of its annual product was lumbering, which employed 1,871 persons in 410 establishments and produced $2,412,996 worth of sawed lumber in 1860. The cotton goods industry, with thirty-three mills employing 2,813 persons and making $2,371,207 worth of products annually, ranked third. Boot and shoe manufacturing, carriage and wagon making, leather finishing, blacksmithing, the production of distilled turpentine, and the manufacture of furniture, woolen goods, and iron products were the other principal industries.[2]

The stimulus of war caused a phenomenal expansion of industry in Georgia, beginning in 1861 and continuing until the Sherman invasion. The greatest industrial activity generated by wartime needs was directed toward the manufacture of munitions and army supplies. Soon after the war began, the Confederate government established in Atlanta a large arsenal, where such munitions as bullets, cartridges, caps, and friction primers were manufactured. Arms and army supplies, including twenty-pounder Parrott ammunition, field gun supplies, knapsacks, and cavalry saddles, were also made at the arsenal. Other Confederate arsenals were operated in Savannah, Macon, Augusta, and Columbus.

Early in the war Atlanta became a veritable hive of industry. The city was the headquarters in the lower South for the Confederate Quartermaster and Commissary departments and was one of the main supply depots of the Confederacy. Machinery and goods of all kinds came in through the blockade at Charleston to Atlanta, where the machinery was set up to manufacture munitions and army supplies. Iron works produced ordnance supplies. A Confederate rolling mill made cannon, armor plate, and rails, and in 1862 the government established a pistol factory there. A foundry produced freight cars, railroad supplies, and other iron products. Buttons, spurs, bridles, bits, and buckles were made in Atlanta, as well as the celebrated "Joe Brown Pikes."[3]

Another great center for the manufacture of munitions and army supplies was Columbus, which in 1861 was one of the largest manufacturing cities south of Richmond. One of the greatest industries in Columbus was the Columbus Iron Works Company, which in 1862 had in operation "twelve or fifteen large and small lathes and customary machinery, also a large foundry." This concern in 1862 was busy building engines and machinery for a gunboat at Apalachicola Bay and was making shot for the defenses there. The foundry had an air furnace capable of melting twenty tons of pig iron "at a heat" and made brass field pieces and tons of shot and shell. The largest sword factory in the South was apparently that of Haiman and Brother of Columbus, which also made tin, sheet iron, and copper wire. Other Columbus manufacturers cast cannon, made military caps and shoes, India rubber cloth, swords, firearms, axes, and army clothing. One of the Confederacy's quartermaster departments was located in Columbus, employing large numbers of women and girls; and the city was the site of a Confederate naval works, under military command, which constructed two gunboats for the government. In the winter of 1861-62 a report from Columbus stated that thirteen new industries had been erected there since the opening of the war.[4]

..INDUSTRY AND TRANSPORTATION

Following the capture of Fort Pulaski by Federal forces, the Savannah Arsenal, under the charge of Colonel R. M. Cuyler, was removed in May, 1862, to Macon, where a foundry was appropriated by the government for the use of the arsenal. More than 350 workmen were kept constantly engaged at the Macon Arsenal, manufacturing cannons, shot, shells, saddle harness, and leather products. Confederate laboratory and armory establishments made smaller munitions, such as cartridges. Other weapons and munitions that were made in Macon and vicinity were swords, sabres, Bowie knives, sheet brass and copper for mountings, muskets, gun carriages, and powder machinery. In addition to these articles of warfare, Macon had industries which manufactured surgical instruments, cotton samplers, plows, wagon boxes, railroad wheelbarrows, camp cots and stools, sword belts, knapsacks, steam engines, tent cloth, and many kinds of clothing.[5]

Augusta became an important center for the making of shoes, clothing, wagons, and other army supplies. The state ceded the Augusta Arsenal to the Confederate government, and under the superintendency of Colonel George W. Rains, a huge powder factory was erected along the Augusta Canal. The factory, said to be the largest establishment of its kind in the world, turned out during the war 2,750,000 pounds of powder. Other busy centers for the manufacture of military supplies were Dalton, where factories for the manufacture of cartouch boxes, swords, knapsacks, canteens, cloth, and shoes sprang up; Athens, where muskets, pistols, swords, and bayonets were made; and Rome, where cannons and batteries were manufactured.

Georgia's thirty-three cotton mills had 85,186 spindles and 2,041 looms in operation in 1860. Three mills were located in Columbus and a similar number in Athens; two were situated in Augusta and two in Roswell; while one factory was located in each of the following towns: Milledgeville, Eatonton, Macon, Thomaston, Sparta, and Lawrenceville. The remaining mills were scattered throughout the state, but mostly in middle Georgia.[6] At the beginning of the war these mills were producing sheetings, shirtings, jeans, and cassimeres and were spinning yarn for hand-looms. They were turning out more than five hundred thousand yards of goods per week. Although the volume of Georgia's textile manufactures exceeded that of any other Southern state, the state was unable to take care of her needs in this respect; and during the upset conditions of war, there was little chance for the textile industry to make great progress. No new cotton mills were opened during the war, but those already equipped were run to their fullest capacity.

In Columbus an old concern, the Eagle Manufacturing Company, operated two large cotton and woolen mills. These factories in 1860 had ten thousand cotton spindles and 1,300 woolen spindles, and employed five hundred persons. A year after the war opened the company had "added several articles to its list of production" and its weekly output of cassimere had been increased from two thousand to twelve thousand yards. The cotton mills in Athens flourished because of the excessive demand for cloth and yarn, and three mills in the vicinity of Thomaston in 1862 were using three thousand bales of cotton annually in the manufacture of yarns and osnaburgs. Two mills at Roswell with ten thousand spindles were employing 350 operatives in early 1861. A mill in Campbell County manufactured cotton thread for use in sewing machines.[7]

Textile manufacturing was handicapped by the scarcity of cards for carding cotton and by the lack of other machinery for the plants. The legislature on December 6, 1862, made an appropriation of $100,000 for the establishment of a state factory to manufacture cotton cards to be used in the home production of cloth. Governor Brown established the factory in the state penitentiary at Milledgeville. He swept the state clean of sheep, goat, deer, and dog skins, and of wire and tacks, and sent an agent to Europe to procure more of these raw materials to be used in the manufacture of cards. By March, 1863, 1,777 pairs of cards had been made, and a year later the factory had a capacity of one hundred pairs per day. The cards were sent out to the counties, where they were sold to the people by the justices of the peace or distributed free to persons who were unable to pay.[8] The production of cotton goods on a large scale was prevented, however, by the scarcity of cards and wire, and the greatest possible service had to be obtained from the old cards. Moreover, the wearing out of machinery which could not be replaced was an obstacle in the manufacture of clothing. An example of such a case was the burning of a cotton mill at Lawrenceville in 1864, the fire having been caused by friction of the machinery.

The manufacture of cotton goods was one of the few major industries that employed more women than men. In 1860, 1,682 women and only 1,131 men were employed in the state's cotton factories. The work did not require skilled labor, and consequently

INDUSTRY AND TRANSPORTATION

the wages were extremely low. In 1860 the Eagle Manufacturing Company paid a total of only $240 a day to its five hundred employees; and "Cracker girls," poor whites from the country, were earning only from eight to twelve dollars a month by piece work in the Columbus mills. Boys of teen age were also employed in the mills. The manager of a mill at Newton Factory advertised in 1862 that he needed the services of three or four apprentices, and offered "a home and good inducements to any deceased soldier's family in which there are three or four boys between the ages of 14 and 18, of good moral habits."[9] A few slaves were employed in the cotton mills, but most of the laborers were relatively uneducated white men and women. Of the 350 employees in the two mills at Roswell in 1861, only three were Negroes.

Georgia had thirty woolen mills in 1860, nineteen that carded wool and eleven that manufactured woolen goods.[10] The capacity of the mills was increased during the war in an effort to supply the state and the Confederacy with woolen cloth. Raw wool was very scarce in the South, and by 1863 the Confederate government's bureaus had obtained a virtual monopoly of the wool on the market and were able to require the woolen factories to make up the whole of it for government account. A man in Macon notified a citizen of Jackson, Mississippi, for whom he was agent for the sale of wool, that there was no possible chance to get the wool manufactured into cloth in Georgia. "The Mills are all under contract," he said, "some with this State and Some with the General Government. This being the Case, I offered the wool for sale at $2.50 per pound, and have succeeded in selling 13,000 pounds, and have delivered and got the money for 4 Bales of it."[11] Later he wrote that he had sold ten thousand additional pounds of wool at the same price.[12] The government's monopoly of the woolen industry was maintained until the end of the war.

Georgia's 125 boot and shoe factories were so busy manufacturing shoes for the army that the people found it difficult to procure shoes and soon began making their own footwear. Gustavus J. Orr, of Oxford, wrote to Alexander H. Stephens in 1861 that the firm of Starr, Orr and Stewart was making shoes for the Confederate government at the rate of about 1,500 pairs per month. He told Stephens that his firm wished to secure a contract with the state to make shoes for the state troops. "We would prefer to take a contract at a fixed percentage upon the cost of manufacture," he wrote.[13] A man in Whitfield County asked Stephens to obtain for

CONFEDERATE GEORGIA..

his friend, James H. Huff, a contract for making army shoes.[14] In addition to making contracts with private manufacturers, the government established its own shoe shops in Columbus and Atlanta. By 1863 the business of making shoes for the army was monopolized by the government shops through their control of hides and leather and their lower cost of production. These shops were unable, however, to supply the demand. "If a sufficient number of shoes could be furnished, our men would be very comfortable," General Joseph E. Johnston wrote to President Davis from his headquarters at Dalton. "They are worn out much faster than received, So that the supply is diminishing rapidly, and the number of men unable to march increasing as fast."[15] The new Confederate Quartermaster-General, A. R. Lawton, also informed Davis of the shoe shortage:

> General Johnston proposed by telegram to detail a large number of shoemakers to work under Major Cunningham, at Atlanta, if the stock of leather at that point was increased. . . . Major Dillard has already forwarded eight thousand pounds and will make it forty thousand.
> As late however as the 26 ult. Major Cunningham states that he was losing good shoe makers and that he had, up to that time, received none from Genl. Johnston.[16]

At the beginning of the war Georgia had only two iron manufacturing companies, and in 1860 the state produced only 2,030 tons of iron and 48,000 bushels of bituminous coal.[17] The increased demand for iron, coal, and other minerals occasioned by the war seemed to offer an opportunity for good investment in mining in north Georgia; and between 1861 and 1863 at least eight different companies were incorporated by the legislature to carry on mining operations in the northern counties. Mark A. Cooper of Etowah, in a letter to the Atlanta *Southern Confederacy* in April, 1862, said that the shortage of "stone coal" to finish iron was limiting the output of products at the Etowah Iron Works near Cartersville. He said that coal was being obtained by requisition of the Navy and War departments, but that at times when the works could not secure coal, many of the laborers had been unemployed and had enlisted in the army. "We are actually standing half our time for the lack of operatives," he wrote.[18] The Atlanta *Southern Confederacy* warned that unless Georgians soon began making iron in large quantities there would be an iron famine. Ten thousand dollars in stock was subscribed by persons in Troup

..INDUSTRY AND TRANSPORTATION

County to form a company to manufacture iron, and a committee was appointed "to visit the mineral regions of the Confederate States, to ascertain the most eligible location for the operations of the company."[19] The Etowah Iron Works were advanced $500,000 in 1863 by the Confederate government in a contract to make munitions, and in January, 1864, an iron company was organized in Athens to operate "at some point above that place." Some of the stockholders of the Athens company agreed to pay their stock in provisions.[20] On account of the increased demand for slate, the Blanceville Slate Mining Company, near Marietta, was unable to fill orders and requested the public to invest in its stock so that it might increase its facilities. Capital was too scarce, however, to make these mining ventures immediately profitable, and few important results came from the operations. In order to secure metals, the Confederate Ordnance Department sent agents over the state to collect or purchase old lead, brass, and iron. Many people donated lead roofs, weights, water pipes, and small metallic articles.

The stimulus of war caused other industries to be expanded and many new enterprises to be established. The Troy Manufacturing Company, of Columbus, in July, 1861, was manufacturing chairs, bedsteads, wooden ware, and mattresses. A new furniture factory in Americus announced in 1862 that it was "prepared to make any kind of furniture that the public may want." The company also stated that "as there is no way now to get metallic burial cases, we have had several sizes of wood coffins made for the accommodation of those who may be in need of them."[21] A LaGrange physician began manufacturing matches, and two men at Americus started making writing ink. A factory in Sandersville manufactured cypress buckets for the government. The Marietta Paper Mill, the largest in the state, made cartridge paper for the Confederacy. Felt was manufactured in Columbus by the Rock Island Paper Mills, and in 1864 this firm, after "months of incessant labor and much expense had succeeded in meeting the demand of the paper manufacturers."[22] A bill to incorporate the Savannah Glass Company was introduced into the Georgia Senate in November, 1863, and in January, 1864, another glass factory was "about to go into operation at Columbus." A factory for the manufacture of oilcloth garments for soldiers was established in Washington, and a company to produce letter envelopes and ink was organized in Marietta. An Americus physician made medicines and oils and announced that he intended "to manufacture medicines on an extensive scale."[23] A machine for the manufacture of ice, installed in Columbus in 1864, supplied the government hospitals in that city with this product. New agricultural implement factories sprang up and old factories were enlarged. A company in Augusta made farm machinery from imported Swedish and English iron, and two Augusta firms manufactured plows.[24]

Soon after the war started, there arose widespread criticism of Georgia manufacturers for profiteering. The war had cut off competition, there was a strong demand for more products than the factories could produce, and prices were rising steadily. An Atlanta paper in March, 1862, noted that there was "a universal complaint of the cotton manufacturers charging most enormous prices for cotton yarns, sheetings, osnaburgs, &c., while they are able to obtain the raw materials at lower rates than ever." The editorial stated that the manufacturers were not altogether to blame for the high prices, for "The dealers in these articles are charging most enormous profits upon the high prices which the factories charge."[25] The manufacturers in many cases were finding larger profits in the rising public markets than in contracts with the quartermasters; hence they either hesitated or declined outright to bind themselves to long term agreements at fixed prices.

A few manufacturers tried to prevent profiteering and speculation. T. L. Holt, agent for the Macon Manufacturers Company, announced in April, 1862, that his company would sell sheetings at eighteen cents per yard cash on delivery, and that they would "be sold by single bales to parties only who will agree to retail them at twenty cents." He said that his company was "unwilling ... to exact the full price which their goods will bring," and that they would appeal to the merchants and factories in the state to unite with them in the effort to prevent speculation and to furnish the people with goods at moderate prices.[26] In October, 1862, the Eagle Manufacturing Company began selling its fabrics at retail to consumers instead of at auction. "It will make speculation and the running up of the goods to twice the price asked at the mills, a very inconvenient business," the company's announcement stated.[27] A majority of the manufacturers, however, demanded increasingly high prices for their products.

Taking cognizance of the apparent profiteering, the Georgia Senate, in an attempt to suppress extortion, enacted a measure on December 7, 1863, which provided "that cotton yarn shall not be

..INDUSTRY AND TRANSPORTATION

sold for more than $2.00 per pound, for No. 6, and up to $3.00 for No. 12, shirting, sheeting and osnaburg, $1.25 to $1.50." When the bill was sent back to the House, it was referred to the Committee on Military Affairs, and the legislature adjourned without enacting the bill into law.[28] This attempt to establish a ceiling price ran counter to the prevailing belief in *laissez faire* economics. Even before the bill was introduced, an Augusta newspaper had said, "We do not know of an instance in which Legislative bodies have undertaken to adjust prices by law in which the evil sought to be remedied was not aggravated. Trade has its own laws . . . and any attempt at artificial diversion certainly produces confusion and disaster."[29]

Prices of manufactured goods became ever higher as the war progressed. Calico which sold for $2.25 a yard in March, 1863, was selling at ten dollars a yard in January, 1864, and fifteen dollars a yard in October, 1864. During the winter of 1865, osnaburgs sold at six dollars a yard; shirtings also brought six dollars a yard; blankets were seventy dollars each; pink satin was seventy dollars per yard; and shoe leather was fifteen dollars a pound. To what extent these prices were due to profiteering it is impossible to say, in view of the inflated condition of the currency. The Columbus *Times* said that "While the public have indulged profusely in abusing the Factories for high prices, extortion, &c., we doubt whether any other enterprises have contributed so largely to the public good. It would have been entirely out of the question to have clothed our armies or those at home, without these useful corporations."[30]

Military adjustments in the cases involving industrial workers were necessary. Confederate statutes of April 21 and October 11, 1862, exempted superintendents and operatives in woolen and cotton factories, shoemakers, tanners, wagon makers, and other mechanics "who may be exempted by the Secretary of War."[31] Besides these exemptions, the Confederacy from time to time detailed men from the army to work in industrial plants. The state government also exempted and detailed many mechanics and other industrial workers from the state militia.

Inevitably the numerous exemptions of Confederate and state industrial employees aroused complaints. A group of Milledgeville soldiers serving in Virginia sent two letters to the Milledgeville *Confederate Union* in August, 1863, criticising industrial workers who used their profession to avoid military service. In a written reply to these complaints, "Mechanic" asserted that the exempted men were organized under orders from the Governor, "there being enough men at home not so *usefully* employed. . . ." He declared that the South was "just beginning to appreciate her mechanics," and "If they had received encouragement in the past we would never have been so dependent on the thieving Yankees. The work they do . . . cannot be dispensed with," he maintained.[32] Undoubtedly some men secured employment in factories in order to avoid the draft, and late in 1863 the pressure for men for the army made it harder to convince the enrolling officers of the necessity for the exemptions. When the Confederacy passed a new conscription act in February, 1864, no provision was made for the exemption of industrial workers, but the President was given authority to grant details of men from the army.

Confederate Georgia had a greater railroad mileage than any other Southern state except Virginia. During the 1850's the number of miles of railroads in the state had increased from 643 to 1,404, and the total cost of constructing the lines had grown from approximately thirteen to twenty-nine million dollars.[33] "I have travelled more than five hundred miles on the Georgia roads, and I am glad to say that all of them seem to be exceedingly well managed," a visitor to Georgia wrote just prior to the war.[34] Eighteen railroad companies operated in the state in 1860. The Central of Georgia, owned by the Central Railroad and Banking Company, was the oldest. Its main line connected Savannah with Macon, with a branch from Gordon through Milledgeville to Eatonton. Another old road was the Georgia Railroad, which joined Augusta with Atlanta. The other principal lines were the Macon and Western, between Macon and Atlanta; the Southwestern, extending south of Macon to Americus and Albany; the Atlanta and West Point; the Atlantic and Gulf, which ran from Savannah to Thomasville; and the Western and Atlantic, connecting Atlanta with Chattanooga. Most important, perhaps, of all the carriers was the Western and Atlantic, owned and operated by the state. Its northern terminus at Chattanooga connected with roads that reached into the Mississippi Valley on the west and to Richmond on the east.

Between 1861 and 1865 practically no progress was made in railway extension further than the granting of charters to several new companies: the Ocmulgee River Railroad from Macon to Griffin; the Atlanta and Roswell Railroad, to connect with the Western

..INDUSTRY AND TRANSPORTATION

and Atlantic; and the Columbia and Augusta Railroad. Just prior to the war the Atlantic and Gulf Railroad began building a line from Thomasville to Bainbridge, but the work was delayed because of the unwillingness of the stockholders to invest their money during such "uncertain times."[35] In 1862 the Atlanta *Southern Confederacy* advocated the construction of railroad lines from Atlanta to the northwestern portion of South Carolina, and from Atlanta to Jacksonville, Alabama, but the projects were never attempted.

Financially, the railroads entered the war years upon a generally sound basis. The Western and Atlantic Railroad had a capital investment of $5,450,000 and owned forty-six engines. In 1861 this state-owned railroad paid from its earnings $438,000 into the state treasury.[36] In 1859 the Central of Georgia's revenue was nearly $1,400,000 and the operating expenses were less than $600,000.[37] The Macon and Western Railroad had a capital investment of $1,500,000, with no bonded debt. The Georgia Railroad possessed a capital stock in 1860 of $4,157,000. The road had a bonded debt of $312,000, but to offset this amount the company had more than a million dollars worth of stock in other railroads.[38]

Immediately after the war commenced, all of the Georgia railroads were thrown into a state of confusion. Many of the newly recruited military units, having no clear conception of their destination, lost time in aimless travel. At Savannah and Augusta the railroads terminating in those cities did not connect with each other, and freight had to be unloaded at one depot, hauled across town, and reloaded on cars at the other depot. Passengers frequently had to wait over night in order to take the next train.[39] The shops of the Georgia Railroad in Augusta and of the Central of Georgia in Savannah were engaged in producing gun carriages and rifled cannon for both the Confederacy and the state.

In the fall of 1861 the Northern stockholders of the Brunswick and Florida Railroad, a short line traversing the southeastern part of the state, refused to carry on the corporate affairs of the company. The Southern shareholders then met in Brunswick and resolved that since "All the money, bonds and assets of the Company are now in the North, and the Southern stockholders are not in condition to raise funds to keep up the road, the railroad be placed in charge of Governor Brown in behalf of the state, to manage and operate until Such time as the Shareholders are in a condition to resume its management." Governor Brown, pronouncing the property necessary for public defense, seized the line on September 26, 1861.[40]

In an effort to break a jam of vital freight in east Tennessee, the Confederate War Department in the fall of 1861 ordered the seizure of a considerable amount of the Western and Atlantic's rolling stock. Writing to Governor Brown from Chattanooga, Assistant Quartermaster William S. Ashe, who had been ordered to make the impressment, said:

... I confidently trust you will strain a point even to assist the Government in this dilemma, and spare me the disagreeable necessity contemplated by my orders ... to impress into the service of the Government ... such engines and cars of your State Road, as may be necessary for the purpose. They will not be required for a long time, it is believed, and will be returned, if loaned, in good order, or damages paid for according to liberal assessment.[41]

Governor Brown at once refused to relinquish the stock, declaring that the Western and Atlantic was the property of the state, and even threatening "by military force if necessary to make counter seizures."[42] The government desisted from making the impressment. Other men objected to the Confederate government's seizure of railroad property. For example, an assistant adjutant-general at Augusta asserted that "The plan of appropriating cars for any special purpose to be controlled by any one outside of the Rail Road managers is one that has never had my approval."[43]

Although the major railroads in Georgia had locomotive and car shops capable of supplying a certain amount of new production, the roads were constantly faced with the problem of securing materials for railroad repairs. The Forest City Foundry in Augusta manufactured railroad car castings, the Atlanta Rolling Mill Company specialized in the re-rolling of rail, and the Etowah Iron Works made car axles, but these companies were inadequate for the proper maintenance of the state's transportation system. The Tredegar Iron Works at Richmond was unable to supply all of the needed materials. Governor Brown said that the east Tennessee roads, which used the roadbed and cars of the Western and Atlantic during the summer of 1861, abused the railroad's property to such an extent that he would be hard pressed for rolling stock the following winter. The heavy government traffic on the Western and Atlantic, the depreciation in the value of money, and the expense of labor to handle the freight caused Brown to declare that the Confederacy would have to do its own loading and unloading.

..INDUSTRY AND TRANSPORTATION

In January, 1864, he asked the Confederate government to return to the state one-fourth of the engines and cars of the Western and Atlantic, which he claimed had been carried off by Confederate officers.[44] He refused also to permit any more cars to be used for the transportation of salt and wood, for two hundred cars had been lost in hauling these products.[45]

Hoping to secure from the Confederate government sufficient iron and coal for the Forest City Foundry to be able to manufacture the sorely needed railroad supplies, the superintendents and managers of several railroad companies in February, 1863, addressed a letter to the Secretary of War. In their letter the railroad officials said that "Any service rendered them [the foundry officials] . . . will subserve the Railroad interest and facilitate the Government transportation."[46] The letter was followed by a petition to the Confederate government from Messrs. Lufborrow and Timmons, proprietors of the Forest City Foundry, explaining that because of their inability to obtain iron and coal, they were casting only fifteen wheels a day instead of making their capacity number of fifty wheels daily. The petition said further:

> The Rail Roads will be further greatly benefited by the Government directing its Agts. at the coal mines of Tennessee to forward to the undersigned at Augusta, Ga., all the coal required to keep their work shops in steady operation. . . .
>
> . . . for the Government to turn over to the undersigned all the pig Iron that can be spared from Guns and other projectiles to be fabricated into wheels and other Rail Road supplies.[47]

Messrs. Lufborrow and Timmons received no encouragement from the government at Richmond and were informed that the government had no materials from guns and projectiles to spare for railroad uses. They then petitioned the Georgia legislature "to direct the management of the Western and Atlantic Rail Road to appropriate to them one train of twelve cars once per month to make a trip from the coal mines of Tennessee to Atlanta, to convey such iron and coal as the undersigned may require, for the manufacture of Rail Road supplies exclusively." Lufborrow and Timmons told the legislature that they had "made ample arrangement for the purchase of all the iron and coal necessary to carry on their work, at the prevailing market price," and that their only difficulty "in rendering further aid to the various Rail Roads is the want of Transportation for their materials."[48] The legislature's "Committee on Transportation" presented to the general assembly on April 9, 1863, a resolution "That the Governor is hereby requested in the management of the W. and Atlantic R. R. to furnish to . . . Lufborrow and Timmons . . . such special facilities of trans- for coal, iron and other supplies as may be in his power. . . ."[49]

Another serious problem to Georgia railroads was military conscription. A Confederate statute of April 21, 1862, exempted the officials, clerks, engineers, conductors, and mechanics of the railroads but did not exempt the porters and unskilled workmen. Confederate draft agents, eager to secure conscripts, occasionally threatened the continued operations of the roads. Governor Brown partially blocked the drafting of Western and Atlantic laborers by the device of mustering them into the state militia, and he wrote President Davis that "the same necessity exists for the exemption of all other railroad officers and workmen which exists in the case of the State Road."[50] Throughout the war the railroads, like the other industries of the state, constantly struggled with the military authorities for control of the steadily dwindling labor supply. In 1864 a Columbus newspaper remarked that it was "the idle dream of theorists and declaimers to substitute disabled soldiers, or others incapable of military service, for men educated for . . . these pursuits. Men unfit for military service are wholly unfit for employment on railroads. No agencies have been more efficient and necessary in carrying on this war than the railroad companies."[51]

Because of obsolete equipment, heavy traffic, and in some cases inexperienced labor, accidents were frequent and schedules irregular. A collision of two trains on the Western and Atlantic in July, 1862, resulted in the deaths of the engineer, fireman, and eight soldiers, and injury to thirty passengers. The breaking of a baggage car wheel on a Central Railroad train in January, 1863, caused a wreck which resulted in the death of three men and the serious injury of three women. In April, 1863, a broken rail caused a Georgia Railroad train to leave the track, but no one was killed. In October of the same year a Georgia Railroad train near Augusta ran off the track, seriously injuring a soldier and killing a Negro. The breaking down of a box car caused the accident. During the same month a passenger train on the Western and Atlantic ran off the track near Marietta, killing a Confederate officer and dangerously injuring another officer. A collision of a freight and passenger train on the Savannah and Augusta Railroad disrupted twenty cars and injured several women. Late in the war a train ran

..INDUSTRY AND TRANSPORTATION

off the track on the Warrenton branch of the Georgia Railroad, killing seven or eight persons, including the baggage master. Soft earth had caused the track to give way when the train came upon it. Primarily because of its poor roadbed, a branch road from Washington to Barnett was in "wretched condition" in February, 1865.[52]

The scarcity of cordwood for the locomotives frequently prevented trains from operating, and occasionally the state militia was detailed to cut a minimum supply of wood. Writing from his headquarters at Dalton in the winter of 1864, General Joseph E. Johnston told President Davis that his army depended upon the Western and Atlantic for bringing supplies to his troops, that rations for only five days had been accumulated, and that the lack of fuel for running the trains was responsible for the supplies not arriving.[53]

Although the railroads had entered the war upon a sound financial basis, their net earnings soon began decreasing. As early as 1861 the revenue of the Western and Atlantic and Georgia railroads started diminishing. In 1863 railroad supplies which reached Georgia through the Federal blockade were commanding prices twenty-five times the prewar levels. With expenses constantly rising, the railroads in 1863 were compelled to make large increases in their freight rates, which were applied to government traffic, regardless of previous agreements. The Western and Atlantic raised its freight rates twenty-five per cent in November, 1863, and the other Georgia railroads made similar increases.[54]

The rate increases were not sufficient, however, to take care of the depreciation and expenses. In an address to the legislature on December 2, 1863, Governor Brown said that the transportation of freight for the Confederate government on the Western and Atlantic Railroad was causing the state "heavy losses," and that he had "notified the proper officer that, in future, the Road will charge one hundred per cent upon the rates now paid for the transportation of Confederate freight." He added that "loaded trains ... are often entered by bands of straggling soldiers and valuable articles taken from them, which the Road is required to pay for."[55] In 1864 the president of the Georgia Railroad reported that his road was running at a heavy loss, and said that it had "made no real profit for the last two years, and is making nothing now."[56] Brown claimed in November, 1864, that the Confederate government owed the Western and Atlantic the sum of $975,774.60, and that although he had made every effort to collect the money, he had been unsuccessful. In January, 1865, the Confederate government owed the Macon and Western Road a half million dollars. "I have been round to the Banks, and enquired if the C. R. R. has declared a dividend lately, but from all I could learn on the subject, I don't think they have . . . ," an Augusta man said in February, 1865.[57]

Near the end of the war accusations were made that private property was being conveyed over the railroads of Georgia at the expense of the Confederate government. Thomas S. McCoy, adjutant of a Mississippi battalion at Augusta, said, "I have discovered . . . that much *private* property has been conveyed on Rail Roads, the transportation being furnished by persons connected with the Quarter Master's Department. . . . No clue can be obtained in the Q Masters Office after the point of consignment, of real ownership in the Property." One of the men accused of making contracts to convey private freight was Major A. M. Bryan, a quartermaster at Milledgeville, but Major Bryan explained that his conduct met the approval of Major Norman W. Smith, Assistant Quartermaster of Field Transportation at Augusta. In a letter to Colonel George W. Brent, Assistant Adjutant-General of the West, Major Smith said that he had authorized Bryan to make the contracts "because of the difficulty of getting subsistence stores to feed the hands." He admitted that the method was irregular, but said that he "considered it for the good of the service."[58]

The invasion of Georgia by Sherman's army in 1864 wrought dreadful havoc on the state's railroads. Sherman's march of destruction followed the line of the Western and Atlantic Railroad from Chattanooga to Atlanta, part of the Macon and Western Railroad between Atlanta and Macon, and almost the entire length of the Central Railroad from Macon to Savannah. Eighty-four miles of the Western and Atlantic between Atlanta and Resaca were destroyed; complete ruin marked the line of the Atlanta and West Point between Atlanta and Fairburn; eighty miles of track, nine depots, and three hundred cars of the Georgia Railroad between Atlanta and the Oconee River were demolished; 139 miles of the Central system between Gordon and Savannah were practically obliterated; and most of the Macon and Western line between Forsyth and Atlanta was wrecked. Serious damage also was done to the Eatonton branch of the Central and to the Augusta and Savannah road between Augusta and Millen. In addition to this

..INDUSTRY AND TRANSPORTATION

widespread destruction, General John B. Hood destroyed three engines and eighteen cars when he evacuated Atlanta in order to prevent their falling into the hands of the enemy.[59]

After Sherman's raid, General P. G. T. Beauregard urged Governor Brown to ask the railroads to use rails from their branch roads in repairing the main lines as soon as possible. By the end of December, 1864, the Atlanta and West Point Road had been repaired, but the line had only one freight engine fit for use. In January, 1865, the Macon and Western Road was repaired from Atlanta to Jonesboro, and the Central had been repaired from Macon to Gordon. Captain L. P. Grant, an engineer directing repairs of the Georgia Railroad, in February, 1865, notified Colonel George W. Brent that the force engaged in repairing the line was inadequate and asked that "400 negroes be impressed and twenty-five four-mule teams and wagons be supplied."[60] Georgia was attempting the impossible, however, and by the end of the war only the Western and Atlantic, which was operated temporarily by Federal military authorities, and portions of the Southwestern Railroad and of the Atlantic and Gulf Railroad, constituted the usable parts of the state's transportation system.

In addition to their destruction of the railroads, Sherman's forces burned or demolished scores of industries between the Tennessee border and Savannah. The Etowah Iron Works was totally destroyed; factories along the Western and Atlantic Railroad and in Roswell were wrecked; the depot, roundhouse, and machine shop of the Georgia Railroad in Atlanta were burned, and the Confederate Arsenal and shops in the same city were destroyed; and the State Arsenal in Milledgeville was demolished. In the early spring of 1865 General James M. Wilson made a cavalry raid from Columbus to Macon and completed the work of devastation.

A comparison of manufacturing in 1860 and 1870 in the counties between Atlanta and Savannah through which Sherman passed shows a general decrease in capital invested in manufacturing. The industries of the state as a whole, however, recovered rapidly from the disasters of the war. Between 1860 and 1870 the number of establishments increased from 1,890 to 3,836, the number of employees from 11,581 to 17,781, capital invested in industry from $10,890,875 to $13,930,125, and the value of the yearly product from $16,925,564 to $31,196,115.[61]

CHAPTER VIII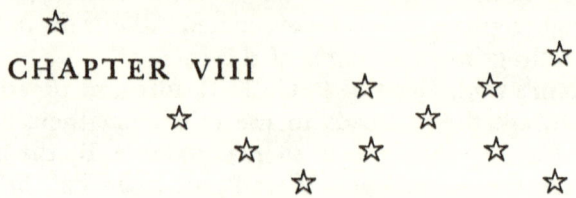

Planter and Slave

KING COTTON RULED GEORGIA IN 1860, but his reign was by no means absolute. Challenging the state's production of 701,840 bales of ginned cotton which sold for more than $25,000,000, were 30,776,283 bushels of corn worth nearly $25,000,000 and slaughtered livestock valued at $11,000,000. Other major farm products were rice, wheat, rye, sweet potatoes, tobacco, peas, beans, cane molasses, honey, butter, and wool.[1]

Although the finer grades of cotton were selling for as high as $12\frac{3}{4}$ cents a pound in the spring of 1861, a higher price than cotton had brought in several years, many people believed that the staple should be dethroned and more foodstuffs raised. "We may be at the commencement of a long war, and it is essential to have full supplies for our people and troops. Plant plenty of provisions and less cotton this year," urged the Savannah *Daily Morning News*.[2] "Southern Agriculture greatly needs . . . a System of Plantation Economy that will render the planting States more independent of the North," another paper said.[3] In an "Appeal to the People of Georgia," Governor Brown urged planters to redouble their energies for the production of all supplies of provisions. "I think of feeding our large steers for the army market," a man wrote to his brother. "I fear meat will be hard to procure for the army."[4]

Aside from the necessity of increasing the production of food, the restriction of cotton cultivation was advocated in order to prevent the staple from being exported. This policy, pursued by the Confederate government during the early part of the war with the expectation that it would cause Great Britain and France to recognize the independence of the Confederacy, aroused much opposition in Georgia. Writing to Vice-President Stephens, a man at Savannah said:

..PLANTER AND SLAVE

The Steamer Bermuda now in our port. Landed . . . clothing and munitions. . . . I am informed the owners desire to reload her with Cotton and would do so, but for public opinion or . . . an irresponsible Vigilance Committee. I regard at this time a free trade in cotton of . . . vital importance to our Government. . . . One weeks supply of cotton for England estimated to be 40,000 Bales is worth two and a half million dollars — a sum sufficient to clothe and arm 50,000 men.[5]

Andrew A. Lipscomb, the chancellor of the University of Georgia, expressed to Stephens a similar view. "It follows, I conceive, that cotton may be best used when left entirely to the instructive direction of trade," he said. "Let us just now have all our ports free. If a vessel will run the blockade, give her cotton with a good, old-fashioned blessing on it."[6]

As the crops were already planted before the war attained the magnitude of a general conflict, the unofficial campaign to limit the cotton crop of 1861 was only moderately successful. "The prospect for our cotton crop is very fine . . . ," wrote a planter in the fall of 1861. "I have not gotten it in as fast as usual, because I have spent more time in saving the provision crop. . . ."[7] The *Southern Cultivator* announced that along the line of the Georgia Railroad "corn and cotton presented everywhere the most flourishing appearance" and that there were "extra large crops of wheat and oats."[8] A planter in DeKalb County said that the crops in his county on the whole were satisfactory: "Our wheat threshed out 75 bushels, our oats were light . . . our Hungarian grass was fine. Our corn . . . excels any that we have had for several years. Cotton was very promising until the heavy rains of August. . . . Our beef cattle . . . look well."[9] A few planters in 1861 plowed up their cotton and sowed corn in its place, and Linton Stephens said that he had "a beautiful crop of wheat and oats and rye and young corn,"[10] but there was comparatively little difference in the acreage devoted to the various agricultural products that year and the preceding year.

In his annual message to the legislature, delivered in November, 1861, Governor Brown recommended that while the ports were blockaded, the planters should turn over their cotton to the state to be deposited in warehouses.[11] He said that the state should advance to each planter two-thirds of the market value of his crop, to be paid in state treasury notes and funded with "eight per cent bonds when presented for that purpose." He declared that this plan "would enable our planters to realize upon their crops a sufficient sum to meet their current expenses."[12] The legislature responded to the Governor's request by incorporating the "Cotton Planters Bank of Georgia." It was hoped that this bank would stabilize the price of cotton and make the staple available "as the basis of a sound circulating medium." The act allowed the planters to become shareholders in the bank by subscribing their cotton at the price of thirty dollars per bale. The legislature also adopted a resolution urging planters to reduce by at least one-half the quantity of their cotton crops for the year 1862 and to grow instead grain and other provisions.[13]

In the spring of 1862 the campaign to persuade the planters to decrease their cotton acreage gained impetus. When Linton Stephens asked Brown for his views concerning the necessity of increasing the growth of provision crops, the Governor stated that "we have more to fear from the production of cotton than from any other disadvantage under which we labor. We should plant double the usual crop of Indian corn and potatoes."[14] Newspapers urged farmers to grow grains instead of cotton, and in many counties the farmers adopted resolutions promising to decrease their cotton production. A group of warehouse and commission merchants in Augusta advised farmers "to plant at least a double portion of corn, peas, potatoes, and every kind of provision for man and beast, and under no consideration plant more than one-fourth of a usual cotton crop this present year."[15] Peterson Thweatt informed Alexander H. Stephens that he had written several articles for the newspapers, "urging our people to cease planting Cotton, and to plant corn and other grain and make meat, &c. I am happy to perceive a healthy change among our Planters and farmers, and I even begin to hope that comparatively little Cotton will be planted in Georgia this year."[16] In a letter to the *Southern Christian Advocate,* the Reverend W. M. Crumbley, the chaplain at the Georgia hospitals at Richmond, expressed a similar hope:

> Under God, I look on the destinies of our country and the result of this war, as now being in the hands of the Cotton planters. They are soon to decide whether we are "to be or not to be." The cotton seed planted will be far more ruinous than minnie balls or Conical shot from the enemy. . . . If much Cotton is planted and we have a bad crop this year . . . famine added to war will annihilate the fairest portion of God's heritage.[17]

The campaign to increase the production of foodstuffs and curtail cotton was much more successful in 1862 than it had been in the preceding year. "As to cotton, very little is planted," averred a Milledgeville paper.[18] An Augusta paper stated that "Col. L. A. Jordan, one of the wealthiest planters in the state, has determined to plant all his lands . . . in . . . grain."[19] "There is so much corn planted that we shall make enough and some to spair [sic]," a woman told her brother. "Cotton is a good price and but few has any to sell."[20] A farmer in south Georgia said: "Our people have planted provision crops almost exclusively—only about 900 acres of cotton . . . for home consumption. Very heavy crops of Corn, Peas, Ground-Peas, Potatoes, Sugar Cane and Rice . . . and the stock of hogs is larger than ever before. . . . Thousands of Beef Cattle are going . . . to our Armies."[21] The Thomasville *Times* affirmed that the grain crop was "immense" in south Georgia and that very little cotton had been planted. A plantation in Columbia County produced only forty-one bales of cotton in 1862, compared to 136 bales raised in 1858, and a planter in Jefferson County sold his fodder, hay, peanuts, and corn for $10,000 while making only $500 from the sale of cotton. The Savannah *Daily Morning News* on February 17, 1863, announced that "the cotton yield in this state for 1862, as shown by the Comptroller General, is 60,000 bales, of 500 pounds each, while ordinarily the production is 700,000 bales."

With the best grades of cotton selling for as high as sixteen and even eighteen cents a pound in 1862, the temptation to plant the staple was more than some people could resist. "By all means get some guide by legislature for the government of planters in reference to planting cotton," a man in Davisboro wrote to Stephens. "We should not be allowed to plant, perhaps, more than one-fourth or one-third of our crop in cotton."[22] Although the Confederate Congress adopted resolutions recommending to planters that they refrain from planting cotton, the matter of limiting cotton production by law was left for each state to determine. Governor Brown, in a message to the legislature in November, 1862, urged planters to cultivate only enough cotton for home consumption and requested that a tax be imposed upon "each quantity of seed cotton sufficient to make a bale of four hundred pounds . . . produced next year . . . over what is actually necessary for a home supply."[23] The legislature did not go so far as to tax the new crop, but it did enact a law which made it illegal for any person to plant "a greater number of acres of land in cotton than three acres for each hand." The penalty for violation of this law was a fine of $500 for each acre planted above the number specified.[24] Although the production of cotton decreased greatly after the law was passed, Brown felt the need of further restriction. In a message to the legislature on March 25, 1863, he recommended that an act be passed which would "make it highly penal for any one to cultivate exceeding one-fourth of an acre in cotton to the hand." He believed that the three-acre limitation virtually invited the production of cotton to that extent. The Governor was disappointed that the legislature failed to follow his recommendation. He made other attempts in November, 1863, and March, 1864, to persuade the legislature to reduce cotton production, but no further action was taken by the assembly.[25]

Despite Brown's failure to persuade the legislature to change the three-acre cotton limitation, Georgia experienced a distinct movement to develop diversified farming during the latter half of the war. "I am dun planting my Corn and Shugar Cane. The time has come when we must raise Everything or do without them," a man in Butts County declared in April, 1863.[26] A large crop of corn was planted in 1863, but on account of a drought the return was not as great as had been estimated. A man in Newton County said that wheat was as good as he had ever seen, and an Augusta paper stated that reports "speak favorably of the prospects of a large wheat crop." In 1864 the corn crop in southwestern Georgia surpassed that of former years, and the wheat crop was "extraordinarily good." One of General Sherman's men said that he daily traversed immense cornfields of hundreds of acres in extent. Near the end of the war a man at Calhoun wrote, "Provisions are as plenty Here as where you are. Wheat looks well Here. Clover is Half leg High.... What few cows are Here are Plum fat. Peoples that Have Horses are planting Corne [sic]."[27] The editor of *The Countryman* made 750 gallons of syrup from sugar cane in 1863, and a man near Milledgeville "realized over $60,000 from the sale of apples." Richard Malcolm Johnston informed Stephens in 1864 that strawberries were being raised "by thousands and tens of thousands" in middle Georgia. Planters began to turn toward stock farming. Essex swine were extensively advertised, and a man near Atlanta raised cattle, brood mares and studs, Cashmere goats, pigs, and hogs.

Labor on the plantations was encumbered with many difficulties, especially with the lack of supervision of the slaves. Overseers were difficult to keep, for many of them joined the army and those who remained demanded higher wages. Relations between planter and overseer became strained. "I got a letter from Fanny yesterday," a soldier wrote to his wife early in the war. "Her overseer has troubled her some. She has turned him off. . . . I knew he had the big head . . . and I reckon it got worse on him as he got things more under his control. Any man that is . . . able to come to the war wont do to attend business at home."[28] A Sandersville man wrote to his father-in-law, "I have not succeeded in getting an overseer for your river place . . . nor have I engaged any for your home place. I shall engage men . . . as soon as possible. . . ."[29] "I think it best that Morison is going to leave, for he would have kilde the mules," a woman explained to her husband. "Hulse has olde man Finley hired and I think he will try to do right."[30] "Uncle Dick went to court today, he is on the jury. I've given him out. I am overseeing a little more," a Sumter County woman despondently said.[31] The body of an overseer, riddled with buckshot, was found on a plantation near the Ogeechee Canal, where he had been killed, probably in an altercation with a planter.

Not only were planters troubled with incompetent overseers, but the overseers themselves were burdened with increasing difficulties, since their employers were absent and they had the problem of training the slaves to wartime economy. In 1862 a disgusted overseer expressed his opinion of his profession:

If there ever was . . . a calling as . . . contemptible as that of an overseer, I would be . . . glad to know what it is. . . . I am just tired of it, and I will quit it, as soon as I find a better business.

If there be good seasons . . . *the master makes* a splendid crop; if any circumstances be impropitious and an inferior crop be made, it is the overseer. If the hands are runabouts, it is the overseer's fault; and if he flogs them . . . or locks them up, or puts them in stocks, he is a brute and a tyrant. If no meat is made, the overseer *would* plant too much cotton, and of course 'tis his fault. If hogs are taken good care of, the overseer is wasting corn. . . . If he does not "turn out" hands in time, he is lazy; if he "rousts" them out . . . why he is a brute.[32]

When Governor Brown in early 1862 was urged to exempt overseers, he declined to do so, for he believed that exemptions "would open the way to abuse," that the duty of overseers to their employers "required them not to volunteer but to stand the chances of draft," and that if overseers were drafted, the law provided for substitutes.[33] A planter told Stephens, however, that there was "danger of Negro riots and starvation unless a few energetic men are allowed to remain upon the plantations."[34]

The Confederate Congress, taking cognizance of the need for

proper control of plantation laborers, passed a law in October, 1862, exempting one owner or overseer for every plantation having twenty Negroes. The storm of protest which this law provoked, coupled with the increasing need of men for the army, led to revisions in May, 1863, and in February, 1864, which drastically reduced the number of exempted overseers.[35] In some sections of southwest Georgia, where the slave population was very large and the white population relatively sparse, overseers continued to be exempted, but according to the report of the Conscript Bureau in December, 1863, the number of exemptions in the entire state was only two hundred and one.[36]

During the second and third years of the war the problem of securing overseers or managers for the farms became extremely difficult. A crippled woman in Glynn County wrote to Governor Brown that her husband had been "in his country's service a year," and that his wages were "our principal income as our negroes are all home on the farm, we have Seventeen in all, not enough to exempt my husband legally, but could not your Honor release him . . . so that he can give some assistance toward his planting interest?" She declared that she could not get anyone to manage the farm, "as every one that is liable to duty has gone in as Substitutes."[37] An elderly man in Oglethorpe County asked Alexander H. Stephens if he could have one of his three sons detailed from the army to attend to his farm. A lawyer in Cuthbert said that "Major Amos E. Ward is . . . one of our best citizens and if he cannot get his son detailed, who is a practical farmer, he will be without an overseer on his Randolph plantation for the present year."[38]

Whatever solution the planter made of his overseer problems, the task of disciplining and controlling Georgia's nearly a half-million slaves remained.[39] In 1861 an overseer wrote to a plantation owner:

> Peter left me Thursday. . . . I attempted to whip him and he refused to submit and walked off. He came back here Saturday . . . and said he had bin to you and that you told him to come back heare and goe to work. I asked him if wars reddey to take a whiping. He said he was not. I told him then he could not work with me until I whiped him. . . . He said he had done nothing to be whiped for . . . and walked off. I wish you would if please come down and let the matter be settle as I do not feel wiling to be runover by him.[40]

Linton Stephens found some of his slaves difficult to control. In

..PLANTER AND SLAVE

a letter to his brother, he explained the trouble that he was having:

> I have got a big row on hand with about 8 or 10 of my negroes for killing my hogs and sheep. . . . I have one of them in jail on bread and water. He tried to cut two of my negroes. . . . He is the worst negro I have and has drawn his knife several times before on overseers. He drew it this time on the overseer. He was brought to me at the camp and the first thing I did . . . was to knock him down and choke him. . . . I would sell him if I could.[41]

Alexander H. Stephens received a letter in 1862 from his overseer regarding a recalcitrant slave:

> I wrote you . . . that Pierce was sick and that I had taken him out of jail. He is now well and I dont think he was much sick at first. I think the most of his sickness was put on in order to get out of jail. . . . I am satisfied that his imprisonment has only tended to harden him. . . . I dont think he will ever reform. . . .[42]

In numerous other letters, as well as in diaries and newspapers, the story is revealed of the troubles Georgians had in managing insubordinate slaves. "Nancy has been very impertinent. . . . She said she would not be hired out by the month, neither would she go out to get work . . . ," an Athens woman wrote.[43] "The servants are so indolent and obstinate it is a trial to have anything to do with them . . . ," asserted Laura Comer.[44] "Some women were in Atlanta to buy food," published the Atlanta *Southern Confederacy* on March 14, 1863. "They did not have twenty negroes and were not entitled to an overseer. The women are unable to control the negroes and make them work. . . ." "I have a great deal of trouble with my negroes. They dont want to go down the country. I sold Big Henry for $2400. I rather have land now than negroes . . . ," a man said in 1863.[45] When a woman in Savannah sent a slave to Atlanta to be sold, she declared, "I am greatly relieved from having sent him away and have written to order him sold at any rate, as his bad example would ruin the other servants."[46] Another woman wrote to her husband regarding their slaves:

> We are doing as best we know, or as good as we can get the Servants to do; they learn to feel very independent as no white man comes to direct . . . them, for Willis speaks shorter to Johnny and orders him about more than any negro on the place; in consequence he seldom tells him to do anything, so sure as he does he [Willis] will make some insulting reply. . . .[47]

Apprehension concerning the state's ability to keep the slaves in proper subjection caused the legislature in 1862 to cancel exemptions from patrol duty. All Negroes going from one plantation to another were required to carry passes from their masters showing that they were absent from home with the owner's consent. The Atlanta *Southern Confederacy* suggested that "military authorities require every male slave of 15 years or upwards to be brought into our lines at every point where the enemy advances."[48] *The Countryman* on October 23, 1863, stated that ". . . the time has come for a stern and rigid execution of the patrol laws. Let negroes be under a strict surveillance, and be strapped well, whenever it is necessary. Let patrols go armed, and let every man keep fire-arms always loaded."

In order to keep the slaves under stricter control, the legislature made several additions to the penal code. An act passed in December, 1861, stated that any Negro who burned a railroad bridge would be deemed guilty of arson and punished by death. Another enactment stipulated that "Any Negro slave or free person of color who shall . . . cohabit with a white woman shall be guilty of adultery or fornication . . . and shall be imprisoned for one week and receive thirty-nine lashes on his bare back, on three several days. . . ." In 1863 the legislature passed a law making it illegal for the owners of slaves to allow them to hire their own time, and requiring the slaves to live on the premises of their owners.[49]

Despite the more stringent regulations, crimes were committed by Negroes. Robbery, arson, murder, and rape were the chief acts of violence. Alexander H. Stephens' Negro, Pierce, was placed in jail for breaking open a man's trunk and stealing his clothing. Several Negroes were caught attempting to break into stores, and a Savannah Negro was arrested for robbing a white woman. Another Savannah Negro, found guilty of robbery, was sentenced "to receive three times thirty-nine lashes, and to be placed in the pillory, and remain there thirty minutes." Several Negro boys attempted to burn dwelling houses and barns, and the Rome *Courier* for July 8, 1861, said that a woman in Chattooga County "was brutally murdered . . . by her negro woman and thrown in the well."[50] Late in the war a Negro man was hanged at Fort Gaines for an assault with intent to kill his master and another man.

Several assaults upon white women and girls occurred. In July, 1862, an enraged mob near Athens hanged a Negro for assaulting the wife of an overseer. During the same year a Negro boy at Savannah was charged with assaulting a white woman. In 1863 a

Negro was hanged at Stone Mountain for committing rape upon an eleven-year-old white girl. A few weeks later the following story appeared in a Savannah paper: "A negro in Ware County, after beating a white woman with a stick, raped her. The negro was soon caught and . . . was tried by a jury. The negro admitted his guilt. The jury rendered a verdict of guilty and recommended that the offender be burned to death. The sentence was accordingly carried into execution."[51]

Rumors of projected Negro insurrections were numerous during the war, and the fear of leaving their families to the mercy of Negroes caused more than one man to hesitate before volunteering. As early as May, 1861, a Negro man was hanged at Kingston for endeavoring to incite an insurrection. In June of the same year southwest Georgia was excited by rumors of a Negro plot. Negroes near Bainbridge collected old guns and pistols, and it was believed that they were planning to "kill all of the men and old women and children and take the younger ones for their wives." Two of the leaders of the proposed uprising were jailed, and a man asserted that if "they ever turn them out we are going to kill them."[52] After a few weeks the insurrection mania in southwest Georgia subsided, but a year later a Negro in Sumter County was hanged for attempting to induce Negroes to escape with him to the Federal blockade on the Florida coast. About the same time several Negroes in that county were discovered having gunpowder in their possession. In 1863 eighteen Negroes were lodged in the Hancock County jail for attempting to incite an insurrection. Approximately one hundred Negroes were reported implicated in the plot. The Milledgeville *Southern Recorder* said that the Negroes had been "inveigled into a secret organization that met after midnight for drill and to adopt some plan by which they could escape to the Federals. The whole trouble was instigated by Negro mechanics who had been permitted to perambulate the county, and make their own contracts contrary to law. . . ."[53] A year later a plot to incite a servile insurrection in Brooks County was discovered by police. The insurrection had been planned by an "infamous white wretch" named John Vickery. He and three Negroes were hanged after being tried in Quitman.

Throughout the war the newspapers published numerous advertisements of rewards for the return of runaway slaves. The approach of the enemy usually encouraged the Negroes to escape from their owners. When several Negroes tried to escape to Fort

CONFEDERATE GEORGIA..

Pulaski in 1863, they were drowned when their boat overturned in the Savannah River. As Sherman's army marched through Georgia, many Negroes followed behind the troops. "The Darkies come to us from every direction. They are looking for freedom but really dont seem to know just what freedom means," one of Sherman's officers asserted.[54] A correspondent to *The Countryman* wrote that "Two of Pa's negroes went off" with Sherman. "Our other negroes behaved splendidly. They were offered every inducement to go. ... All of Uncle J.'s negroes left but one."[55] Another writer said, "Andrew went off; he was young; I think they told him great tales, and thus got him off. I judge he is dead before this, as he was just out of a spell of pneumonia."[56]

Other Negroes were turned adrift by the Yankees to support themselves or perish. Captain David R. Conyngham, of Sherman's army, described the plight of the Negroes:

> The waters of the Ogeechee and Ebenezer Creek can account for hundreds who were blocking up our columns, and there abandoned, ... after being encouraged "to gwine along." Many of them died in the bayous and lagoons of Georgia. Wheeler's cavalry charged upon many negroes, driving them pellmell, into the waters, and mothers and children, old and young, perished alike![57]

A Brookhaven newspaper stated that the Negroes who accompanied the Yankees "received the first rude shock but a few miles from town, when they were compelled to dismount and trudge through the mud. Fatigued, hungry and cold, they strived ... to keep up with the mounted apostles of liberty. ... The first to succumb were the children, being deserted by their brutish mothers to perish on the wayside."[58] Late in the war a group of Negroes, while attempting to float down the Savannah River in a raft to join the Yankees, were killed when their raft struck a torpedo. Governor Brown in March, 1865, wrote Joseph E. Johnston that large numbers of Negroes were "going off daily to Savannah to the enemy." He said that the legislature had asked him to place a line of pickets between the Savannah and Ogeechee rivers, but that he was unable to do so, and requested Johnston to send a small force of men to the southeastern section of the state.[59]

On the other hand, many Negroes remained docile and even intensely loyal to their masters. Harrison Berry, an educated slave belonging to S. W. Price of Covington, published a pamphlet in which he defended slavery. He declared that abolitionist agitators

..PLANTER AND SLAVE

were the worst enemies of the slave. When a Negro woman in Columbus was told that the North planned to march an army through the South, she replied, "Do they think we are all 'sleep here? Every nigger . . . will rise to stop em."[60] An old Negro in Atlanta frequently managed his master's store during the latter's absence. About midway of the war a Decatur girl said that "Nothing on the plantation had visibly changed. The field-hands went out to their work at dawn. . . . The house women spent the days in the workroom spinning and weaving. . . ."[61] When Federal soldiers visited a home at Danielsville, a slave woman knocked a Yankee off a stolen horse. A slave at Eatonton pursued two Yankees into the woods and captured them. A Negro boy near Milledgeville captured a Yankee wagon filled with stolen goods and delivered it to Confederate authorities. A Confederate private, entombed in a cave in Atlanta, the mouth of which had been blocked by the explosion of a shell, was rescued by a faithful Negro.

Moreover, one finds much evidence of affection between master and slave. Joseph LeConte, the famous scientist, said that "the Negroes are extremely kind . . . to me and to Sister's family."[62] "The Negroes all wish you to come home very badly," G. F. Bristow wrote to Alexander H. Stephens.[63] "My love to all friends and the negroes," a soldier wrote to his father. "We *all* miss you very much, even the little negroes . . . ," a man told his brother. Another man wrote to his sister, "Nan makes quite a companion of little Diana. She is teaching her to sew and to be a good girl, and, by her gentle influence, is doing more for this little daughter of Ham than the Puritan missionaries of Port Royal could accomplish with all their arts."[64] "I have just finished teaching the servants as is my habit on Sunday eve'g," Laura Comer wrote.[65] Alexander H. Stephens in 1862 said that he had a strong desire to raise tobacco next year for his Negroes. One of Mrs. Howell Cobb's faithful slaves scribbled an affectionate letter to her mistress: ". . . I have not forgotten you and if you plese mam send your old servant some sugar and coffee and give my love to all the children. . . . Give my love to all my collord friends in the yard and recive the greates portions for yourself."[66]

The problem of caring for the Negro confronted the planter throughout the war. "I have a supply of negro clothes, shoes, &c, bought early in the summer, seeing that there would likely be a scarcity of such things. It was very fortunate I did so too, for those who put it off, have been unable to purchase at any price," a

CONFEDERATE GEORGIA..

planter in 1861 wrote.⁶⁷ John B. Lamar told his brother-in-law, Howell Cobb, that he was having difficulty in securing clothing and other necessities for his slaves:

> I have some wool and next May's dip will add some to it, making ... 800 lbs or more, which will make about half our negro cloth. Shoes I can get at some price I expect. As to bagging, rope and twine, we can do without, by packing seed cotton away in pens and letting it lay until the English send us bagging. But salt we must have or starve. I suppose enough will be made on the ... coast during the year.⁶⁸

"I've sixty yards of negro cloth spooled now. Going after dinner to warp it and will draw it in tomorrow for Liza to weave," a woman said. "Will you ... let me know if you have any cloth on hand ... for servants clothes?" a man asked. A woman wrote to her husband, "I just got out a piece of cloth yesterday. It is for the negroes." A planter said that it was "a great advantage to have Capt. Winn's family on the plantation, for Mrs. Winn attends the sick ones ... which relieves me ... of the anxiety about the negroes and place."⁶⁹ In 1864 a man in Cuthbert requested his mother to send her Negro boys there. "I have a farm now and I would try and feed them for you ... ," he said.⁷⁰

Within a few months after the war started, desirable slaves became more difficult to purchase. "I have been all over the City [Savannah] to every house where negroes were kept for sale, and a girl or cook cannot be bought," an officer wrote to his wife in February, 1862.⁷¹ By 1863 the labor shortage had become acute; and this fact, together with inflationary prices, caused the prices of slaves and of wages paid for hired Negroes to increase. "I have hired some of my negroes to a factory near Macon. Get fine wages for them," a man in Savannah disclosed in 1863. "I understand that you wish to hire a negro boy.... I have a very good boy that I will hire you," another man wrote. "Wanted to hire ... 7 or 8 Negro men to work at my saw mill," a man advertised.

Slaves sold in 1862 at prices ranging from about $550 to $1600 each; in 1863, from $650 to $3500; in late 1864, from $1,000 to $4,700; and in early 1865 from $2,700 to $5,500. An Atlanta newspaper in 1863 declared that "Negroes ... have become as high as able-bodied substitutes over 45,"⁷² and the Columbus *Daily Times* on January 22, 1864, said that "We are at a loss to determine upon what basis ... such prices for slaves can be predicated." The high

..130

cost of slaves was more apparent than real, however, for the general cost of living in the South during the latter half of 1863 was nearly double that of April, 1861, and in the spring of 1864 it was more than three times as high. Early in 1865, when there was a noticeable increase in the advertisements offering Negroes for sale, the prices of slaves began declining. Slave owners may have realized that the ownership of slaves was no longer an asset.

The economic and social life of the free Negro, of whom there were 3,500 in Georgia in 1860, was difficult during the war. Free Negresses in Savannah made clothing for the soldiers and free Negroes were impressed by a state law to help construct fortifications near the city. A newspaper announced that "Among the subscribers to the Confederate loan in Columbus was a free negro, who took bonds to the amount of two or three hundred dollars."[73] Several free Negroes, however, petitioned the legislature for permission to return voluntarily into slavery by becoming the slaves of specified white persons. In each case the petition was referred to the legislature's judiciary committee for consideration, after which the legislature usually voted to allow the Negro to become a slave. For instance, the legislature on December 17, 1861, passed an act authorizing Elmira Mathews, a free Negress in Greene County, "to sell herself into perpetual slavery" to John D. Doherty. The act said that the woman would be "subject to all the incidents of slavery, except the liability of being sold during the lifetime of said Doherty, by himself or his creditors for his debts: The sole consideration for which voluntary enslavement on her part shall be the obligation thereby incurred by her master of feeding, clothing and protecting her."[74]

The legislature in November, 1863, considered enacting a law "to sell all free negroes of African descent into slavery," but the judiciary committee to which the bill was referred reported adversely and the measure was not voted upon. Free Negroes were required to register their names with the county ordinaries, and those who failed to comply were subject to penalties. In some cities free Negroes were compelled, like the slaves, to secure passes from their employers if they wished to leave their homes at night. Free Negroes were required to have white guardians, and a few free Negroes who had no guardians petitioned the legislature to appoint specified persons for that purpose.

Regardless of the strict patrol regulations, many Negroes seem to have enjoyed as much, if not more, freedom during the war than previously. A traveller near Macon in 1862 said that "Crowds of slaves in gayest attire" got on and off the train "at every country stopping place." He stated that the slaves were "merry, noisy, loquacious creatures, wholly unconscious of care or anxiety."[75] In Columbus Negro parties were held frequently at night, and a Columbus paper thought that the frolicking was an "unmitigated nuisance." Another paper announced that "Macon is filled . . . with Negroes" who act "as if they were free people . . . perambulate the streets, smoke cigars, swear, and steal."[76] Negroes congregated on the streets of Savannah on Sunday afternoons to play "uproarious games." The slaves also enjoyed barbecues, picnics, church services, and an occasional dance in the cotton shed or sugar house. Late in the war a woman complained that she was getting tired of Negro weddings, "for all of them thinks we must give them a big supper."[77]

The first use of the Negro by the army, other than as personal servants, was in the summer of 1862, when the Confederacy began impressing slaves for work upon the Savannah fortifications. General H. W. Mercer, commanding the construction of the fortifications, in August, 1862, called upon the slaveholders of Georgia, especially those in the neighborhood of Savannah, to send twenty per cent of their able-bodied slaves to work on the fortifications. Transportation and wages were furnished by the Confederate government. General Mercer wrote Secretary of War G. W. Randolph that he had collected a thousand Negroes to work upon the fortifications and that he could secure five hundred additional slaves but did not have tools for them. "Not the slightest force has been used," Mercer declared; "the great mass of the planters are patriotic and respond cheerfully."[78]

Soon "a howl of indignant condemnation" arose, however, from slave owners all over the state. Many planters said that they had no objection to contributing their slaves voluntarily but that they would not submit to impressment. Richard F. Lyon of Atlanta wrote to Stephens that he believed the impressment was illegal. "If my negroes are carried to Savannah under this order, I abandon them," he declared. "I do not want them to return to the plantation to demoralize the balance."[79] In November General Mercer notified Governor Brown that the Secretary of War had withdrawn from him "all power to retain the Negroes" and requested that the state should furnish him with fifteen hundred slaves to work on the defenses. The legislature enacted laws authorizing the Gov-

..PLANTER AND SLAVE

ernor to impress the slaves. In April and August, 1863, General Mercer made further requests upon slave owners for slaves. County sheriffs collected the Negroes and sent them to Savannah.[80]

The use of Negroes as laborers was never entirely satisfactory to the army and continued to be condemned by many Georgians. The Augusta *Chronicle and Sentinel* did not "like the idea of Negro coadjutors in the war for independence" but was willing for slaves to be used as teamsters, cooks, and nurses.[81] The Atlanta *Southern Confederacy* on January 27, 1863, complained that "Either the military or city or county officers are constantly seizing negroes . . . and putting them to work without giving the owners notice." Governor Brown himself, in April, 1863, said that Negroes should not be taken from the plantations in the spring of the year. Approximately 150 of the Negroes employed at Savannah were sick daily, according to the medical superintendent of the forces building the fortifications. Planters worried for fear that their slaves would be overworked, demoralized, or would run away. The Savannah *Daily Morning News* said that a few Negroes did run away from the work at the fortifications. Captain J. W. Mallett, supervisor of the Confederate laboratories in Macon, where impressed slaves constructed earthworks, received letters from slave owners requesting that their slaves be allowed to visit home occasionally. An Americus slave owner wrote that "As Isham has a wife and is very anxious to See her, I should be glad if he could come home immediately. In fact, I fear he may run away if not permitted to do so."[82]

Despite its unpopularity, the impressment of Negroes continued until the end of the war. In December, 1864, Negroes were being impressed at Columbus to work upon railroads and fortifications, and in February, 1865, slaves were impressed to rebuild the Georgia Railroad and the Macon and Western Railroad.

A movement to arm the slaves, which began in 1863, was almost universally condemned in Georgia. The Atlanta *Southern Confederacy* stated that "It would be the sacrifice of the principle which is the basis of our social system."[83] The Savannah *Daily Morning News,* the Milledgeville *Southern Recorder,* and the Macon *Daily Telegraph* believed that there was danger in putting arms in the hands of Negroes. "The proposition to make soldiers of our slaves [is] the most pernicious idea that has been suggested," General Howell Cobb wrote to Secretary of War Seddon in January, 1865. "You cannot make soldiers of slaves, nor slaves of soldiers."[84] In a message to the legislature in February, 1865, Governor Brown said, "I am satisfied that we may profitably use slave labor, so far as it can be spared from agriculture, to do menial service in . . . the army . . .: but . . . any attempt to arm the slaves will be a great error."[85] On the other hand, Joseph Addison Turner, editor of *The Countryman,* did not believe that there was any truth in Brown's assertion that slaves could not be relied upon to fight. Nevertheless, resolutions in favor of arming the slaves were rejected by the legislature in March, 1865. The Confederate Congress, at the instigation of President Davis, adopted a measure on March 13, 1865, "enrolling slaves in the Confederate army, each state to furnish its quota"; but before more than 3,486 Negro troops could be furnished from Georgia, the war had ended and the slaves were free.

The relative scarcity of slaves and the absence of white men caused work on the plantations to fall largely upon old men, women, and children. A young officer sent these instructions to his wife: "So soon as Litt [a slave] gets through hauling straw . . . make them haul out as much manure as you want in the garden, and the balance have hauled out into the corn field. . . . Make Litt crowd up while he has Sam to help him. Always get Mr. Greer to show him how to do everything."[86] In another letter he asked his wife to tell his son David to "see to everything, horses and hogs being fed."[87] A woman wrote to her soldier-brother, "Everybody has out their wheat. . . . Ma has got hers out. She thinks she will make her seed."[88] A few months later another sister wrote to the same brother, "Ma had her wheat out last week, it is not very good. Therefore we will not eat much biscuit next year. The corn looks very well, but we are deep in the grass . . . we have tried to get help but can not."[89] A soldier advised his wife to borrow money and buy corn if she could not sell their cow. Another man wrote to his wife, "You stated that you had not bought a horse yet. You need not be in a hurry about a horse if you can get your wheat sowed."[90] "You must write me which debts to pay first as I am determined to settle all I can," a plantation mistress requested of her soldier-husband.[91]

Farming necessarily became more and more of a co-operative enterprise. "Many planters are making arrangements to attend to the farms and fields of their neighbors, who have gone into the army and have not left laborers at home," announced the *Southern Cultivator.*[92] "I am nearly done cutting my wheat," a planter wrote. "I was to help the Rev. L. P. Davis today but it is Raining very hard at this time. . . . If your Wheat is not Ready to cut, let me know and . . . I will . . . help you. . . ."[93] A woman in Bulloch County informed her husband that "We get along very well considering the hindrance we have had through log rolling this week. Last Saturday, at your Father's and the cow pen logs, here Thursday. At Grandmother's Friday. At Rebecca Pridggens, Saturday, and at Nancy Waters. I hope this will end the log rolling for this spring."[94] A farmer wrote to a friend: "If you are in a tight place to get your wheat cut let me know and I will . . . give you a lift. I know Polly Ann will have a good dinner and . . . very likely the old man will draw out his bottle that has bin [sic] hid away for nearly a year."[95] A soldier told his wife to lend salt to their friends after she had kept as much as she would need for the following year. Writing to his wife, another soldier said, "I . . . will do my best to get the barrel of sugar to be divided between them [members of the family] and you."[96]

Although the war left untouched no phase of Georgia's economic and social life, its greatest effect was upon agriculture, for more than three-fourths of the population was engaged in farming. As the war ended, many planters, finding themselves destitute, migrated from north and middle Georgia to the southwestern part of the state, a region untouched by the enemy. Other planters moved to western areas of the United States. Planters who did not join the exodus to the newer regions were faced with rebuilding their dilapidated plantations and caring for the emancipated Negroes. Near the close of the war a Thomasville planter described his bewildering situation:

> I went home and found everything ruined, mules, horses, oxen, waggons. . . . Willie Winn has brought out some forty of my Negroes and I dont know what to do with them. . . . Your place and Maj. Porters has not half open land enough for your Negroes. . . . I have no home for my family and dont know what I shall do. I am riding every day hoping to find some shelter.[97]

Thousands of Negroes flocked into the towns to loaf, steal, and do generally as pleasure dictated, while others, attracted by stories of higher wages, began departing for Mississippi and Louisiana. A majority of the freedmen, however, soon drifted back to the plantations and sought to renew their relations with their former masters. Many planters and Negroes found it mutually advantageous

CONFEDERATE GEORGIA..

to sign temporary contracts which stipulated the obligations of each. Typical of such contracts was one made by an Eatonton planter:

... the said Irby H. Scott agrees to furnish said freedman ... now members of his family with food and clothing and to treat them in every way humanly and to give them one-sixth part of the whole crop raised on his plantation this year 1865 ... and in consideration of the above, we the undersigned freed-men and women do bind ourselves to continue to perform the work on his plantation ... until the 25th of December next ... and in the meantime to be ... obediént to said Irby H. Scott ... and not to leave said plantation without permission. . . .[98]

A great slump in farm values occurred as a result of the war. The amount of improved land increased slightly in the mountain section and in portions of south Georgia, but there was a decrease in the other regions, especially in middle Georgia, which prior to the war had been the most prosperous part of the state. The number of farms increased everywhere, but they were smaller in size and worth only about one-half as much per acre as before the war. During the decade between 1860 and 1870 the total cash value of the farms in Georgia declined from $157,072,803 to $94,559,468, and the value of farming implements and machinery decreased from $6,844,387 to $4,614,701.[99]

CHAPTER IX

Disloyalty and Desertion

WHILE THE VAST MAJORITY OF Georgians were loyal to the Confederacy, many of them had Union sympathies, enlisted in the Federal military or naval forces, gave aid and comfort to the enemy, or attempted to remain neutral.[1] "It will be a very fortunate circumstance, if bands of tories and robbers can be kept down," a citizen of Dalton wrote to Vice-President Stephens early in the war. "There are too many spies in our midst."[2] Throughout the war many Georgians felt that the state had made a tragic mistake in seceding. Less than a year after the war began, an Atlanta man wrote Stephens that "Every man . . . knows that secession . . . involved us in war, and that the only escape from its further ravages is at once to renounce Secession as no remedy for any evils of which the South complained; . . ."[3]

At the beginning of hostilities Union sympathizers and "Tories" were so numerous in Georgia that "vigilance committees" were organized in many counties. In a letter to Governor Brown in May, 1861, the Kingston Home Guards said it was "absolutely necessary that there should be an armed body of discreet persons, not only to scare suspicious characters, but to protect those unjustly suspected." Even the leader of the vigilance committee at Kingston was accused of treason.[4] A few months later a woman wrote, "Our church and Mr. Hinton's house burned by incendiaries. . . . Yankees among us, no doubt."[5]

When the war began, nearly seven thousand persons of Northern birth resided in Georgia, and their sympathies were divided. Some Northerners returned to their native section, but many remained in Georgia and either were loyal to the South or attempted to give assistance to the Union cause. For those with Northern sympathies scant freedom of speech or action was permitted. "I think there are numbers of Yankees here but they keep very quiet and they cannot return if they go North . . . ," wrote a man at Savannah, in July, 1861.[6] In Macon a Northern carpenter, found guilty of using treasonable language, was warned to leave the city. At Rome a man was imprisoned "for expressing treasonable sentiments," and an Augusta citizen was arrested for selling passes to slaves with which they might reach the Union lines. A deaf and crippled "clock cleaner" was arrested in Burke County under suspicion of being a spy. The Augusta *Chronicle and Sentinel* reported that he had been tampering with Negroes. "When occasion requires, his lameness and deafness are cured instanter, but are decidedly aggravated disorders when a white man approaches," the paper stated.[7]

The Atlanta *Southern Confederacy* warned that Atlanta would attract a class of people who would "form a nucleus . . . for any . . . disloyal sentiment. . . ." The editor said that there were a few men of Northern birth in Atlanta, "who are still *Yankees,* who ought to be back in their native land . . . and those may, in some cases, even wish our arms to be successful . . . still they are not *Southernized* in their . . . feelings, and hence are incapable of making good Southern citizens."[8] A few weeks later five men and three women residents of Atlanta, all of Northern birth, were arrested "on suspicion of being dangerously unfriendly to us."[9] When the pickery at a factory in Roswell, north of Atlanta, burned, the fire was attributed to "Yankee hands or Yankee money."

Savannah, the chief city and seaport of the state, contained many individuals of Northern or foreign birth who were hostile to or indifferent toward the Confederacy. In February, 1862, the Milledgeville *Southern Federal Union* said that "there is a vast deal of traitorous material" in Savannah,[10] and a short time later the mayor offered a reward for the detection of anyone furnishing the enemy with Southern papers. "Traitorous parties in Savannah have been holding communications with the enemy," disclosed the Savannah *Daily Morning News* on February 16. Captain George A. Mercer of Savannah said in August of the same year that "The Enemy derive many advantages from northern born men in our midst; a large proportion of them are hostile. . . . These men become guides, spies, and informers."[11] As late as March, 1865, a man charged with using treasonable language in Savannah was sentenced to pay a fine and to leave the city immediately.

In 1862 several hundred aliens, in order to avoid conscription, presented affidavits to the clerk of the Inferior Court at Savannah, saying that they did not intend to become citizens of the Confed-

..DISLOYALTY AND DESERTION

erate States.[12] The Prussian consul at Savannah, I. N. Hudtwalcker, wrote Governor Brown in March, 1862, that "several subjects of the German states in Savannah were drafted after taking an oath of non-intention to become citizens of this country" and asked that they be released. Adjutant-General Wayne ordered the men to be released immediately.[13]

In Augusta numerous persons were suspected of disloyalty. The Augusta *Constitutionalist* said that the New York *Herald* contained a description of Augusta, its foundries, distance on the river, and other facts concerning the city. "This may have been furnished to the *Herald* by some one in New York, who has . . . resided in Augusta; but it is not . . . improbable that some traitor now in Augusta has . . . furnished it . . . ," the paper declared.[14] In 1863 an Augusta policeman was arrested for treason, and a year later several Augusta women were apprehended for communicating with the enemy. Near the end of the war the editor of the Augusta *Chronicle and Sentinel,* who came to Georgia from Connecticut after the war began, ostensibly as an exile banished for his anti-abolition proclivities, was accused of being a Federal spy.[15]

Disaffection toward the Confederacy was most evident, however, in the mountain sections of north Georgia, where a strong Union sentiment prevailed throughout the war. Many reasons have been given for this Union feeling, probably the most important being that since a majority of the mountaineers owned no slaves, their social and economic interests and problems were not similar to those existing in other sections of the state. Shortly before the war began, Governor Brown received a strong protest against secession from a man in Walker County, in northwest Georgia:

> We the people of Walker Co and Dade Co Ga DeKalb Co . . . do not in tend to Submit to . . . Secession . . . which has been taken out of the hands of the People and has fallen in to the hands of Dimegougs and office Seekers pickpockets and vagrants. . . . If Surtern Georgia want to leave the union let her go but we the people of Cheroke want to Stay in the union So I hope you will let us go in peace. . . . if not we will try what venture there is in flint and steel We have 2500 volunteer now they are seun [sworn] to Stan to each other. . . .[16]

A citizen of Gainesville who asked Howell Cobb to obtain for one of his friends an appointment as a Confederate surgeon stated that the appointment would have "a good effect upon the politicks [*sic*] in that mountain region in aiding us to Satisfy . . . the tremendous union feeling. . . ."[17]

Governor Brown, who had lived in north Georgia, knew the character of the mountain people and by using tact kept down trouble for a while. When Harrison W. Riley, a leading politician of Lumpkin County, early in 1861 threatened to seize the United States mint at Dahlonega and hold it for the Federal government, Brown, instead of using force, quietly notified the superintendent of the mint that the state now possessed it.[18] The United States flag continued to fly in Pickens County, but Brown refused to send troops to tear it down, and soon the flag was removed by the people themselves. Practically every county in north Georgia raised at least one company of troops for the Confederacy, and Brown gave the mountain companies preference in place, arms, and equipment. Priority in the selection of officers was in some cases ignored in order to give positions to men from the mountain counties. Despite Brown's lenient policy toward the Unionists and the apathetic, disloyalty in the mountain section continued in an aggravated form until the end of the war.[19]

Scarcely had the war started when men began deserting from the army or absenting themselves without leave.[20] In April, 1861, a group of men was ordered to attend a court martial at Griffin to answer a charge of non-attendance at a company muster. At Thomaston a deserter who was discovered working in a factory soon "commenced boarding in the jail." "Privates Steele and Caudle left Camp yesterday noon without leave. Steele has just returned, and been placed in the Guard Tent," wrote Captain C. R. Hanleiter of the Jo Thompson Artillery at Savannah.[21] In a letter to his wife, a Georgia officer at Fort Pulaski said that "Two men (Germans) from this Fort deserted . . . and have doubtless posted the enemy with our ways . . . of getting a mail. . . ."[22] The Atlanta *Southern Confederacy* told the story of two young men who, pretending to be machinists, engaged work in the state road shop, but did not prove to be as good workmen as they had represented themselves to be. "They slipped out (at night) from the boarding house, carrying off . . . articles that did not belong to them." The men were believed to be deserters.[23]

Many of the deserters were of the lawless class who would have caused trouble under any circumstances. As early as May, 1861, Governor Brown was informed that a group of men in Murray County, with lawless leaders, was making up a company of "home guards." He was told that the men would apply to him for guns and that he should be scarce of arms when they applied.[24] An

..DISLOYALTY AND DESERTION

entire cavalry company at Camp Spaulding, composed of the "lowest classes from Savannah," was arrested for mutinous and disorderly conduct. "My heart bled to observe, at Dress Parade, ... Privates Devlin, Hornsby and Payne each marching ... up and down the line, with ball and chain, as a punishment for their recent insubordination," said Captain Hanleiter.[25] When a man in Savannah was wounded from a pistol shot, the captain of the city guard told General Henry R. Jackson that two other men were implicated. "It has been stated ... that they united themselves with the Company, merely for the purpose of winning money from the Crackers, and the first opportunity desert to the enemy—also they are New York rowdies and pickpockets, ... bad men to be in our Army ... ," the captain alleged.[26]

Some men deserted because they disliked their officers, many of whom during the first year of the war spent too much time idling about the quartermaster's and commissary quarters. One soldier, after sending in his resignation, wrote to his mother: "I was badly treated in Savannah. . . . Those old army officers rendered my situation in the regular army exceedingly unpleasant and while I am . . . anxious to serve the country, I am not willing to remain longer with them."[27] "There is entirely too much Demagogueism in this Department of the Army," wrote Captain Hanleiter. "Almost every officer is trimming his sails for future political use." Dissatisfaction concerning their pay was also a cause of men's desertion. "Gov. Brown having refused to pay the Sappers and Miners agreeably to the terms of their enlistment, . . . they swear they 'don't care a damn' whether the Yankees take the island [Skidaway] or not—they will not work extra hours unless paid for it," said Hanleiter.[28] A Savannah newspaper in 1863 declared that desertions were frequent and inquired if the troops had been regularly and promptly paid.

Other factors, such as poor food, homesickness, and ignorance caused men to desert. "We are living quite hard, we have poor beef and fresh Shoat meat . . . ," an officer wrote from Camp Wilson, Savannah, in early 1861.[29] "Our Company is without Meat—there being none in Savannah," another soldier wrote in 1862.[30] One soldier attributed the food shortage to the fact that officers had their families with them and were "feeding them off the government." Some men deserted when they received gloomy letters from their families. Others were Union men at heart. A private wrote to his father in 1863: "I am this day as strong a

Union man as ever walked the soil of Virginia. I would hate to desert but if I ever get a good chance I will be sure to do it. I never expect to kill a Union man."[31]

With the passage of the first conscription act on April 16, 1862, the number of desertions rapidly increased. Men conscripted for service were potential material for desertion, for their hearts were not devoted to a cause for which they had not volunteered. "The people of Georgia regard the draft as disgraceful," Captain George A. Mercer said.[32] "The army here is in great excitement at the passage of the conscript law. . . . I find every body opposed to this tyrannical conscription law," Edward R. Harden wrote to his mother from Camp Jackson.[33] Conscripts hid themselves or moved quickly from one county to another in order not to be discovered. "In Savannah I have seen several refractory Conscripts brought to the Barracks under military guard," Captain Mercer said in 1862.[34] In Murray County a man who desired to avoid conscription laid his right hand upon a stump and with an axe cut off two of his fingers. A party of six men in Marion County was in armed resistance to conscription. Governor Brown in July, 1862, issued a proclamation calling for the arrest of deserters, but the evil continued. A month later Captain Mercer said that "Four of Millen's Battle. [Battalion] are supposed to have deserted to the enemy's Gun Boats; they were all northern men and suspected. Nearly all the deserters . . . have been northern born."[35]

In addition to conscription, the tax-in-kind and impressment laws tended to arouse disaffection. Many of the poorer people had never paid any direct taxes, and when someone appeared and took one-tenth of their farm products, they resented it. Disaffection due to the inordinate impressment of supplies spread to the army and contributed to desertion. "The impressing agent has gone around, and, in many cases, robbed the families of their meagre support . . . ," said Toombs, and consequently "the soldiers . . . have become discontented and desertions have taken place."[36] The criticisms of the Confederate government by Brown, Stephens, Toombs, and other prominent men probably added to the feeling of discontent and tended to encourage desertions. When Congress, in October, 1862, passed an act exempting one white man for every plantation of twenty or more slaves, many of the poorer men who were drafted to replace the exempted ones either deserted or swore that they would not fight.

The exemption of men engaged in so-called vital occupations

..DISLOYALTY AND DESERTION

also caused resentment. The Atlanta *Southern Confederacy* avowed that there were men who could fill the places of exempted railroad and express men, teachers, millers, and ferrymen. "Teachers are exempt, and under this provision . . . schools have sprung up in abundance—gotten up, in many instances, by men who are no more fit for teachers than they are for Generals," this paper asserted. "The ladies can teach, and . . . thereby relieve able bodied men and let them go into the army." According to the *Southern Confederacy,* it was "nonsense" to exempt printers and pressmen and not editors; and religious sects, such as Quakers and Dunkards, who were conscientiously opposed to the war, should not be exempted.[37] Moreover, the Confederate government's policy of exempting all boys attending military schools caused resentment. A citizen of Henderson wrote Alexander H. Stephens that he knew "several wealthy gentlemen" in his county "whose sons are at the conscript age, and who are in the school [Georgia Military Institute] at Marietta to keep . . . out of the army."[38]

In addition to the Confederacy's numerous exemptions, Governor Brown, using his authority to exempt all civil and military officers necessary for the administration of state affairs, included judges, sheriffs, tax-collectors, treasurers, mayors, employees of the state railroad, and numerous other state employees. His many exemptions added to the discontent. In January, 1864, an Augusta newspaper stated that 5,579 Georgians had been exempted because they were in "essential occupations"; 1,499 had been exempted for physical disability; and that five thousand Georgians had secured substitutes.[39] The Bureau of Conscription reported a total of 8,229 exemptions up to February, 1865.[40]

While the wealthy conscripts were able to hire substitutes, the less fortunate men seldom were able to do so; but many of the poorer classes were glad to hire themselves out as substitutes.[41] "Wm. A. Weldon . . . has now taken a notion to go to the war and to go as a Substitute . . . ," a man wrote to his brother.[42] "Willis has rote to him [her father] to come to richmond and get him A substitute and he thinks some times he will go and Again he thinks if he gets one for Willis he mus get for all and he says he is not able to hier substitutes for all," Mollie Evans of Butts County wrote her husband, who was in the service.[43] In another letter to her husband, Mrs. Evans remarked:

Betty Thaxton was looking for James home last week but she got a letter from James . . . and he stated that he could not come: James is geting very tierd of the ware he rote to Betty to send him money to get him a substitute Betty was very much pestered about it she says she will give every thing she has . . . for money enough to get him out of the ware. . . .⁴⁴

In Atlanta the dread of having to fight caused many business men to procure substitutes, said to be worth in 1863 from four to five thousand dollars. From eight to ten thousand men in Atlanta capable of bearing arms were reported to be "listless lookers on while a conflict is pending. . . ." "A number of foreigners and men of Yankee proclivities have left Macon recently by underground railroad for Lincolndom," announced the Augusta *Chronicle and Sentinel*. "Many of them have furnished substitutes for the army, and have amassed fortunes at home, but now as substitutes will be abolished . . . they Vamouse the ranch to foreign ports."⁴⁵ The Savannah *Daily Morning News* declared that many "carpers and grunters" were smugly hiding away and that other rich and able-bodied men, instead of doing their duty, were "a curse and a fire-brand in camp."⁴⁶

A Fort Valley woman protested to Governor Brown concerning the "slackers" in her community:

It appears that all the poor from here has gone and the rich remains who has the Slaves it is those . . . that has remain home who is benifited [sic] after the war it is the rich they have no mercy on the Soldiers familys I heard a lady in this place before her Husband Should go she would gave all her property away I think if She was tried she would Sing her tune quite differently. . . . I am like my friend Dr. McGhee of Houston he made a Speech on fry day in this place and he made the very Speech I wanted to hear for such men he told them they did not have the grit and such ought to be boiled up in Soap greese.⁴⁷

Late in 1862 the northeastern counties of the state became the refuge of a band of deserters and Union sympathizers. Headed by a deserter, Jeff Anderson, these men hid in the mountains and engaged in stealing, harboring runaway slaves, and terrorizing the surrounding country. Governor Brown sent reserve troops to disband them; some fifty of the leaders, including Anderson, were arrested, and several hundred deserters were returned to their commands. At the same time, however, the ringleader of a band of deserters and murderers near Marietta had not been captured. Soon after Anderson was arrested, he escaped from jail in At-

..DISLOYALTY AND DESERTION

lanta and resumed his leadership of a band of armed deserters in the mountains. Early in 1863 a large number of enlisted men from northeast Georgia were skulking in the mountains. Consequently, a company of Georgia State Guards, with instructions to avoid bloodshed if possible, was ordered to Dahlonega by Adjutant-General Wayne to "scour the mountains for the arrest of deserters and other persons . . . inciting rebellion." The order stated that in sections of northeast Georgia large numbers of deserters and other disloyal citizens were "Committing acts of robbery and threatening to . . . do other acts of violence."[48] On the same day that Wayne sent the troops to Dahlonega, Governor Brown commanded all Confederate officers and privates in Georgia who had deserted to return to their commands immediately.

The Georgia State Guards, commanded by Captain E. M. Galt, and aided by the safety committee at Dahlonega, arrested many of the deserters; and several hundred men from northeast Georgia enrolled at Atlanta as volunteers. The Dahlonega *Signal* for March 7, 1863, said that "the deserters have nearly, if not all, returned to the army, whilst the disloyalists, if there are any left find it best to keep still."[49] The Atlanta *Southern Confederacy* maintained, however, that "A few persons in Northeast Georgia were cautiously speaking their treasonable sentiments, . . . secretly . . . encouraging men to . . . resist . . . enrollment as conscripts . . . and a few ignorant men to violate private rights, plunder, commit rape, break open jails . . . thus placing themselves in a position of . . . rebellion."[50]

The impression should not be given, however, that a majority of the people in northeast Georgia fought against the Confederacy. In Pickens County, where the United States flag continued flying for several weeks following secession, more than 550 men enlisted in the Confederacy, or approximately one-eighth of the county's entire population in 1860. By March, 1862, Lumpkin County had "more than 500 men armed and arming." The many accusations of disloyalty in northeast Georgia caused a citizen of Clarkesville to write a letter to the Atlanta *Southern Confederacy* in which he declared that Habersham County had furnished more than six hundred soldiers out of a voting population of about eight hundred and fifty. The letter said further:

> I am well satisfied that there are not 25 deserters in the county. . . . There were some, however, liable to conscription refusing to go, and a few — a *very few*, who were disloyal. In White and Rabun counties the average was about the same, only that there were a few more of

the disloyal in the lower part of White county. The people of North Eastern Ga. have furnished as much *sound* fighting material as any other portion of the State of the same population.[51]

Despite such refutations, disloyalty increased throughout northeast Georgia during 1863. Governor Brown on May 26th ordered the officers of the state troops to be active in arresting all deserters and to deliver them to Colonel G. W. Lee, commanding a Confederate post at Atlanta. The latter telegraphed a message to Governor Brown regarding deserters:

There is considerable trouble in North Eastern Georgia, especially in Fannin County. The loyal Citizens arrested a number of deserters, who were rescued by other deserters and tories, Killing and wounding Several. Only one of the deserters Killed. If you can spare one company . . . send it there. Supposed to be one hundred and fifty tories and deserters in a body and Camped. They are plundering and burning. . . .[52]

Brown replied that "a company or two should be raised in Fannin County to protect their homes and drive out deserters."[53] Adjutant-General Wayne in August ordered the home guards of eight counties in northeast Georgia to "act together, or in such separate organizations as may be effective, to put down the tories and deserters infesting those Counties." By September, 1863, the situation in northeast Georgia had become so critical that the Confederate government ordered Colonel Lee to proceed to north Georgia in order to operate against the deserters. Adjutant-General Wayne notified Colonel Lee that Lumpkin County was "overrun with Deserters, Tories, and Rogues, who are stealing and running off horses, mules and cattle. . . ."[54]

Although disloyalty and desertions were greater in the mountain counties than elsewhere, they were by no means confined to northeast Georgia. An official of the Adjutant-General's office in Milledgeville notified a conscription officer that deserters from both the Confederate army and the state militia were hiding in the mountains of Pike County, in central Georgia, committing depredations and evading the enrolling officers. The southeastern corner of Georgia, especially the Okefenokee Swamp, was a favorable retreat for deserters. An island in the Okefenokee Swamp, known today as "Soldier Camp Island," was used alternately as a camping place for deserters and by soldiers searching for deserters. The mountains of northwest Georgia also served as a secure retreat for

..DISLOYALTY AND DESERTION

deserters; and on June 9, 1863, General S. B. Buckner, in command of the Department of East Tennessee, requested Brown to instruct the sheriffs and militia officers of the counties in that region to arrest all persons absent from the army without leave.[55]

General Gideon J. Pillow in July, 1863, said that there were twenty-five to thirty thousand men liable to duty in Georgia and that the state was full of able-bodied men and refugees. In November Benjamin H. Hill issued an appeal for the absentees from General Bragg's army to return promptly to duty, declaring that more than half of the officers and privates were absent. "They . . . are spending their time on railroads, at hotels, at . . . houses . . . and taking pleasure walks and rides with thoughtless women," Hill asserted.[56] The legislature on December 15th passed an act to punish by fine or imprisonment or both, "any person who may hereafter conceal, or assist any deserter in resisting a legal arrest in this State."[57]

Besides the organized bands of deserters and the men who were absent without leave, a disloyal organization known as the Peace Society existed in the state and was especially strong in west Georgia along the Alabama border, where the society had its greatest strength. Among the members were persons living in Columbus, West Point, and Meriwether County. The objects of the order were to organize a political party opposed to the administration; to get the people at home and as many soldiers as possible to join the society; to overturn the state government and compel it to make peace; and to break down the Confederate government. Men known as "eminents" travelled over Georgia, secretly giving the "degree" to all whom they considered fit subjects. The society kept no records and had no regular time or place of meeting; and since each member was an "independent," it was difficult to deal with the order. Some of the members may not have intended to be disloyal, but the society was a dangerous instrument in the hands of disloyal, designing politicians.[58]

There were also men in Georgia trading with the enemy. The Atlanta *Southern Confederacy* warned its readers "that enemies and traitors . . . are now engaged in buying our cotton, with not only the knowledge and connivance of the Lincoln authorities, but with their . . . authority." The public was cautioned not to allow cotton to be purchased by anyone beyond the enemy's lines unless it was known that the owner was loyal to the Confederacy.[59] Commenting on this illegal trade, Captain Mercer declared that "The

Yankees possess a potential weapon for converting lukewarm Southerners into warm Lincolnites, and they use it without sting; this is the granting of commercial privileges and trade monopolies to those they wish to purchase. . . . It is the love of money that is . . . making traitors among us."[60]

Adventuresome Georgians were selling cotton to France and England in spite of a blockade which Governor Brown placed upon its exportation. "The steamer Emma of this port started out to run the blockade—got aground last night and the Federal barges put off after her and the men on board set her on fire. She had on board 600 or 700 Bales Cotton all lost," Aaron Wilbur wrote from Savannah in August, 1862.[61] Trading through the blockade was the most lucrative business a person could engage in prior to 1863, when Brown became convinced that the cotton embargo was unwise and chartered fast blockade runners.

Commenting upon the activities of speculators and blockade-runners, Captain Mercer said:

The German Jews . . . are a most noxious element; they swarm in every town and village, escape service as Aliens, . . . think only of accumulating wealth. . . . These are the "good union men," who take the oath of allegiance to our invaders. These men are all speculators and extortioners, blockade-runners, and brokers; they have done more to depreciate our currency than all the rest of the community. It is an anomaly to see safely embosomed among us a people more hurtful than our Yankee foes. [Aliens] are now reaping all the benefits of the war, while our own people are actually bearing all the burdens.[62]

As the war entered its fourth year and the fortune of the Confederacy continued to wane, desertions and disloyalty increased among the disconsolate soldiers and citizens. General Johnston in January, 1864, said that "Many persons in Georgia . . . are recruiting for cavalry, ostensibly under authority of the War department. Many of these persons never complete their companies—having no other object than to keep themselves and a few friends out of service. . . . Desertion is becoming more frequent."[63] A few days later the Adjutant-General's office at Milledgeville sent the following dispatch to an officer who was attempting to conscript men for the state militia: "Your letters detailing your difficulties in the enrollment of your Senatorial District, especially Chattooga, were duly rec'd. . . . in such districts or localities, as it is impracticable . . . to enroll the citizens, you are authorized to suspend enrollment."[64]

Numerous private letters reveal the extent to which desertions

..DISLOYALTY AND DESERTION

had grown by early 1864. Writing to her husband from Santa Lucah, Georgia, a woman said, "They have took up John Whitner and sent him off. I heard that they told him he could go back to his co. but he told them he would go to the yankees first." A few weeks later she wrote:

> John Whitner was at home the last account the Cavalry started to take him off but he jumped the cars and beat them back home. it is thought that K deington is lying around home. . . . I dont know where Bill Greenman is. I dont think he is about Ellijay now if he is I haven't heard any talk of him.[65]

A citizen of Greensboro sent the following information to an attorney in Macon:

> If Oglethorpe County is in your Dist for Sequestration you will have a rich case in Mr. Wright . . . who deserted . . . to the Yankees. . . . He came home and sold his property . . . and put out for Yankeedom and the Northern papers mentions the fact of Lt. Wright . . . and 40 others having arrived Safely in their camps . . . he has a Suit or two in this County for money he loaned before the War. . . . I wrote you the other day about H [?] Wattemeyer that had gone the same road also.[66]

A sailor who was on a steamer near Savannah in April, 1864, wrote to his mother that "yesterday a boat went down the river below Ft. Pulaski with two Midshipmen in command, in search of oysters, and two of their men deserted to the Yankees."[67]

The Georgia press also related the extent to which desertion had grown. The Columbus *Times* published a story of the hanging of a deserter from Coffee County, who in conjunction with other deserters had been committing depredations in Florida. The Savannah *Daily Morning News* said that "Last week some seventeen deserters . . . were captured in Screven County. Savannah and other sections are being thoroughly scoured, and have become too insecure for the safety of deserters."[68] According to the Atlanta *Appeal*, a battalion of sharpshooters, composed of deserters and renegades, had been mustered into Federal service. "Three parties of aliens have been captured attempting to escape to the enemy at Pulaski," stated the Savannah *Daily Morning News*. "Many more have gone to South Carolina to avoid Gov. Brown's enrolling officers."[69]

As Sherman's army entered Georgia, the feeling of disaffection increased, and some of the Confederate troops at Dalton threatened not to fight. A Confederate soldier near Marietta admitted to his wife that "The men is all out of heart and . . . are going to the Yankees by the tens and twentys and hundreds most every night. Johnston's army is very much demoralized. . . ."[70] During the Atlanta campaign a Georgia "traitor" furnished Sherman with information concerning the railroads and resources in the territory between Atlanta and Savannah. Brigadier General M. D. Leggett, of the Federal army, addressed the following letter to Sherman's aid-de-camp in order to arrange for the interview between the Georgian and the Northern commander:

Capt.:
Permit me to direct your attention to the bearer, James C. McBurney, a citizen of Macon, Ga., who accompanied Gen Rousseau in the capacity of Guide and A. D. C. on his recent raid.

He is desirous of having a conversation with Genl. Sherman, as his business has been such as to make him familiar with the localities and resources of Southern Georgia. . . . His statements will be found reliable.[71]

After Sherman's army had departed from Atlanta and had begun its march to the sea, deserters, robbers, bushwhackers, and even citizens from the surrounding country for fifty miles away flocked into the city and joined in the work of exploitation. "While I regret the loss of Atlanta . . . as a military base . . . I can scarcely regret that the nest of speculators and thieves &c is broken up," wrote a Confederate officer at Atlanta.[72] As Sherman's troops marched across the state, many Georgians were ready to submit to almost any terms in order to prevent the devastation of the country. Some disaffected planters were said to have awaited the approach of the invaders, making no attempt whatever to hide their property from the Yankees. Desertions increased and many soldiers went home to stay.[73] Governor Brown called on every man in the state to rally to the cause, but the response was half-hearted, for in October, 1864, probably not more than one-third of the men fit for duty were in the field.[74] Major Joseph B. Cumming recounts an interesting story of an attempted mutiny along the road between Decatur and McDonough:

While I sat there I noticed the sudden disintegration of the head of my column — men . . . starting off in the direction of our march. I . . . ordered them to halt. No attention was paid to the command, and the disorder increasing . . . I . . . galloped . . . until I passed the first deserter, then ranged my horse broadside across the narrow country road. I drew my pistol and threatened to shoot if they did not

..DISLOYALTY AND DESERTION

halt. Like all other mobs, when met by resolute opposition, *my* mob halted. . . . One old fellow, however, . . . said . . .: "By God, if there is going to be any shooting, I'll shoot, too!" The question of the moment was whether I should shoot the old fellow, running the risk of . . . killing somebody else, or ignore him. . . . The latter course was followed. . . . I then . . . made the men a speech, the key-note of which was not honor . . . but self-preservation.

Soon all of the men were back in the ranks, and the march was resumed.[75]

In the meantime virtual anarchy existed in portions of north Georgia as bands of lawless men committed outrages. "Stealing, robbing and other lawless deeds are becoming quite common in the vicinity of Rome . . . ," said the Augusta *Chronicle and Sentinel*. "Straggling vagabonds infest that section of the country, and . . . commit . . . depredations. . . ."[76] "Our Cavalry behave very badly, taking everything they can lay their hands on," Kate Cumming wrote in January, 1864, when she was in north Georgia.[77] A north Georgian described to his sons the lawlessness in his community:

The Caviler has kiled albert ward . . . and dole and gust got home the night before had on ther Yanky uniform the Caviler took all ther money I supose they had fore thousan dollars they shot his wife thumb of . . . in shooting at him dock got away from them it wold bin a good deed if they had a got him too they have kiled Seven men over on tienetaly [?] lately.[78]

A north Georgia woman mailed this note to her husband:

I was glad to find that you was in such fine Spirits your letter was so different from the sentiment of the people here in general though they are in much better spirits here now than they wer when you was here the disloyal citizens talks quite different to what they did though I know it isn't the sentiment of their heart when they Speak in favor of the Government and I know if they had the chance they would show themselves again.[79]

Many families in north Georgia were forced to leave their homes on account of the bushwhackers. Governor Brown's aid-de-camp in July, 1864, asked Howell Cobb to send troops to Dawson County "to suppress if possible this devastation and marauding." He said that similar complaints were being received from adjacent counties.[80] A man wrote to Governor Brown that there was ambush fighting in the vicinity of Tallapoosa and Buchanan. He said further:

I regret to report . . . this Section . . . is infested with robbers and murderers. Soon after the evacuation of Rome they entered the place, and commenced hanging the old men to make them give up their money. Two of the best citizens, Mr. Ombrey and Judge McGuire attempted to rescue them when they killed Mr. Ombrey and shot at Judge McGuire. I immediately detached a company Capt Wimberly Comdg. and ordered him to proceed to Rome . . . to . . . arrest all such characters.[81]

Two unofficial guerrilla bands, "McCollum's Scouts" and "Jordan's Gang," committed numerous murders and robberies in Cherokee and Pickens counties in 1864. The chief class of victims were citizens sympathetic to the Union who had given information to Sherman, but some of the actions of the gangs seemed to be in total disregard of the victim's affiliations. It was rumored that their favorite way of disposing of Tories was to bring them to a river near their camp and shoot them off their horses into the stream.

Three similar bands of terrorists operated in extreme northwest Georgia. A man named John Gatewood was the leader of the most important of these bands, and his operations were directed mainly against Union sympathizers. He scoured the country with his band of irresponsibles, pillaging and killing. The next band of guerrillas in importance was one headed by John Long and Sam Roberts. Union in their sympathies, this band was similar to Gatewood's group except that they persecuted persons who were loyal to the Confederacy. Deadly enmity existed between the bands of Long and Gatewood. The third band of guerrillas, the "Doc Morse Gang," operated mainly in Tennessee and in the region of Georgia east of Walker County. Not much is known about this band, but it was dreaded in the vicinity of its operations.[82]

In the fall of 1864 bands of Tories were plundering northeast Georgia. An Augusta paper reported the difficulties prevailing in that section:

The company of tories . . . in Fannin county . . . have been . . . driven to the mountains.

In Gilmer county there are three companies of the same stamp.

In Pickens county the . . . tories were dispersed by Wheeler. Those who escaped are banding together again . . . for plunder. . . .

. . . most of the tories in North East Georgia were born and raised there. . . .[83]

Governor Brown regretted that conditions in upper Georgia were so unfavorable. He asked Colonel William Phillips, com-

..DISLOYALTY AND DESERTION

manding a camp of reserve troops at Newnan, to co-operate with Colonel J. R. Griffin of the state militia, in arresting deserters and sustaining the civil authorities. He announced in a proclamation that no one had the right to impress supplies unless duly authorized, and he requested General Beauregard to arrest straggling bands of cavalrymen who were plundering.[84]

During the last months of the war the situation in Georgia almost reached an open rebellion. Writing to President Davis in January, 1865, Howell Cobb said that "It is useless to disguise the fact that there is a deep despondency in the public mind—extending in too many instances to disaffection . . . the march of Sherman . . . brought out a latent feeling that had its previous existence in a spirit of discontent." Cobb urged Davis to abolish conscription and to return to the volunteer principle of maintaining the army.[85] Desertions were becoming even more frequent. A soldier wrote to his wife on New Year's Day that "Two men went to the Yankees last night out of our Company; but that is nothing uncommon. They will go Somewhere in larger companys than two if our rations dont get better."[86] While Sherman was in Savannah, he received resolutions from a group of disloyal citizens in Liberty and Tattnall counties, stating that the occupation of Georgia by the Federal army met with their approval. At Savannah citizens drew up resolutions asking the Governor to call a convention to see whether the war should be continued, and in several counties west of Savannah the Confederacy was openly denounced in Union meetings. An enrolling officer in Upson County wrote Howell Cobb that a meeting would be held in Thomaston to request the Governor to call a convention and to resolve that the county would pay no more Confederate taxes. "In my opinion this is treason," the officer said.[87] Another man told Cobb that it was impossible for an enrolling officer in Paulding County to "execute the duty of his office without a guard."[88] Writing to his wife from Augusta in January, 1865, General Cobb said, "I find the people depressed, disaffected, and too many of them disloyal."[89]

The chaotic conditions which prevailed in southeast Georgia during the last part of the war are clearly depicted in an official report submitted to the Conscript Service of Georgia by the Confederate inspector commanding the First Congressional District of the state. Writing from Ware County in February, 1865, the inspector stated that the number of deserters in the counties south of the Altamaha River had greatly increased and that they were banded together to resist arrest and to commit lawless acts. "They have sworn to shoot or hang any En Officer who ventures . . . to enforce . . . the law," he said. "Seven times within 2 weeks they visited Blackshear . . . and deliberately breaking open the Stores . . . robbed them of their contents. . . ." He declared that not only the deserters but a number of citizens in Blackshear refused to pay their Confederate taxes, and that some of them cursed the government. According to his report, the conditions in several counties north of the Altamaha River were equally as bad.[90]

Throughout north Georgia thieving and murdering were widespread. Thousands of deserters were prowling through the country, robbing for their living. Many of them were mounted and passed as scouts, claiming to be Texans. A letter written by a north Georgia woman is indicative of the conditions there in January, 1865:

The country is plum full of Cavalry just . . . stealing all the time, Bud Freeman is in there with an independent company. The Keys are all going to move off to Yankeedom also Daltons and Baites' wife, Johnson has given Sharp leave to move them, the bushwhackers slips in every once in awhile and plunders. . . .

. . . they are pressing every man in to searvice for seven days all over the State to take up straggling cavalry, they took up a company at Cleveland and like to had had a little row, they took them up again at Clarkesville and they did kill one man. . . . I believe it will come to . . . guerrilla warfare.[91]

Colonel James J. Findley, of the Georgia militia, notified Brown that many soldiers from north Georgia had deserted, "Some even since the fall of Vicksburg," and that the mountain people desired peace. He asked the Governor to influence General Cobb to suspend conscription in north Georgia.[92] After visiting northeast Georgia, General A. W. Reynolds informed General Cobb that "Col. Findley's command . . . is scattered over the country as if quartered at home. . . ." General Reynolds added, however, that he saw no disloyalty in northeast Georgia, and that if the people there "could be protected from the roving bands of deserters . . . they would prove . . . faithful friends."[93]

With north Georgia filled with predatory bands of Tories, deserters, and raiders, the Confederate War Department on January 23, 1865, appointed General William T. Wofford to assume command of the Confederate forces in north Georgia with headquarters in Atlanta. Wofford was instructed to break up unauthorized military organizations, arrest deserters, and restore civil and

..DISLOYALTY AND DESERTION

military law. He secured seven thousand men, many of whom were deserters, and obtained corn which he and General Henry M. Judah, of the Federal army, distributed among the people, the two generals having made a truce for the purpose. Wofford's men scoured the country arresting deserters, murderers, and Tories, and a semblance of order gradually was restored. Until the end of the war, however, conditions in north Georgia remained chaotic. A woman in that section wrote to her husband: ". . . if the troops are ordered to the front this spring, . . . the bushwhackers will be worse than they ever have been, . . . the company that went from here are home half their time. It does hurt me . . . to see so many men lying about doing nothing, knowing the privations . . . others are going through. . . ."[94]

A conscript officer at Gainesville described the situation in north Georgia at the close of the war:

> In two or three counties above this, the Conscript law has been suspended for nearly twelve months, in consequence of their having been overrun by tories and bushwhackers. Soon after the occupation of North Georgia by Sherman . . . this portion of the state became a favorite retreat for deserters . . . because . . . of the natural protection which they found in the . . . mountainous region. Since then it has been a theater for the lawless depredations of prowling bands of cavalry. . . .[95]

As late as April, 1865, bushwhackers still had full sway in many sections of north Georgia, plundering both friend and foe. Brown told the legislature that several hundred deserters had been arrested within a single week. ". . . there was a little raid of Torys and Hog Backs about 12 miles above here last week and used up 2 or 3 farmers provisions," a citizen of Calhoun wrote on April 7, 1865.[96] The feuds between the Tories and the Confederates were a long time in dying out.

CHAPTER X

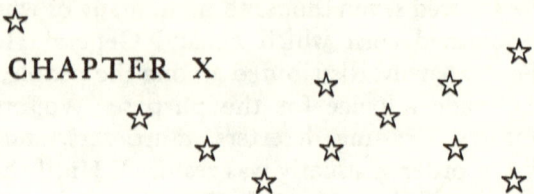

The Sherman Invasion

"To assume the offensive from this point we must move either into Middle or East Tennessee," General Joseph E. Johnston wrote to Jefferson Davis from Dalton on January 20, 1864. "To the first, the obstacles are Chattanooga, now a fortress, the Tennessee River, the rugged descent of the Cumberland Mountains and an army outnumbering ours more than two to one. The second course would leave the way into Georgia open." Johnston explained that he had neither the subsistence nor field transportation for either march.[1]

After General Grant had defeated the Confederates at Chattanooga, he went to Virginia to fight General Lee, leaving General William T. Sherman in Chattanooga with an army of approximately 99,000 men. Sherman on May 4th crossed into Georgia and began a campaign to capture Atlanta and to strike a fatal blow at the heart of the Confederacy. Opposing his invasion was Johnston's army of approximately 43,000 men, reinforced as much as possible since the Confederate defeat at Missionary Ridge. His headquarters were at Mill Creek Gap, along the summit of Rocky Face Ridge, twenty-five miles southeast of Chattanooga.[2]

The deadly contest to capture Atlanta began near Dalton when Sherman attacked through Ringgold to Dug Creek Gap. Finding this direct route to Dalton too strong, Sherman marched his army through Snake Creek Gap to attack the defending army's communications at Resaca, eighteen miles to the rear of Dalton. Skirmishing occurred near the gap, but Johnston's forces were outnumbered, and he was compelled to retreat from Dalton to Resaca. In a letter to his brother, General Sherman explained this phase of the campaign: "Johnston had chosen Dalton as his place of Battle, but he had made all the Roads to it so difficult that I resolved to turn it. So I passed my army through a pass 20 miles South of

..THE SHERMAN INVASION

Dalton and forced him to Battle at Resaca."[3] A heavy loss of men at Resaca caused Johnston to retreat on May 15th to Cassville. "The enemy has out a strong skirmish line and sharpshooters behind every tree and shelter. They shell us continually and to expose your head one second is to draw a dozen bullets," Lieutenant A. J. Neal of Zebulon wrote to his father.[4] A few days later Cassville also was deserted by the Confederates as they continued their slow retreat southward along the Western and Atlantic Railroad.

Sherman next made a flanking movement to Dallas, hoping thus to cut off Johnston's supplies. General Joseph Hooker attacked A. P. Stewart's division of the Confederate army at New Hope Church on May 25th, but the Federal troops were repulsed with heavy losses. Writing to his sister from near New Hope Church, Lieutenant Neal said: "It is reported that the Yankees are falling back. They are certainly short of provisions.... Our skirmishers went into Dallas yesterday and report that the enemy has destroyed everything. They killed for food every cow, calf and hog and took all food from the citizens leaving them in great distress."[5]

By June 8th the Federal army was near Acworth and the Confederates were near Marietta. Sherman wrote to his brother from Acworth, saying:

... all of Georgia except the cleared bottoms is densely wooded with few Roads, and at any point enterprising enemy can ... make across our path formidable works, whilst his sharp-shooters ... in the guise of peaceable farmers can ... kill our wagonmen, messengers and couriers.

It is a Big Indian War. Still thus far I have won some strong positions, advanced a hundred miles and am in possession of a large wheat growing Region and all the Iron mines and works of Georgia.[6]

The Confederates were forced to abandon Pine Mountain, near the center of Johnston's army, and then Lost Mountain, on the left, but they remained intrenched at Kennesaw Mountain on the right. The Battle of Kennesaw Mountain, a continuous struggle lasting from June 10th to July 3rd, then began. "The Yankees has fought gallantly.... They captured 300 of our skirmishers yesterday. Hot times are expected in a few days," a Confederate soldier at Kennesaw Mountain wrote to his brother.[7] On June 27th Sherman recklessly hurled his men against the Confederate position at Kennesaw, sustaining casualties of 2,500 veterans, while the Confederates were losing approximately eight hundred men. Despite this victory, the Confederate position on Kennesaw was abandoned because of lack of ammunition, and because Sherman sent General James B. McPherson to flank Johnston's army by crossing the Chattahoochee River east of Marietta, thus forcing the Confederates to retreat across the river and to fall into intrenched positions directly before Atlanta.[8]

In two and a half months of fighting Johnston had lost approximately ten thousand men, including those killed, wounded, captured, and missing, while Sherman's losses numbered about seventeen thousand. According to President Davis, demands were pouring in from many quarters for Johnston's removal, including a request from Secretary of War Seddon, who had favored Johnston's appointment. Johnston had just completed plans to intercept a move toward Atlanta by General George Thomas when, on July 17th, he was ordered by Davis to relinquish his command to General Hood. Lieutenant-Generals Hardee and Stewart joined General Hood in sending a telegram to President Davis, requesting that the order of Johnston's removal be postponed until the fate of Atlanta was decided, but the President replied that he "could not suspend the order without making the case worse than it was before the order was issued." After describing to Hood the course of action he had in mind, Johnston retired to Macon.[9]

Davis' act in relieving Johnston aroused widespread interest. In Georgia, as elsewhere, public opinion was divided. The Savannah *Daily Morning News* said that the "change of policy under the new Commander indicates that our fortunes may yet be retrieved...."[10] The Sandersville *Central Georgian* declared, "Our confidence in Gen. Johnston has not been shaken . . . neither do we entertain . . . the idea that any feeling but a sincere desire to promote . . . the Confederacy influenced the President in making the change."[11] Disapproval of Davis' act was expressed by the Augusta *Chronicle*.

In the meantime, as Sherman's army was penetrating deeper into Georgia, Governor Brown on May 18th and 21st and June 24th called out a part of his newly organized militia and sent them to Johnston's assistance. The mayor of Atlanta requested that every male citizen in the city report to the marshal of Atlanta for duty, and newspapers throughout the state urged every man who was able to wield a musket "to fly to the rescue of the commonwealth." The Sandersville *Central Georgian* believed that if the Governor "would issue his proclamation calling upon the people

..THE SHERMAN INVASION

to rally to the defence, he himself taking command of them in person ... Johnston will have men enough and to spare."[12] Wild rumors circulated throughout the state, and the Columbus *Times* assured its readers that "The report that Joe Brown is about to assume command of the Army of Tennessee, with Bill Arp [the humorist] as Chief of Staff, is unfounded."[13] The Macon *Daily Telegraph* believed that Sherman's army would be destroyed, but called attention to the Yankees' devastation. "Rome they gutted, and ran mad in a drunken riot over the place ... ," the *Telegraph* stated.[14]

Sherman's forces were, in truth, devastating the country north of Atlanta. A Cartersville woman said that at her home the Yankees "tore down the fencing, burnt rails, and took everything they could get their hands on. ..."[15] Another woman stated that at her farm Federal troops "took all the grain, forage ... stripped us bare of everything to eat; drove off all cattle, mules, horses; killed chickens; and ... turned their horses into a wheat field so that what the horses could not eat, was destroyed by trampling."[16]

Governor Brown on June 28th appealed to President Davis for reinforcements to defend Atlanta, but Davis notified him that he had given the state all of the troops he could spare. The Governor then attacked Davis vehemently, claiming that Confederate troops who should be fighting Sherman were scattered from Pennsylvania to Texas. Having failed to secure the desired response from Davis, Brown on July 9th issued a proclamation calling out every man able to bear arms from fifty to fifty-five and from sixteen to seventeen years of age, including Confederate exempts and details.[17] Several thousand men reported to Adjutant-General Wayne in Atlanta, and an intense effort was made to make the city impregnable. Engineer officers, with a large force of Negroes, worked to strengthen the city's fortifications. The state militia, consisting of more than ten thousand troops under the command of Major-General Gustavus W. Smith, with General Robert Toombs as Chief of Staff, was ordered to the trenches around Atlanta.

Sherman on June 27th dispatched General George Stoneman with a force of five thousand men to move around Atlanta, destroy the Macon railroad at Lovejoy's Station, and then to proceed to Macon and Andersonville and release prisoners confined at those points. According to the plan, General Edward M. McCook was to go southward via Fayetteville with four thousand men and meet Stoneman at Lovejoy's Station on the night of June 28th.

Stoneman moved southward through Monticello, capturing horses and Negroes, and reached the east bank of the Ocmulgee River opposite Macon, where he found that a severe freshet had washed the bridge away. A railroad bridge, about a mile lower down, was still intact; but before Stoneman could recover from his surprise, General Howell Cobb, in command at Macon, had called on all the able-bodied men to assist in defending their homes. Among those answering the call were Thomas Dabney, a former Mississippi planter, and his son, Thomas, Jr. The latter wrote the following recollections of the defense of the city:

Father and I ran to the arsenal and got . . . ammunition . . . and then ran . . . to the bridge. . . . We were among the first to arrive, but soon old men and boys began to pour in. . . . A considerable number of convalescents from the numerous hospitals located in Macon joined us. We were none too soon, for already could be seen the long lines of the enemy not over a half-mile from the bridge, and every few moments shot and shell whistled over the heads of the defenders of that bridge.[18]

Prevented from crossing the bridge, and learning that Confederate cavalry was pursuing him, Stoneman hastily retreated and was defeated about fifteen miles from Macon by General Alfred Iverson's cavalry. Stoneman and seven hundred of his men were captured on July 29th. Writing to his wife after his surrender, General Stoneman said: "My horse shot, my Command was driven off the field except the Artillery and Portion of our brigade—which I held together to cover the rest of the force. This and myself were forced to surrender after having used up our ammunition."[19]

An account of how Stoneman's men devastated a plantation was written by the grandniece of Louise Reese Cornwell of Hillsboro, whose home was used by Stoneman as his headquarters during his march:

Before the house was appropriated . . . the family saw everything outside destroyed. A gin house containing 190 bales of cotton was burned, all the stock taken away, cows butchered . . . hogs . . . killed. . . . Pigeons . . . chickens, turkeys killed. . . . The smoke house was salvaged. . . . Dirt put in lard, lime in syrup, wine in casks appropriated. . . . All out houses burned, the fence . . . set afire. . . .[20]

The Macon *Daily Telegraph* made the following bitter comment concerning Stoneman's raid:

Perhaps there never was a more consummate band of plundering thieves. . . . The officers themselves . . . joined in . . . pillage. They entered private houses and stripped ladies . . . of rings and pins; broke open drawers and trunks; and stole silver and plate of every description. In many instances house girls were ravished. . . . No savage dog . . . ever . . . committed more fiendish brutalities.[21]

A less exaggerated account of the raid was given by a young girl who watched Stoneman's army as it marched past her plantation sixty miles below Atlanta:

Just at noon . . . a negro boy ran across the yard screaming, "The Yankees . . . are coming!" Before you could think the negro men were on the stock making for the swamps, with . . . screaming women, children and dogs following. In the meantime the most jaded, worn crowd of men in blue, mounted on all kinds of horses . . . among them our buggy horse, swarmed everywhere. It was General Stoneman on his famous raid. . . . They were so closely followed by Wheeler's cavalry they only took time to eat up everything that was cooked for white and black.[22]

One objective of Stoneman's raid was Andersonville, which he had hoped to reach in order to liberate the Federal troops imprisoned there. Andersonville, isolated from the area of warfare, had been chosen as the site for the prison when the scarcity of provisions and the danger to Richmond had made it necessary to remove the prison from Virginia. The selection of Andersonville for the prison was commented upon by an Augusta paper: "A site has been selected near Andersonville, Sumter County, Ga., for . . . Yankee prisoners, hiving out from Belle Isle., Richmond, Va. The situation is on the Southwestern railroad, about half way between Oglethorpe and Americus, and in . . . a fine agricultural region, where supplies are . . . abundant."[23]

In February, 1864, prisoners began to arrive at Andersonville, and by the end of July there were over thirty-one thousand men imprisoned there. Because of various circumstances, more than twelve thousand prisoners died. As it became obvious that Sherman's army would take Atlanta, the prisoners were removed hastily to Savannah and Charleston, and finally to a new prison at Millen, Georgia.

Inasmuch as the name of Andersonville is somewhat odious, since many soldiers died there, it is interesting to note that a majority of the letters written by Georgia soldiers serving as guards at the prison testify that the prisoners were treated with kindness and consideration. Although one Georgian told his wife that "the prisoners were dying from hunger and thirst,"[24] another soldier declared that "The federal prisoners were well cared for. I never . . . heard of any complaints . . . as to short rations."[25] A brigade drummer explained that "the prisoners were cared for as well as possible. Our . . . supplies were exhausted. They were fed on a coarse food but as good as we soldiers had."[26] Another guard said that ". . . the soldiers at Andersonville were treated with all the care possible to prisoners of an impoverished Confederacy."[27]

After the war Captain Henry Wirz, the Confederate officer in command of the Andersonville prison, was tried by a military commission, condemned, and executed. In his defense it was said that war conditions, not vindictive cruelty, were responsible for the frightful sufferings of the prisoners.

Reminiscences of Georgians who were at Andersonville affirm the opinion that Captain Wirz was not cruel or negligent. One soldier stated that Wirz "was a good man. . . . He furnished them [the prisoners] with every convenience that was possible. I have not heard of him having any one of them punished. He looked after them being fed. He would ride his . . . horse in front of the commissary wagon to see that it was properly distributed."[28] Another former prison guard declared that he "never saw nor heard of Captain Wirz mistreating a prisoner. . . ."[29]

Two days after General Hood assumed command at Atlanta, he attacked Sherman at Peachtree Creek, the Confederates pouring through the woods and "yelling like demons." Within five hours the Confederates had lost about five thousand men while Sherman's casualties were only 1,800. In the Battle of Atlanta, two days later, the Confederates again were repulsed after repeatedly attacking the Federal army, and Hood withdrew behind the fortifications of the city and assumed the defensive. The forty-day siege of Atlanta then began, the Federals keeping up a constant bombardment; and the citizens burrowed into cellars, caves, and railroad cuts for protection. As Sherman moved to the south side of Atlanta to capture the railroads there, he was attacked by Hood at Ezra Church on July 28th, but the Confederates again were unsuccessful.[30]

Fearing that his communications would be cut, Hood divided his forces into two distinct armies, sending one, under General Hardee, to Jonesboro, twenty-two miles to the south. Sherman, aware of the movement, forced his superior numbers wedge-like into the gap and effectually separated the wings. Then he struck

THE SHERMAN INVASION

in detail. In the Battle of Jonesboro, fought on September 1st, the Confederates attacked with vigor, but Hardee was unable to make any impression upon Sherman, and the Federal commander cut off Atlanta's communications by capturing the Georgia and the West Point railroads as well as the line leading to Jonesboro. Weakened and unable to check Sherman's movements, Hood on September 1st evacuated Atlanta, after blowing up about seventy carloads of ammunition and destroying locomotives in the shops and roundhouses, and joined Hardee near Lovejoy.[31]

Chagrined because of his failure to defeat Sherman, General Hood in his official report of the battles depicted General Hardee as a disgruntled leader who failed to carry out properly his commands. On the other hand, Hardee, in a letter to Johnston, said that the officers and troops had confidence in Johnston but not in Hood; and in his official report, Hardee made a devastating reply to Hood's charges that he had lacked zeal in obeying instructions in the three main engagements at Atlanta. He attributed the loss of that key city to Hood's own incompetence.[32]

Sherman's army began occupying Atlanta on September 3rd, and a few days later he notified Hood that all civilians residing in the city must be removed at once. The Federal commander offered to provide food and transportation for civilians who wished to go to Tennessee, Kentucky, or farther north, and to provide transportation to Camp Rough and Ready, a few miles south of Atlanta, for the remainder. "Atlanta is no place for . . . non-combatants, and I have no desire to send them north if you will assist in conveying them south," Sherman declared.[33] An angry correspondence between the two generals ensued, with Hood accusing Sherman of committing an "act of barbarous cruelty."[34] Mayor James M. Calhoun and two city councilmen addressed a petition to Sherman, asking that he reconsider his decision, but the order was carried out. From 1,600 to 1,700 men, women, and children were moved to Camp Rough and Ready or to points north.[35]

Immediately after Sherman occupied Atlanta, Governor Brown withdrew from Hood's command his state militia, consisting of ten thousand or more troops sometimes dubbed "Joe Brown's Pets," and gave them a furlough of thirty days. The furlough ostensibly was for the purpose of gathering the autumn crops, but was in reality to prevent the state troops from being enrolled in Confederate service. With the Governor's furloughing of the state troops, and with Georgia practically at the mercy of the Northern army,

Sherman believed that he might induce Brown to withdraw Georgia from the war and make peace. He was aware also of the hostility that existed between Governor Brown and President Davis. Accordingly, he entered into communication with three Georgia Unionists, Joshua Hill, R. K. Wright, and William King, and asked them to invite Brown and Stephens to a conference with himself in Atlanta. Sherman's offer was to spare Georgia, confine his troops to roads in crossing the state, and pay for supplies for his army if Brown would withdraw the state troops from the Confederacy.[36] Stephens, urged by his friend Toombs to ignore Sherman's offer, notified the general in a letter addressed to William King that although he desired peace, neither Sherman nor himself had authority in the matter.[37] Brown refused to meet Sherman, and, like Stephens, pointed out that neither he nor Sherman had authority to make peace. He declared that Georgia could "through a convention negotiate treaties and declare peace," but that the state had "conferred no such power upon the Governor."[38]

Alarmed on account of Sherman's communications with Brown and Stephens, Davis went immediately to Georgia, where he visited Hood's army, held war rallies, and expressed his contempt for "croakers" who would not fight. Peace meetings were held throughout the state, however; and it was generally believed, in view of the expected defeat of Lincoln, that the war might be arbitrated.

The peace negotiations caused much excitement and varied comments. In his *Autobiography* Herschel V. Johnson remarked that "In September, 1864, appearances were gloomy; the hearts of many failed; they looked to the election of Genl. McClelland President of the United States with much anxiety; they desired and thought that something might be done, in that direction, by inaugurating a peace movement in the South."[39] The Milledgeville *Southern Recorder* believed that Lincoln "with a show of reason would call for an armistice," but noted with regret that a few newspapers in Georgia advocated that each state should "make the best bargain it can with Mr. Lincoln. . . ."[40] The Columbus *Daily Times* declared that "the mere whisper of . . . peace is criminal — he who would entertain it with no abatement by the foe, is a traitor, . . ."[41] The Atlanta *Intelligencer* thought that peace would come only after Sherman's defeat and that Sherman was in a dangerous situation. According to the Macon *Telegraph and Confederate*, Sherman could be defeated and the South would gain her independence.

After remaining in Atlanta for more than two months, Sherman ordered that the principal buildings in the city be destroyed. Just prior to the devastation, one of Sherman's officers wrote that "The houses are vacant; there is no trade . . . the streets are empty. Beautiful roses bloom in the gardens of fine houses, but a terrible stillness and solitude cover all, depressing the hearts even of those who are glad to destroy it."[42] Sherman detailed two regiments to destroy all railroad depots, warehouses, machine shops, and other buildings of use to the enemy, but not to injure dwellings. A machine shop and iron foundry were set on fire, and a nearby oil refinery became a fierce blaze. Next followed a freight warehouse, in which were stored bales of cotton; and soon the depot, machine shops, and roundhouse of the Georgia Railroad were a fiery mass. Numerous other buildings were blown up, and an immense amount of government property, which the Federals were unable to transport to the rear, was destroyed. The night of September 15th was made hideous by bursting shells and explosions, and the heart of the city was in flames all that night. "Clouds of heavy smoke . . . hang . . . over the doomed city," a soldier noted in his diary.[43] Fire swept Atlanta and consumed every house with the exception of about four hundred dwellings. Eleven-twelfths of the mills, factories, and other public buildings went up in flames, while thousands of carcasses of dead animals strewed the streets. Stores, hotels, Negro marts, theatres, and grog shops were burned. "The heaven is one expanse of lurid fire; the air is filled with flying, burning cinders; buildings covering two hundred acres are in ruins or in flames," Sherman's aid-de-camp recorded.[44] Houses which escaped destruction were piled high with looted goods awaiting opportunity for removal. Except for approximately fifty families, all of the remaining civilians in the city fled, frightened by the conflagration and the dread of violence.

Even more of Atlanta would have been destroyed except for the heroic work of Father Thomas O'Reilly of the Church of the Immaculate Conception. When Father O'Reilly refused to relinquish his parsonage to the Yankees, a number of Catholics in the Federal army volunteered to protect his church and parsonage, and would not allow any adjacent houses to be fired that would endanger them. Not only was the Catholic church saved by Father O'Reilly, but also the Second Baptist, Second Presbyterian, Trinity (Methodist), and St. Philip's Episcopal churches, as well as the city hall and several blocks of residences.

After evacuating Atlanta, Hood had moved northward into

Tennessee, hoping that Sherman would follow him in order to protect the Federal line of communications. Sherman pursued Hood nearly to Gadsden, Alabama, dispatched General Thomas with an ample force to fight Hood's army, and then decided to carry out a long-contemplated project of marching to the seacoast. In preparing for the march, Sherman left behind all disabled men and made up an army of sixty-two thousand veterans, of whom five thousand were cavalrymen. Each brigade had an organized party of foragers, called "bummers," who were authorized to take necessary provisions, horses, and mules, but were ordered not to enter dwellings or commit any trespass. In districts where the army was not opposed, mills, cotton gins, and houses were not to be molested; but they were to be destroyed where the march was interrupted. These orders were very poorly obeyed, the soldiers apparently being encouraged to believe that they were at liberty to do as they pleased.[45]

Sherman divided his army into two equal divisions. The left wing, under General H. W. Slocum, went via Decatur, Covington, Madison, Eatonton, and Milledgeville to Sandersville, where it joined the right wing, under General O. O. Howard, which proceeded through Jonesboro and Gordon with a feint at Macon. The cavalry was commanded by General Judson Kilpatrick, whom Sherman made independent of Slocum and Howard and directly responsible to headquarters. Dashing around the advancing columns of troops, Kilpatrick devastated a wide area in central Georgia. The army spread out over an expanse from forty to sixty miles wide, marched from ten to fifteen miles a day, and lived on the country, stripping it of provisions and destroying what it did not consume.

Within a few days after the army departed from Atlanta, independent "bummers" in addition to the regular foraging parties were being sent out by companies, platoons, and in some instances by individuals. These "bummers" were the most venturesome men in the army and were not always under "discreet officers." Although some of the raiders took only what they needed to eat, others ransacked houses, ripped open featherbeds, smashed looking glasses and crockery, and tumbled tables and chairs, frightening women and children. Sometimes they came in with fresh horses loaded with provisions. Hitchcock says that "At or near every farmhouse we hear constant shooting — of pigs and chickens. . . ,"[46] Foragers in Newton County ran a mill for several days and loaded wagons

..THE SHERMAN INVASION

with forage, furniture, and bedding, with which they said they "intended to fit up good winter quarters." As rumors of the approaching troops reached the frightened inhabitants, frantic efforts were made to conceal valuable personal articles. Some of these goods were hidden in swamps, other treasures were buried in gardens, and occasionally cemeteries were selected as the best places of security. By one means or another, the Yankees discovered many of the hidden goods.

Among the plantations raided by the Yankees was the Burge residence near Covington. Mrs. Burge, a widow, was left on the plantation during the war with her little daughter and her slaves, numbering about one hundred. After spending several sleepless nights prior to the raid, she saw Yankees approaching her home on November 19th and met them at the gate to claim protection. She described what happened:

But like demons they rush in! My yards are full. To my smoke-house, my dairy, kitchen, and cellar, like famished wolves they come, breaking locks and whatever is in their way. The thousand pounds of meat in my smoke-house is gone in a twinkling, my flour, my meat, my lard, butter, eggs, pickles . . . wine, jars, and jugs are all gone. My eighteen fat turkeys, my hens, chickens, and fowls, my young pigs, are shot down. . . .

The invaders also stole Mrs. Burge's buggy horse, her mare, two colts, a mule, and her sheep. She said that Sherman's army left her poorer by thirty thousand dollars "and a much stronger Rebel!" "They robbed every house on the road of its provisions," Mrs. Burge related.[47]

Hoping to lessen the devastation, General Gustavus W. Smith's Georgia militia kept in front of Sherman's army. Lieutenant John H. Ash, of the Georgia Hussars, recounted a skirmish which occurred near Griffin between the Hussars and General Howard's advanced troops:

Near Bear Creek Station met and encountered the overwhelming numbers of Sherman's advance, killing and wounding a great many of the advancing enemy, but we were unable to check them, as our Reg could only muster 48 guns. We were so completely run over that we were scattered in every direction, those of us who were not killed and captured.[48]

General Howard's wing marched to within a few miles of Griffin, creating "quite a commotion there," made a feint at Macon, and proceeded on to Gordon, a village just south of Milledgeville. In the meantime, General Slocum's wing sacked Madison and Eatonton and approached Milledgeville. At Madison stores were ripped open; goods, valuables, and plate disappeared. The jail, depot, and commissary were burned. "Pianos were consigned to the flames, and most likely the houses with them," one of the Federals narrated.[49] In Eatonton a cotton mill was burned, merchandise establishments were raided, and nearby plantations were stripped of provisions. "You never saw such a complete wreck of pa's store. There was not a five cents' worth left in it," wrote "H. M." at Eatonton shortly after the raid.[50] Another inhabitant of Eatonton described the raid made upon his plantation:

The Yankees took all my hams, and chickens, and turkeys, and all my lard, and sugar, except a little. They broke open my closets, took my tin ware, some of my china, and nearly all of my blankets. The negroes ran over, and told me about it. I sent, immediately for an officer, and he came over, and put a stop to it. . . . They took my handsome piano cover, but Jane (Negro girl) begged them to give it to her, and they did so.[51]

Near Milledgeville lived a wealthy planter who wished to hide a quantity of gold money before Sherman arrived. Calling some slaves, he said, "Boys, I want to place new gate posts to the driveway." He timed things so that when the dinner bell rang the work was complete except for placing the new posts in position. After the slaves had left, he put the money in the holes and covered it with fresh earth. When the Negroes returned, the posts were put in position with the money beneath them. No one suspected the hiding place, and later the man recovered the gold.[52]

Telegrams from Generals Wheeler and Cobb on November 16th warned Brown that Sherman had left Atlanta and was moving toward Macon. From Tuscumbia, Alabama, General Beauregard wired Brown to aid General Cobb, commanding the reserve troops in Macon, "with all the force you can." Brown replied, "I will do all in my power to aid Genl. Cobb. I fear we have not force to stop the . . . enemy."[53] On the following day Brown informed the legislature, then meeting in Milledgeville, that Sherman had burned Atlanta and was on his way to Milledgeville. He requested quick legislation permitting him to call out the entire population of the state to repel the invaders. The legislators agreed only after exempting themselves and the judges, but Brown adjourned the legislature "to the front . . . to meet again if we should live, at such place as the Governor may designate." Hurrying to the penitentiary, Brown informed the convicts that those who were willing to join the militia would be pardoned. Only four of the 126 prisoners refused the offer. The most valuable official records were quickly gathered together and carried to a place of safety in southwest Georgia.[54]

Governor Brown, state officials, and legislators fled by rail, carriage, or afoot.[55] The last train had scarcely disappeared before the left wing of Sherman's army reached Milledgeville on November 21st and encamped on a plantation ten miles away. Two days later Sherman himself arrived. He ordered that the magazines, arsenals, depots, factories, and the penitentiary be destroyed; but he spared the city except for the desecration of the capitol by soldiers, who scattered in all directions books and official papers, and who in a mock session of the legislature repealed the secession ordinance. In recounting Sherman's invasion of the capital, a Milledgeville paper declared that "A full detail of all the enormities . . . would fill a volume, and some of them would be too bad to publish. In short if an army of Devils; just let loose from the bottomless pit, were to invade the country they could not be much worse than Sherman's army."[56] Peterson Thweatt some months later described to Stephens the wreckage of his home by the invaders:

All our provisions, crockery, silver, bed clothing, our own clothing, &c &c were taken or destroyed. Our parlour furniture given away to negroes, and most of what we had, when they left, was what was returned to us by our own or other negroes. Our nurse was taken and has never been heard from since. My wife and children lived on Potatoes for several days, and the negroes fed them from the leavings of the Yankees. . . .[57]

In nearby Clinton and Gordon, Howard's infantry and Kilpatrick's cavalry were wreaking widespread vengeance. "Everything had been swept as with a storm of fire," a Macon paper stated. "One third of Clinton is in ashes. The whole country around is one wide waste of destruction."[58] A letter written from Clinton to a Savannah newspaper related: "Many of us are utterly ruined, hundreds without anything to eat, their cattle and hogs killed; horses and mules . . . taken off . . . our schools, lodges, and most of the churches burned . . . clothes taken off the backs of some of the contrabands, and female servants . . . villified . . . by their officers."[59]

The devastation would have been even greater had not Federal officers often placed guards around certain houses to protect the occupants. "Gen. George Spencer put a guard . . . around this little house and brought nice meals to us and our maids . . . ," one woman said.[60] Another woman recounted that after the Yankees had devastated her plantation, the following incident occurred:

> Maj. Gen. Howard and staff officers came at tea time. We managed to have something to eat . . . and while Gen. Howard sat at the table and asked God's blessing, the sky was red from flames of burning houses. His staff officers . . . played on the piano . . . and sang several songs. . . . Gen. Howard kindly offered us a guard . . . as the army passed. . . .[61]

The march was resumed from Milledgeville on November 24th, Sherman's army harrying a wide stretch of country and passing through Sandersville, Tennille, Louisville, and Millen. In the lower section of the state, Sherman was opposed by small bodies of infantry under various commanders and by a small force of cavalry under General Joseph Wheeler. At Sandersville the Yankees drove Wheeler's men away and burned the courthouse because it had been used as a Confederate fort. In Millen the hotel, railroad building, and a few other structures were destroyed. Numerous other engagements occurred between Sherman's army and small forces of Confederates as the Federal troops approached Savannah. The general purpose of the Southern soldiers was to restrict the area ravaged by the Federal foragers. Nevertheless, the destruction in lower Georgia was thorough, as is revealed in a letter from Alexander C. Walker, a Burke County planter, to Governor Brown:

> From Brier Creek to the Ogeechee . . . is a scene . . . desolation. I will give my own case, which with occasional exceptions is as favorable as any. They took every working animal . . . also my fattened hogs, about 18,000 lbs. pork, were driven some 20 miles & slaughtered — to drive them they took seven of my negro men — of these I learn all have returned but one. They burned the gin house and screw, with about 30,000 lbs. of cotton . . . they killed every turkey and chicken. . . .

Walker complained to Brown that "A dozen active scouts falling back before them . . . and giving even 2 hours notice of their approach would have enabled us to have saved our hogs and horses."[62]

Some Georgia newspapers affected joy at Sherman's southward march and predicted his destruction. The Augusta *Constitutionalist* asserted that "The hand of God is in it. The blow, if we can give it as it should be given, may end the war."⁶³ "Favorable *grounds* . . . exist for checking the advance of Sherman towards Savannah — grounds soft and moist," remarked the Columbus *Daily Times*.⁶⁴ In another editorial the *Times* said: "Sherman . . . has many days hard marching before . . . he will be able to respond visibly to the rockets of his friends on the coast, with a good prospect of having to fight his way through the entire distance."⁶⁵

Sherman's army was not the only one guilty of reprehensible conduct, for Wheeler's cavalry frequently stole horses and destroyed private property. The Savannah *Daily Morning News* said that "Gen. Wheeler . . . has . . . demonstrated to every man in the Confederacy, except the President and Gen. Bragg, that he is not capable of commanding 10,000 cavalrymen. . . ."⁶⁶ Alexander C. Walker informed Brown of the outrages perpetrated by Wheeler's cavalry and asked him "if there was any power by which Wheeler's command could be made to assemble at a given place, with notice to the people to come forward and claim their stolen property."⁶⁷ Referring to Wheeler's men as a "plundering band of horse stealing ruffians," Walker told Brown that two plantations not in the path of the Yankees had been completely ruined by Wheeler's cavalry.⁶⁸ In a letter to General Beauregard, Brown affirmed his respect for Wheeler as "a gentleman and soldier," but expressed surprise that Wheeler "should pronounce all the important charges of horse stealing, breaking open houses, and stealing property of citizens, which are made against his Command, to be false." General Howell Cobb forwarded to Beauregard evidence of approximately forty well authenticated cases of wanton depredations committed by Wheeler's cavalry.⁶⁹

Alarmed by the reports of Wheeler's conduct, General Beauregard on December 28th sent Inspector-General Alfred Roman to make an inspection of Wheeler's corps. The report which Roman submitted to Beauregard defended as a whole Wheeler's command from the charges of depredations, but recommended that Wheeler should be relieved from his command, "not as a rebuke, but for the good of the cause, and for his own reputation." Roman said further: "My honest conviction is, that General Wheeler would be a most excellent Brigade or even Division Commander; but I do not consider him the proper man to be placed at the head of a large, independent Cavalry corps. Under him, and in spite of his . . . soldierly qualities, no true discipline will ever be perfected in his command. . . ."⁷⁰

After destroying three hundred miles of railroads, and property valued at approximately one hundred million dollars located in forty counties throughout central Georgia, Sherman reached the vicinity of Savannah on December 10th. He was temporarily prevented from communicating with the nearby Federal fleet on account of Fort McAllister, situated near the mouth of the Great Ogeechee River; but on December 13th a force under the command of General W. B. Hazen captured the fort, which was defended by Major George W. Anderson with a small command of Confederates. General Hazen's official report of the assault said:

Just outside the work a line of torpedoes had been placed, many of which were exploded by the tread of the troops, blowing men to atoms, but the line moved on without checking, over, under, and through abatis, ditches, palisading and parapet, fighting the garrison through the fort to their bomb proofs, from which they still fought, and only succumbed as each man was individually overpowered.[71]

General William J. Hardee, with a nondescript force of about ten thousand men, defended Savannah; but on December 19th Sherman forced a landing on the South Carolina side of the Savannah River, forcing Hardee to evacuate the city. By means of hastily constructed pontoon bridges, he withdrew into South Carolina on the night of December 20th. "Tho' compelled to evacuate the city, there is no part of my military life to which I look back with so much satisfaction," Hardee declared after the war.[72] On the following day Sherman entered Savannah, the city was placed under military government, and the citizens drew up resolutions asking the Governor to call a convention to decide whether the war should be continued. Although newspapers in the state called the resolutions "shameful treason," Georgians were longing for peace. The Savannah *Daily Herald* claimed that meetings were held in fifteen counties in which the spirit of the Savannah resolutions were adopted; and an Augusta paper announced that similar resolutions were sent to Governor Brown from Jackson County. Throughout the state many people were at the point of starvation, and predatory bands were stealing at random.

At the headquarters of the Georgia reserves in Macon, General Cobb continued to muster recruits in a desperate attempt to continue the fruitless struggle. He wrote Confederate General W. W. Reynolds that the latter's "proposed movement on Dalton met with his approval, but that Genl Beauregard had directed that no such movement be made at this time." He urged Reynolds to get as many men as possible organized as reserves.[73] When Adjutant-General S. Cooper wired him from Richmond to remove his headquarters from Macon to Augusta, Cobb replied that railroad communications between Augusta and Macon had been cut and that "almost the whole of that portion of the State from which recruits to the army can be had, is cut off from Augusta." He reminded Cooper that if his headquarters were removed to Augusta, the defense of southwestern Georgia, "the grainery of the Confederacy," would be left without troops. He stated that "In Cherokee, Georgia, the establishment of posts, organization of local companies, and enforcement of the Conscript law are . . . within my reach from this point. I shall go at once to Augusta but will not move my office fully until I hear further from you."[74]

By the end of March, 1865, all of the Georgia coast was completely free of Confederates, and the Federal forces were in entire control. On April 9th, the day of Lee's surrender, General Cobb notified Governor Brown that President Davis had directed him to give Governor Thomas H. Watts of Alabama "all the assistance in his power," but that he had not decided whether he should send the state troops out of Georgia.[75] A few days later General J. H. Wilson, following a skirmish at Girard, Alabama, captured Columbus, destroyed the city's military supplies and shipyard, and moved rapidly toward Macon. General Cobb sent out a flag of truce and Macon was surrendered on April 20th. On May 3rd General Wilson summoned Governor Brown to surrender all of the troops and military stores under his command, each soldier being allowed to return home after he swore not to take up arms against the United States.[76]

CHAPTER XI

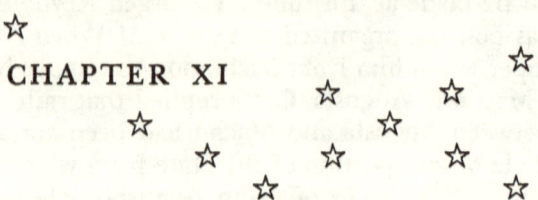

Women's Wartime Activities

"I OFTEN CATCH MYSELF WISHING THE Yankees had minded their own business and 'let us alone' and all my troubles would not have been. But on second thought I am perfectly willing to undergo almost any privation for the sake of our Confederacy and our rights," a woman in Newnan wrote to a friend in November, 1862.[1] Before the war ended, the women of Georgia did undergo almost every privation, not only suffering the loss of male relatives and friends but also experiencing indescribable hardships and dangers. Besides the perils of fire and shell, they faced loneliness, starvation, disease, lawlessness, destruction of property, personal insults, and the sacrifice of the innumerable comforts which are prevalent in times of peace.

Hardly had the mobilization of troops begun when co-operative agencies, known as "soldiers' aid societies," were organized by women in all parts of Georgia. The purpose of the societies was to furnish the soldiers with clothing, food, articles of comfort, and hospital stores by means of voluntary contributions of money, materials, and labor. Collective activity afforded the pooling of resources and the division of labor. Meetings were held in private homes, courthouses, town halls, churches, and schoolhouses.[2]

There is no way of estimating the total value of the contributions made by the Georgia societies, but contemporary manuscripts and newspapers reveal the devotion of the women to the Confederate cause. "The following articles were sent last week to the Baldwin Blues from the Ladies Soldiers Aid Society in this place," the *Southern Federal Union,* of Milledgeville, announced on July 16, 1861; "150 pairs of socks, 75 shirts, 75 pair of drawers, 40 pair of pants." A Milledgeville woman, Martha Low Fort, says in her *Memoirs* that her mother was elected president of the "Soldiers' Relief Society" of that community, and that the girls made shirts coats, socks, and even cartridges.³ The Macon *Daily Telegraph* announced that "A small company of ladies assembled at the Milledgeville Hotel, on the 4th instant, and celebrated that great holiday by making upwards of three thousand cartridges for the Confederate army."⁴ According to a Milledgeville paper, "52.05 taken in at the young Misses Concert and Tableaux on Monday evening was turned over to the Ladies Relief Society of this city."⁵

The activities in Milledgeville, the capital, were characteristic of the work of the soldiers' aid societies throughout the state. In Macon the Soldiers' Aid Society raised and disbursed during the first seven months of its operation $7,391.95, not including a large quantity of material for camp and hospital service. In 1862 a group of Macon citizens purchased an old hotel and placed it in charge of the relief society, which converted the hostelry into a hospital and eating house for disabled soldiers. The women in Savannah held fairs at which they raffled off their jewelry, plate, and other valuables, using the proceeds to supply equipment and comforts for the soldiers and hospital supplies for the invalid troops. Many Savannah women cut up their India rubber piano covers in order to make blankets for the soldiers. A newspaper in Americus announced: "The President of the Soldiers' Aid Society urged all Americus women to meet in the Methodist Church at 8 o'clock Monday morning, 'prepared to say what she can and will do' to furnish clothes for the soldiers."⁶ At Sandersville the women met in the courthouse each Friday morning in order to sew garments for the soldiers. In many towns the women held bazaars as a means of raising money, selling family valuables and wearing apparel. Amateur theatricals, staged by women in private parlors and public buildings, likewise served the double purpose of raising money and affording amusement.

A report of the Soldiers' Aid Society of Athens reveals that by October 9, 1861, the Society had furnished the soldiers with the following supplies: "Coats, 301; pants, 97; shirts, 724; drawers, 624; socks, 348 pairs; canteen covers, 160; havelocks, 60; extra garments, 65; total number, 2695. Linen sheets contributed for bandages. Carpets for covering. Lead pipes . . . to mold bullets."⁷ When the Soldiers' Aid Society at West Point learned one Saturday night that a company of forty men, without coats, would pass through the town on the following Monday morning, the women worked all day Sunday and had the coats ready for the men when they arrived. "I have been hard at work — soldier's work — and my hands . . . ache with sewing on their stout uniforms," a woman wrote. "I assure you our 'Relief Association' is . . . anything but a mere pastime assembly of talkative women."[8] "We school girls are preparing a Tableau for the benefit of the soldiers. I hope we will succeed with it," a Milledgeville girl recorded in her diary.[9] Another woman made the following entry in her "Journal": "Mrs. Seward went to the sewing Society this morning and brought home three coats to make for Capt. Spencer's Company. Lucius Bryan also sent her six pairs of pants. Ma is helping her to sew. The girls will have Tableaux tomorrow."[10]

An interesting account of the sewing activities of women in Decatur is given by a participant:

. . . At the midnight hour the weird click of knitting needles chasing each other round and round in the formation of socks . . . was no unusual sound. . . .

When the knitting of a dozen pairs of socks was completed, they were washed, ironed and neatly folded . . . and I then resumed the work of preparing them for destination. . . . Usually a pretty necktie, a pair of gloves, a handkerchief and letter, . . . enlarged the package.[11]

Another woman stated that "From 1861 to the close of the War . . . our busy hands were never idle. Carpets and piano covers were cut up and sent to the tents to sleep on, having already given up blankets and quilts in abundance. Boxes of eatables were sent. . . ." She said that the women, even during their carriage drives, would take their crochet and knitting along.[12]

A few women refused to assist the societies. An instance of such a case is indicated in a letter written by a woman to her husband:

A committee waited on Mrs. Bond to see if she would contribute something to our society fund . . . but Mrs. B. could not be inspired with much enthusiasm. She said she thought there was no danger or probability of any fighting to be done. . . . I told her her money ought to flow like water in this cause. That I had *sent my all* and her whole fortune was a paltry sum in comparison with my sacrifices. I have no patience with these kind of people. . . .[13]

Not only by co-operating with the soldiers' societies but also by their individual efforts, Georgia women industriously made the necessary clothing for the soldiers, for their families and slaves, and for themselves. A woman in Calhoun County said that while her husband "was on the firing line I was at home, and under the direction of my mother, spun the warp and filling for the family

..WOMEN'S WARTIME ACTIVITIES

clothing and bed covering and bed comforts, and all the suits of clothes for the Davis family, and the contributions we made to the Confederacy."[14] A fifteen-year-old girl in Stewart County "helped card, spin, sew, knit and even went into the swamps to collect barks . . . to dye the cloth for the soldiers clothes and comforts."[15] "The thread to be woven into my father's uniforms, his blankets, his underwear, his saddle blankets . . . knapsacks . . . was spun by my mother . . . ," another woman recalled.[16] In the diary of a Thomasville girl are found the following notations: "I stitched four pair of pants today, on the machine, for Robert and Gaston. This morning I hemmed two dozen towels and six table cloths. . . . I have been sewing on the negro clothes all day and have made three pairs of britches and one dress for Malinda."[17]

"Blessed will be the women after the war, for a great many will have but one sock to knit," exclaimed an Americus editor.[18] The Augusta *Chronicle and Sentinel* remarked that "Any one would suppose that sewing was the most peaceful occupation in the world, yet it is horrifying to hear ladies talk of stilettos, bodkins, gatherings, surgings, hemmings, gorings, cuttings, whippings, lacings, cuffings and basting!"[19]

Ingenious methods were devised by the women in their efforts to supply their own wardrobes. Attics were ransacked for cast off garments, old clothes were turned and dyed, and silks of ancient pattern and homespun cotton dresses became fashionable. As for millinery, any old straw was a bonanza. One woman recalled that "Gentlemen's beaver hats were cut down to medium and low crowns. Palmetto hats were very jaunty; rye straw was plaited, and made an admirable imitation of Milan braid. . . . Many shirred hats and bonnets were worn."[20] A woman recollected that she "had a friend who swapped a silk dress for baby clothes. . . . We often turned our skirts up side down, and wrong side out . . . and were awfully proud of our 'new dresses.' "[21] Another woman gave the following reminiscence:

> I recall a faded gray merino, on which I set a great store. Magenta was a favorite war color. So an idea occurred to dye it. A walk of several miles found me in possession of plenty of poke berries. Under the manipulations of mother and the dye-pot; it was transformed into a thing of beauty. Combined with odds and ends of black lace, velvet and silk, I felt as proud as a Duchess. . . .

The same writer said that her sister secured a cloak in a singular way:

Taking a walk in a grove she found a sheep's skin, lost by some luckless rider, who had probably used it for a saddle blanket. Unlike Mary's little lamb, whose fleece was white as snow, this was as black as a crow. Nothing daunted, she . . . carried it home. The wool was clipped from the skin, washed, mixed with cotton, dyed, spun by mother and myself, and woven. It made pretty, gray material, which being cut into a "paletot" or Russian circular, and decorated with braid, was much admired.[22]

In desperation, one girl asked her grandmother for a few scraps of clothing:

The young ladies here wear hats altogether and are having them made out of old white leghorn and straw bonnets trimmed with ribbon, lace and flowers. I expect it will take two straw bonnets . . . to make a hat. . . . I have neither hat nor bonnet for the summer . . . please ask Aunt Mary Harden if she has some flowers that she does not need, any color will do and also if she has some ribbon that I could trim a hat with, a sash or anything will do so it is ribbon. I wish you could get a box Grandma and send me anything you can rake or scrape in the way of clothes.[23]

In the spring of 1862 there originated a movement called "The Ladies' Gunboat Association," the purpose of which was to obtain funds with which to construct an additional warship to protect the Georgia coast. Soon women in all parts of the state were collecting money with which to build the boat. "The ladies of Savannah . . . have already raised over $3,600, after two days effort, toward this object" of building a gunboat, announced the Sandersville *Central Georgian* on March 9, 1862. "What will the ladies of Washington County do . . . ?" Women in Americus prepared a tableau and charade exhibition and gave the proceeds to the gunboat fund. In Athens all the women and young girls were requested to bring forth their gunboat money. "I am . . . gratified to see you have contributed towards building a gun boat for Savannah," a soldier at Fort Pulaski wrote to his wife.[24] Within a few months sufficient funds were raised to construct a small iron-clad boat.

At almost every railroad junction in Georgia women established places called "wayside homes" to provide food and comfortable lodging for the constantly passing soldiers, especially for those who were sick or wounded. The Savannah wayside home within six months fed and lodged 3,750 soldiers. The wayside home in Macon was praised by a hospital matron as "one of the most useful institutions we have." The home at Millen was built by public

..WOMEN'S WARTIME ACTIVITIES

subscription, and the work was entirely under the auspices of the women of Burke County. Thousands of soldiers came to it, and a nurse was always on hand to attend to the sick.

As the bitter consequences of war became more apparent, soldiers suffered from the scarcity of medical attention and supplies. To meet this situation, hospital relief societies were formed by women to furnish the hospitals with the necessities to alleviate suffering. In addition to money, the principal articles sent to the hospitals were sheets, towels, medicine, cooking utensils, and cutlery. A group of Americus women in July, 1862, assembled at the Methodist church and raised one hundred dollars for the hospitals at Atlanta. They resolved to contribute an equal sum monthly. At Columbus the proceeds of a fair given by the women were devoted to the aid of the soldiers. Similar fairs were held in other cities and towns. The Sandersville *Central Georgian* stated that "The ladies of Sandersville . . . prepared a quantity of lint, bandages, &c., which was . . . sent to Atlanta for the . . . wounded."[25] At Atlanta the St. Philips Hospital Society (Episcopal) was active in making contributions to aid the sick and wounded men. "The ladies of Atlanta are doing their whole duty to the gallant sick and wounded defenders of the country," an Atlanta paper affirmed. "Committees are appointed for a particular daily work in the hospitals, which work is so arranged that everything goes on smoothly and regularly."[26] In other communities the women were equally as active in raising funds for local hospitals and in taking care of the wounded soldiers.

There were times, however, when the desire of the women to help proved fatal to the convalescing men. Fannie Beers, a hospital matron, says in her *Memories* that a young soldier who was ill of dysentery in a hospital at Ringgold craved "apple turnovers" such as his mother used to make, but on account of his critical condition, the physicians denied his request. One day, while Mrs. Beers was absent, an old lady gained access to the ward and gave the soldier the turnovers which he desired. Before morning the boy was dead.[27]

Not only were the women meritorious in their aid to the hospitals, but many of them served as nurses. Despite the widespread prejudice against women serving in hospitals, many women braved public opinion and volunteered for hospital work. Scarcely had the war begun when five young women in Columbus addressed a letter to the *Daily Sun* of that city:

During these perilous times we, the *unengaged* young ladies of Columbus, feel it only our duty to offer our humble services in the anticipated engagements, as Florence Nightingales to the brave companies who have so nobly marched from our city to the defense of our country.... Our company being now organized, we number twenty. If our services are accepted, we are at any moment ready to march to the post of duty.[28]

The Atlanta *Weekly Intelligencer* on September 18, 1861, said that "Two ... ladies of our city left for Richmond to assume in the Georgia Hospital there the position of nurses." A judge in Dougherty County sent two of his daughters to be army nurses, one of whom served through the entire war. Scores of other Georgia women volunteered and served as nurses in Virginia, Georgia, and other states, the most famous of whom was Madame M. C. Cazier, who organized and supervised a hospital in Savannah.

Throughout the war women were confronted with the problem of producing sufficient food to meet the needs of themselves and their families. "These hard times learn housekeepers lessons of economy that will be useful to them as long as they live," noted a Milledgeville paper.[29] In the spring of 1862 many women in northwest Georgia were busy planting corn, and when they were asked why they were so engaged, they answered that "the men folks here have all gone to the war, and we intend to make our bread."[30] "The Time may come yet when youl have to get along all most by your self so all you can learn now about farming cant be any disadvantage to you," a Georgia soldier wrote to his wife. "You must be man and woman both while the war lasts."[31]

Letters written to and from Georgia women to their soldier-husbands indicate the complexity of problems and duties confronting the women in managing the plantations and crops. "Last week we gathered Willis' crop, hauled in 160 bushels of corn and two good stacks of fodder," a woman in Sumter County penned to her husband. "We gather [sic] it before we wanted to. Bill Levington brought his hogs down there, and they were destroying it. We are now picking peas in the new ground and want to gather corn as soon as they can put the hogs there."[32] Later she wrote, "I dont know yet where I will boil syrup. Mr. Little says that his mill is now running and will be untill [sic] Christmas. I am going to see Bro G. He is now grinding, perhaps he will grind mine."[33]

The same woman was advised by her husband "to fatten that old red ox and pickle him up this winter if you think you can get

..WOMEN'S WARTIME ACTIVITIES

salt and have enough feed to spare to fatten him. If you undertake it put him in a small pen and fatten him like a hog. Make every shift you can to get a plenty to eat for next year. . . ."[34] In another letter she was told by her husband to "trade for two good cows and calves if you can get young ones. Uncle thinks you had best not sell my horse at any price."[35] "If you are a mind to let your stock run in the field do so. . . . I want you to save all your corn and wheat and not sell any of it," another soldier instructed his wife.[36] "Save every thing that you can . . . in the way of provisions as next year will be hard year again. . . . Do not kill the hogs until late so as to make them as fat as possible," was the advice a soldier in Virginia sent to his wife.[37]

Despite the women's toil and sweat, food became scarcer as the war wore on, and many accustomed edibles became unattainable. As substitutes for coffee, the women made a drink from chicory and ground peas, from potatoes and rye, or from okra seed. Tea was made from dried raspberry leaves or from sassafras. Parched peanuts were made into cocoa. Sorghum replaced sugar. Occasionally, in desperation, bands of women raided food stores. A group of Milledgeville women in April, 1863, attempted to seize goods from merchants, but the mob was soon dispersed and the goods were returned. In March, 1865, a party of fifty women, claiming to be soldiers' wives, raided the tithing depot at Colquitt and appropriated a hundred bushels of government corn.

In addition to their work of supervising the plantations, sewing, rendering assistance to the soldiers, and securing food, the women were faced with a multitude of other duties. Excerpts from letters written by a lieutenant to his wife give an insight into the tasks confronting one woman:

Fair . . . will have a colt about the first of April. . . . Jack Williams promised to take charge of her, so send her over to his house about 1st of March next.

What will you do for a cook when Julia leaves? Can you make out with Maria . . . ?

I am owing . . . Duncan some $600. . . . Get the money from Mr. Greet and send David . . . to pay it.

Have me one extra heavy comfort made and a large jar of Chow Chow so when we do send, it can be sent to me.

I do not know the time you expect to be confined. I hope, however, you will have an easy time of it. . . . Send me some fishing lines. . . . Buy me a bag of . . . shot — 2 boxes of good percussion caps & one of

CONFEDERATE GEORGIA..

my square boxes of powder, also send me several quires of letter paper—tell Saml Hall to send me both Vols of Abbotts history of Napoleon.... Keep Floyd going to school. . . .

Please . . . send me a receipt for curing stone bruise and toe Itch....

Get me some ten gallons of Peach brandy and put it away.[38]

The utter loneliness and anxiety of the women is disclosed in the voluminous manuscripts of the period. A wife in Dahlonega grieved for her husband, who was a captain in the army, until her mind became deranged. Citizens requested that the husband be granted a furlough in the hope that if he could visit his wife, she might recover. The request stated that "her confinement is not far off. . . ."[39] A mother in Eatonton communicated to her brother:

I am all the time uneasy and I fear if the war last much longer some of our children will be left on the Battlefield or die in the Hospitals. My children is all the comfort I have and if they get kill what will I have to live for. My path has been hilly, bumpy and stumppy and it don't seem to get any smother, but I drive dull care away and think I have live nearly fifty years and can make out the ballance of my days.[40]

In another letter she said that her sons had emerged safely from the battles near Richmond, but that ". . . Goodwin and Sid Shivers will go in Sept. and then I shall be left alone with no one but Mari. Mari is about as she was when you saw her last, large, heavy and helpless. She has to be put in the bed and taken up like a child."[41]

A Butts County wife wrote to her soldier-husband concerning her loneliness:

I am very lonesom evry Sunday since you left. I am lonesom all the time but I am worse evry Sunday. I wish you was her to go to meeting with me to morrow and next day.

I had rather you was home and I and you living in A doll house then to live in the finest house in the state with out you present. I think of you often in the day and my last words at night is A prayer in behalf of you. . . .[42]

To her soldier-cousin a girl wrote, "We are all beginning to think that it is now your time to come home. I do not like to insist too much . . . but if you can prevail on them to spair [sic] you a few weeks; my word for it, we will give you a glorious reception. . . ."[43]

When faced with peril, women frequently exhibited great courage and fortitude. Aside from those women who gained information for the Confederates through casual contacts with the Federals, Mrs. Harriet Chivers of Decatur, the widow of Dr. Thomas

..WOMEN'S WARTIME ACTIVITIES

Holly Chivers, the poet, served as a Confederate spy.[44] It was the alertness of Mrs. Charles Wallace Howard of Kingston that kept the colonial documents of Georgia, which her husband had secured at state expense in London in 1838, from being destroyed during the war. As Sherman began his invasion of the state, Mrs. Howard, whose husband had possessed the documents before he enlisted in the army, shipped the valuable papers to Governor Brown for safety.[45] When Yankees invaded a home near Toombsboro, a Negro man began climbing up the side of the house in an attempt to reach the loft, where was hidden food which he intended giving to the visitors. A woman grabbed an iron fire poker and told him to come down or she would break his back. The Negro descended quickly.[46] At another home a woman spied a group of Yankees throwing off her hog pen rails in order to capture a fat hog. "She had no gun, but had a spell of insane anger," a writer recalled. "With flaming eyes . . . she started to rush toward them. . . . She dashed one to the ground, then grabbed their guns. . . . Perhaps they thought to kill a woman for a hog wasn't worth the lard."[47] Before the Yankees entered a house in Walton County, a girl placed a piece of leather, which was very scarce, in a chair and then put several shawls around her to keep the Yankees from getting them. When the Northerners saw her sitting in the chair, one of them exclaimed, "My, what a fat girl"; and another soldier opined, "You can't tell a book by its binding."[48] After Federal soldiers had entered a house in Fannin County and wounded a man whom they were trying to arrest, his sister stabbed the assailant to death.

An Atlanta woman invited several women to her home to enjoy what probably would be their last good meal. Just after being seated at the table, several Union soldiers appeared and demanded that the women leave the table, for the Yankees wanted to eat the meal. Among the women was a peculiar old lady, who, when the soldiers attempted to sit down, raised her chair over her head and said, "The first damn Yankee that sits at this table I will kill." They threatened to kill her, but the hostess told the soldiers that the woman was "crazy and very wild at times and would not hesitate to kill them." Reluctantly the Yankees departed, leaving the women to eat their meal in peace.[49]

When Federal soldiers visited a plantation in Monroe County for the purpose of capturing a man named Benier Pye, who was known as "the keeper of Confederate supplies," and an escaped

Confederate prisoner, Pye's daughter hid the two men in the garret of the house. Although the Northerners searched the garret, they failed to detect the hidden men. Later, while Yankee guards were asleep, the girl helped the Confederate soldier to escape. The next day she borrowed from a neighbor an old dress, a calico bonnet, and a large plaid shawl, which she quietly handed to her father, still hidden in the garret. On the following morning the man's wife was seen by the Yankee guards walking toward the garden, accompanied by an old "woman" whose long skirt and shawl enveloped her bent form, while her face was hidden beneath the bonnet. She leaned upon her walking stick and carried a basket on her arm. Thus, the man, disguised as an old woman, escaped.[50]

A Georgia woman recounted an interesting story told to her by her aunt, who had been sent by her mother to a spring to get water for a Union officer:

As I stepped out of the house, hot as a freshly cooked ginger cake and round as I was long, I saw the officer conceal a broad smile. . . . I pranced before him, in my indignation . . . never once glancing at him.

"Are all the young rebels as plump as you, Miss?" he asked, as he caught up with me.

Before I had time to give vent to the wrath that was overwhelming me, he began again, "I would certainly like to have your picture to show up North as the hottest little rebel I ever met!"

"I am sure the pleasure of meeting me is all yours. I wish I had a picture of you also. Perhaps that would help keep the crows away, as Sherman says that is all that will live here when his march to the sea is over. I may have a heated appearance, but I can act with coolness."

As my lips closed on those words, with a quick twist of my arm, I drenched him and his trim uniform.

"Is it a picture of a hot rebel or a cool Yankee that you like best today, sir?" I flung over my shoulder as I flew up the hill. Before he recovered his composure, I was out of sight.[51]

The bravery and determination of Georgia women were exhibited in other ways. Allie McPeek, a widow upon whose farm the battle of Jonesboro was fought, exposed herself during the battle to the fire of both armies, moving fearlessly about among the wounded and dying, impartially helping both friend and foe. The death of a little boy in Gwinnett County presented the women of that community with the problem of burying his body. Two Negro men made a coffin and dug a grave in a cemetery three miles away. The women procured a blind mule, hitched him to a wagon, and started to the cemetery with the body. When half way to their destination, they were stopped by Yankee cavalrymen, who unhitched the mule and led him away. One woman, stepping into the place vacated by the mule, said, "I will pull and you push." The day was exceedingly hot, but the forlorn procession finally reached the cemetery, where the two Negroes assisted in the burial.[52]

A woman had a harrowing experience in 1864 while refugeeing with her children from Atlanta to West Point:

We travelled all night . . . over bad roads. The night was dark and stormy. Our horses stopped and by the lightening we saw the bridge washed away. We waited there till morning, turned back. . . . We took the train to Columbus. . . . We were attached to another freight car. From Columbus we went to West Point. The only vacant room in the hotel . . . was one in which a man had just died of small pox, so we slept . . . on the floor in a widow's home.[53]

Negro women sometimes were as alert in meeting unexpected situations as were their mistresses. When a small group of Confederate soldiers in Jasper County saw a company of Yankees in the distance, the Confederates quickly galloped off toward Macon, leaving two ladies and two Negro maids behind. As the Federal soldiers reached the spot where the Confederates had been, they yelled, "Where are those Damn Rebels that were with you?" Maud, one of the maids, ran up the *left* road screaming, "Come back, Marse Taylor, and give up. These Yankees will kill you." She misled the Northerners. They ran for miles and came back cursing, for the Confederates had taken the *right* road to Macon.[54]

LaGrange had the distinction of having a company of women soldiers, the "Nancy Harts," under the captaincy of Mrs. J. Brown Morgan. The company was organized by Mrs. Morgan for the protection of the homes and children in the absence of the men. In 1865 when a detachment of Wilson's raiders rode through the town, the "Nancy Harts" lined up for action, but they surrendered when the officer in command of the raiders promised to spare the city from looting and destruction.

A woman in Resaca was instrumental in creating the first Confederate cemetery in the state. After the battle of Resaca, many dead Confederates were left lying on the field, a short distance from where Mary Green lived. With the help of a Negro cook, she dug a grave in her flower garden and buried two of the bodies. At the close of the war the idea occurred to Mary Green and her sisters that they should collect the Confederate dead and inter them in a plot of ground which their father donated for the purpose. As they had no money with which to do the work, they secured small donations from their friends throughout Georgia. The women then decided that it was not fair to call on Georgia to bury the dead of other states; consequently, a list of the dead and the states they were from was published in newspapers throughout the South, accompanied by an appeal for aid. Contributions poured in. Men were employed to landscape the ground, and when the work was completed in 1866, each state had a plot in which her men lay.[55]

Another Georgia woman, Mary Elizabeth Rutherford of Columbus, was responsible for beginning the custom of observing an annual Confederate Memorial Day throughout the South. Miss Rutherford in January, 1866, suggested to the members of the Columbus Soldiers' Aid Society that since their work of aiding the soldiers had ended, the Society should be reorganized into a "Ladies' Memorial Association." The object of the Association was to set apart one day in each year for especially caring for the soldiers' graves and decorating them with flowers. Letters were sent by the Association to patriotic societies throughout the South, urging them to unite in making the observance of Memorial Day a universal custom. States in the lower South selected April 26th as the date of Memorial Day for two reasons: it marked the anniversary of General Joseph E. Johnston's surrender, and flowers were most abundant during the latter part of April.[56]

In their numerous letters to the soldiers, the women endeavored to encourage the morale of the men. "We have plenty to eat, and know that it's only you that's having a hard time," began a letter written by a woman to her soldier-husband.[57] Writing from Richmond to a Georgia woman, an officer remarked: "Your letters . . . have given me more *real pleasure* during the toils of this terrible campaign than anything else. On the battlefield . . . on the march, when sick or worn down . . . they have come . . . to cheer my drooping spirits. . . ."[58] When a soldier at Fort Pulaski received two letters from his wife, he was so happy that he "cried and shouted like a child." One woman wrote disgustedly to her brother that her husband was entering the army to cook and attend to the horse of another soldier, and that if she were a man, she would take her gun and fight until she died before she would go as a "waiting boy." A girl admonished her brother to "be a good boy Jimie and shun bad company. You know my brothers all ways was my pride,

..WOMEN'S WARTIME ACTIVITIES

and if any of them was bad, it would hurt me so bad."[59] Near the close of the war a woman wrote to her soldier-husband:

> I am just what I was when the war first began, I was a Rebel then and I am yet and my best wishes are for the Rebels, the Old Veterans, long may they live, for subjugation will be unknown so long as we have Veterans in the field. . . .
> I hope our arms will be successful another year. I also hope the Lincoln Govt may see their former blindness, and know that ours is not a people to be subjugated.[60]

Unfortunately, not all women conducted themselves in an exemplary manner. In the spring of 1864 one of General Johnston's staff officers wrote to the post commander at Dalton, "Complaints are daily made to me of the number of lewd women in this town, and on the outskirts of the army. They are said to be impregnating this whole command."[61] The situation became so serious that General Johnston issued an order to have Dalton and the surrounding country searched, so that all women who were unable to give proof of their respectability could be sent to points beyond the reach of soldiers. Strict measures were invoked to guarantee that the women did not return, but it is doubtful that the regulations met with any considerable success. The Federal army was also confronted with the evil of illicit sexual indulgence. While he was in Marietta in the summer of 1864, one of Sherman's officers stated that the Federal army had captured four hundred young women who had been working in a factory at Rossville, making cloth for the Confederate government. He said that the girls would be sent away. "Some of them are tough," he declared, "and it's a hard job to keep them straight and to keep the men away from them. General Sherman says he would rather try to guard the whole Confederate Army, and I guess he is right about it."[62] Another Northern soldier, while in Savannah, said, "I'm on duty every other day; but the reason of it is because there are so many hore houses in town which must have a Sentinel at each door for to keep them Straight."[63]

CHAPTER XII

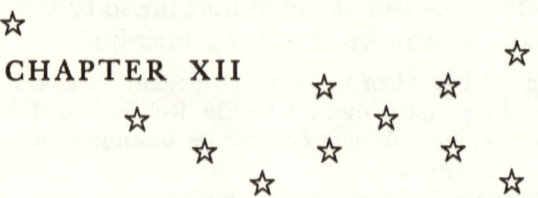

Social Life and Diversions

DESPITE THE SORROWS AND TRIBULATIONS of war, Georgians enjoyed a fairly varied program of social activities and diversions. Concerts, tableaux, and plays served the double purpose of raising money for the soldiers and acting as safety valves to relieve the high pressure of excitement and dread which was characteristic of the time. Besides the theatrical attractions, there were such diversions as attending weddings and dances, canoeing, playing cards, backgammon, and chess, participating in corn shuckings and quilting parties, fishing, horse racing, dueling, gambling, and drinking.

A majority of the theatrical performances were comedies and farces, designed to relieve the anxiety and tension which prevailed. A review of the titles of plays presented in Savannah in 1863 reveals such amusing names as *The Spectre Bridegroom, The Limerick Boys, Black-Eyed Susan,* and *Idiot Witness.* Dramatic performances in Augusta included such original productions as *The Viviandiers, The Scouts, The Prisoner of Monterey,* and *King Linkum the First,* the latter a comical burletta on the cabinet at Washington.[1] Musical shows of the minstrel type were very popular. The "Taylor Troupe" entertained the citizens of Columbus with the popular comedy, *Bamboozling,* the laughable afterpiece, *The Eton Boy,* and with poems and songs. "A fine bill is promised to theatre-goers tonight in Forrest's great play of 'Metamora,' and the roaring farce of 'The Political Candidate,' to be interspersed with popular songs," the Columbus *Daily Times* announced.[2] In 1862 "The Queen Sisters," a troupe of comedians, gave a series of entertainments to "well filled houses" in Savannah. Frequently a double-bill was offered, consisting of a tragedy followed by a short farce.

Occasionally, a more dignified dramatic program was presented. Bulwer-Lytton's *Richelieu* and a tragedy, *Ingomar,* were per-

..SOCIAL LIFE AND DIVERSIONS

formed at Augusta. After a successful season of seventy nights, the "Thespians," a theatrical troupe, closed their stay in Augusta with *Still Waters Run Deep,* by Tom Taylor, and *The Veteran,* an adaptation from the French, by John Hill Hewitt. Presentations were given in Macon of Shakespeare's *Merchant of Venice, Camille,* and *Pocahontas,* the last a famed extravaganza by John Brougham of London.³

Many of the theatrical performances had as their themes military plots and events pertaining to the war, performed for the purpose of inspiring patriotism and a feeling of martial enthusiasm. Determined to give the public a "real treat," the "Dramatic Society" of Sandersville presented *Jacob Haines,* or *The Volunteer,* a new production written expressly for the society. At Savannah a new war drama, *Roll of the Drum,* abounding with incidents of the war, proved popular;⁴ and in Augusta the seventh presentation of "The Queen Sisters" was entitled *The Vigilance Committee.* A member of the "Thespians," the Augusta theatrical troupe, offered three hundred dollars for the best melodrama in three acts, and two hundred dollars for the second-best, "founded on events of the present war."⁵ Other plays, such as *The Drunkard,* or *The Fallen Saved,* attempted to portray the virtues of morality.

Most of the entertainments were presented by amateur actors, but several professional organizations appeared in the larger cities. An Augusta paper announced that "tonight affords the last opportunity of witnessing the performance of Mr. and Mrs. Dalton and troupe, on which occasion a powerful cast of 'Lucretia — critia Borgia' is announced, including Mr. Keeble. The bill also includes music by the Palmetto band, a song by Miss Virginia Kemble, and the laughable farce of 'The Two Lovers.' "⁶ The director of the "Grand Ball" advertised in Atlanta that tickets for the entertainment could be purchased at "Dr. Taylor's Drug Store, or Wood and Bro's jewelry store." Professional and amateur actors sometimes combined their skill to make a cast, as when "The Confederate Philharmonic Association" gave a concert in Augusta combining the "artistic skill of the professional gentlemen belonging to this association" with that of "lady and gentlemen amateurs."⁷

Among the amateur companies which afforded entertainment were groups of Negro singers and actors. When "Booker's Negro Minstrels" of Macon gave two concerts in Milledgeville, a newspaper report of the attraction said that "The negroes sing well, and are quite equal in talent to many of the Yankee stragglers who have heretofore attempted to delineate negro character."[8] Early in 1862 a band of "colored musicians," all slaves except one, performed in Athens; and in 1864 "Blind Tom," the Negro pianist, gave a series of concerts in the same town.

Although the funds from a majority of the concerts were used to aid the soldiers, an occasional entertainment was presented in order to secure money for other purposes. For example, students of the Atlanta Female Institute gave a concert in order to secure money for the school library. In announcing the event, an Atlanta paper stated:

> The Anniversary of the "Isabella Society," of the "Atlanta Female Institute," will be celebrated tonight, when a concert will be given by the young ladies, assisted by the professors of the Institute. This musical and literary feast is designed to raise a fund, which will be appropriated to the "Library of the Society,"— therefore, a gentleman, accompanied by a lady, will be charged 50 cents for admission.[9]

At the military camps in Georgia the soldiers enjoyed a variety of amusements. "Now while I write there is . . . one party playing at leap frog and singing spiritual songs, some dancing, some cursing, some reading the bible, some drinking whiskey and all sorts and more evil than good . . . ," a soldier at Camp Walker wrote to his wife.[10] A soldier encamped at Thunderbolt, near Savannah, wrote:

> The night is the only time that we have any excitement. The days are rather dull, varied with any quantity of hard work. . . . But despite all that, a jollier crowd couldn't be found any where in this country. We have some first rate musicians with us, and at night they get together with their flutes, violins and guitars and "discourse sweet music" until the drum at nine o'clock sends us all to bed.[11]

A correspondent at Camp Bartow said, "If you could hear the jokes they crack around the campfire and the hearty, merry peals of laughter, you would almost be tempted to envy the soldier his happy lot."[12]

Friends and relatives of the soldiers frequently visited the camps, especially during the first months of the war. When a grand review of the troops at Camp McDonald took place in July, 1861, people from the entire upper part of the state crowded into the little town of Big Shanty to witness the review and maneuvers. After several young women had visited an encampment near Atlanta to ascertain if they could do anything for the soldiers, some of the men

..SOCIAL LIFE AND DIVERSIONS

called upon the women in the evenings at their homes and requested them to play such songs as "Home, Sweet Home," "Annie Laurie," and "The Girl I Left Behind Me."[13]

Whenever soldiers, convalescing or on furlough, returned home, social activity was incited to a quicker tempo. The presence of two young soldiers in Sparta caused a dance to be given for their special benefit, and a "sociable" or two was planned. Although a correspondent described Milledgeville as "a small, dilapidated town with a decayed theatre," whenever the legislature was in session weekly dances occurred, and the young women invited any soldier-friends who were nearby to attend.[14] One writer said that most of the parties were "starvation parties," but that "if one of our boys came home on a furlough . . . we would run the gauntlet and boil syrup and have a candy pulling."[15] Another woman recalled:

We lassies were permitted to stroll afternoons after our work was over for the day. How we would primp, dressed within the traditional inch of our lives, and . . . with a certain quick step make for the house with the cool veranda where we always saw convalescent soldiers. What a joy that hour was! To and fro in the twilight we strolled . . . while beyond were the purple hills, silhouetted beneath the golden rays of the setting sun.[16]

Some of the men, however, found the parties uninteresting. One such case was that of a young officer in Savannah, who, after attending "a pleasant picknick [sic] party the day before yesterday, and . . . a sociable last night," found himself "this morning feeling much like a 'witch.' " In a letter to his mother, he said:

I am far from liking parties. Now, last night, there were present many ladies who were strangers to me, and although I am not often at a loss for small talk, yet I became completely disgusted with myself before the evening was through, catching myself saying the same things and to different ladies, and now and then finding myself desperately bored. . . . Let me set your mind at rest at once by stating that my sweethearts (I have three) here, are two of them bigoted Presbyterians and the third an equally ardent Episcopalian.

The fact is . . . I find that my stock of sentimentalism constantly diminishes. The romantic light which clothes all the female tribe as "angels" on earth, in my boyish imagination, is being . . . entirely dissipated.[17]

Regardless of the war, love and romance continued and marriages were solemnized. Early in the war Lou Burge,[18] a senior

CONFEDERATE GEORGIA..

at Wesleyan Female College in Macon, made the following entry in her diary:

Lucia, E. Smith, and I went to ride in Mr. Gunn's carriage; had a wonderful time; . . . drove all over Macon. . . . As we were returning to College saw John H. Boss lying full length on the grass in front of Mrs. Franklin's talking to a crowd of girls, all sitting or reclining on the grass. A nice position for a young man to be in the presence of young ladies! . . . Em Bellamy spent nearly the whole evening in my room crying about the war and John H. Boss who leaves tonight. . . . The girls are almost all crying. Guinn Gothin's feelings have overcome her; she has gone to bed, sick with crying about Bush Lumsden who doesn't care a snap for her. . . . I am glad that I am not *in love* if that is the way I would have to do if my sweetheart should leave for the wars. I have received a letter from Ed Beecher renewing the offer of marriage that he made to me in August last. I refused even more decidedly than I did then. Gabriella Howeson regrets so much that I am not out of college so that I could flirt with him. She vows her intention of doing so should he ever address her. Miss Mattie says that he has been engaged to . . . and flirted with nearly every young lady in Macon.[19]

Writing to her brother, a girl said, "Jo you ought to just see the love letters I have recive from Hardy and House. They did not pass them throw your hand if they had i would not recive them. these are better than them three were, this was bettern than Miss Margo."[20] Another woman informed a friend, "I don't think you will suit well for an old maid. Though I think if this war lasts much longer, there will be more old maids than you can count. What do you think?"[21] One girl wrote to a soldier-friend:

You say that all the Boys says that the girls may look out for they do all intend to Marry — when they come home, and I suppose you to be *one* of the *Boys,* for Miss Elizabeth Holt Says that She had rather look at you one minute than to *live* two years — and be fed on Sugar or be toted all the days of her life.[22]

A Columbus man declared that several boys in his city were in competition for the love of an attractive girl:

A good many boys are here now, and old man Hargraves daughter seems to be the attraction. Bob Bacon, Briggs, Clapp and Doe Cody are earnestly seeking her favors, but she seems to sport with the whole party and lead them a merry round. Each one is confident of success, and go it with a perfect rush courting both the old man and his daughter. I hope Cody will succeed, for though very pompous and conceited he is a true Confederate soldier. . . .[23]

..SOCIAL LIFE AND DIVERSIONS

The exchange of Valentine greetings was popular during the war. "After supper we amused ourselves getting up Valentines," wrote a young woman. "Everybody in the neighborhood has agreed to send one to Jim Chiles, so he will get a cartload of them."[24] In sending a Valentine to a male friend, a woman wrote, "As this is leap year I have a notion of sending a love letter to somebody. If I was not afraid of being found out I would."[25]

Officers were usually considered a better "catch" by the women than were privates. In a letter to an Americus girl, an officer inquired if all the handsome men were officers, and he expressed sorrow for the privates if none of them was considered handsome. Continuing, he said: "With most ladies now-a-days, it takes a field officer to be called 'Handsome,' the personal appearance of a General . . . being considered indescribable; Captains are usually termed 'Good Looking' . . . and Lieutenants 'tolerable,' while privates are considered as being almost disgusting."[26]

Although public opinion tended to condemn hasty war marriages, the excitement and social contacts of war had a stimulating effect upon the number of weddings. A letter written by a Georgia girl late in the war mentioned that marriages were frequent:

> It seems the war does not stop the girls from marrying. They are marrying all around me, but it does not make me at all despondent, for I think we have enough to grieve about without a husband. Some of the girls who have married say they have one consolation — if the war lasts ten years they will not be old maids, but I think happy is the girl who has no husband.[27]

"Fanny Graham is now in Upson helping Miss Lou H into the matrimonial noose," a mother communicated to her son. "She has been gone already two weeks, having attended a wedding in Atlanta on the way. She is so happy with her young friends. . . ."[28] Writing to a soldier-friend regarding a local marriage, a woman commented, "Mary Carmichael and George Wolf married last Thursday night. William Bankstone says there was a Wolf taken one of his yew lambs. So I dont now [sic] whether she is a yew or wether [sic] Wolf will haft to find that out."[29]

Some of the weddings were elaborate affairs, for an effort was made to keep them on an equality with peace-time nuptials. Kate Cumming gives a description of such a wedding in Newnan in the spring of 1864:

> The affair was quite a grand one for the times. Dr. Quintard came

from Atlanta to perform the ceremony, which took place in the Presbyterian church at 11 a. m. The church was darkened and lit with lamps and candles. . . . There were nine bridesmaids and an equal number of groomsmen. Many of the latter came from the army, as that number of young men could not have been found in the whole country. On looking at the ladies' dresses, which were made of brand new swiss muslin, I could not keep from thinking of the cost, and wondering where such a quantity had been gotten.[30]

On the other hand, some of the weddings were simple affairs, lacking in display and splendor. Such a ceremony was described by a person who lived in Walthourville:

I was considerably bored by the person who performed the ceremony. He was one of the prosiest kind of presbyterian preachers. He amused us by eulogising, preaching a regular funeral oration, on the good qualities of the couple he was marrying. He finally finished, and instead of offering his congratulations at once to them, he backed off and left us standing there. So I took his place.[31]

With a majority of the men away from home, the few civilian men enjoyed a respite in their courting competition and found themselves fully occupied in entertaining the local girls. "William is flying around extensively courting the girls. Miss Maxwell is the cynosure of his affection," a woman wrote to her husband.[32] Disturbed on account of the large number of girls who desired his association, a young Madison boy confided the complexity of his problems to his uncle, who was fighting in Virginia:

Uncle Birdy you may tell Jo that I think I will cut him out, while he is gon.
. . . we have hard times and wars a coming but I am still flying around with the girls. I tell you they keep me steried up. I went to meeting last meeting at Union and coming home I had to keep company with about a dozen girls, and you know that they keep me stirede up. I want you to make haste and kill those old Yankees by Christmas and come home to help me out for I tell you that I have my hands full but I will try to entertain them the best I can.[33]

A Marietta girl disclosed to her brother the courting activities of one of the local men:

You told me to tell you what old John G. was doing at this time. I dont know what he is doing at that time. He was last night corting Miss Elica Willingham at the corn pile like he never thought of the poor voluntere. about two weeks ago he was working at Mr. Applings

..SOCIAL LIFE AND DIVERSIONS

in day and staid at our hous evry other night and potended to help Pa shuck corn and cortid Line tell she looked as pale as ashies. she got so week on the Stranky of it. She got so she cood not weve a yard of cloth an day. Mother said go home till I get my little bour pig fat and I will let you know but he wont wate and it frets the old lady.[34]

Another young woman wrote:

Mollie there was the grandiest [sic] old Widower stayed here last night you ever saw he lives in Heard Co. there was two young ladies also stayed he was taking on about one of the girls she promised to marry him last night and this morning she kick him and sent him up the road as fast as two horses could take him.[35]

In addition to the usual affairs of the heart, many young men and women appreciated friendship and unromantic association with members of the opposite sex. While on a visit to her uncle's home in Oxford, a girl mentioned in her diary:

Spent the evening with Henry [Graves] — had a nice long talk with him. Every day I am more and more convinced . . . that he is one of the best friends that I have. We are very intimate and outsiders suppose us engaged. I don't answer, nor does he; 'twould be a pity to deprive them of something to gossip about.[36]

A Milledgeville girl, Anna Maria Green, said that soon after her return home from school "Dr. Robert Campbell of Augusta came to the asylum as a patient and has been a private boarder in our family. Most of my stay at home was spent with him, either reading French, playing chess, talking or riding. His company was extremely agreeable to me. . . ."[37]

Some of the noncombatant men became illicit lovers of the unmarried girls. A soldier revealed to his wife some gossip in which he thought she might be interested:

Molie I want to write to you about some things but I am all most afraid to do so for fear it aint so, but I will risk it.
Rich Thaxton said that Aunt Sarah Camp's oldest daughter was ruin and also Fannie Tennet was likely to bring forth. He said several others was in the same fix. he said it was thought that John Aikins was the Gent that Spoiled those Girles.[38]

Picnics, fox hunts, corn shuckings, quilting parties, and fishing increased the social pleasures. In the winter of 1865 a girl said, ". . . we spent the afternoon planning for a picnic at Mrs. Henry Bacon's lake . . ." and that she had ruined her riding habit "in those fox hunts at Chunnenuggee Ridge last fall."[39] ". . . we was at Mr. Welsis at a cornshucking last night and we had a fine time you ma [sic] depend," another girl related. "ther [sic] was 9 Girls and boys."[40] Another young woman penned to her brother:

> Liz, Mat and I went to Mr. Younk Elder's . . . to a quilting, which was given especially for Alonzo, who had been sick all the winter, but is now able to be up. The girls made his quilt of homespun. We were invited to a Valentine drawing the next night at the mountain Academy. We did not go as we thought the crowd would be rude, since then I have heard it was very much so.[41]

A Jones County woman divulged to a friend an inkling of the few social pleasures prevailing in her community:

> . . . the dullest times I ever saw. We young folks had a very nice time yesterday on the river fishing. If you had of been there you would laugh heartily, one of the girls caught an eel, it frighten her so bad she thundered from below. Mollie I laugh until I thought I never would get home. We were all in a canoe, boys and girls, you never heard people laugh so, and a few days before that we all went a fishing and one of the girls fell over the fence and showed her you know what it look like a new moon. You never saw boys skedaddle so in your life.[42]

As an increasingly large number of wounded soldiers came to the Georgia hospitals, entertainment was provided for their benefit. In the spring of 1864 Newnan and LaGrange had become enlivened with parties for the convalescent men. Fannie Beers says that when she was nursing the soldiers at Ringgold she kept in her office "a great many books for the convalescents, who were my most constant visitors." At Newnan she brought an ownerless piano into her room, and it "contributed largely to the pleasure of the soldiers, also serving for sacred music when needed."[43] Eliza Frances Andrews and several other young women sang war songs outside of the windows of a hospital in Cuthbert. She said that "The poor fellows were so delighted when they heard us that all who were able . . . came out on the terraces, while others crowded to the windows and balconies. They sent a shower of roses down on us, and threw with them slips of paper with the names of the songs they wished to hear."[44] Another woman said that she "Felt very little like it, but played the piano for a dozen soldiers, who seated themselves on the green, evidently to hear music!"[45]

Many Georgians found pleasant diversion in reading, and the titles of the books read suggest that the classics and other serious

..SOCIAL LIFE AND DIVERSIONS

works were more popular than light fiction. A Forsyth girl read "a very entertaining book, 'White Kitten,' showing the power of God." She also read poetical quotations from numerous authors on varied subjects.[46] Among the many books perused by a young Thomasville woman, some of which she read to her sick husband, home on furlough, were: *The Last of the Barons, The Count of Monte Cristo,* Thomas Macaulay's *History of England, Memoirs of Napoleon Bonaparte,* by the Duchess d'Abrantes, *Oliver Twist, Guy Mannering, Jane Eyre,* and *Devereaux*.[47] In writing to her sister, another woman commented:

> And so you are reading Miss Evans' [Augusta Evans Wilson] last. I shall be glad to read it. I have been reading Dickens' Household Works (four vols. in one) lately. What a flood of new books there will be when peace is made — new to us I mean. Why we will feel like we have been taking a nap with old Rip Van Winkle.[48]

Yet apparently the number of women in Georgia who read widely was considerably limited. An officer at Savannah expressed astonishment when he discovered how few of the women were educated. "In nine hundred cases out of a thousand," he declared, "they seem to think that books — except love stories — pertain to the school room alone." He said that of all the girls he knew, "ninety out of every hundred are as shallow in mind and character as our 'Spring Branch' and as artificial as the paint with which they daub their cheeks."[49] A few months later he confessed that he knew ladies who were "refined and very pleasant, kind and attractive," but that he found "something lacking in almost every case. *Sense, brain* is the thing most wanting . . . ," he declared. Despite these criticisms, he knew several women in Savannah whose friendship he valued highly. He said that of all his acquaintances "Fannie" was the sweetest tempered and that he considered himself very fortunate in gaining her friendship. Another of his friends, a sixteen-year-old girl, had "a great passion for reading — and solid reading." He said that in this respect her influence upon him was "stimulating," and that she "has also a great passion for music." A third friend whom he admired was a young married woman. Writing of her, he remarked:

> I will tell you of another of my *Sweet* friends. A *married* lady but *not a whit* the less interesting and loveable from that cause. The Bible says "do not covet thy neighbor's wife." I am dangerously near this forbidden ground sometimes. Do not become alarmed. She has been

married several years and her oldest boy is 8 or 9. I visit her occasionally and have very quiet delightful evenings. Her husband is a Capt, stationed in the city and a very pleasant gentleman.[50]

Although dancing was condemned by many of the churches, and a religious periodical, the *Child's Index,* said that the practice was "bad for society because it leads to evil consequences," girls of aristocratic lineage danced and attended dancing schools. When one of the sisters of General Henry R. Jackson asked him if he thought she should take dancing lessons, he replied, "I would strenuously advise both you and Sister to do so. I would advise you under no circumstances to be discouraged, and to practice continually both at home and in the dancing school. Tell Sister from me, by all means to go, and not to talk about her principles being opposed to it."[51] "I am thankful that we have the spirits for dancing, and are not as many households are, shrouded in gloom," stated a woman who resided near Savannah. A little later she recorded, "Went last night over to the Constantine's house to see the dancing party. . . . Some funny dancing! A very amusing and nice time."[52]

An officer notified his sister that he was looking forward with pleasure at the thought of the "nice music you will give me some of these days." He said that he had heard no new music since he had seen her, and that as he knew no ladies in Savannah whose acquaintance he cared to cultivate, he had no one to give him music. Continuing, he wrote:

I want you to give me a list of all the music you have, both songs and instrumental music. If Ma and Pa go to Terrill you must go to Augusta and spend the winter and take music lessons. I am afraid you are losing precious time. You ought to read a great deal and practice too. I had rather you were accomplished and poor when you are grown, than that you should be worth a half million and be a dunce.[53]

Christmas, traditionally celebrated with the popping of firecrackers and the happy exchange of Christmas gifts, continued to be observed during the war, but anxiety and the absence of many men lessened the gaiety of the occasion. "Christmas very quiet — spent it at home. Santa Claus brought me $10.00. Very different from last which I spent in Eatonton," a girl recorded in her diary.[54] Another young woman, in writing to a friend, dismissed briefly the subject of how the Christmas of 1861 was celebrated, by saying, "Well, Lack posted you all about how we spent Christmas. I guess

..SOCIAL LIFE AND DIVERSIONS

Suffisit it to Say that it wente finely with us Gals (All Rite)."[55] After the devastation wrought by Sherman, many families in 1864 were not visited at all by "Old Saint Nick." The sadness of Christmas during that year is depicted with heart-rending words by a woman whose home was invaded:

> This has usually been a very busy day with me, preparing for Christmas not only for my own tables, but for gifts for my servants. Now how changed! No confectionery, cakes, or pies can I have. We are all sad; no loud, jovial laugh from our boys is heard. Christmas Eve, which has ever been gaily celebrated here . . . is an occasion now of sadness and gloom. I have nothing even to put in Sadai's stocking, which hangs so invitingly for Santa Claus.[56]

During the war men enjoyed drinking and gambling, horse races, and to a limited extent billiard playing and bowling. A saloon, built in the basement of a Savannah hotel in 1862, was said to "compare favorably with the most fashionable establishment of the Northern cities." A year later a gambling establishment in Augusta was suppressed by the police and the owner of the firm was killed in a duel. Horse races were held over the Chattahoochee course, near Columbus, during the spring of 1864. The races continued for five days and the stakes were declared large.[57] Billiard rooms were reopened in Savannah in February, 1865, and as the war ended, two tenpin alleys were opened to the public in the same city.

Although dueling as a means of deciding points of honor was fast becoming obsolete and was a dubious form of "diversion," two men at Savannah in 1863 crossed to the South Carolina side of the river and "exchanged a couple of fires."[58] In the same year at LaGrange a duel took place between two army officers. The weapons used were navy pistols, and the distance was twenty paces. At the second fire one of the officers was slightly wounded, whereupon the disagreeable matter was amicably adjusted.

Toward the end of the war an atmosphere of gloom and despondency was manifest in nearly all social gatherings, except among the refugees in southwest Georgia. That section, remote from the scene of military operations, became more cosmopolitan as refugees from all parts of the South crowded into the little towns. Parties and theatricals gave the region a spirit of gaiety. As late as January, 1865, a Georgia girl, refugeeing near Albany, said that "While the gentlemen lingered over their wine after dinner, we ladies sat in the parlor making cigarettes for them. The evening was spent at cards. . . ." A month later she remarked, "We danced eighteen sets, and I was on the floor every time, besides all the round dances."[59]

CHAPTER XIII

The Press and Literary Pursuits

WHEN JOEL CHANDLER HARRIS IN 1863 submitted a manuscript to the editors of *The Commonwealth* at Atlanta, he closed his accompanying note with these words, "Hoping that you may receive a thousand reams of nice paper. . . ."[1] Not only was a shortage of paper a recurrent obstacle to the publishing business in Georgia, but many other difficulties plagued the state's publishers. Presses were not manufactured in the South, few Georgians were trained in designing illustrations for periodicals, transportation and postal facilities often were disrupted, and many pressmen were serving in the armed forces.

Publishing in Georgia was divided chiefly among Macon, Augusta, Savannah, and Atlanta. Burke, Boykin and Company in Macon, the leading publishing firm in the state, was an extensive publisher of local authors. Macon was also the home of J. C. Schreiner (formerly of New Orleans), a publisher of sheet music almost exclusively. Another New Orleans music firm, A. E. Blackmar and Brother, moved to Augusta early in the war and became one of the leading publishing firms of that city. Literary works were produced in Augusta by Stockton and Company, the Augusta *Constitutionalist,* and by Blome and Tehan. The firm of W. B. Smith and Company of Augusta published one of the South's leading weeklies, the *Southern Field and Fireside.* Considerable fiction was printed in this periodical.[2] The press of the Atlanta *Intelligencer* published pamphlets containing much of the correspondence between Governor Brown and President Davis. John M. Cooper and Company of Savannah published many of the sermons and addresses delivered by Stephen Elliott, a prominent Savannah Episcopal minister. The state printers, Boughton, Nisbet, and Barnes of Milledgeville, published the legislative journals and laws.

Early in the war a prospective publisher in Dalton addressed a letter to Alexander H. Stephens regarding his publishing ambitions:

> I am using my energy to establish a *publishing house*, with the view of supplying, in part at least, our country with textbooks. I have a number of works now ready for the press, and I hope to bring them out very soon, I know of no house that has the capital to publish books, hence I am trying to induce capitalists to embark in the enterprise, and I have some hope that I will succeed.[3]

The man's expectations were too sanguine, however, for there is nothing to indicate that he succeeded in his project.

Two useful volumes were produced by publishers in Griffin. *Grier's Almanac for the States of Georgia, South Carolina, Alabama and Tennessee, for the Year 1862* was published early in the war by Brawner and Putnam. The almanac contained the "usual Astronomical Calculations, with the time of High Water at Savannah . . . to which are annexed the Chief Officers of the State of Georgia . . ." and "the times of holding Courts in the State. . . ." In 1863 H. P. Hill and Company, of the same city, published the *Confederate States Railroad and Steamboat Guide*, a one-hundred-page booklet containing schedules of the railroads in the Confederate states. The Atlanta *Southern Confederacy* stated that the guide was "as neat a job as any one can turn out. It fills the place of Appleton's in every way."[4] The Savannah *Daily Morning News* declared that the guide contained "a variety of valuable information."

The newspaper press had made rapid advancement during the decade prior to the war. Whereas in 1850 there were fifty-one newspapers and periodicals in the state, by 1860 the number had grown to 105, with an increase in subscribers of from 64,155 to 180,962 during the decade. The daily papers had increased from five to twelve during the period. Exclusive of the periodicals, Georgia had seventy-two newspapers in 1860. The daily papers had a circulation of 18,650, while the circulation of weekly publications was 127,322, making a total average circulation of 145,972. Within the decade the total annual circulation of newspapers and periodicals rose from 4,070,866 to 13,415,444 copies. Undoubtedly, the secret of this rapid growth lay largely in the increasing interest of Georgians in politics. Of the 105 newspapers and periodicals in the state in 1860, seventy-five were classified as political journals.[5]

At the beginning of the war the Savannah *Daily Morning News*, edited by William T. Thompson, had the largest circulation of

..THE PRESS AND LITERARY PURSUITS

any daily paper in the state. Under Thompson's leadership the *Daily Morning News* had become one of the most important newspapers in the South, boldly enterprising and independent, with leanings toward "Southern rights."[6] The local rival of the *Daily Morning News* was the Savannah *Republican,* a conservative journal which had formerly supported the Whig party. In Augusta the *Constitutionalist* was a militant Democratic paper strongly favoring Southern rights. Owned by James Gardner, a prominent politician, the *Constitutionalist* was one of Georgia's most powerful political sheets. Another Augusta paper, the *Chronicle and Sentinel,* established in 1785, was an important, but politically conservative, publication.

In the central part of the state, the leading papers were the Macon *Daily Telegraph,* the *Federal Union* of Milledgeville, and the *Southern Recorder,* also published in Milledgeville. The Macon *Telegraph* and the *Federal Union* were Democratic journals favoring secession; the *Southern Recorder* was a conservative pro-Union newspaper which supported the Constitutional Union party in 1860 but was loyal to the South after the state seceded. Three papers were published in Columbus: the *Daily Sun,* the *Enquirer,* and the *Times.* The *Daily Sun* and the *Enquirer* were conservative, Whiggish publications and the *Times* was Democratic. Of the three papers, the *Daily Sun* had the largest circulation in 1860, but the *Times* seemed to be the most vigorous exponent of Southern rights. The principal papers published in Atlanta were the *Southern Confederacy,* a rabidly secessionist paper, and the *Intelligencer,* the leading Democratic organ of north Georgia. James B. Hambleton, the editor of the *Southern Confederacy* when the war began, was a "fire eater" who at one time printed what he called a "black list" of Northern merchants with whom he urged the Southern people not to trade. The *Intelligencer,* owned by Judge Jared I. Whitaker and edited by Major John H. Steele, was Atlanta's oldest daily paper and was a strong factor in the politics of the state, aiding the Democrats to win victory after victory.[7]

Some of the principal papers published in the smaller cities were the Athens *Banner,* one of the oldest papers in the state, the LaGrange *Reporter,* the Gainesville *Eagle,* the Sandersville *Central Georgian,* the *North Georgia Citizen* of Dalton, the Americus *Sumter Republican,* the Albany *Patriot,* and the Rome *Courier.* Except in Savannah and Brunswick, no papers were published in the southeastern portion of the state, a section sparsely inhabited at the time of the war.

The difficulties of the press began immediately after secession. Publishers, editors, and printers' devils joined the volunteer companies, leaving mostly old men, women, and children to publish the papers. In the latter part of April, 1861, the call of war had taken away nine of the twenty employees of the Macon *Daily Telegraph*. By the spring of 1862 the Augusta *Chronicle and Sentinel* had furnished fourteen men to the ranks of the Confederacy. "The proprietors and journeymen of the *Georgia Forester*, published at Waresboro, being 'Wire Grass Minute Men,' which company has been called into service by Gov. Brown, the paper is offered for sale on easy terms," a Columbus paper announced.[8] Due to its employees' going off to the war and the postal routes being temporarily deranged, the *Southern Baptist Messenger* in May, 1861, was late in reaching its subscribers. The Macon *Citizen* on September 12th announced suspension, saying that the establishment was for sale at "panic prices." In the fall of 1861 the *Upson Pilot*, published at Thomaston, was slowly dying. The patriotism of the editor would not permit him to remain safely behind the editorial desk when his services were needed at the front. A few more issues were produced, but with the close of the year 1861 the paper expired.

Publishers who remained to conduct the papers were soon harassed with a multitude of additional difficulties. When the war began, only about five per cent of the American paper mills were in the South and only four small paper mills were in Georgia. The supply of paper from the Georgia mills and from mills located in other parts of the South was not large enough to take care of the demand, and transportation delays were troublesome. By the fall of 1861 the paper problem became acute and newspapers began offering high prices for linen and cotton rags. Due to the impossibility of securing a supply of paper, many newspapers began issuing only half sheets. Other papers, such as the *Harris County Enterprise*, were half sheets some weeks and full sheets other weeks, depending on the supply of printing paper available. In January, 1862, the Savannah *Daily Morning News* printed three issues on brown paper, the only substitute available.

As paper became increasingly difficult to procure, newspapers were forced to raise their subscription and advertisement rates and to go on a strictly cash basis. On account of "inflationary prices in

..THE PRESS AND LITERARY PURSUITS

labor and materials," the Savannah *Daily Morning News* in January, 1863, increased its subscription rate to $6.00 for six months or $10.00 a year, and in November of the same year announced that "The increased price of paper, labor and subsistence renders it indispensable that rates be increased" to $13.00 for six months. Two dollars was charged for ten lines of advertising. Similar increases in the subscription and advertising rates were made by other papers. The weekly edition of the Augusta *Chronicle and Sentinel* advanced its subscription rate from three to four dollars a year on March 1, 1863. Two years later this paper was selling for 50¢ a copy.

The increased price of subscriptions and advertisements resulted in a diminishing circulation and advertising revenue. The volume of advertising and the number of subscriptions steadily decreased, especially toward the end of the war, and advertisers and subscribers frequently delayed in paying their bills. Whether the editors were able to meet the expenses of publication with the advertising receipt is very doubtful. The numerous complaints from the editors concerning the high prices of paper, ink, and labor do not seem to indicate any surplus earnings. The editor of the Waynesboro *Independent South* wrote Governor Brown that he was not making any money and had a large family to support. "And I wish to know if you will give me a Ticket to pass over the State Road free, and I will retalliate [sic] in any advertising," he inquired.[9] Another editor made the following comment in regard to the financial predicament of the publishers:

We believe it may be safely assumed that there are but two classes of men in the Confederacy, not in the army, who are not "speculators" or "high price men," in some way or other. The parson still preaches to his congregation, at a salary which barely keeps soul and body together, while publishers of newspapers are working for the public gratis and boarding themselves.[10]

Near the close of the war the editor of an Augusta paper remarked, "If ever there was 'a hard road to travel' it is publishing a newspaper in war times. That is our experience — and we think most of the fraternity will say 'Amen' to it."[11]

In addition to their financial troubles and the scarcity of paper and ink, the publishers of Atlanta were confronted in the spring of 1864 with a strike among the printers, who demanded an increase of fifty per cent in their wages. On account of the depreciated currency, the real earnings of the printers had decreased. The

Columbus *Times* declared the demands of the Atlanta printers to be unreasonable and said that "The difficulties of securing printers will doubtless force upon publishers the necessity of employing girls and boys to do the work heretofore done by men." This statement by the *Times* brought forth a rebuke from the printers' "local" of the Columbus *Enquirer*. The printers maintained that the employment of women and children would prove demoralizing to their profession.[12] Although the printers, like the editors, were not subject to conscription, the Atlanta editors asked a conscript officer to draft the printers. The officer was willing, but he began his work by conscripting the editors, who, he said, were no longer at work. As the editors did not wish to be conscripted, they consulted with their employees and arranged a compromise.

The Georgia newspapers experienced many changes and mergers during the war. Two Atlanta papers, the *Confederacy* and the *Gate City Guardian*, were merged in 1861 and became known as the *Southern Confederacy*, but the paper died at Columbus in 1864 during the Sherman invasion. The *Intelligencer*, the only Atlanta paper to survive the war, fled to Macon and for a time was published from a box-car, which could quickly be moved from place to place. The publisher of the Augusta *Chronicle and Sentinel*, Dr. William S. Jones, sold his paper in 1862 to N. S. Morse of New York. Under the editorship of Morse, the *Chronicle and Sentinel* was at times rabidly anti-Davis. The Macon *Telegraph* became the Macon *Daily Telegraph and Confederate* on September 19, 1864, when it was consolidated with the *Daily Confederate*. The *North Georgia Citizen* at Dalton was partially destroyed by Sherman and was suspended for some time, and the Rome *Courier* was suspended from May, 1864, to September, 1865. The Milledgeville *Confederate Union* escaped the pillage of Sherman when its press was hurriedly taken to the woods, and the Columbus *Enquirer* continued publication throughout the war with the exception of a few weeks.[13]

When Federal forces took possession of the daily press at Savannah and Macon, they published army organs from the confiscated offices. The Savannah *Republican* was published in the interest of the Federal government from December, 1864, to October, 1868, by John E. Hayes, the war correspondent of the New York *Tribune*. The Savannah *Daily Morning News* was published by a Northerner, S. W. Mason, under the title of Savannah *Daily Herald* until 1868, when J. H. Estill purchased the paper and re-

THE PRESS AND LITERARY PURSUITS

sumed the original name. When General Wilson's cavalry entered Macon on April 21, 1865, the editors and printers of the Macon *Daily Telegraph and Confederate* vacated their offices; and no paper was edited in Macon until May 4th, when the Macon *Evening News* was established, published by a combination of printers under military surveillance. The *Telegraph* appeared again on May 11th under the new ownership of Clayland and Dumble, who made no reference to the exciting scenes which had occurred during the paper's suspension. When the Federals captured Athens, they brought out an issue of the *Southern Banner* filled with propaganda. The Athens citizens were enraged, thinking the editor had turned traitor. Every paper in the state, except the *Southern Cultivator,* was obliged to suspend operations at times, and a total of fifty-three newspapers which were founded before the war ceased to exist.

In addition to her own newspapers, Georgia was host to several peripatetic papers during the latter part of the war. The Memphis *Appeal* was published in Atlanta for a few weeks in 1864, and the Chattanooga *Rebel,* keeping safely in advance of the Union Army, moved southward to Marietta, Atlanta, Griffin, and Columbus. The Knoxville *Register* was also published in Atlanta during a part of the war. When Federal forces occupied Fernandina, Florida, in 1862, the editor of a newspaper there moved his press to Thomasville, Georgia, where he established a new weekly paper.

A perusal of the meager columns of telegraphic items contained in the Georgia newspapers of the war period discloses the difficulty with which the news was obtained. The newspapers were not entirely free of censorship imposed by the Confederacy. In January, 1862, the Confederate Congress made it a crime to publish any news of "the numbers, disposition, movements, or destination of Southern land or naval forces." As a result of this censorship, and of failures in the telegraph and mails, the news quality of Georgia papers was relatively poor. Editors frequently were unable to decide whether an article was authoritative or based on mere rumor; consequently, they often quoted several authorities for a news story, thus protecting themselves in the event the article was not true.

The unsatisfactory arrangements for news reports by telegraph caused a group of Southern publishers to organize "The Press Association of the Confederate States" at Augusta in February, 1863. The purpose of this association was to maintain reporters in the field to transmit news dispatches and to operate a system of news agencies for the common benefit of the members of the organization. Although forty-four Southern newspapers, including twelve of the largest papers in Georgia, were members of the association in 1863, the organization was frequently unable to supply the desired news. "Why is there no Associated Press at Dalton?" inquired the Savannah *Daily Morning News* on December 1, 1863. "If the Association cannot obtain army news it fails to accomplish the object for which it was formed." At a meeting of the directors of the association in Atlanta on May 14, 1863, J. S. Thrasher, the superintendent of the association, said that "lax discipline observed in many of the telegraph offices" was preventing many of the association's news reports from being kept private. He added, however, that the Milledgeville Telegraph Company had performed a satisfactory service in sending "to the whole country" the proceedings of the extra session of the Georgia legislature.[14] The association continued to function until the end of the war and in view of the chaotic conditions rendered a valuable service.

Despite the government's attempt at censorship, the Confederate authorities seldom interfered with the Georgia press. Although the Georgia editors were divided in their opinions concerning the controversies engaged in by Governor Brown and the Confederate administration, neither Brown nor the Confederacy made any attempt to stifle the freedom of the press. Even when the Georgia papers disagreed with Confederate policies, they were loyal to the Southern cause and were usually careful not to divulge facts that might be of aid to the enemy.[15] Early in the war the Augusta *Chronicle and Sentinel* on June 9, 1861, said, "We want to give the enemy no information of the number of men we have in service, nor of their position or destination, when our Government thinks such information might benefit the enemy or prejudice our cause."

The newspaper editorials did much to preserve a high morale among the people and were almost universally optimistic regarding the South's possibility of winning the war. The editors published propaganda to the effect that the North was losing, often criticized harshly Lincoln and the Yankees, and frequently referred to the Federal troops as "a horde of barbarians." As late as February, 1865, the Columbus *Daily Times* said, "People from the mountains to the seaboard are resolved, with the voice of one man, never to submit to the demands of Lincoln, Seward and the abolition crew, who require us to bend our necks to the yoke they have made for us."[16] A month later the same paper asserted, "We must go on with this revolution as a united people until our independence is acknowledged, or we are ruined."[17] The Atlanta *Daily Intelligencer* declared that "with all the energies we possess as a firm, united people, we should press forward, sacrificing every private interest for the public good . . . and . . . we will soon witness the joy . . . of success."[18] On the very day that Johnston surrendered to Sherman, the Sandersville *Central Georgian* said, "We are not of those who cry *whipped*."[19]

The newspapers apparently recorded the true history of public opinion in Georgia as it was during the war. "The Confederate press during the whole of the present conflict has reason to be proud of its fidelity to principle, while its utterances have shown that it has been a no less faithful exponent of that public sentiment it has represented," said the Atlanta *Southern Confederacy* in January, 1863.[20] Near the close of the war the Columbus *Daily Times* declared, "While the papers have been the advocates of the war they have not been so much the originators as the reflectors of public opinion. Public sentiment all the while has been in advance of the press. . . ."[21]

Another literary pursuit of significance in Georgia during the war was the publication of periodical literature.[22] The periodicals welcomed an era free from the competition of Northern magazines. One of the leading periodicals was the *Southern Field and Fireside,* published in Augusta, with its decidedly varied reading matter. Less widely known were the *Georgia Weekly* of Greenville, *The Countryman* of "Turnwold," and the *Southern Literary Companion* of Newnan. The most colorful journalistic figure of the war years was Joseph Addison Turner, the editor of *The Countryman.*[23]

The *Southern Field and Fireside,* a weekly folio of eight pages to an issue, made its initial appearance in Augusta on May 28, 1859, with James Gardner as proprietor. It was composed of three parts: literary, agricultural, and horticultural. Gardner published the work in conjunction with the *Constitutionalist* until the first part of 1864, when he sold his interests to Stockton and Company, who in turn sold out in October, 1864, to William B. Smith and Company of Raleigh. Its importance to Georgia ceased with the removal. The editors of the *Southern Field and Fireside* were interested in developing the latent literary talent of the South and continually offered prizes for poems, tales, and essays. Serial stories were also important features. For example, Augustus Baldwin Longstreet's *Master William Mitten* ran serially for twenty-six consecutive numbers in 1859; and William Wilberforce Turner's *Jack Hopeton and His Friends* ran serially for weeks. Although the periodical was unable to maintain its original standard of excellence during the war, it had at least thirteen thousand subscribers in 1864.

A quarterly of literary importance in Georgia was *The Plantation*, edited by Joseph Addison Turner at his home near Eatonton. The first number of *The Plantation* appeared in March, 1860, but the war forced Turner to abandon its publication in 1862. The primary purpose of *The Plantation* was to defend the institution of slavery, but it also contained many pages on politics, social life, amusements, and industries.[24]

Although the war stifled *The Plantation*, Turner on March 4, 1862, issued the first number of *The Countryman*, printed on his own press at his plantation, "Turnwold," near Eatonton. In announcing *The Countryman*, Turner said that he was attempting to revive Hezekiah Niles' famous *Register*, and that *The Countryman* would not only have all the features of the *Register*, but also would be stamped with an independent Southern tone. "It is our aim to fill our Little Paper with Essays, Poems, Sketches, Agricultural Articles, and choice miscellany ... ," the announcement stated.[25] The Augusta *Chronicle and Sentinel* noted that the periodical was "handsomely printed, spicy, and entertaining."[26]

Because of war conditions, contributions to *The Countryman* came from only a few writers. The writings of Turner, however, were the most interesting appearing in the periodical. Turner wrote mediocre poems and also tried his hand at drama in blank verse. The best of his dramas is *Joseph: A Farce in One Act*, a humorous satire on the controversy between Joseph E. Brown and Jefferson Davis concerning states' rights. Three acts of his work *West Point — a Tragedy in Five Acts* appeared in ten numbers of *The Countryman* from December 22, 1862, to March, 1863.[27]

On the Turner plantation Joel Chandler Harris came in contact with the African folklore that produced the Uncle Remus stories. When Harris was only thirteen years old, he became a member of the Turner establishment, where in addition to his work in the printing office, he came in contact with Turner's slaves. Harris

THE PRESS AND LITERARY PURSUITS

contributed more than thirty articles to *The Countryman,* including miscellaneous poems and short stories. While at Turnwold the youth made his first attempt at literary criticism, "Henry Lynden Flash," a review of the poems written by the editor of the Macon *Daily Confederate.*

The *Southern Cultivator,* a monthly published in Augusta (it moved to Athens in 1865) by Dr. William Louis Jones, was one of the few agricultural periodicals published in the South, and it had a large circulation. From its pages were expressed the buoyant expectations of the Southern planters. The scarcity of paper caused the periodical to be issued every other month after March, 1863, but it continued to be published throughout the war.

The *Southern Literary Companion,* published in Newnan, was a weekly folio devoted to literature, arts, the sciences, and agriculture. Little can be learned about the periodical, for only a few issues are extant. War conditions forced the *Southern Literary Companion* to discontinue publication early in 1865. Another periodical, the *Georgia Literary and Temperance Crusader,* was published in Atlanta from 1859 to November, 1861, and contained original prose and poetry.

Several periodicals of lesser note were published. For the benefit of the soldiers, two periodicals were published in the state, the *Soldiers' Friend* in Atlanta, and the *Army and Navy Herald* at Macon, both of which were weeklies. Five educational periodicals appeared between 1859 and 1865, published either in the general interest of education or by students of some educational institution.[28] The *Wesleyan Christian Advocate,* a Methodist organ, was published monthly in Atlanta during the war; and the *Christian Index,* the oldest Baptist paper in the South published continuously, was issued at Macon and was suspended for only a few weeks. *The Child's Index,* a periodical for children, was published monthly in Macon and contained stories and poems of a moral and religious nature. It was a Baptist publication, with eleven thousand subscribers in November, 1863, but the war caused the circulation to decrease in 1865. A mediocre humorous magazine, the *Bugle-Horn of Liberty,* was published in Griffin for a few months in 1863.

The vicissitudes of war did not entirely deter Georgians from writing books. Charles C. Jones, Jr., of Savannah published in 1861 a little volume entitled *Monumental Remains of Georgia,* a study of Indian mounds; and during the same year, the Reverend

John H. Caldwell, pastor of a Methodist church in Savannah, wrote a religious novel, *The Thurstons of the Old Palmetto State, or Varieties of Southern Life*. In 1862 John M. Richardson, a teacher at the Georgia Military Institute in Marietta, published *Manual of Military Reconnaissances*, and Henry W. R. Jackson produced *Confederate Monitor and Patriot's Friend*, a book containing sketches and events of the war. Augustus Baldwin Longstreet, the author of *Georgia Scenes*, in 1864 published a new book, *Master William Mitten, or a Young Man of Brilliant Talents, Who Was Ruined by Bad Luck*.[29] During the same year, the Reverend E. W. Warren of Macon wrote a novelette in favor of slavery, entitled *Nellie Norton: or Southern Slavery and the Bible*; and Colonel James M. Folsom of Gordon published *Heroes and Martyrs of Georgia*. Another Georgian, Richard Malcolm Johnston, in 1864 published at Augusta his *Georgia Sketches ... from the Recollections of an Old Man*, by Philemon Perch. This volume contained "Mr. Israel Meadows and His School," "Judge Mike and His Court," "How Bill Williams Took the Responsibility," and "Miss Pea, Miss Spouter and the Yankee." These humorous stories were intended to illustrate characters and scenes among the simple rural folk of middle Georgia as they were during the time of Johnston's childhood.

During the gloom of war, Major Charles H. Smith of Rome, Georgia's rustic philosopher and humorist, wrote numerous stories for the newspapers under the pseudonym of "Bill Arp." Written in the backwoods vernacular of the "cracker," his letters and stories were read at countless firesides and gave the people a needed relaxation from the momentous events of the war. After the war, his collection of stories was published in a book entitled *A Side Show of the Southern Side of the War*.

Intense emotions found expression in lyrical poems. A native of Baldwin County, Dr. Francis Orray Ticknor, wrote the immortal poem "Little Giffin" in honor of a Tennessee youth, who, after running away from home to join the army, had been seriously wounded and was recuperating at a hospital in Columbus. The opening stanza reveals the rhythm of the poem:

> Out of the focal and foremost fire,
> Out of the hospital walls as dire;
> Smitten of grape-shot and gangrene
> (Eighteenth battle, and *he* sixteen!)
> Spectre! such as you seldom see,
> Little Giffin, of Tennessee!

..THE PRESS AND LITERARY PURSUITS

One of the best known war poets was Carrie Belle Sinclair, born in Milledgeville in 1839. During the war she was living in Augusta, where she wrote a poem, "The Homespun Dress," which was sung to the tune of "The Bonnie Blue Flag" and portrayed the life of the civilian population. In addition to this poem she wrote "Dreaming" and "Georgia." Poems in memory of General Albert Sydney Johnston were written by the Reverend E. P. Birch of LaGrange and by Louise Rogers of Atlanta. The former also wrote "The Devil's Visit to 'Old Abe,'" written on the occasion of Lincoln's proclamation for prayer and fasting after the First Battle of Manassas. Henry Lynden Flash, a war correspondent and editor of the Macon *Telegraph and Confederate,* wrote the poems "Zollicoffer," "Stonewall Jackson," and "Leonidas Polk." His poems, reflecting a weird vein, were published in several Southern papers. Marie LaCoste of Savannah published a poem, "Somebody's Darling," in 1863, reflecting the ravages of the war on the families of the soldiers.

Besides these popular poems, Georgia's newspapers published much doggerel written by the state's pseudo poets. Most of the poems had either a martial air or expressed a feeling of pathos:

LINES TO GEORGIANS

Sons of the empire State awake!
  Your country calls you forth;
Go forth to make the tyrant quake,
  Go forth to show your worth.

The vandals now pollute our land,
  And their cry is subjugation;
Away to the field with sword in hand,
  And spurn such degradation!

Go forth and meet him as he comes,
  With muskets true in hand,
O, drive him back from Georgia's shores
  Ye noble! patriot band![30]

The following stanzas expressed the patriotic sentiments of a Georgia woman when she was asked by her lover if she wished him to volunteer:

I need not say I love with all
  The warmth of woman's heart,
And agonizing is the thought
  That we should ever part;

> But though with you all joy should go
>   That gladdens up my way,
> I would not have you for my sake,
>   I would not have you stay.
>
> But who can penetrate the veil
>   Futurity doth wear,
> And death may come, then let us now
>   To meet our God prepare;
> Then, should you fall on battle-field,
>   Or I should droop and die
> Ere you return, we'll meet again
>   In that blest world on high![31]

Many songs with a military background appeared. "Secession Quick-Step" was the name of a piece of music composed by Herman L. Schreiner of Macon, and "We Conquer or Die" was the title of a song composed for the piano by James Pierpont of Savannah. The most popular Georgia writer of songs during the existence of the Confederacy, however, was John Hill Hewitt, a music teacher in Augusta. Hewitt's song-sheets appear on the lists of the leading Confederate music publishers. Among his productions of that period are musical settings for "Rock Me to Sleep, Mother," the popular ballad by Elizabeth Akers; and "All Quiet Along the Potomac Tonight," by Ethel Lynn Eliot Beers. Ballads with both words and music by Hewitt are "The Unknown Dead," "When Upon the Field of Glory," "You Are Going to the Wars, Willie Boy!," and "The Young Volunteer." Hewitt published during the war one of his three full-length books, *War: A Poem, with Copious Notes, Founded on the Revolution of 1861-62*.[32]

In addition to his popularity as a composer of songs, Hewitt won fame as a writer of drama. His principal productions of the war period were *The Scouts, The Log Fort, The Vivandiers, The Prisoner of Monterey,* and *King Linkum the First*. The last named play, a satire of Lincoln, is the only one of Hewitt's productions which has appeared in print. While *King Linkum the First* is of little merit as drama, it does reflect the extreme propaganda that prevailed in the South during the war years. A critic of Hewitt's works says that his "plays are uniformly sensational in conception, wooden in treatment. . . . But the very number hints of some success. . . ."[33]

Georgia in 1860 had 364 libraries which were listed by the official census reports as "libraries other than private." These

THE PRESS AND LITERARY PURSUITS

libraries, divided among public libraries, Sunday school libraries, college libraries, and church libraries, contained a total of 272,935 volumes.[34] The number of libraries and the volumes they contained had grown tremendously since 1850, when the census reported only thirty-eight libraries, other than private ones, with a total of 31,788 volumes.[35] Georgia had also many superior private libraries. Joseph Addison Turner's home near Eatonton contained a library of nearly two thousand volumes. Israel K. Tefft, founder of the Georgia Historical Society, had an unrivaled collection of historical documents, signatures, and portraits in his library at Savannah. The library of A. A. Smets of Savannah, who was treasurer of the Georgia Historical Society from 1855 until his death in 1862, contained manuscripts of the ninth to the fourteenth centuries, volumes printed in the sixteenth century by Gutenberg, Fust, and Schoffer, works from the press of William Caxton, and manuscripts of Horace Walpole, Laurence Sterne, Joseph Addison, and others.[36] The valuable library and manuscripts belonging to George Wymberley Jones DeRenne, near Savannah, were entirely destroyed by Sherman's troops, but in later years his son built up another great collection.

The activities of the Georgia Historical Society, founded in 1839, did not cease during the war. The twenty-fifth anniversary of the society was celebrated in February, 1863, at the society's library hall. Charles S. Henry was elected president for the ensuing year. A newspaper announced in October, 1864, that the society had held its regular monthly meeting. The library of the society was open to the public three afternoons each week. The librarian in March, 1865, requested all persons having in their possession books belonging to the society to return them to the library, "as the library is now being arranged and books catalogued."[37] Despite the havoc of war, Georgia's press and literary pursuits did not entirely languish.

CHAPTER XIV

Education

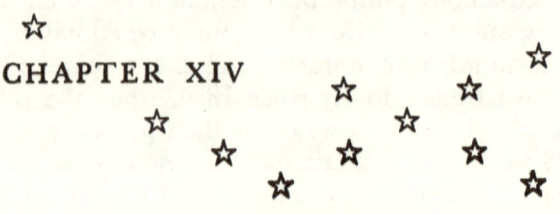

THE IMPACT OF WAR CRITICALLY disrupted the colleges and schools of Georgia. Virtually all of the institutions for the higher education of men were suspended; several of the women's colleges ceased to operate; the academies and private schools were seriously impaired; and the establishment of a contemplated public system of primary and secondary schools was necessarily postponed.

Both the students and faculty of the University of Georgia at Athens were in a state of frenzied excitement during the winter and spring of 1861. The academic year opened with 123 students enrolled; but when the war began, they began leaving college, with or without permission of parents or faculty, in order to enlist. There were drilling and studying of tactics, marching and countermarching. The law students organized a military company and tendered their services to the Governor. A member of the faculty, Richard Malcolm Johnston, explained to Alexander H. Stephens the situation at the university as it existed in May, 1861:

> We have but a little over forty students in college. Fifteen or twenty have already gone to war. Last week the Junior Class with Brooke at their head resolved that they could not study and all but six left. Two students left to-day. More will leave tomorrow. If the war continues, we shall be obliged to do, as they have done in S. Carolina College, close up.[1]

A senior at the university described to Stephens the changed atmosphere brought by the war:

> Of course we are very much excited by the troubled condition of our country.
> Our furor for the news comes on at half past eight in the morning. I think the college has at last settled down into a state of comparative tranquillity. We have between thirty five and forty boys here now. We

..EDUCATION

have a much pleasanter time though . . . than when all the students are here. There is no noise, no inconsiderate babbling. . . . The Senior Class . . . obtained from the faculty a shortening of our time here so we get out on the 15th of May.[2]

Before midsummer, seventy-five students had enlisted and nearly all of the others were preparing to volunteer. Chancellor Andrew A. Lipscomb decided to put the university on a wartime footing and to keep it open if possible; but conditions went steadily from bad to worse. In June, 1861, the Law School adjourned for the duration of the war; and when the trustees met in Athens on July 5th, Professors Johnston and W. D. Walsh tendered their resignations, to take effect at the end of the year. The faculty members agreed to remit twenty per cent of their salaries in consequence of the reduced receipts of the institution. In May, 1862, examinations were given to the two remaining seniors.

With the attendance rapidly decreasing, Chancellor Lipscomb petitioned President Davis to exempt from conscription all students under twenty-one years of age, but Davis replied that he had no control over the matter. As times grew harder, the salaries of the few remaining professors were reduced at first twenty per cent and then one hundred per cent, and the Chancellor was paid only $250 a year in Confederate money. In October, 1863, the university was closed when Governor Brown issued a proclamation calling out state troops and home guard companies for the defense of Georgia. During the remainder of the war the buildings were used for military purposes, and when the trustees met in July, 1864, no effort was made to reopen the university. An announcement stated that "The Professors were all retained in office without salary, but allowed to occupy their present residences free of rent, and to employ themselves in such pursuits as they may find useful to the country, until recalled to their posts."[3]

Under the leadership of President James R. Thomas, Emory College, a Methodist institution for men located at Oxford, was making considerable progress when the war began. Dr. Thomas was an avowed secessionist. In a letter to an Atlanta newspaper in March, 1861, he warned that if the South should be defeated, "the phrase 'colonial vassalage' had no . . . meaning to convey the slightest idea of what will be our real condition. . . . The present condition of Southern slaves will be a paradise in comparison with what these malignant fanatical marauders have in store for us, if they succeed in their wicked purposes." He urged a general uprising "from one end of the Confederacy to another," and declared the Confederacy to be "the last hope of Freedom and the last hope of a pure Gospel."[4]

The enthusiasm of Dr. Thomas for a "general uprising" soon permeated the entire faculty and student body. "Six students from Oxford College, Ga., arrived at Montgomery . . . on the way to Pensacola to join the Oglethorpe Infantry," the Columbus *Daily Sun* announced on April 19th. A few days later an Emory student described the spirit which dominated the campus:

> There is a great deal of excitement prevailing here. We are expecting the college to close in a few days. President Thomas says if the excitement continues, he will be compelled to disband. One of the Professors is Captain of a Company, and is looking for orders every day to leave for Pensacola or Fort Pulaski. A number of the boys left here last night for Fort Pickens . . . and about 20 leave tonight for Pensacola. A great many of the students are going home. I think by Friday, the College will be broken up entirely; what boys are not going to the wars, are going home.[5]

When the trustees met on July 17th, there was not a quorum present, but the secretary recorded the unofficial suggestions of the group. The faculty had prepared to continue the college, receiving whatever fees came in as their remuneration, and the trustees advised the faculty to give military instruction to students who desired it. The trustees met again in November, and upon finding that most of the students had joined the army, and that the college had no funds, voted to close the college for a year. An unsuccessful attempt was made during the following summer to open a preparatory school in the college buildings, but the Confederacy appropriated the buildings for hospital purposes. The trustees appointed the Reverend W. J. Parks as an official agent to take care of the college interests, but he was unable to prevent much ruthless destruction of property. As President Thomas said after the war, "Troops of the enemy, officers, and attendants of our own hospital, and I am sorry to say, rowdy boys and negroes in and around Oxford were co-sharers in these burglarious and thieving achievements." Not until January, 1866, did old Davie, the college janitor, again ring the bell for classes and three professors begin teaching a small group of twenty students.[6]

Mercer University, a Baptist college at Penfield, kept its classes going throughout the war while every similar institution in the state was closed. The senior class of 1861, consisting of thirty-one

..EDUCATION

members, was the largest one up to that time graduated from the institution. Although the class entered the army almost in a body, the trustees resolved to continue the college for the benefit of students who might be able to remain. When Governor Brown in February, 1862, called for twelve additional regiments, many students volunteered, for they were determined not to be drafted. "All of our class but three . . . who are under age . . . were quite ready to start," a Mercer student told a friend, "when . . . came a notice from the Governor exempting the students . . . from the Draft, and from militia duty . . . and the mighty ebullition of our patriotism suddenly cooled down . . . and now here we are . . . plodding the daily round of college life. . . ." Instead of all students leaving immediately, they left by degrees. "I expect College will suspend after this term," the student wrote, "but cannot say certainly. . . . The Trustees will decide the matter in April. They have already given the Faculty the six months notice necessary before suspension; but they may not suspend at all." A month later he wrote: "I think there is no doubt at all of suspension. . . . Our number has been reduced to twenty, and may dwindle to nothing before long. The Military spirit is again infusing itself into the boys, and we have at last succeeded in resuscitating the cadets, so far as drilling is concerned. . . ."[7]

In the fall of 1863 twelve students entered Mercer, but by the middle of the school year nine of them were in the army. For the remainder of the war only a skeleton of the college organization was preserved, and with the close of the war came temporary confusion and demoralization.[8]

At Midway near Milledgeville was Oglethorpe University, a Presbyterian college. Soon after Georgia seceded, students organized a volunteer corps, called the "University Guards," and were furnished with muskets by the state. Eighteen students received diplomas in 1861, but the attendance steadily declined, and the class of 1862 was the last one to be graduated during the war. From the spring of 1862 until the latter part of the war the college was only nominally kept open. A few students were in attendance in 1863-64, and General Henry R. Jackson was asked in 1863 "to deliver the Oration before the two societies of Oglethorpe College on Commencement Day."[9] Exercises were suspended toward the close of the war because of the small enrollment and the lack of necessary funds. Most of the university's assets were in Confederate securities and were lost.

Between 1836 and 1860 many institutions for the higher education of women had been established in Georgia. The women's colleges usually had evolved from seminaries. Although they retained many characteristics of the seminaries, they constituted a marked advancement in the education of women. The financial stringencies of the war and the absence of men teachers caused many women to adopt teaching as a profession. Partly for this reason, and because the war did not make large inroads in enrollment, the women's colleges fared somewhat better than did the colleges for men.

Wesleyan Female College in Macon remained open during the war except for two or three weeks when General Sherman passed near Macon on his way to the sea, and for two or three days when General Wilson took possession of the city. During the 1861-62 session Wesleyan had "158 students in the literary and 104 in the ornamental department." A newspaper reported in June, 1862, that the college had 158 students, and a year later the same paper stated that "Wesleyan . . . has 223 students in the Literary and 169 in the Ornamental Departments. . . . The faculty was 'comprised of the ablest teachers. . . .' "[10] In 1864 the college had 244 students. Three other Methodist colleges suffered calamity during the war. In 1863 Madison Female College had a curriculum which included courses in music, a literary department, and a preparatory school, but the college was destroyed by fire during the following year. LaGrange Female College was accidentally burned in December, 1863, and Andrew College in Cuthbert was used by the Confederacy for a hospital.

A Baptist college for women, Monroe Female University at Forsyth, maintained a small enrollment until 1865, when the school building became an army hospital. Sherman's march wrote *finis* to two Baptist colleges, Woodland Female College at Cedartown, and the Cherokee Baptist College in Cassville. The Baptist Female College at Cuthbert continued a precarious existence. In 1864 the building was used for a government hospital, and the president used a part of his own dwelling for classes.

Georgia Presbyterians maintained colleges for women at Griffin, Rome, and Greensboro until 1863, when the whole program of female education was temporarily abandoned by the Presbyterian synod. The war was only partly responsible for the failure, for the institutions were involved in financial difficulties before the war began. Griffin Female College was used as a hospital and was acci-

..EDUCATION

dentally burned in 1864, and Rome Female College became a nondenominational institution in 1863. The president of Rome Female College explained to Governor Brown in 1863 some of his difficulties in maintaining the college:

> I have . . . a letter from the Roswell Cotton Factory, in which the Agent declines to send me a few bunches of thread. His reasons were, that they could not now sell by retail without being taxed with *another* clerk, and that you have forbidden the shipment of thread on the State Road. . . .
> I . . . ask of you . . . a permit to ship a bale of thread to this place. I will sell it for what it may cost me, reserving what may be needed for my own family. . . . I have ten persons to clothe, and considerable cloth is needed . . . for the accommodations of Pupils boarding in the college. My wife presides in the school room and cannot attend to spinning. We charge a low price for board and cannot afford to pay the high price asked by the speculators for thread and cloth.[11]

A year later the college ceased operations when the contending armies approached Rome.

Lucy Cobb Institute at Athens, a girls' school named in honor of the daughter of General Thomas R. R. Cobb, continued to enroll students throughout the war. The rates of Lucy Cobb in 1862 for one-half of a scholastic year were "$300 for board, with washing, light, fuel and instruction in English classes, Mathematics, and Scientific Course." Additional fees were charged for "instruction in harp, piano, and guitar, art, modern language, pencil and crayon drawing. . . ."[12]

The training of physicians in the medical colleges of Georgia practically ceased during the war. The financial tension which prevailed just before the outbreak of hostilities reduced the student body and the income of the Atlanta Medical College, and the summer session of 1861 was the last term of the college until 1865. The college was converted into a Confederate hospital. The Medical College of Georgia, located in Augusta, was closed from 1863 until 1866 and used as a hospital.[13] Operation of the Georgia College of Eclectic Medicine and Surgery at Macon was stopped. When Sherman captured Savannah in 1864, work at the Savannah Medical College was suspended until 1866.

In the fall of 1861 a joint committee of the legislature visited the Georgia Academy for the Blind in Macon and "found it located in a spacious and elegant building." The committee reported that the blind pupils "made rapid progress in reading, arithmetic, and other subjects."¹⁴ Two years later, however, the academy was converted into a government hospital; and the former inmates were removed to Fort Valley, where the school was operated until it was brought back to Macon in 1865.

Prior to 1868 there was no organized system of common schools in Georgia supported by public taxation. Efforts had been made in 1845 and again in 1856 to inaugurate a state school system, both of which had been unsuccessful. At Governor Brown's request, the legislature in 1858 set apart $100,000 annually of the net earnings of the Western and Atlantic Railroad for educational purposes and passed an act "to provide for the education of the people of the State between certain ages, and to provide an annual sinking fund for the extinguishment of the public debt." The act allowed the people of any county to establish free schools and to use their share of the funds for this purpose; and in 1860 one county, Forsyth, did establish free schools.¹⁵ The measure contemplated the realization of a fund sufficient to establish free schools throughout the state, an anticipation which probably would have been realized but for the war, which caused the school funds to be largely used up in aiding the families of soldiers.

Educational matters were, therefore, still left largely to the counties and towns, except for a "poor school fund" appropriated by the state to pay the tuition of paupers in private schools. In addition to the poor school fund, a law passed in 1843 by the legislature permitted the county courts to levy a local tax for the education of the poor. Although the legislature did not exercise any compulsion in the matter, eighty-four counties in 1859 did levy and collect a direct tax which was designated as a supplement to their school funds received from the state. Many Georgians felt that it was disgraceful, however, to accept aid from the state or county for educational purposes; and in 1859 only 82,800 white children out of 107,825 between the ages of eight and eighteen were actually in some kind of school. Because of these factors, there were 44,257 persons over twenty years of age in the state in 1860 who could neither read nor write.¹⁶

Despite the lack of a state system of public education, Georgia's schools and academies had advanced rapidly during the 1850's. Public schools increased their total annual income from taxation, public funds, and other sources from $182,231 in 1850 to $449,966 in 1860. At the same time the number of such schools rose from 1,251 to 1,752, the enrollment from 32,705 to 56,087 pupils, and

..EDUCATION

the number of teachers from 1,265 to 1,884. The total attendance at schools of all kinds increased from 77,016 to 94,687 during the decade. Of the 94,687 students in school in 1860, 50,552 were males and 44,128 were females.[17]

By far the greater number of common schools were of elementary grade. As a rule only the larger towns, such as Savannah, Augusta, and Macon, could offer secondary schooling. High school education was supplied only by the private academies and seminaries, by a small number of public high schools, supported by local taxation, and by denominational schools similar to the academies. The number of academies increased during the 1850's from 219 to 242, the number of teachers from 318 to 375, and the attendance from 9,059 to 11,075 pupils. Not only were the academies growing in number, but their total annual income jumped from $108,983 to $237,373 during the decade.[18]

The fate of the public schools and academies during the war varied according to circumstances. Most of the public and private schools in Savannah remained open, and the city retained many strong teachers. Both the male and female departments of the Chatham Academy in Savannah were kept in operation. The Academy of Saint Vincent de Paul, conducted in Savannah by the Sisters of Our Lady of Mercy, was still conducting classes in 1864. In the latter part of that year a "French and English Boarding and Day School for Young Ladies" in Savannah was advertising for students. The Academy of Richmond County, in Augusta, remained open until late in the war, and the Augusta Select Academy for Boys and Girls continued to offer "a thorough English and classical education." The Collegiate Institute at Athens prospered, and many sons of refugees from Charleston, Savannah, and Augusta were sent there. An Americus paper in 1862 announced that "Dr. Randall has had as many as seventy-four pupils . . . during the current term. He is instructing a number of children of soldiers. . . ."[19] A report issued by the superintendent of a school established in Columbus by the Eagle Factory showed that 190 boys and 168 girls were attending the school in June, 1864. The Columbus Free School also continued to function.

Many new schools, most of which were privately owned, were started. An Americus teacher announced in 1862 that "At the solicitation of my friends, I will open a school for Boys and Girls at the Red Store . . . where . . . a good plain English education will be taught. . . ."[20] In Columbus, Miss Julia C. Jewett opened a school for boys and girls at the Wynnton Male Academy. One of the most successful schools, however, that was established during the war was a boarding school conducted by Richard Malcolm Johnston on his plantation near Sparta. Johnston resigned his position at the University of Georgia in 1861 and the following year opened a select school for boys in Hancock County. "Rockby," as the school was called, was conducted upon an honor system, rather than upon the "espionage" system then prevailing in most schools. In a letter to Vice-President Stephens, Johnston explained his plans:

We have been at work day and night to get ready for our boys. . . . I expect them in two or three days. There will be twenty of them, and we shall have our hands full of work. . . . I am going to try to keep a school in which there is no humbug. It is entirely a new undertaking and I have my fears that my little public wont like it. But if I succeed, I should be tempted to praise myself. I have received about Sixty applications, and this embarrasses me somewhat, because it is an evidence that I am expected to do my work right. I have had a good house built and a neat schoolroom. . . . I intended to spend about twenty-five hundred dollars. I have already spent four thousand, including board of workmen. But my buildings are good, and put up with some regard to·taste.[21]

Johnston's school became widely known for its thoroughness and high moral tone. Although the cost of attendance, five hundred dollars, was comparatively high, the enrollment was more than fifty. At the close of the war Johnston saw his estate swept away, and he moved to Baltimore.

Many other schools and academies, however, were forced to close because of financial difficulties, scarcity of students, and the invading armies. The Georgia Military Institute at Marietta suspended operations in 1864 when the cadets were placed in active service, and the Hearn Institute, near Rome, closed in 1863 because of the proximity of military operations. The dearth of teachers and the incompetency of those available were also major factors in causing many schools to close and the education of children to suffer. Secondary education in ante-bellum Georgia had been largely in the hands of "Puritan" schoolmasters and schoolmarms from the North, but during the war many Georgia schools would not employ native Northerners to teach. For instance, a Savannah paper announced that "The Rev. Mr. Pryse has expressed a determination not to employ teachers from North of Mason & Dixon's

..EDUCATION

line, and we commend him for it." The same paper advertised: "Teachers wanted to fill vacancies in Huntington Hall, Savannah, Ga. All must be natives of the South, or some European country, and at Peace with the Southern Confederacy."[22]

Newspapers printed numerous notices of teaching vacancies. "Teacher wanted, for the Union Society Orphan Institution at Bethesda, ten miles from Savannah," one advertisement read. "A single man preferred, and one capable of giving instruction in Vocal Music." Another notice in the same paper said that "A male or female teacher, who is willing to take charge of a small School in Bryan County . . . at a fair salary, can hear of an opportunity for employment by application to the Editor of the *Republican*."[23]

On the other hand, many men and women found teaching to be an attractive, if not lucrative, means of eking out a livelihood during the troublous times. A LaGrange paper announced that "Prof. R. S. Proppen, having been discharged from the army . . . is now engaged in the Southern Female College, and will give Private Lessons in Music, at the residences of his Pupils. He will also give instruction in the French Language."[24] "A young gentleman, a Southerner by birth and education, wishes to obtain a School . . . ," another teacher advertised. A woman in Americus published that she would reopen her school and would seek to support her family by teaching while her husband was in the army. A man informed Vice-President Stephens that he found teaching a rather satisfactory employment during the war:

> I have just returned from Crawfordville to Jefferson to take charge of the School again. . . . I know of no other employment . . . that would pay me as well as teaching, notwithstanding, it does not pay very much at this state of affairs, but find the . . . school room more pleasant than I thought for, and also equivalent to any years Schooling, I concluded to try it again. . . . My salary above board last year, was $375.00, but I have succeeded in getting in but very little of that amount.[25]

With many men teachers serving in the army and with school boards reluctant to employ teachers of Northern birth or sentiments, the burden of teaching fell largely upon inexperienced and frequently incompetent men and women. When the Confederate Congress in September, 1862, exempted from military service all teachers engaged in teaching twenty or more pupils, a Georgia newspaper remarked that men were becoming teachers who were not qualified to teach. Often the teachers knew little more about the subjects they were teaching than did their pupils. When a girl asked her teacher to explain algebraic equations, the teacher, not understanding how to work the problems, told her, "Get your bonnet . . . and go out in the shade and work it out yourself . . . it will do you more good."[26] A mother noted in her diary, "Heard Anna her lessons *thoroughly*, we are at Eng. and French Grammar. I hope to get her well 'grounded' before she begins school again, as the teachers are so careless."[27] In order to make teaching a more attractive occupation, the legislature in December, 1863, enacted a measure which granted to county boards of education the right "to increase the per diem pay of school teachers entitled to the benefit of the poor school fund of this State."[28]

All levels of education, from the elementary grades to the colleges, survived the war only with tremendous difficulty. School attendance was irregular, for parents frequently kept their children at home to help with necessary duties. The teachers were confronted with a multitude of problems; and if a teacher resigned, a school might be suspended indefinitely. A teacher in a girls' school at Forsyth recorded in her diary a few of the troubles that beset her:

> Quite a small opening, owing to the War and Lincoln blockade.... A slight change in the programe [sic]. Have a class sit in my room all the time.... Have as much to do in the school room as I can possibly do. Never was busier. Paucity of pupils do not lighten my duties.... Had to hear a lesson for Mr. Wilkes.... It seems Mr. Wilkes thinks I am made of India rubber, can stretch to any number of duties.[29]

Another woman wrote that "Mr. Schringers School is quite thin. Miss Hansun has taken her children from School. No one knows why."[30] A soldier wrote to his son, "I am sorry to hear that the school is broken up as well as Mrs. Willis death. I hope, however, Mr. Willis will commence his school again as I dont want Mollie to lose a day from school and I fear we shall never get another teacher as Mr. Willis."[31] Near the close of the war an Athens teacher said: "My school has opened with *14 babies* for which I ought to be thankful considering the intense cold weather.... I trust that as spring approaches the no. may increase, for with . . . corn at 20 or 25 per bushel and flour at $2 per lb., that number would afford a scanty subsistence."[32]

Some teachers, even when offered more attractive positions elsewhere, conscientiously remained in schools that paid meager salaries. An example of such a case is disclosed in the following letter, written by a teacher at Sylvan Home, Georgia, in reply

..EDUCATION

to an invitation from her uncle and aunt to teach in Eatonton:

> I had so much rather teach such a school as you offer, than the one which I will have here, which I know will be small. But it is getting late, and I have said that I would commence on Monday. I know that it would be to my interest to go. I would not only make more, but also have the advantages of society. . . . Were it not for Polkie and Jennie I would leave this school. . . . They . . . have both lost time from school. . . . It will not do for them to stay at home this year and it is too far for them to go to town. If I thought that we could get a teacher here I would not hesitate a moment. But I do not think that it would be right for me to sacrifice their good to my interest.[33]

Besides all the other multifarious difficulties of education during the war, Georgia was confronted with the problem of securing textbooks. A Columbus paper in August, 1861, said that since textbooks had "been obtained heretofore from the North . . . it behooves us to be making some provision to supply our schools with books. . . . Never again shall the children of the South receive instruction from Northern teachers and Northern books."[34] Early in the war Georgia newspapers published numerous advertisements of school books for sale at book stores, but such notices became less and less frequent after 1863, when the supplies of books became almost exhausted. In an attempt to supply the needed books, several Georgia publishers printed textbooks. Burke, Boykin and Company of Macon led all other Georgia publishers in the number of textbooks issued — publishing spellers, readers, grammars, and primers. J. J. Toon and Company of Atlanta in 1863 published *The Revised Elementary Spelling Book* by the Rev. Robert Fleming of Thomasville, Georgia; and in 1865 the same company issued *Browne's Arithmetical Tables*. A new descriptive geography, compiled by John H. Rice, was published in Atlanta in 1862, and *The Southern Confederacy Arithmetic* was published at Augusta in 1864.[35]

In spite of these publications, a textbook deficiency continued. A report issued in 1864 by the superintendent of the Columbus Free School said, "We labor under some disadvantage in not having suitable text books — such as mental Arithmetics and Primary Geography; otherwise we are well and cheaply supplied."[36] Although some of Georgia's textbook requirements were filled by publishing firms in Nashville and other out-of-state cities, a serious shortage of books existed during the latter half of the war.

Clearly indicated in the correspondence of soldiers with their families is the deep concern of Georgians that their children should secure as adequate an education as was possible during the war. "I am glad that you are sending the children to school," a soldier wrote to his wife. "I want to know how they are getting on, if they learn fast. I would be glad if you could spare Marcus if you would send him to school some."[37] Another soldier in writing to his wife expressed a determination to educate their son:

> I have always known that he [his son, John Thomas Stillwell] was smart and I tell you now Tom will fill a page in the history of the world yet and I want to live to educate him. I will work all night to do it. . . . Always teach him that an education is worth more than fortune. . . . I don't say what he shall follow for he ought to choose that himself but give him an education and he is ready for anything and be sure to give him for his first book the bible and for his second the life of Jo Brown and if he never sees any others these two are enough.[38]

Writing to his son, a soldier said, "You must study at home until school commences. Don't idle away a day, when you are not seeing to the affairs and business about home take your book and be studying."[39] To his three children he wrote, "Molley must study hard and learn to write . . . and David must be particular in his spelling, he must take a dictionary by him when he goes to write and see that he spell evry [sic] word correctly. He improves in his hand writing. . . ."[40] A wife in Meriwether County wrote to her soldier-husband: "You . . . wanted to know how much the children had learned, they are getting along tolerable well. Henrietta is reading, writing and studying geography, and dictionary, Buddy can spell in three syllables very well. . . ."[41]

A young north Georgia girl explained her school activities to her father:

> Your letter to Bud, Mattie and myself have been received. . . . We are going to school yet and I will go all the year if you wish me to but I dont have much to do when I go only of weeks when we have to write compositions. Then I help some of my friends . . . write their compositions. I write my own in a copy book which I will show you when you come home. Mattie is very smart at school but dreadful lazy at home. She can beat Bud reading and her spelling class is composed of about 15 little urchins all older than herself and she stands head of them nearly all the time.

A year later she wrote, "I go to school but do not like to one bit.

..EDUCATION

I do not like Mr. Mitchell and will quit school when this quarter is out if you will let me."[42]

The problem of educating the orphans of the war began to be considered by Georgians in 1863. In that year the Georgia Baptist Convention appointed a committee to request the legislature to enact a measure for the education of the orphans of soldiers. The committee memorialized the legislature;[43] but, as the memorial effected no result, the Baptists in 1864 requested the committee to renew its petition to the legislature. The legislature failed, however, to pass the desired act; and in May, 1864, Georgia Baptists began planning to establish their own orphanage. The burden of educating orphans and the children of needy soldiers remained primarily a private enterprise. For example, the LeVert Female College at Talbotton announced in March, 1865, that it would educate free of charge five daughters of indigent soldiers,[44] and Enoch Steadman, a wealthy textile manufacturer, made large contributions to educate orphans.

At historic Bethesda, ten miles from Savannah, the Union Society maintained an orphanage for boys. The war caused the orphanage to be moved in 1863 to Bethany, a town in Jefferson County, where a small group of orphans continued to be educated. Near the end of the war the legislature authorized Governor Brown to allocate thirty thousand dollars to help support the orphans of the Union Society.[45]

CHAPTER XV

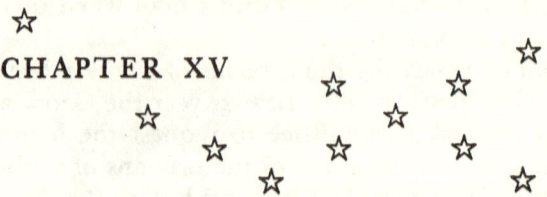

The Churches During the War

BAPTISTS AND METHODISTS DOMINATED the religious life of Georgia during the war. These two denominations had far more churches than all of the other sects combined, and approximately nine out of every ten church members were either Baptists or Methodists. Third in number of churches was the Presbyterian, followed in order by the Union,[1] Episcopal, Christian, Lutheran, and Catholic churches. Except for the Lutheran church, the decade before the war had witnessed a rapid growth both in membership and in church property valuation among all of the major denominations. The number of Baptist churches had increased from 879 to 1,141, the Methodist from 795 to 1,035, the Presbyterian from ninety-seven to 129, and the Episcopal from twenty to twenty-five. With property valued at $796,138, the Methodists continued to lead in the valuation of their churches, followed by the Baptists and the Presbyterians, with property valued at $787,198 and $445,005, respectively.[2]

As shepherds of the flock, the clergymen generally were recognized for their moral and intellectual leadership; and when war clouds appeared upon the horizon in 1860, people naturally looked to their ministers for political, as well as for spiritual, guidance. Many clergymen opposed secession. Bishop George F. Pierce, of the Methodist church, was a "Union man" and had voted for Bell and Everett in 1860. He dreaded the results of secession, but when the crisis came, he took his place with his people as an advocate of state independence. Another Methodist minister, George G. Smith, had no love for secession, but he said that "When it became evident that . . . the States in the North were determined to destroy slavery . . . I saw no hope of escape from absolute ruin but withdrawal from the Union."[3] A Presbyterian minister, Nathaniel A. Pratt of Roswell, believed that secession and war would jeopard-

THE CHURCHES DURING THE WAR

ize the security of the people of Georgia. A former Presbyterian pastor, Charles Wallace Howard, opposed secession but served as a captain in a Georgia regiment. Dr. Alexander Means, a Methodist minister and teacher, had opposed immediate secession, but he voted in the secession convention with the majority. The rector of Saint John's Episcopal Church in Savannah declared that his heart trembled when he contemplated a dissolution of the Union, but that if no other remedy of the nation's problems could be found, "we will sing the requiem of these United States."[4]

Other members of the clergy, however, were leaders in promoting secession. Preaching to his congregation on Sunday, December 9, 1860, the Reverend R. K. Porter, pastor of the Waynesboro Presbyterian Church, referred to the Union as a voluntary agreement, and asserted that "If the compact fail of its ends it is potentially dead."[5] Several days prior to the secession of Georgia, Stephen Elliott, the bishop of the Episcopal Diocese of Georgia, instructed the Episcopal clergymen that in the event of secession they should omit from their prayer the words "President of the United States" and substitute the words, "thy Servant, the Governor of the State of Georgia."[6]

The secession of Georgia found the clergy, in general, not only co-operative but also frequently preaching militaristic sermons, some of which were published by the newspapers or circulated in pamphlet form as propaganda. The letter of the Reverend James R. Thomas, President of Emory College, urging a general uprising against "malignant fanatical marauders," has already been cited.[7] Bishop Stephen Elliott constantly used his pulpit in Christ Church, Savannah, for the purpose of delivering sermons in support of the Confederate cause. At the close of a militant sermon to the "Pulaski Guards" on June 9, 1861, Bishop Elliott said: "And now, soldiers, I send you forth with the Church's benediction. . . . Your cause is just. . . . Who can doubt the issue if you will but keep the Lord on your side?"[8] On the following Thursday, a day appointed by President Davis for "humiliation, fasting, and prayer," Elliott again preached in Christ Church and declared that the South was engaged "in one of the grandest struggles which ever nerved the hearts . . . of a heroic race."[9] While Bishop Elliott was uttering these words of exhortation, Bishop George F. Pierce was urging the people of Sparta to subscribe to the Confederate produce loan. Pierce saw in the anti-slavery movement the overthrow of the South's civilization and the demoralization of the Negro. In a sermon delivered to the "Rome Light Guards," a Presbyterian minister, the Reverend J. Jones of Rome, asserted: "You are engaged in a holy war! If the rescue of the holy sepulchre from the infidel Moslem, induced three millions of men to lay their bones in the East, shall we not willingly contend to snatch the word of God from the modern infidel. . . ?"[10]

When state conventions and conferences were held by the churches to decide their future policy, they invariably endorsed the Confederacy. The Georgia Baptist Convention assembled at Athens on April 27, 1861, and avowed that Georgia Baptists would "not be behind any class of our fellow citizens in maintaining the independence of the South. . . ."[11] Approximately one-half of the delegates to the Southern Baptist Convention, meeting in Savannah in May, were Georgians; and the convention unanimously pledged its entire confidence in the Confederate government. The Cherokee Baptist Convention, representing Baptist churches north of the Chattahoochee River, met at Calhoun and adopted the opinions of the Southern and Georgia Baptist conventions.

When the Methodist Conference of Georgia met at Atlanta in December, 1861, it adopted a resolution of gratitude to God for the "brilliant victories we have achieved by our arms," and resolved that "there is no such thing as a Union party among us. . . ."[12] A year later the Methodist Conference, which was held at Macon, adopted resolutions of confidence in the Confederate government and condemned "the character of our invaders and their unprincipled modes of warfare."[13]

The Presbyterian church in Georgia was also loyal to the Confederacy. Twenty delegates from eleven Presbyteries throughout the South met in Atlanta on August 15, 1861, and adopted a resolution urging all Presbyteries in the Confederacy "to send commissioners to a General Assembly to be held in Augusta on December 4." The Presbytery of Georgia, meeting in Darien in November, 1861, unanimously adopted a resolution "That the Presbytery of Georgia does now dissolve all connection with . . . the General Assembly of the Old School Presbyterian Church of the United States. . . ."[14] When the Presbyterian Synod of Georgia held its annual meeting at Marietta in November, the following report of the "Committee on the Minutes of the General Assembly and State of the Church," made through its chairman, the Reverend James Woodrow, was unanimously adopted:

THE CHURCHES DURING THE WAR

From authentic, though unofficial sources, we have learned enough of the measures of the General Assembly [of the Presbyterian Church of the United States] to show us that we can never have any further interest in what it may do hereafter, except as we may be interested in any other branch of the Presbyterian Church in any other foreign country, and with which we have no ecclesiastical connection. . . .

We hail with delight the prospect of the early organization of a General Assembly of the Presbyterian Church in the Confederate States....[15]

Acting in accordance with these and similar resolutions, delegates from ten Presbyterian synods from Virginia to Texas assembled in Augusta on December 4, 1861, and organized the Presbyterian Church in the Confederate States.[16] The assembly adopted a resolution in vindication of its withdrawal from the Presbyterian Church of the United States and declared that "the existence or non-existence of slavery is a question which exclusively belongs to the State."[17]

No less active in supporting the Confederate cause and in advocating the organization of independent Southern churches were the Episcopalians and the Lutherans of Georgia. In a letter to the Episcopal clergy of Georgia, Bishop Elliott in August, 1861, enclosed a program for the reorganization of the Episcopal church and urged preparations to defend the state from possible invasion. Ranking first in seniority among the Episcopal bishops of the South, Bishop Elliott in the following year summoned a general council of the Southern Episcopalians to meet in Augusta. The council assembled in November, 1862, and enacted a body of canon laws for the administration of the Protestant Episcopal Church in the Confederate States.[18] Georgia Lutherans favored the separation of the Lutheran church in the South from the Northern church; and Lutherans from Georgia were among the delegates who convened in Concord, North Carolina, in May, 1863, and organized the "General Synod of the Evangelical Lutheran Church in the Confederate States." The Lutheran congregations in Georgia loyally supported the Confederacy, and at many of the Lutheran services collections of money were made for the benefit of the Confederate government.

The Roman Catholics of Georgia heartily supported the war without adopting resolutions or establishing a new ecclesiastical organization. A notice of masses at the Catholic Church of Saint John the Baptist in Savannah requested that "all members attend and offer their fervent prayers for . . . the Southern Confederacy in repelling the aggressive invasion of Northern barbarians."[19] A sum of money was sent by this church to Secretary of the Treasury C. G. Memminger for "the sustenance of our Confederate army." Following Confederate victories in 1862, Catholic churches in Georgia sang or read the hymn of thanksgiving, "Te Deum," in solemn thanks to God.

Throughout the state congregations were organized to collect and distribute food, clothing, and medicine for the soldiers. For instance, Bishop Elliott, explaining that military preparations were imperative, sent instructions in August, 1861, to all clergymen within his diocese:

Each Parish to organize under its Rector, and some gentleman who will act as treasurer and secretary. . . .

The purpose . . . shall be to prepare . . . clothing . . . medicines and nourishment . . . and . . . hospital attention when sick or wounded, if the troops [are] from . . . Georgia.

Each Rector to exhort every person in his Parish to do what he can towards this prospective fund by contributions in . . . clothing, in blankets, provisions, medicines, money. . . .

Each Parish to report monthly to the Bishop . . . the condition of the Parish, the articles and funds collected, distributed, and on hand. . . .[20]

Although the clergy was exempted from conscription, many ministers believed it their patriotic duty to volunteer. A company of troops was organized in Talbot County with a Baptist minister as captain. A Methodist minister who was a veteran of the Mexican War resigned from his circuit and organized a company of troops. "Rev. F. McMurray, Pastor of the Presbyterian Church, Union Springs, has been chosen Captain of a new military company . . . and will soon be in active service," announced a Columbus paper.[21] The Reverend C. P. B. Martin of Montpelier notified Governor Brown that if the Governor would make him a brigadier-general, he could raise a regiment.[22] Among the casualties at the First Battle of Manassas was a Methodist preacher from Meriwether, who, when the war began, raised a company in his native county, composed of his friends and "brethren." Another Methodist minister, Samuel E. Randolph of Valdosta, volunteered in 1861 and died in military service before the year ended.

Instead of becoming soldiers, however, a majority of the clergy served as chaplains, hospital commissioners, and agents of organizations for distributing Bibles, religious tracts, and supplies to the soldiers.[23] A young Methodist minister at Cedartown was "restless

THE CHURCHES DURING THE WAR

and anxious to go to the army," and when he was offered the position of chaplain of "Phillips Legion," he accepted it.[24] By 1863 there was more than a score of Methodist chaplains in the army; and when the Georgia Methodist Conference held its annual meeting at Columbus in November, 1863, it voted in favor of a resolution "That the Board of Managers of the Missionary Society of this Conference . . . appropriate all the funds remaining in hand . . . to the support of Missionaries to the Army, to the number of one for each Brigade composed . . . of Ga. troops, and that further Collections be taken . . . by all the preachers for the same purpose."[25] Before the war ended, Georgia Methodists had furnished twenty-three chaplains and fourteen preachers serving in the capacity of soldiers or officers. A Baptist minister, J. H. Campbell of Griffin, writing to Alexander H. Stephens that two Georgia regiments had applied to the War Department for the appointment of his son as their chaplain, requested Stephens to secure for the son a military commission.[26] Exact records for the Baptist church are not available, but hundreds of Baptists attended the armies of the Confederacy and labored as missionaries, evangelists, or chaplains. The Episcopalians furnished eight chaplains in addition to a few men who served irregularly. Other denominations were no less active, particularly the Roman Catholics, whose Sisters of Charity nursed many sick and wounded soldiers. A Catholic priest, Father Peter Whelan, was in Fort Pulaski during the siege by Federal forces in 1862, and by his calmness and cheering words encouraged the members of the garrison during the ordeal.

Ministers were inevitably chosen to administer many benevolent enterprises. Some of them delivered addresses in behalf of "Wayside homes." Charles Wallace Howard was notably active in appealing to the public for funds for the homes. A Forsyth minister served as an agent for a Savannah hospital, and a Marietta clergyman went to Augusta to solicit donations of articles needed in the hospitals. George G. Smith's first duty as chaplain was to solicit supplies in north Georgia for the sick soldiers. A Baptist minister at Fort Gaines went to Marietta in 1864 to serve in a Confederate hospital and to convey supplies from a soldiers' aid society. Another minister was agent for the Baptist Orphans' Association and secured donations of money and land valued at $150,000 in inflated Confederate currency.

Even politics called upon the clergy for aid. The prominent Methodist minister, Alexander Means, who formerly had been president of Emory College, was urged by friends to present his name as a candidate for Congress. He said that he declined the offer "from prudential motives, the chief consideration being an unwillingness to take a position which would subject my ministerial character to imputations. . . . There would scarcely have been ground for a doubt of success, had I consented."[27]

Military leaders realized the value of the clergy in sustaining morale and in inspiring the soldiers to a greater patriotism. One Methodist minister reported that the "camp rang with old Methodist songs, and revival fires burned with the camp fires of the soldiers."[28] The chaplain of a Georgia regiment stationed near Savannah wrote to the editor of the *Southern Christian Advocate* concerning religious activities among the troops:

> We had a series of religious meetings of nights last week. . . . The good Lord blessed us greatly. . . . Brother L. R. Redding of the Georgia Conference, Capt. of the Bartow Guards, preached from the text, "Who is on the Lord's side?" Ex. xxxii, 26. In response to the startling question of the text, nearly one third of a large congregation embracing many officers, came forward, acknowledging their allegiance to the Lord. . . . We carry our place of worship with us, — a large canvass tent. . . . We are occupying an advanced post in full view of . . . the enemy's vessels in Warsaw Sound, trusting in the Lord to deliver us from their evil intentions.[29]

During the winter and spring of 1864 a revival lasted for four months among the soldiers at Dalton. They organized Bible classes and built log cabins in which to conduct their services.

Thousands of religious tracts, filled with reading material adapted to the soldiers, were published at Macon by the Soldiers' Tract Association. The Association was a joint enterprise of the major denominations in Georgia and distributed religious literature among the soldiers. Money for publishing the tracts came from voluntary donations, and the various denominations collected and distributed the funds. The Methodist church, for instance, collected $24,782 in 1863. A Baptist minister, J. W. Burke, was the Association's treasurer. The churches also took an active part in the Confederate States Bible Society, the purpose of which was to supply the soldiers with Bibles. When the Bible Society was organized at a convention held in Augusta in March, 1862, Bishop George F. Pierce delivered a sermon to the delegates. In addition to their contributions to the Soldiers' Tract Association, the churches made donations to the Bible Society. Because of the diffi-

THE CHURCHES DURING THE WAR

culty of having Bibles printed, many Bibles were imported from England. Bishop Elliott in January, 1863, said that the "British and Foreign Bible Society . . . has . . . generously placed a large amount of Bibles at the disposal of parties in the Confederate States, who are taking means to have them introduced thro' the blockade."[30] Besides providing the soldiers with tracts and Bibles, the Methodists and Baptists issued periodicals for the soldiers. At Macon the Methodists published a semi-monthly paper entitled the *Army and Navy Herald,* and the Baptists published in Atlanta a paper called the *Soldier's Friend.* These periodicals were designed specifically for camp readers and were devoted largely to reading material that created an abhorrence of evils most common to army life and inspired the soldiers to Christian living.

The Episcopal church experienced difficulty in securing prayer books for the soldiers. When the General Council met at Augusta in November, 1862, a committee was appointed to consider the subject of publishing a new prayer book; but in the meantime, Bishop Elliott placed an order with R. I. Maynard, an Atlanta publisher, for five thousand copies of a collection of services and prayers, to be called the "Mission Service."[31] He told another clergyman that "the 'Mission Service' contains much more . . . than is contained in the N. York publication and . . . will contain all that will be needed in Camps, Navies, Hospitals, besides being a substitute for the Book of Common Prayer until we can see our way clear to the publication of a perfect edition."[32] Upon receiving a copy of the "Mission Service," however, Bishop Elliott was "deeply mortified at its appearance." He wrote Maynard that the book was "not according to contract," that the quality of paper used was the "commonest newspaper trash," and that the publisher had "made the cover of a Prayer Book a vehicle for the advertisements of a Firm." He instructed Maynard to suppress "that cover in all the copies not yet issued" and to use a plain note cover instead.[33]

Families of soldiers were usually anxious that the men not neglect their spiritual life. In the knapsack of many a volunteer a Bible, donated by a mother, wife, or sweetheart, was tucked away. A mother wrote to her soldier-son, "My desire is, that you will be able to resist temptation, that you will be rigidly Temperate . . . and . . . live a Christian life. . . ."[34]

The first two years of the war were a period of spiritual growth and of increased religious activities in the churches. A Methodist minister in Forsyth urged Christians to be more united, and in the same community a Cherokee Indian preacher endeavored "to stir up the hearts of Christians in behalf of Indian missions."[35] An Atlanta pastor in June, 1862, delivered to large audiences a series of lectures upon such subjects as "The Theatre, its Moral Influence." Religious services for the prisoners at the Milledgeville penitentiary were held on Sunday afternoons. A Waynesville minister asked Alexander H. Stephens if he or President Davis would "write me or the children through me a few thoughts on the Sunday School." He said that he wanted "to use every inducement to get the uprising generation interested in the Sabbath School cause."[36] In March, 1863, a new Catholic church was dedicated in Savannah. As for the Episcopalians, it was stated that wherever Bishop Elliott went, he was "received into communities where the Church is hardly known, with open arms . . . children and adults baptized, and numbers confirmed."[37]

Revivals, prayer meetings, and special services were frequent in the evangelical churches. The Baptist, Methodist, Presbyterian, and Lutheran churches of Savannah in February, 1862, held a union service to supplicate the protection of God upon the Confederacy. An Americus paper announced that a "meeting has been progressing for several days past at the Baptist Church in this city. Much interest is manifested. . . ."[38] "They are having a great revival there [in Macon]," Colonel Aaron Wilbur wrote in August, 1862.[39] At Augusta the mayor ordered that the fire alarm bell be tolled at one o'clock each day to remind the people to unite for prayer. Union prayer meetings were held in the Methodist and Baptist churches of Columbus. In fact, these two denominations vied with each other in holding religious revivals.[40]

Large numbers of the people observed the numerous fast days ordered by the Confederate government and concurred in by the Georgia legislature. "Several of the Baptist churches of this county have agreed to observe the first Sabbath in March next as a day of fasting, humiliation, and prayer," a Sandersville paper stated in February, 1862.[41] "We have seldom seen Fast Day observed more universally by this community than on Friday last," the same paper said in April, 1863.[42] A few individuals, however, objected to keeping the fast. "Julia and Mary and I went to Hard Rock last Sunday to hear them talk about fasting as some of them do not believe in it," a Marietta man wrote to his brother.[43] William L. Beebe, the editor of the Atlanta *Southern Confederacy*, was opposed to "any

THE CHURCHES DURING THE WAR

President, Governor, or other public officer" requesting days of fasting and prayer. He said that "if by fasting or other self-denial people hoped to win divine favor, they thereby were denying the all-sufficiency of the blood of Jesus Christ."[44]

As the war progressed, the departure of clergymen and laymen for the army, and the approach of the invading forces, caused many religious activities to be disrupted. The fact that candidates for the ministry were not exempt from military service made it difficult to replenish the supply of clergymen. This condition is reflected in the decrease in the number of ministers entering the Methodist church. In 1858 twenty-seven were admitted; in 1861, ten; in 1862, six; in 1863, six. The 1864 conference did not meet until January, 1865, and at that session only three preachers were admitted. "We have no preaching here now. Don't know when we will have any," a man wrote in June, 1862.[45] "We have rather a dull prospect for meetings this year as our singers are all gone, or at least our leaders," a woman wrote in 1863.[46] The Evangelical Lutheran Church in Savannah was closed for some time on account of having no minister. Attendance at church services dwindled because of the absence of men and because of the difficulties of travel.

Yearly and quarterly conventions and conferences were held with difficulty, if at all. As early as 1861, Bishop Pierce, in writing to another bishop, remarked that the conferences were difficult for ministers to attend:

> The war has cut me off from all my Conferences. Bishop K has written to me requesting me to hold the Miss. and Louisiana Conferences for him. I am willing to do so but would prefer a different arrangement, as follows. Would it suit you for me to hold Ga. and Florida and turn over Miss. and La. to you? This I think would be a convenient arrangement for both of us. . . . Money is scarce and I would like to avoid expense. . . .
>
> Some of the Ga. Preachers have written to me — desiring to change the Conference from Sav to Atlanta. Hard time, expense of travel, yellow fever the reasons assigned.[47]

When a state Bible convention met in Athens in October, 1862, delegates from distant portions of Georgia were unable to attend. Quarterly meetings of the Dahlonega Station Methodist Conference were suspended from October, 1863, to June, 1866. The Georgia Baptist Convention was held annually except in 1865, when Columbus, the city in which their session was scheduled to be held, fell into the hands of the enemy. In 1864 the Methodists were forced to postpone their state conference until January, 1865.

The clergy continued, however, to offer sermons in behalf of the Confederacy and to encourage the public morale. The Reverend H. A. Tupper in September, 1862, told a congregation in Washington, Georgia, that "this struggle only makes us rejoice . . . that we have escaped from an unnatural and destructive union."[48] In a sermon to the Georgia legislature on March 27, 1863, Bishop Pierce said: "This war is not of our seeking. . . . Our propositions for amicable adjustment were rejected with subtlety and guile. We are fighting for liberty and home and family. . . ."[49] In the summer of 1864 Bishop Elliott delivered a sermon at Macon in behalf of the Confederate cause.

The religious press also persisted in its propaganda. A Baptist periodical, the *Child's Index,* in an article entitled the "Landing of the Pilgrims," said that from the Pilgrims of 1620 had "descended the Yankee nation, which is now trying to deprive us not only of our religious liberty, but of every kind of liberty." The account said further:

They refuse to let us have Bibles. . . . They drag our preachers from our pulpits, and send them to prison.

They deprive us of our churches, and burn them or use them as stables or store-houses. They send preachers of their own to preach wherever they have taken . . . our towns, and if they conquer us they will take away all our churches . . . and not even let us pray in our families as we wish. . . . They are blinded by fanaticism and infidelity.[50]

Despite revivals and other religious activities, many Georgians seemed to suffer a spiritual relapse. When the Presbyterian Synod met in Macon in November, 1862, a report of the church stated that ". . . many of our people and churches are allowing the trials and troubles of our country to engross all their feelings, resources and energies, to the neglect of the salvation of the soul, and the building up of God's kingdom in the World. The tendency of this neglect must be to aggravate and prolong our calamities."[51]

The Columbus *Times* announced that when the young men and women of Columbus attended church, they indulged in conversation, smoked pipes or cigars, chewed tobacco, and even expectorated on the carpets and steps. "This bloody war and the languid state of the Church fills my heart with double cares, and also with double fears," a Methodist minister stated.[52] "When I came into the pulpit and for years after," an eccentric old pastor declared, "religion used to be the principal topic preached upon; now, it is

..THE CHURCHES DURING THE WAR

all rum and niggers!"⁵³ Another minister complained that "the Sabbath was utterly disregarded" and that "trains were run on the Sabbath with the plea of necessity."⁵⁴ "I care nothing myself about going to church," declared Linton Stephens. "Very much out with church people generally. It would trouble me to count fifty church people who have my confidence in their sincerity. They are a vast crowd of hypocrites, whited sepulchers full of dead men's bones."⁵⁵ Near the end of the war the Savannah *Republican* stated, "Most people are a little shy of religion. They give it a day entirely to itself, and make it a stranger to the other six."⁵⁶

As Georgia became one of the principal areas of military and naval operations, church services were frequently interfered with. Federal naval operations in 1861 and 1862 caused many of the churches located near the coast to be abandoned. Some of the churches in the path of Sherman's army were destroyed or occupied by the Federals for military purposes, and many churches were used as hospitals by the Confederates. In 1863 all of the churches in Ringgold and Newnan were used as hospitals, and the Methodist church at Oxford was used as a hospital from 1862 through 1864.⁵⁷ The proximity of the enemy also prevented many services from being held. "No church, our preacher's horse stolen by the Yankees," a woman wrote at the time of Sherman's raid.⁵⁸

The work of the chaplains was also seriously impaired. A medical director near Marietta sent the following message to an Episcopal chaplain, John W. Beckwith: "I think . . . that you can do most good by remaining in Atlanta and ministering to the sick and wounded sent to the rear. You would find but few very sick and few wounded in the field hospitals here. They are sent as fast as practicable to the rear."⁵⁹ Writing from his post at Atlanta, the Reverend Beckwith explained to his wife the situation:

> I have asked Hardee for a candid opinion as to the ability of a Missionary to do work in the Army while this Campaign is going on, and he tells me it is simply impossible. . . . He says that if the men were brought together for service it wd. at once attract the attention of the enemy who wd. open fire upon us . . . and cause a useless sacrifice of life. He therefore advises me to confine my operations to the Hospitals, for nothing can be done here outside of his Staff. . . .
>
> I had an interesting service this morning: the Gen. and Staff were around me and joined me in the services. I did not preach, and the service was short, for fear of interruption, no man being able to tell what half hour may bring forth.⁶⁰

Upon occupying Georgia towns, Federal commanders frequently ordered all ministers to take an oath of allegiance to the United States government as a condition for allowing church services to be held. A Union captain at Madison issued such an order, but S. P. Richardson, the Methodist minister, hesitated to take the oath, although he was advised by his friends to do so. Finally, he did offer supplications to the Almighty. "I prayed for the President," he said, "that the Lord would take out of him and his allies the hearts of beasts, and put in them the hearts of men, or remove the curses from office. The little captain never asked me any more to pray for the President of the United States."[61] While Sherman was in Savannah, a Presbyterian minister, S. Edward Axson,[62] omitted the prayer for the President and passed directly on from the preceding prayer to the litany without pausing.[63]

The war awakened the churches to an increased interest in the welfare and religious training of the slaves. Political union with states hostile to slavery had tended to keep the Southern churches on the defensive, but a sense of security engendered by the creation of the Confederacy caused the churches to feel freer in giving religious training to the Negroes. In spite of many difficulties, the churches worked diligently during the war to give spiritual training to the black members, and frequently white congregations went without pastors in order that the Negroes might be supplied. In an address delivered to the General Assembly of the Presbyterian church at Augusta in December, 1861, the Reverend Charles C. Jones declared that "The importance of the instruction of the negroes under our present circumstances cannot be too highly estimated." He urged the ministers to divide their preaching "in just proportion between the whites and the blacks."[64] The general council of the Episcopal church, upon meeting in Augusta in 1862, adopted a resolution recognizing its obligation to provide for the spiritual wants of the slaves.

Baptists, Methodists, and Presbyterians were leaders in agitating for the repeal of a statute which forbade persons from teaching Negroes to read and write. The Georgia Presbytery in November, 1862, resolved that the law should be repealed. The Cherokee Baptist Convention in June of the same year appointed a committee to petition the legislature for the repeal of the statute, and the Central Baptist Convention, meeting at Madison, concurred. President N. M. Crawford of Mercer University said that the statute "for a generation has been a stigma upon our state." Samuel

THE CHURCHES DURING THE WAR

Boykin, the editor of the *Christian Index,* also plead for the repeal of the law. Bishop Pierce, preaching in Milledgeville in March, 1863, denounced the law. Counter protests within the Baptist denomination brought the campaign for repeal of the statute to a halt, but a Baptist minister at Columbus in writing to a colleague expressed regret that the law prevented "a Christian master the privilege of teaching his slave to read the Gospel."[65]

Baptists were also active in promoting the right of Negro ministers to preach. A group of Baptists early in 1863 sent to the legislature a protest against an enactment in the Code of Georgia which made it unlawful to license a Negro to preach, whether free or slave. This protest, written by the Reverend H. H. Tucker, assisted in procuring the repeal of the obnoxious law, but the legislature left in force the old law requiring permission to be obtained from the inferior court before a slave could be licensed to preach.[66]

Although the statute forbidding persons from teaching Negroes to read and write was not repealed, and the churches did nothing to encourage the emancipation of the slaves, the war had a salutary effect in arousing greater interest in the social and moral status of the Negro. In November, 1862, the Presbytery of Georgia expressed "the pleasing hope that the day is not far distant . . . when the entire slave code of our own and other Confederate States shall be thoroughly revised. . ." Bishop Pierce, in his sermon to the legislature in 1863, said that "all laws . . . which . . . allow arbitrary interference with the connubial relations of slaves ought to be rescinded." He declared that husbands and wives "are subject to all the contingencies of time and circumstances . . . of passion and caprice. . . . It is . . . a stigma upon our civilization. . . ."[67] In 1864 the Georgia Association of Baptists resolved that the institution of marriage should be maintained "among all classes of people . . . and that . . . the law of Georgia, in its failure to . . . protect this relationship between our slaves . . . ought to be amended."[68] Late in the war Columbus newspapers criticized the continued use of Negro churches for army hospitals. "The poor African . . . worshipped at the churches now occupied who could never have been religiously benefited at other places," one paper said. "There are comparatively few sick and wounded among us. Then why not evacuate these churches at once?"[69]

Financially the churches suffered greatly in the war. Many of the assets of the denominational colleges were invested in Confederate and state securities and were lost. Missionary work among

CONFEDERATE GEORGIA..

the Cherokee Indians in north Georgia and in the territories was completely broken up, and the missionary contributions received by the churches were devoted almost entirely to domestic work in the armies and in providing Bibles and religious reading for the soldiers. In 1863 Bishop Elliott wrote the treasurer of the Domestic Missions of the Episcopal Church: "The Missionary Committee has not been idle . . . but the distances by which we are separated and the slowness of the mails makes communication very tedious and prospects very slow."[70] When the Methodist Conference met in Athens in January, 1865, no report was made of any missionary money collected, and possibly there was none. Contributions for church expenses declined greatly, and the preachers were pressed to get means of subsistence. Bishop Elliott expressed to another minister in 1863 the troubles he was having concerning pastoral salaries:

My own salary and traveling expenses have been fixed heretofore by the Domestic Committee at $1800. I am content to receive any thing the Church may give. I have no other income.

I have been obliged, since the war began, to apply to the salaries of the missionaries and of myself, a special fund solicited personally by me and not intended to be thus applied. Of this there remained some $700, which I desire to use for the assistance of feeble Parishioners.[71]

A few months later Bishop Elliott was greatly pleased to be able to pay the salaries of two bishops in advance and to be able "to reserve a small balance in favour of each."[72]

Toward the end of the war financial hardships forced many ministers into other pursuits for a livelihood. The story of the Methodist clergyman, George G. Smith, is indicative of the trials of the ministry during wartime. In the spring of 1861 he taught school for a teacher whose health had become impaired. In September he became a chaplain, served in Virginia and Maryland, and was wounded. Upon returning to Macon in 1862, he was appointed to preach to Negroes there. He was slowly recovering from his wound when he resigned his position in order "to save the country" his salary. He then began to trade:

I exchanged Cotton yarn and cloth for Beeswax and Honey. I made candles and sold them. I had a little farm and raised some supplies. I had some pigs . . . turkeys, chickens. I succeeded in making some very good ventures in trade. . . . I found a young fellow who was refugeeing with a team and a wagon. We went into partnership and I furnished

..THE CHURCHES DURING THE WAR

him snuff tobacco, yarns, cotton . . . wool cards and other supplies and he bought back bacon, lard, homespun, sugar, etc., and so I got my supplies.

In 1864 Smith moved to Lowndes County, where he held revivals in Valdosta and Quitman, preaching in a schoolhouse in the former town and in an old store in the latter. "I preached on Sundays and traded in the intervals," he said. "I . . . shipped my barter to Macon and we lived."[73]

Although the war seriously impeded the growth of the churches in Georgia, the number of churches continued to increase, but at a relatively slower pace. The Baptist church in 1861 had 1,015 churches and 540 ordained ministers. In 1866 it had 1,435 churches and 757 ministers, but the number of Baptist church members was approximately the same as in 1860. The Presbyterian church began the war with sixty-nine ministers, 106 churches, and 6,274 members; and five years later it had seventy ministers, 117 churches, and 6,279 members, a gain of only one minister, eleven churches, and five members. By 1870 the situation was much brighter for all denominations. The number of Baptist churches had grown during the 1860's from 1,141 to 1,308; the Methodist, from 1,035 to 1,158; the Presbyterian, from 129 to 134; the Episcopal, from 25 to 27; the Lutheran, from nine to ten; the Christian, from 15 to 33; and the Catholic, from eight to eleven. The number of Universalist and Jewish churches remained the same as in 1860. The total number of churches increased during the decade from 2,393 to 2,873, and their property valuation grew from $2,440,391 to $3,561,955.[74]

The churches of Georgia thus played a significant role in the Confederate drama. Every denomination loyally supported the Confederacy. Although the ministry was divided in regard to the wisdom of secession, the clergy gave unstinted help to the South and labored untiringly to maintain civilian morale. Prior to Sherman's raid, religious activities generally increased; yet some Georgians seemed to suffer a spiritual relapse consonant with wartime conditions. The churches manifested a greater desire to improve the social welfare and religious training of the slaves. Despite large financial losses, the number of churches did not stop increasing.

NOTES

CHAPTER I

1. Allen D. Candler, ed., *The Confederate Records of the State of Georgia*, I, 19-57 (hereafter cited as Candler, ed., *Confederate Records*); *Journal of the House of Representatives of the State of Georgia . . . 1860*, 35 (hereafter cited as *Georgia House Journal*); "Minutes of the Executive Department of the State of Georgia" (January 2, 1860, to July 10, 1866. MS. in the Georgia Department of Archives and History, hereafter cited as Georgia State Archives), 100-117.
2. Candler, ed., *Confederate Records*, I, 19-57.
3. *Ibid.*, I, 58-156; Isaac W. Avery, *The History of the State of Georgia from 1850 to 1881*, 136, 149; Ulrich B. Phillips, *The Life of Robert Toombs*, 209, 210.
4. "From the Autobiography of Herschel V. Johnson," *American Historical Review*, XXX, 2 (Jan., 1925), 323.
5. Candler, ed., *Confederate Records*, I, 157-205.
6. Ulrich B. Phillips, ed., *The Correspondence of Robert Toombs, Alexander H. Stephens, and Howell Cobb*. American Historical Association *Annual Report*, 1911, II, 505-516 (hereafter cited as Phillips, ed., *Correspondence of Toombs, Stephens, and Cobb*).
7. The Georgia Platform stated that although Georgia was not entirely satisfied with the Compromise of 1850, she would accept it as she was anxious to remain in the Union.
8. Alexander H. Stephens, *A Constitutional View of the Late War Between the States*, II, 278, 300.
9. Candler, ed., *Confederate Records*, I, 206, 208, 211, 740-747.
10. "Minutes of the Executive Dept., 1860-66," 148.
11. Nov. 16, 1860.
12. Nov. 21, 1860.
13. Nov. 30, 1860.
14. Albany *Patriot*, Dec. 13, 1860.
15. Dec. 12, 1860.
16. Augusta *Daily Chronicle and Sentinel*, Dec. 22, 186J.
17. Jan. 12, 1861.
18. Those who opposed immediate secession and hoped for a compromise within the Union advocated a convention of all the Southern states and were known as co-operationists.
19. Hill to Johnson, Dec. 3, 1860, in Benjamin H. Hill Papers.
20. Eliza Frances Andrews, *The War-Time Journal of a Georgia Girl, 1864-1865*, 176.
21. *Acts of the Gen. Assem. of Ga., 1860*, 26, 27.
22. Augusta *Daily Constitutionalist*, Dec. 5, 1860.
23. The former governors favoring secession were Howell Cobb, George W. Crawford, Charles J. McDonald, and Wilson Lumpkin. Herschel V. Johnson was the former governor who opposed secession. Justices Joseph Henry Lumpkin and Richard F. Lyon of the Georgia Supreme Court favored secession, but Justice Charles J. Jenkins was opposed.
24. Candler, ed., *Confederate Records*, II, 13-16.
25. *Ibid.*, I, 212-219.
26. Kate Haynes Fort, ed., *Memoirs of the Fort and Fannin Families*, 69.
27. *Journal of the Georgia Convention*, 10-13.
28. *Ibid.*, 305, 306. Contrary to the general impression, Johnson and not Stephens led the fight against immediate secession.

247 ..

29. *Ibid.*, 15-20. Nisbet stated in the convention that the Ordinance of Secession was written by Robert Toombs.
30. Candler, ed., *Confederate Records*, I, 241-244.
31. An absent delegate voted two days later for the ordinance, making the total 209 to 89.
32. *Journal of the Georgia Convention*, 32-39.
33. Candler, ed., *Confederate Records*, I, 16, 17.
34. *Ibid.*, I, 349-361.
35. Jan. 22, 29, 1861.
36. Jan. 26, 1861.
37. Feb. 8, 1861.
38. Feb. 27, 1861.
39. Benjamin H. Hill, Jr., *Senator Benjamin H. Hill of Georgia*, 41.
40. "From the Autobiography of Herschel V. Johnson," *American Historical Review*, XXX, 2 (Jan., 1925), 327.
41. Andrews, *War-Time Journal*, 176, 177.
42. *Journal of the Georgia Convention*, 60 ff.
43. Candler, ed., *Confederate Records*, II, 24-31.
44. Herbert Fielder, *A Sketch of the Life . . . of Joseph E. Brown*, 182.
45. Candler, ed., *Confederate Records*, I, 294, 295, 422-447.
46. *The Planters' Weekly*, Apr. 3, 1861.
47. *Journal of the Georgia Convention*, 242-248.
48. *Georgia House Journal, 1861*, 32. This was the first constitution of Georgia upon the adoption of which the people voted directly.
49. July 3, 1861.
50. Milledgeville *Federal Union*, Jan. 22, 1861.
51. Mar. 13, 1861.
52. Phillips, ed., *Correspondence of Toombs, Stephens and Cobb*, 554, 555.
53. *Journal of the Georgia Convention*, passim.
54. Milledgeville *Southern Federal Union*, Apr. 2, 1861.
55. Sandersville *Central Georgian*, Apr. 10, 1861.
56. Rebecca Latimer Felton, *Country Life in Georgia in the Days of My Youth*, 80.
57. Apr. 17, 1861.
58. Apr. 16, 1861.
59. Apr. 23, 1861.

CHAPTER II

1. April 23, 1861.
2. Columbus *Daily Sun*, May 4, 31, July 16, 1861.
3. Thweatt to Stephens, Apr. 29, 1861, in Alexander H. Stephens Papers (Lib. of Cong.).
4. Johnston to Stephens, May 2, 1861, *ibid.*
5. Johnston to Linton Stephens, May 21, 1861, *ibid.*
6. James A. Nisbet to Stephens, July 8, 1861, *ibid.*
7. James Cooper Nisbet to L. P. Walker, July 8, 1861; and James A. Cooper to A. H. Stephens and Robert Toombs, July 8, 1861, *ibid.*
8. Avery to Stephens, Oct. 29, 1861, *ibid.*
9. J. D. Waddell to Stephens, Apr. 22, 1861, *ibid.*
10. James S. Martin to Stephens, July 18, 1861, *ibid.*
11. George W. Ray to Stephens, Sept. 11, 1861, *ibid.*
12. O. C. Gibson to Brown, Apr. 7, 1861, in Telamon Cuyler Collection.
13. R. L. Warthen to Brown, Sept. 26, 1861, *ibid.*
14. John M. T. Gullett to Brown, October, 1861, *ibid.*
15. William R. Davis to Cobb, Feb. 21, 1861, in Howell Cobb Papers (private possession).
16. Robert N. Ely to Cobb, Aug. 13, 1861, *ibid.*
17. J. D. Frierson to Cobb, Aug. 13, 1861, *ibid.*
18. Samuel W. Pruitt to Cobb, June 19, 1861, *ibid.*
19. Crawford to J. P. Benjamin, Oct. 21, 1861, in Telamon Cuyler Collection.
20. William Howard Russell, *My Daily North and South*, 158.

..NOTES

21. Henry C. Wayne to H. R. Jackson, Mar. 29, 1862, in Henry R. Jackson Papers; Ella Lonn, *Foreigners in the Confederacy,* 92; Jews were prompt to enlist.
22. Brown to Stephens, June 25, 1861, in Alexander H. Stephens Papers (Emory Univ. Lib.).
23. A term loosely used by volunteer military organizations to designate a mixed unit of infantry, cavalry, and artillery slightly larger than a regiment.
24. Candler, ed., *Confederate Records,* II, 87, 313; *ibid.,* III, 193; *Official Records of the Union and Confederate Armies,* Ser. IV, Vol. I, 788-790. All troops enlisted prior to May, 1861, were twelve months' companies; and prior to the Confederate Conscription Act of April, 1862, many men continued to enlist for only one year.
25. Brown to Walker, Apr. 24, 1861, in Brown Papers (Georgia State Archives).
26. Thomas R. R. Cobb to Howell Cobb, June 15, 1861, in Cobb Papers (private possession).
27. See letter of Robert H. May to Brown, May 8, 1861, in Brown Papers (Georgia State Archives).
28. July 2, 1861.
29. Cary Cox to Stephens, Jan. 18, 1862, in Stephens Papers (Lib. of Cong.).
30. Quoted in Columbus *Weekly Times,* July 4, 1861.
31. Henry C. Wayne to Cuyler, Mar. 18, 1862, in "Savannah Ordnance Letters."
32. W. G. Gill to W. W. Paine, Sept. 20, 1861, in "Augusta Arsenal Letters." Confederate arsenals and laboratories were located in Atlanta, Macon, Augusta, Columbus, and Savannah.
33. E. B. D. Riley to Cuyler, Mar. 17, 1862, in "Atlanta Arsenal Letters."
34. M. H. Wright to Cuyler, Sept. 4, 1862, *ibid.*
35. *Official Records,* Ser. I, Vol. LII, Pt. II, 97, Candler, ed., *Confederate Records,* III, 143-145.
36. Atlanta *Daily Intelligencer,* July 3, 1861.
37. *Ibid.,* Aug. 21, 1861.
38. Candler, ed., *Confederate Records,* III, 126, 127.
39. *Ibid.,* II, 56, 57, 109, 365; *Ibid.,* III, 90.
40. McIntosh to Jackson, Jan. 6, 1862, in Jackson Papers.
41. Capers to Jackson, Jan. 5, 1862, *ibid.*
42. Thweatt to Stephens, Mar. 10, 1862, in Stephens Papers (Lib. of Cong.).
43. McIntosh to Jackson, Mar. 13, 1862, in Jackson Papers.
44. Candler, ed., *Confederate Records,* II, 199-201, 345, 346, 351, 353. The pike had a six-foot staff to which was attached an eighteen-inch knife.
45. In 1862 Atlanta became the headquarters in the Lower South for the Quartermaster and Commissary Departments of the Confederate and state governments.
46. See "Miscellaneous Georgia Poor Relief Papers, 1861-1865."
47. Atlanta *Southern Confederacy,* Apr. 28, 1861.
48. Thomas H. English, ed., *Autobiography of "The Countryman," 1866, by Joseph Addison Turner,* 18.
49. Aug. 20, 1861.
50. Atlanta *Daily Intelligencer,* Sept. 25, 1861.
51. "Adjutant-General Letter Books, 1862, No. 12," 384, 385.
52. Candler, ed., *Confederate Records,* II, 266, 332-335, 354, 355.
53. M. A. Quillin to E. A. Davis, Sept. 14, 1861, in E. A. Davis Papers.
54. Irby Goodwin Scott to Irby H. Scott, Feb. 2, 1862, in Irby H. Scott Papers.
55. Montfort to his wife, Mar. 2, 1862, in "Letters from Confederate Soldiers," II, 78 (Georgia State Archives).
56. J. H. Alexander to Adam Leopole Alexander, Sept. 8, Nov. 14, 1861, in Adam Leopole Alexander Papers.
57. *Report of the Executive Committee of the Georgia Relief and Hospital Association . . . Oct. 29, 1862.*
58. Tucker to Brown, Sept. 6, 1861, in Brown Papers (Georgia State Archives).
59. *Report of the . . . Georgia Relief and Hospital Association,* 22-31.

60. Letter of Rev. W. M. Crumley published in *Southern Christian Advocate,* Jan. 16, 1862.
61. "Journal of Anna Maria [Green] Cook," Nov. 19, 1861.
62. Robert H. May to Brown, May 8, 1861, in Brown Papers (Georgia State Archives).
63. Johnston to Alexander Stephens, Aug. 9, 1861, in Stephens Papers (Lib. of Cong.).
64. Milledgeville *Southern Federal Union,* June 18, 1861.

CHAPTER III

1. Milledgeville *Southern Federal Union,* Feb. 23, 1861.
2. Quoted in Avery, *History of Georgia,* 193, 194.
3. In 1857 Brown was nominated for governor on the Democratic ticket. He defeated Benjamin H. Hill, the American Party's candidate, and two years later was re-elected governor.
4. Whitaker was the grandson of Jared Irwin, the only governor in the history of the state who had been elected for three terms.
5. Atlanta *Weekly Intelligencer,* Aug. 21, 1861.
6. Thweatt to Stephens, Aug. 19, 1861, in Stephens Papers (Lib. of Cong.).
7. In a letter to her husband, Mrs. Howell Cobb remarked: "*Have* you see the *last* Federal Union? Do read the editorial.... It is solely intended for the illiterate constituents of Gov. Brown.... But people are already beginning to say, 'He'll be elected.'" Mary Ann Cobb to Howell Cobb, Aug. 30, 1861, in Howell Cobb Papers (private possession).
8. July 18, Aug. 5, Sept. 23, 1861.
9. Sept. 18, 1861.
10. Moses W. Davis to E. A. Davis, Sept. 13, 1861, in E. A. Davis Papers.
11. Nisbet represented Bibb County in the Secession Convention, and was a member of the Confederate Provisional Congress.
12. See Savannah *Republican,* July 8, Aug. 20, Sept. 20, 1861; and Atlanta *Southern Confederacy,* Aug. 13, 23, and Sept. 20, 22, 29, 1861. The charge of speculating probably referred to the fact that Brown had purchased for Georgia and resold to the Confederacy saltpeter and sulphur, making a profit of $22,132.70 for the state.
13. Aug. 19, 1861. The Savannah *Republican,* Aug. 20, 1861, said that although Jared Irwin had been elected governor for three terms, Brown concealed the fact that they were not three consecutive terms.
14. Sept. 16, 1861.
15. Quoted in Columbus *Weekly Times,* Sept. 23, 1861.
16. Quoted in Columbus *Weekly Times,* Sept. 26, 1861.
17. Sept. 5, 1861.
18. Atlanta *Weekly Intelligencer,* Sept. 18, 25, 1861.
19. Phillips, ed., *Correspondence of Toombs, Stephens, and Cobb,* 574, 577.
20. Atlanta *Southern Confederacy,* Sept. 24, 1861.
21. Candler, ed., *Confederate Records,* I, 703-731; II, 125.
22. Phillips, ed., *Correspondence of Toombs, Stephens, and Cobb,* 580.
23. Candler, ed., *Confederate Records,* II, 83-85, 94-125, 149-168; *Acts of the Gen. Assem. of Ga., 1861,* 141.
24. Phillips, *Toombs,* 241, 242. In 1862 Dr. Lewis resigned and Herschel V. Johnson was elected to fill the vacancy.
25. Thweatt to Stephens, Jan. 9, 1862, in Stephens Papers (Lib. of Cong.).
26. Candler, ed., *Confederate Records,* II, 263-265; *Acts of the Gen. Assem. of Ga., 1862,* 10-16.
27. Candler, ed., *Confederate Records,* II, 94, 96, 500-504, 588, 589, 765, 766; *Acts of the Gen. Assem. of Ga., 1862,* 10-16; *ibid., 1863,* 5-11.
28. Brown to Jackson, Jan. 31, 1862, in Jackson Papers.
29. Brown to Hardee, Dec. 16, 1863, in Aaron Wilbur Papers (Emory Univ. Lib.).

..NOTES

30. Johnson to Wilbur, Jan. 20, 1864, *ibid.*
31. Johnson and Brothers to Wilbur, Feb. 6, 1864, *ibid.*
32. Candler, ed., *Confederate Records*, II, 433-439; *ibid.*, III, 332, 333.
33. *Ibid.*, II, 202-207; *ibid.*, III, 309, 471.
34. *Acts of the Gen. Assem. of Georgia, 1862*, 25, 26.
35. Waters to J. W. Mallett, July 2, 1862, in "Macon Arsenal Letters."
36. Brown to A. H. Stephens, Mar. 28, 1862, in Stephens Papers (Lib. of Cong.).
37. *Acts of the Gen. Assem. of Ga., 1862*, 25, 26; Candler, ed., *Confederate Records*, II, 541, 591, 592, 871.
38. Quoted in Sandersville *Central Georgian*, Nov. 13, 1861.
39. "Minutes of the Executive Dept., 1860-66," p. 293.
40. J. Henly Smith to Stephens, Dec. 16, 1861, in Stephens Papers (Lib. of Cong.).
41. Jan. 4, 1862.
42. *Acts of the Gen. Assem. of Ga., 1861*, 1, 2.
43. Candler, ed., *Confederate Records*, II, 223, 277, 280-283, 595.
44. Thweatt to Stephens, Jan. 31, 1863, in Stephens Papers (Lib. of Cong.).
45. Phillips, ed., *Correspondence of Toombs, Stephens, and Cobb*, 610, 611.
46. When the South in 1862 sought through voluntary agreements among planters to restrict cotton cultivation in favor of grains, Toombs refused to co-operate. His opposition to the administration rather than his cotton crop prevented his nomination for governor.
47. Thweatt to Stephens, May 14, 1863, in Stephens Papers (Lib. of Cong.).
48. James R. Sneed, editor of the Savannah *Republican*, hoped that Howell Cobb might be elected governor. See letter of Sneed to Cobb, June 28, 1863, in Cobb Papers (in private possession).
49. James Gardner, owner of the *Constitutionalist*, said that the Confederacy could best be served by retaining Brown in office and thus preventing political controversies.
50. Milledgeville *Southern Recorder*, June 2, 1863.
51. Quoted in Savannah *Republican*, June 23, 1863.
52. June 4, 1863.
53. August, 1863.
54. Hill to Adair, Thrasher, and Calhoun, in Milledgeville *Southern Recorder*, Sept. 8, 1863.
55. Americus *Sumter Republican*, Sept. 11, 1863. Furlow had been a railroad promoter. As a member of the secession convention, he had voted for secession. From 1861 to 1863 he was a member of the state senate. He was known as a friend of education, a school in Americus having been named for him.
56. Sept. 15, 1863.
57. Milledgeville *Southern Recorder*, Sept. 8, 1863.
58. Sept. 12, 26, 1863.
59. Oct. 5, 1863.
60. Brown to Stephens, Aug. 22, 1863, in Phillips, ed., *Correspondence of Toombs, Stephens, and Cobb*, 628.
61. Furlow carried Baldwin County (Milledgeville) but no county north of the capital.
62. Thomas Hardeman, Jr., to Cobb, Nov. 16, 1863, in Cobb Papers (private possession).
63. Toombs' candidacy was due primarily to his desire to combat Confederate policies. See letter of Toombs to A. H. Stephens, Nov. 27, 1863, in Cobb Papers (Univ. of Georgia Lib.).
64. Candler, ed., *Confederate Records*, II, 488-500, 514-517.
65. *Ibid.*, II, 587, 655; *Official Records*, Ser. IV, Vol. III, 234, 235; *Acts of the Gen. Assem. of Ga., 1864 (extra sess.)*, 152-154. The Confederate Conscription Act of Feb. 17, 1864, lowered the conscription age limit to seventeen and raised it to fifty.
66. See letter of Henry C. Wayne to Col. A. Wilbur, Mar. 31, 1864, in Wilbur Papers (Emory Univ. Lib.).
67. John A. Cobb to his wife, June 5,

CONFEDERATE GEORGIA..

1864, in Cobb Papers (private possession).
68. Macon *Telegraph and Confederate* (n. d.), quoted in Columbus *Daily Times*, Feb. 28, 1965.
69. Quoted in Savannah *Daily Herald*, Mar. 2, 1865.
70. Mar. 24, 1865.
71. "Minutes of the Executive Dept., 1860-66," 780; Candler, ed., *Confederate Records*, II, 884, 885; *ibid.*, III, 717-726. Brown, having been a prisoner in Washington for nine days, was released by President Johnson. He returned to Georgia and resigned as governor. Stephens was paroled after being held prisoner at Boston for several months. Toombs fled to Europe.
72. Secretary of State William H. Seward wired Johnson: "It gives me especial pleasure to convey to you the President's acknowledgments of the fidelity, the loyalty, and discretion, which have marked your administration." Seward to Johnson, Dec. 19, 1865, telegram in Telamon Cuyler Collection.
73. In 1853 Jenkins had been the unsuccessful Whig candidate for governor.

CHAPTER IV

1. U. S. Census Office, 8th Census, 1860, *Statistics of the United States*, 295-298; *Report of the Comptroller-General of Georgia, 1860*, 3-7, 11. The bonds consisted of $2,073,750 six per cent, $72,000 five per cent, and $525,000 seven per cent bonds. Georgia's slaves in 1860 were worth $454,042,282 and had an average value of $671.61 per slave.
2. *Report of the Comptroller-General of Georgia, 1860*, 7, 8.
3. Brown said that he had been unable to raise money on the six per cent bonds without offering them at a considerable discount.
4. *Confederate Records*, II, 39-43, 96-99. Secretary Memminger announced in November, 1861, that all of the $15,000,000 Confederate bonds had been purchased.
5. *Ibid.*, II, 245-248.
6. "Governor's Letter Books, 1861-65," 344-353.
7. Thweatt to Stephens, Jan. 27, 1862, in Stephens Papers (Lib. of Cong.).
8. *Official Records*, Ser. IV, Vol. I, 328, 329. Cotton brokers and other experts served as government agents for purchasing the produce. Market prices were paid at rates adjusted between the parties and agents of the government. See C. G. Memminger, *Instructions for the Agents for Collecting ... the Produce Loan*.
9. Thian, ed., *Reports of the Confederate Treasury*, App., Pt. III (1861-1865), 48.
10. N. G. Foster to A. H. Stephens, Sept. 20, 1861, in Stephens Papers (Lib of Cong.).
11. Smith to Stephens, Oct. 16, 1861, *ibid.*
12. George W. Lamar to A. H. Stephens, Oct. 1, 1861, *ibid.*
13. D. Ponce to Stephens, Aug. 24, 1861, *ibid.*
14. William C. Butler to Stephens, Nov. 11, 1861, *ibid.*
15. V. H. Oppert to Cobb, June 4, 1861, in Cobb Papers (private possession).
16. Hussey to Cobb, June 14, 1861, *ibid.*
17. William B. Shelton to Cobb, June 24, 1861, *ibid.*
18. Thomas M. Harris, *et al.*, to Stephens, Oct. 3, 1861, in Stephens Papers (Lib. of Cong.).
19. Crawford to Stephens, Nov. 3, 1861, *ibid.*
20. Thian, ed., *Reports of the Confederate Treasury*, App., Pt. III (1861-1865), 49-52.
21. Augusta *Weekly Chronicle and Sentinel*, Oct. 30, 1861.
22. *Journal of the Congress of the Confederate States of America, 1861-1865*, I, 478, 479.
23. Nov. 27, 1861.
24. Thian, ed., *Reports of the Confederate Treasury*, App., Pt. III (1861-1865), 129-132.
25. "Address of Alexander H. Stephens at Crawfordville, Georgia," Nov. 1,

..NOTES

1862, in Stephens Papers (Lib. of Cong.).
26. *Official Records*, Ser. IV, Vol. II, 219, 237, 238, 320, 347, 376, 452.
27. Candler, ed., *Confederate Records*, II, 381-394.
28. *Georgia Senate Journal, 1863 (extra sess.)*, 108, 178.
29. Reynolds to Cobb, Jan. 22, 1865, in Cobb Papers (Univ. of Georgia Lib.).
30. "Jennie" to her cousin in the army, Mar. 8, 1864, in E. A. Davis Papers.
31. Feb. 19, 26, 1864.
32. Candler, ed., *Confederate Records*, II, 595-600.
33. Mar. 29, Apr. 8, 1864.
34. Quoted in Americus *Sumter Republican*, Mar. 18, 1864.
35. Memminger to Brown, Aug. 13, 1862, in Joseph E. Brown Papers (Duke Univ. Lib.).
36. Candler, ed., *Confederate Records*, II, 100, 101.
37. A total of $867,550 of seven per cent bonds and of $2,441,000 of eight per cent bonds were sold.
38. Candler, ed., *Confederate Records*, II, 243-245; *Acts of the Gen. Assem. of Ga., 1863*, 15, 16. A certificate of deposit was a non-circulating note which did not bear interest.
39. *Acts of the Gen. Assem. of Ga., 1860*, 13.
40. Thweatt to Stephens, Aug. 19, 1861, in Stephens Papers (Lib. of Cong.).
41. *Acts of the Gen. Assem. of Ga., 1861*, 80; *ibid., 1862*, 56-60; *ibid., 1863*, 79. Taxes were paid in both Confederate and state treasury notes.
42. *Ibid., 1861*, 88; *ibid., 1863*, 79; *ibid., 1864*, 22-44.
43. *Ibid., 1863*, 80, 81; *ibid., 1863 (extra sess.)*, 176-178; *ibid., 1865 (extra sess.)*, 66, 67.
44. *Report of the Comptroller-General, 1863*, Pt. I, 29, 30, 34.
45. Thweatt to Stephens, Apr. 14, 1864, in Stephens Papers (Lib. of Cong.).
46. *Report of the Comptroller-General, 1860*, 27-34. Bank stock paid a tax of 39 1/16 cents on the one hundred dollars.
47. Quoted in letter of Hiram Roberts to Joseph E. Brown, Apr. 11, 1861,

in Brown Papers (Georgia State Archives).
48. Roberts to Brown, Apr. 11, 1861, *ibid.*
49. *Memorial of the Banks of Savannah to the . . . Senate and House of Representatives of the Confederate States.*
50. The suspension continued until Jan. 1, 1865, when the legislature re-enacted a law which provided for the forfeiture of charters of banks which did not resume specie payments. *Acts of the Gen. Assem. of Ga., 1861*, 18, 19, 25-27; *ibid., 1862*, 19-21.
51. *Ibid., 1861*, 19-28; *Report of the Comptroller-General, 1863*, Pt. I, 21; *ibid., 1864*, 7; *ibid., 1865*, 12.
52. July 26, 1862.
53. R. A. McGiboney to Memminger, Mar. 10, 1864, in Thian, ed., *Correspondence of the Treasury Dept.*, App., V (1863-1865), 326, 327.
54. William C. Butler to Stephens, Nov. 11, 1861, in Stephens Papers (Lib. of Cong.).
55. *Acts of the Gen. Assem. of Ga., 1861*, 66, 67.
56. Nov. 18, 22, 1862.
57. Brown to Vance, Sept. 26, 1862, in Joseph E. Brown Papers (Lib. of Cong.).
58. Quoted in Savannah *Daily Morning News*, Mar. 25, 1863.
59. Quoted in *ibid.*, June 24, 1863.
60. S. Collins to his brother, Feb. 17, 1862, in Miscellaneous Soldiers' Letters (Duke Univ. Lib.).
61. W. Sparks to his brother (n. d.), in Evans Papers.
62. Columbus *Enquirer* (n. d.), quoted in Savannah *Republican*, Mar. 20, 1863.
63. Atlanta *Southern Confederacy*, Feb. 14, 1863.
64. Savannah *Republican*, June 9, 1864.
65. "George A. Mercer Diary," Sept. 14, 1863.
66. Mar. 4, 1865.
67. *Acts of the Gen. Assem. of Ga., 1861*, 10-16; *ibid., 1862*, 13, 14; *ibid., 1863*, 5-11; *ibid., 1864*, 6-11; Candler, ed., *Confederate Records*, II, 399-406, 503, 504, 588, 589, 765.

68. *Report of the Comptroller-General, 1863*, Pt. I, 19-21; *ibid., 1864*, Pt. I, 41.
69. James H. Bass, "Civil War Finance in Georgia," *Georgia Historical Quarterly*, XXVI, 3 and 4 (Sept.-Dec., 1942), 224.
70. *Acts of the Gen. Assem. of Ga., 1861*, 30, 76.
71. *Georgia Senate Journal, 1861*, 226, 230.
72. O. H. Smith to Wier Boyd, Sept. 4, 1862, in Boyd Papers.
73. The counties appointed treasurers of soldiers' relief funds. See "Miscellaneous Georgia Poor Relief Papers, 1861-1865."
74. *Report of the Comptroller-General, 1863*, Pt. I, 7-9; *ibid., 1864*, Pt. I, 8; *ibid., 1865*, Pt. I, 6.
75. *Ibid., 1864*, Pt. I, 22; *ibid., 1865*, Pt. I, 23.
76. Joseph S. Anderson, *et al.*, to Brown, Feb. 22, 1865, in "Military Records, Depredations, 1865."
77. *Report of the Comptroller-General, 1865*, Pt. I, 1, 9, 12.
78. *Ibid., 1866*, Pt. I, 5-11.

CHAPTER V

1. Moses W. Davis to E. A. Davis, Sept. 13, 1861, in E. A. Davis Papers.
2. Candler, ed., *Confederate Records*, III, 28, 29, 52, 53.
3. Brown to Stephens, May 4, 1861, in Stephens Papers (Emory Univ. Lib.). See also letter of Henry C. Wayne to Jefferson Davis, May 3, 1861, in "Georgia Portfolio," II, 144, 145.
4. The coastal defenses consisted of Fort Beaulieu, on the Vernon River, erected to defend Savannah from the rear; Fort Rosedew, on the Ogeechee River; Fort Brown, on St. Simons Island; Fort Jackson, also known as Fort Oglethorpe, about 3½ miles west of Savannah; Fort Pulaski, a brick structure built by the U. S. Government during the first half of the nineteenth century on Cockspur Island to command the Savannah River at its mouth; and Fort McAllister, located on the west bank of the Great Ogeechee River, 26 miles south of Savannah.
5. Roberts to Brown, Apr. 11, 1861, in Brown Papers (Georgia State Archives).
6. Sept. 4, 1861.
7. Pope Barrow to Mrs. Howell Cobb, June 19, 1861, in Cobb Papers (private possession).
8. *Official Records*, Ser. I, Vol. VI, 30-73.
9. Sept. 18, 1861.
10. "Minutes of the Executive Dept., 1860-66," 256-281, 290, 296, 297. On Nov. 19, 1861, there were 5,500 Confederate soldiers and 8,000 state troops on the Georgia coast.
11. *Official Records*, Ser. I, Vol. XII, 362, 363.
12. *Official Records*, Ser. I, Vol. VI, 32, 33; *Official Records, Navy*, Ser. I, Vol. XII, 326-365. Rear Admiral S. F. DuPont commanded the squadron and Brigadier-General T. W. Sherman the army.
13. Lawton to Jackson, Jan. 27, 1862, in Jackson Papers.
14. *Official Records*, Ser. I, Vol. XII, 487.
15. Jackson to Henry C. Wayne, Dec. 25, 1861, in Jackson Papers.
16. R. E. Lee to Jackson, Jan. 3, 1862, *ibid*.
17. *Ibid.*, Mar. 2, 1862.
18. Brown to Jackson, Feb. 5, 1862, in Jackson Papers.
19. Henry C. Wayne to Jackson, Feb. 15, 1862, *ibid*.
20. T. W. Montfort to his wife, Feb. 8, 1862, in "Letters from Confederate Soldiers," II, 56 (Georgia State Archives).
21. Lawton to Jackson, Apr. 13, 1862, in Jackson Papers. Stones were placed on board of vessels, which were towed down the river and sunk across the channel.
22. G. W. Gormany to Jackson, Feb. 20, 1862, *ibid*.
23. "P. M. L." to Brown, Dec. 18, 1861, in Brown Papers (Emory Univ. Lib.).
24. Candler, ed., *Confederate Records*, II, 52, 53; *ibid.*, III, 20, 28, 29, 33, 34, 48-50, 145.

..NOTES

25. *Official Records,* Ser. I, Vol. VI, 167, 332.
26. *Ibid.,* Ser. I, Vol. VI, 33, 35. Tattnall already had supplied the garrison with six months' provisions.
27. T. W. Montfort to his wife, Feb. 17, 18, 1862, in "Letters from Confederate Soldiers," II, 66, 69 (Georgia State Archives).
28. T. W. Montfort to his wife, Mar. 12, 15, 1862, *ibid.,* II 79, 81.
29. T. W. Montfort to B. A. Thornton, Apr. 6, 1862, *ibid.,* II, 101-103.
30. *Official Records,* Ser. I, Vol. VI, 133-169. Gen. Q. A. Gillmore was the engineer officer in charge of the attack. Tybee Point was three-fourths of a mile from Fort Pulaski, and until the bombardment army authorities believed that the maximum distance a fort could be successfully bombarded was from 600 to 900 yards.
31. "Mercer Diary," Apr. 11, 1862.
32. Apr. 17, 1862.
33. *Official Records,* Ser. I, Vol. VI, 133-139.
34. Candler, ed., *Confederate Records,* II, 213-215.
35. "Adjutant-General Letter Books, 1861-1864, Vol. B-44, A. G. O.," Pt. I, 320.
36. May 7, 1862.
37. Candler, ed., *Confederate Records,* II, 236-239, 311-313, 375, 376; *ibid.,* III, 194, 325-328, 334 *ff.*
38. *Official Records,* Ser. I, Vol. XIV, 317-319.
39. *Ibid.,* Ser. I, Vol. XIV, 3, 198, 211-223, 757, 811. The attack was the seventh attempt by the Federal navy to capture Fort McAllister.
40. Mercer to his sister, Mar. 11, 1863, in Walker-Mercer Papers (Emory Univ. Lib.). In June, 1863, the ironclad steamer *Fingal* got aground in Warsaw Sound, riddled by shot from Northern monitors, and surrendered.
41. "Mercer Diary," June 11, 1863.
42. *Official Records Navy,* Ser. I, Vol. XII, 633, 634; *ibid.,* Ser. I, Vol. XIII, 19-21; *ibid.,* Ser. I, Vol. XIV, 150.
43. William Pittinger, *The Great Locomotive Chase,* 102-112.
44. *Ibid.,* 115-119. To inquirers along the route Andrews declared that he was running a powder train through to General Beauregard, then at Corinth, Miss.
45. See *Official Records,* Ser. I, Vol. X, Pt. I, 630-639; and Pittinger, *The Great Locomotive Chase,* 143 *ff.*
46. *Official Records,* Ser. I, Vol. XXIII, Pt. I, 281-295; *ibid.,* Ser. II, Vol. V, 549, 737, 946, 952, 960, 969.
47. Atlanta *Southern Confederacy,* May 6, 10, 1863.
48. *Official Records,* Ser. I, Vol. XXX, Pt. I, 37, 38, 55-58, 136.
49. *Ibid.,* Ser. I, Vol. XXX, Pt. I, 38, 39, 60, 61; *ibid.,* Ser. I, Vol. XXX, Pt. II, 288. "Looking back one can see the mistake that was made by the Confederates in . . . fighting the enemy about Snodgrass Hill instead of pressing the routed army in its disorderly retreat to Chattanooga . . . ." "Joseph B. Cumming War Recollections," 46.
50. For details of the battle see *Official Records,* Ser. I, Vol. XXX, Pt. I, 27-1071; *ibid.,* Ser. I, Vol. XXX, Pt. II, 3-543.
51. Andrew Jackson Neal to John Neal, Sept. 21, 1863, in A. J. Neal Papers.

CHAPTER VI

1. Candler, ed., *Confederate Records,* III, 30-60. A Confederate act of Feb. 28, 1861, stipulated that the President with the consent of Congress should appoint the general officers.
2. Linton Stephens to A. H. Stephens, May 31, 1861, in Alexander H. Stephens Papers (Manhattanville College). The brackets were in the original manuscript.
3. Brown to A. H. Stephens and Thomas R. R. Cobb, July 20, 1861, in Brown Papers (Emory Univ. Lib.).
4. Thweatt to Stephens, July 3, 1861, in Stephens Papers (Lib. of Cong.).
5. Candler, ed., *Confederate Records,* II, 93-95; 131, 132, 138-144, 146, 154.
6. "Minutes of the Executive Dept., 1860-66," 261-264, 314-318.
7. *Ibid.,* 310, 334, 335.

8. Dec. 17, 1861.
9. "Minutes of the Executive Dept., 1860-66," 225.
10. L. P. Walker to Brown, May 22, 1861, in Telamon Cuyler Collection.
11. *Official Records,* Ser. IV, Vol. I, Pt. I, 368, 406-416.
12. Lachlan H. McIntosh to Henry R. Jackson, Mar. 13, 1862, in Jackson Papers.
13. *Official Records,* Ser. IV, Vol. I, Pt. I, 617, 618, 624, 625, 668, 1046, 1058, 1059; *ibid.,* Ser. I, Vol. VI, 318, 319.
14. Wayne to Jackson, Dec. 31, 1861, in Jackson Papers.
15. *Ibid.,* Jan. 6, 1862.
16. Lawton to Jackson, Jan. 30, Feb. 3, 1862, in Jackson Papers.
17. Lawton to Jackson, Feb. 17, 1862, *ibid.*
18. Lawton to Jackson, Jan. 27, Mar. 11, 1862, *ibid.*
19. Brown to Jackson and Purse, Feb. 15, 1862, *ibid.*
20. Wayne to Jackson, Feb. 12, 1862; and telegram of Brown to Jackson, Feb. 15, 1862, *ibid.*
21. Wayne to Jackson, Apr. 17, 1862, *ibid.* Lawton to Jackson, Apr. 16, 1862, *ibid.;* "Minutes of the Executive Dept., 1860-66," 385.
22. "From the Autobiography of Herschel V. Johnson," *Amer. Hist. Rev.,* XXX, 2 (Jan., 1925), 332.
23. Phillips, ed., *Correspondence of Toombs, Stephens, and Cobb,* 629. Toombs wrote his wife: "Davis has no capacity, and his generals but little more . . . and if it possible to ruin our cause by imbecility they will do it . . . ." Robert Toombs to "Julia," May 13, 1862, in Toombs Papers.
24. Candler, ed., *Confederate Records,* II, 301; *ibid.,* III, 192-198.
25. Brown to G. W. Randolph, June 17, 1862, in Telamon Cuyler Collection.
26. Randolph to Brown, June 18, 1862, *ibid.*
27. Smith to Stephens, June 21, 1862, in Stephens Papers (Lib. of Cong.).
28. May 21, 1862.
29. June 21, 1862.
30. Oct. 1, 1862.
31. "The Supreme Court delivered a decision here yesterday *sustaining* the constitutionality of the Conscription Act. The case was a sham, one got up with a previous knowledge of what the decision would be and intended for effect upon the Legislature." Linton Stephens to A. H. Stephens, Nov. 12, 1862, in Stephens Papers (Manhattanville College).
32. Browne to Cobb, Jan. 21, 1862, in Cobb Papers (Univ. of Georgia Lib.).
33. Candler, ed., *Confederate Records,* II, 215, 216, 447-449, 507, 508; *ibid.,* III, 325-327.
34. Bettie R. Brown to her "soldier friend," February, 1863, in Bettie R. Brown Papers.
35. "Governor's Letter Books, 1861-65," 451.
36. Cobb to his wife, Sept. 9, 1863, in Cobb Papers (Univ. of Georgia Lib.).
37. "Howell Cobb's Letter Books, 1863-65," No. 57, Sept. 14, 1863.
38. Candler, ed., *Confederate Records,* III, 504-509, 515-517, 529-573.
39. *Ibid.,* II, 601-607.
40. *Ibid.,* II, 792-799.
41. "Governor's Letter Books, 1861-65," 694, 695.
42. *Official Records,* Ser. I, Vol. LII, Pt. II, 687, 710-712, 736, 754, 760, 778, 796, 803; *ibid.,* Ser. IV, Vol. III, 1138.
43. *Ibid.,* Ser. IV, Vol. II, 30, 211, 469-471, 559-561.
44. Savannah *Daily Morning News,* Nov. 11, 1863.
45. *Ibid.,* June 29, 1863.
46. *Official Records,* Ser. IV, Vol. III, 594, 595.
47. The legislature on Dec. 11, 1862, made it unlawful to plant a greater number of acres in cotton than "three acres for each hand."
48. Candler, ed., *Confederate Records,* II, 516; *ibid.,* III, 438, 439.
49. *Official Records,* Ser. IV, Vol. III, 829.
50. Henry Cleveland, *Alexander H. Stephens, in Public and Private,* 788.
51. *Official Records,* Ser. IV, Vol. III, 594-597, 622, 663.
52. Brown to Seddon, Nov. 14, 1864, in Telamon Cuyler Collection.

..NOTES

53. Candler, ed., *Confederate Records,* II, 766, 767, 829, 830.
54. Phillips, ed., *Correspondence of Toombs, Stephens, and Cobb,* 622, 623. Herschel V. Johnson approved of scarcely any Confederate financial measures.
55. *Official Records,* Ser. IV, Vol. III, 967.
56. Candler, ed., "Confederate Records," V, Pt. I, 294.
57. *Official Records,* Ser. IV, Vol. III, 78-82. The purpose of the regulations was to control imports and exports for benefit of the Confederacy.
58. Brown to Wilbur, Apr. 15, 1864, in Wilbur Papers (Emory Univ. Lib.).
59. Candler, ed., *Confederate Records,* III, 329-331, 450-458, 463-466.
60. *Official Records,* Ser. IV, Pt. I, 954; *ibid.,* Ser. IV, Pt. II, 121; *ibid.,* Ser. IV, Pt. III, 203, 204.
61. Cleveland, *Stephens,* 747.
62. Candler, ed., *Confederate Records,* II, 305-307.
63. Stephens to Johnson, Mar. 14, 1864, in Charles C. Jones, ed., "Autograph Letters and Portraits of the Signers of the Constitution of the Confederate States."
64. "Autobiography of Herschel V. Johnson," *Amer. Hist. Rev.,* XXX, 2 (Jan., 1925), 333, 334.
65. *Official Records,* Ser. IV, Vol. III, 234, 235. "Joe Brown has been here the guest of Linton Stephens and little Aleck likewise. The Legislature is to be convened in Special session, and Toombs, Stephens & Co., will no doubt put Joe Brown up to some factious issue with the Confederate government." James A. Nisbet to Howell Cobb, Feb. 28, 1864, in Cobb Papers (Univ. of Georgia Lib.).
66. *Georgia House Journal, 1864,* 51, 52, 58, 97, 98.
67. Candler, ed., *Confederate Records,* II, 649-654; *Official Records,* Ser. IV, Vol. III, 235-237. Alexander Stephens said that it should be "the earnest desire of our Government to end the war . . . and to adjust all matters of difference with the Government at Washington upon the principles of State Sovereignty. . . ." Alexander H. Stephens to Jefferson Davis, Apr. 9, 1864, in "Georgia Portfolio," II, 50.
68. See Chapter X.
69. Candler, ed., *Confederate Records,* II, 748; *Georgia Senate Journal, 1864,* 33, 44.
70. Candler, ed., *Confederate Records,* II, 817, 851-853; *Acts of the Gen. Assem. of Ga., 1865,* 84.
71. Feb. 19, 1864.
72. Quoted in Macon *Daily Telegraph,* Mar. 24, 1864.
73. Mar. 24, 1864.
74. Quoted in Macon *Daily Telegraph,* Mar. 28, 1864.
75. Mar. 24, 1864.
76. Watterson to Stephens, Apr. 3, 1864, in Stephens Papers (Lib. of Cong.).
77. Foster to Stephens, Apr. 4, 1864, *ibid.*
78. Thomas to Stephens, Apr. 9, 1864, *ibid.*
79. Thweatt to Stephens, Apr. 9, 1864, *ibid.*
80. Stephens to Johnson, Apr. 8, 1864, *ibid.*
81. Cleveland to Stephens, June 28, 1864, *ibid.*
82. Feb. 21, 28, 1865.
83. February, 1865.
84. *The Countryman,* Mar. 21, 1865.
85. Published in *The Countryman,* Apr. 4, 1865.
86. Jefferson Davis to Mrs. Howell Cobb, Mar. 30, 1865 (manuscript formerly in possession of the late Miss Mary Lamar Erwin, Athens, Ga.).

CHAPTER VII

1. U. S. Census Office, 8th Census, 1860, *Manufactures of the United States,* 729, 730; *ibid., Statistics of the United States,* 331.
2. *Ibid., Manufactures of the United States,* 82.
3. V. T. Barnwell, comp., *Barnwell's City Directory,* I, 24.

4. *De Bow's Review*, XXXIII (1862), 78.
5. *Ibid.*, 77, 78.
6. U. S. Census Office, 8th Census, 1860, *Manufactures of the United States*, xiii, 61; *De Bow's Review*, XXXI (1861), 556, 557.
7. *De Bow's Review*, XXXIII (1862), 76-80.
8. Candler, ed., *Confederate Records*, II, 395-398, 450-453, 666, 667.
9. Atlanta *Southern Confederacy*, May 7, 1862.
10. U. S. Census Office, 8th Census, 1860, *Manufactures of the United States*, 82.
11. Isaac Scott to J. C. Johnson, February, 1863, in Scott Papers.
12. *Ibid.*, Feb. 21, 1863. The only manufactures over which the Confederate government sought control were those which directly supplied the army. The government never devised any civil machinery for control of the factories, for the supply of the army was regarded as solely a military problem.
13. Orr to Stephens, Nov. 29, 1861 (Georgia State Archives).
14. P. L. Wade to Stephens, Oct. 7, 1861, in Stephens Papers (Lib. of Cong.).
15. Johnston to Davis, Jan. 23, 1864, in "Georgia Portfolio," II, 115 (Duke Univ. Lib.).
16. Lawton to Davis, Mar. 1, 1864, *ibid.*, II, 135. Major G. W. Cunningham was in charge of the government's depot and shops in Atlanta.
17. U. S. Census Office, 8th Census, 1860, *Manufactures of the United States*, clxxxiii.
18. Atlanta *Southern Confederacy*, Apr. 5, 1862.
19. *Ibid.*, Mar. 18, 1863.
20. Augusta *Daily Chronicle and Sentinel*, Jan. 8, 1864.
21. Americus *Sumter Republican*, Jan. 31, 1862.
22. Augusta *Daily Chronicle and Sentinel*, June 24, 1864.
23. Americus *Sumter Republican*, July 11, 1862.
24. A Georgian invented a corn and pea planter, and a man in Sylvania invented a "plow stock and plow."
   See W. L. Benton to A. H. Stephens, June 10, 1861; and G. C. Dixon to Stephens, June 13, 1861, in Stephens Papers (Lib. of Cong.).
25. Atlanta *Southern Confederacy*, Mar. 29, 1862.
26. Americus *Sumter Republican*, Apr. 25, 1862.
27. Columbus *Daily Sun*, Oct. 13, 1862.
28. *Georgia Senate Journal, 1863, passim.*
29. Augusta *Daily Chronicle and Sentinel*, Nov. 4, 1863.
30. Columbus *Daily Times*, Feb. 13, 1864. Wages apparently did not increase as rapidly as the cost of living. In an attempt to keep the "real" wages of its employees from declining, the Eagle Manufacturing Co. sold food to its employees at lower than market prices. *Ibid.*, Apr. 25, 1864.
31. *Confederate Statutes at Large*, 1st Cong., 1st sess., chap. 74; *ibid.*, 1st Cong., 2nd sess., chap. 45.
32. Milledgeville *Confederate Union*, Aug. 22, 1863.
33. U. S. Census Office, 8th Census, 1860, *Statistics of the United States*, 331.
34. Frederick L. Olmstead, *The Cotton Kingdom*, I, 272.
35. Savannah *Daily Morning News*, Feb. 15, 1861.
36. *Reports of the Superintendent and Treasurer of the Western and Atlantic Railroad to Joseph E. Brown, Governor, October 1, 1864*, 9.
37. Savannah *Daily Morning News*, Jan. 7, 1862.
38. Peter S. McGuire, "The Railroads of Georgia, 1860-1880," *Georgia Historical Quarterly*, XVI, 3 (Sept., 1932), 182.
39. *Proceedings of the Convention of Railroad Presidents Association, Held at Chattanooga, Tenn., June 4, 5, 1861.*
40. "Minutes of the Executive Dept., 1860-66," 244-246.
41. Ashe to Brown, Oct. 3, 1861, in Brown Papers (Georgia State Archives).
42. Brown to Ashe, Oct. 3, 1861 (telegram), in "Governor's Letter Books, 1861-65," 97.
43. William M. Wodby to J. W. Mallett,

..NOTES

Mar. 5, 1863, in "Macon Arsenal Letters."
44. Candler, ed., *Confederate Records*, III, 132-134, 484.
45. *Ibid.*, II, 415, 416.
46. Superintendents and managers of a group of Southern railroads to the Secretary of War, Augusta, February, 1863.
47. "Petition of Lufborrow and Timmons to the Confederate Government," Richmond, Va., March, 1863.
48. "Petition of Lufborrow and Timmons to the Georgia Legislature," Richmond, Va., March, 1863.
49. *Georgia House Journal, 1863,* 157.
50. Candler, ed., *Confederate Records*, III, 192-198.
51. Columbus *Daily Times,* Jan. 21, 1864.
52. Augusta *Daily Chronicle and Sentinel,* Oct. 7, 28, 1863; Columbus *Daily Times,* Feb. 10, 1865; Norman W. Smith to George W. Brent, Feb. 9, 1865, in Brent Papers.
53. Joseph E. Johnston to Jefferson Davis, Jan. 20, 1864, in "Georgia Portfolio," II, 113.
54. See *Official Records,* Ser. IV, Vol. I, 269, 538; *ibid.,* Ser. IV, Vol. III, 616-618.
55. Candler, ed., *Confederate Records,* II, 556-558.
56. Charles C. Jones, Jr., and Salem Dutcher, *Memorial History of Augusta, Georgia,* 494.
57. Charlie Alexander to his father, Feb. 1, 1865, in Alexander Papers.
58. McCoy to George W. Brent, Feb. 6, 11, 1865, in Brent Papers.
59. *Official Records,* Ser. I, Vol. XXIV, 56, 159, 792; *ibid.,* Ser. I, Vol. XLIV, 13.
60. Grant to Brent, Feb. 13, 1865, in Brent Papers.
61. U. S. Census Office, 8th Census, 1860, *Manufactures of the United States,* 80, 81, 729; U. S. Census Office, 9th Census, 1870, *The Statistics of Wealth and Industry of the United States,* 392, 506.

CHAPTER VIII

1. U. S. Census Office, 8th Census, 1860, *Agriculture of the United States,* 22-29. Only Alabama, Mississippi, and Louisiana exceeded Georgia in the quantity of cotton produced.
2. Apr. 19, 1861.
3. *Southern Field and Fireside,* May 11, 1861.
4. M. W. Davis to E. A. Davis, Sept. 13, 1861, in E. A. Davis Papers.
5. W. R. Fleming to Stephens, Oct. 3, 1861, in Stephens Papers (Lib. of Cong.).
6. Andrew A. Lipscomb to Stephens, Oct. 23, 1861, *ibid.*
7. C. A. Alexander to his father, Nov. 23, 1861, in Alexander Papers.
8. *Southern Cultivator,* XIX (August, 1861), 240.
9. Moses W. Davis to E. A. Davis, Sept. 13, 1861, in E. A. Davis Papers.
10. Linton Stephens to A. H. Stephens, May 1, 1861, in Stephens Papers (Manhattanville College).
11. Although the Confederate Congress passed several acts which bore traces of embargo sentiment, no outright cotton embargo law was ever passed. An embargo *was* placed upon the exporting of cotton, not by Congress, but by state and local officials and by public safety committees. See *Journal of the Confederate Congress,* I, 205, 251, 264, 288, 290.
12. Candler, ed., *Confederate Records,* II, 100-102.
13. *Acts of the Gen. Assem. of Ga., 1861,* 20-22, 137. The bank was located in Thomasville, and the act gave the directors the power to establish branch banks.
14. Savannah *Daily Morning News,* Mar. 3, 1862.
15. *Southern Cultivator,* XX (April, 1862), 85.
16. Thweatt to Stephens, Mar. 10, 1862, in Stephens Papers (Lib. of Cong.).
17. Apr. 10, 1862.
18. Milledgeville *Southern Federal Union,* May 13, 1862.
19. Augusta *Constitutionalist* (n. d.), quoted in *Southern Cultivator,* XX (April, 1862), 85.

20. M. E. Marshall to Irby H. Scott, July 27, 1862, in Scott Papers.
21. O. H. Smith to Wier Boyd, Sept. 4, 1862, in Boyd Papers.
22. J. R. Price to Stephens, Aug. 21, 1862, in Stephens Papers (Lib. of Cong.).
23. Candler, ed., *Confederate Records*, II, 268, 269.
24. *Acts of the Gen. Assem. of Ga., 1862*, 20-22. Brown sent a copy of the act to President Davis and to the governor of each cotton state, accompanied by an appeal to bring the question to the attention of the legislature of each state. See letter of Brown to Jefferson Davis, Dec. 30, 1862, in Jefferson Davis Papers.
25. Candler, ed., *Confederate Records*, II, 367, 368, 504-507, 591; Joseph E. Brown to Gov. M. L. Bonham of South Carolina (telegram), Apr. 11, 1863, in Pickens Papers.
26. W. Sparks to his brother, Apr. 5, 1863, in Evans Papers.
27. E. W. Brown to Joel Strickland, Apr. 7, 1865, in J. R. Brown Papers.
28. S. G. Pryor to P. T. Pryor, Sept. 7, 1861, in "Reminiscences of Confederate Soldiers," III, 58 (Georgia State Archives).
29. W. W. Carter to Thomas J. Warthen, Nov. 21, 1861, in Warthen Papers (Duke Univ. Lib.).
30. S. J. Boyd to Wier Boyd (n. d.), in Boyd Papers.
31. Penelope T. Pryor to S. G. Pryor, Oct. 14, 1861, in "Reminiscences of Confederate Soldiers," III, 75 (Georgia State Archives).
32. *Southern Cultivator*, XX (July and August, 1862), 136.
33. Henry C. Wayne to Henry R. Jackson, May 5, 1862, in Jackson Papers.
34. J. R. Price to Stephens, Aug. 21, 1862, in Stephens Papers (Lib. of Cong.).
35. *Confederate Statutes at Large*, 1st Cong., 2nd sess., chap. 45; *Official Records*, Ser. IV, Vol. II, 690, 691; ibid., Ser. IV, Vol. II, 691; ibid., Ser. IV, Vol. III, 180.
36. One of Howell Cobb's sons wrote him that three of the four overseers on the Cobb plantation near Athens had been drafted. "It is an outrage and . . . you ought not to submit to it," he declared. John A. Cobb to Howell Cobb, Aug. 9, 1863, in Cobb Papers (private possession).
37. Mrs. M. E. Houston to Brown, Mar. 27, 1863, in Brown Papers (Georgia State Archives).
38. Edward R. Harden to James A. Nisbet, Apr. 24, 1861, in Nisbet Papers.
39. In 1860 there were 462,198 slaves in Georgia, owned by 41,084 persons, an average hold of 11.2. This was a larger number than the average in Virginia and North Carolina and smaller than in Alabama. There were approximately 15,000 landowners working without slave labor. The plantation system was gaining strength, for the number of overseers in Georgia had increased from 2,166 in 1850 to 4,909 in 1860. In 41 counties the slaves outnumbered the whites. U. S. Census Office, 7th Census, 1850, *A Statistical View of Each of the States*, xxxiii, xxxiv, 365; U. S. Census Office, 8th Census, 1860, *Agriculture of the United States*, 226, 227, 247; ibid., *Population of the United States*, 72-74, 598-604, 670.
40. J. H. Taylor to D. C. Barrow, Oct. 27, 1861, in Barrow Papers.
41. Linton Stephens to A. H. Stephens, Jan. 22, 1862, in Stephens Papers (Lib. of Cong.).
42. G. F. Bristow to Stephens, Jan. 22, 1862, *ibid.*
43. Mary Ann Harden to her son, Sept. 27, 1863, in Harden Papers.
44. "Laura B. Comer Diary," Aug. 16, 1862.
45. Edward R. Harden to his mother, Aug. 9, 1863, in Harden Papers.
46. Henrietta J. Wayne to "Mamma H.," Jan. 17, 1863, *ibid.*
47. Sallie Jackson to Asbury H. Jackson, Aug. 23, 1863, *ibid.*
48. Aug. 23, 1862.
49. *Acts of the Gen. Assem. of Ga., 1861*, 68, 69; *Georgia Senate Journal, 1863*, 120.
50. Quoted in Columbus *Daily Sun*, July 13, 1861.
51. *Savannah Republican*, Jan. 27, 1864.

NOTES

52. G. H. Davis to D. C. Barrow, June 21, 1861. See also J. H. Taylor to D. C. Barrow, June 16, 1861, in Barrow Papers.
53. Oct. 27, 1863.
54. O. O. Winther, ed., *With Sherman to the Sea*, 136.
55. *The Countryman*, Jan. 10, 1865.
56. *Ibid.*
57. Conyngham, *Sherman's March*, 276-278.
58. Brookhaven *Telegraph* (n. d.), quoted in Columbus *Daily Times*, Dec. 14, 1864.
59. "Governor's Letter Books, 1861-1865," Mar. 14, 1865.
60. Columbus *Daily Sun*, May 2, 1861.
61. Matt Crim, *Adventures of a Fair Rebel*, 109.
62. Joseph LeConte, *'Ware Sherman*, 32.
63. Bristow to Stephens, Oct. 8, 1861, in Stephens Papers (Lib. of Cong.).
64. George A. Mercer to his sister, Mar. 11, 1863, in Walker-Mercer Papers.
65. "Comer Diary," Mar. 2, 1862.
66. Jenny Lamar to Mrs. Howell Cobb, 1863, in Cobb Papers (private possession).
67. Charles A. Alexander to his uncle, Nov. 19, 1861, in Alexander Papers.
68. Lamar to Cobb, Nov. 3, 1861, in Cobb Papers (private possession).
69. Charles A. Alexander to his uncle, Nov. 19, 1861, in Alexander Papers.
70. Edward R. Harden to his mother, Oct. 18, 1864, in Harden Papers.
71. T. W. Montfort to his wife, Feb. 1, 1862, in "Letters from Confederate Soldiers," II, 51 (Georgia State Archives).
72. Atlanta *Southern Confederacy*, Feb. 14, 1863.
73. Columbus *Daily Sun*, Apr. 20, 1861.
74. Candler, ed., *Confederate Records*, V, Pt. I, 69.
75. C. C. Hopley, *Life in the South; from the Commencement of the War*, II, 336, 337.
76. *The Countryman*, Sept. 20, 1864.
77. Anna Niles to Alice Niles, Jan. 30, 1865, in Niles Papers.
78. Mercer to Randolph, Aug. 16, 1862, in Stephens Papers (Lib. of Cong.).
79. Lyon to Stephens, Aug. 23, 1862, *ibid.*
80. Candler, ed., *Confederate Records*, II, 311-314; *ibid.*, III, 334-336; *Acts of the Gen. Assem. of Ga., 1862*, 54, 55.
81. Jan. 4, 1863.
82. James A. Hill to J. W. Mallet (n. d.), in "Macon Arsenal Letters."
83. Aug. 23, 1863.
84. Cobb to Seddon, Jan. 8, 1865, *Amer. Hist. Rev.*, I, 1, (Oct., 1895), 98.
85. Candler, ed., *Confederate Records*, II, 832-835.
86. T. W. Montfort to his wife, Jan. 27, 1862, in "Letters from Confederate Soldiers," II, 48 (Georgia Archives).
87. T. W. Montfort to his wife, Nov. 1, 1861, in *ibid.*, II, 27.
88. Delia Davis to James Davis, June 10, 1862, in E. A. Davis Papers.
89. Donie Davis to James Davis, June 20, 1862, *ibid.*
90. J. E. Jeffares to Sarah Ann Jeffares, Dec. 2, 1863, in "Confederate Diaries," VIII, 176 (Georgia State Archives).
91. P. T. Pryor to S. G. Pryor, Dec. 5, 1862, in "Reminiscences of Confederate Soldiers," III, 257 (Georgia State Archives).
92. *Southern Cultivator*, XX (May and June, 1862), 117.
93. L. I. Chesnut to Alexander Chesnut, June 3, 1862, in Chesnut Papers.
94. Rutha Hodges to Asbury W. Hodges, February 27, 1863, in "Confederate Diaries," VII, 249 (Georgia State Archives).
95. W. A. Weldon to Alexander Chesnut, Apr. 26, 1863, in Chesnut Papers.
96. Charles A. Alexander to his wife, June 3, 1864, in Alexander Papers.
97. Abial Winn to Charlie Alexander (n. d.), *ibid.*
98. "Irby H. Scott Contract," Aug. 9, 1865, in Scott Papers.
99. U. S. Census Office, 8th Census, 1860, *Agriculture of the United States*, 26; U. S. Census Office, 9th Census, 1870, *Statistics of Wealth and Industry of the United States*, 120; U. S. Census Office, 12th Census, 1900, V, 688.

CHAPTER IX

1. Among the native Georgians who served as officers in the Union army or navy were John M. Berrien, John M. Cuyler, George B. Dandy, Henry K. Davenport, Montgomery C. Meigs, Clarke Merchant, E. T. Nichols, Edward E. Stone, and H. D. Wallen.
2. A. S. Warrell to Stephens, May 15, 1861, in Stephens Papers (Lib. of Cong.).
3. J. A. Stewart to Stephens, Nov. 5, 1861, *ibid.*
4. Lucy J. Cunyus, *The History of Bartow County*, 214, 215.
5. "Diary of Dolly Sumner [Lunt] Burge," in "Confederate Diaries," X, 35 (Georgia State Archives).
6. H. J. Wayne to "Mamma H.," July 15, 1861, in Harden Papers.
7. Apr. 18, 1862.
8. Atlanta *Southern Confederacy*, Mar. 5, July 30, 1862.
9. *Ibid.*, Sept. 3, 1862.
10. Quoted in Savannah *Daily Morning News*, Feb. 12, 1862.
11. "Mercer Diary," Aug. 31, 1863.
12. There were 11,671 persons of foreign births in Georgia in 1860 out of a total free population of 583,417. Most of the foreigners were natives of Germany and the British Isles.
13. Hudtwalcker to Brown, Mar. 11, 1862; Henry C. Wayne to Hudtwalcker, Mar. 12, 1862; Hudtwalcker to Wayne, Mar. 13, 1862, in Wayne Papers.
14. Quoted in Atlanta *Southern Confederacy*, Mar. 5, 1862.
15. At times innocent persons were arrested. An Augusta man wrote Stephens that "Wm. H. Byrd, a native Georgian, was confined to the Conf. States jail as a Spy. *Malicious and secret ill feelings has been the sole cause of arrest*, and no single act can be proven on him for which he is charged. . . ." John H. Byrd to A. H. Stephens, Oct. 18, 1861, in Stephens Papers (Lib. of Cong.).
16. James W. Ailes to Brown, Feb. 15, 1861, in Telamon Cuyler Collection.
17. Jonathan Martin to Cobb, Apr. 15, 1861, in Cobb Papers (private possession).
18. Samuel H. Gibson, commanding a volunteer company at Dahlonega, denied a false impression that his company was involved in Riley's reported intention of seizing the mint. See letter of Gibson to William Martin, Jan. 29, 1861, in Gibson Papers (Georgia State Archives).
19. A man in Rome wrote Howell Cobb that "The Representative from this District is . . . using his influence to discourage the people . . . we feel deeply troubled that we have got to fight such an enemy at home." Charles H. Smith ["Bill Arp"] to Cobb, Nov. 13, 1862, in Cobb Papers (private possession).
20. Georgia deserters from the Confederate army totalled 79 officers and 6,797 men during the war, but 5,173 of these deserters were returned to the army. *House. Ex. Doc.*, 39th Cong., 1st sess., No. 1, IV, Pt. I, 139-141.
21. "C. R. Hanleiter Diary, 1861-1862," Dec. 10, 1861.
22. Theodorick W. Montfort to his wife, Mar. 28, 1862, in "Letters from Confederate Soldiers," II, 98 (Georgia State Archives).
23. Mar. 2, 1862.
24. S. R. McCancy to Brown, May 21, 1861, in Brown Papers (Georgia State Archives).
25. "Hanleiter Diary," Feb. 23, 1862.
26. Lyde Goodwin to Jackson, Apr. 6, 1862, in Jackson Papers.
27. Edward R. Harden to his mother, Aug. 3, 1861, in Harden Papers.
28. "Hanleiter Diary," Feb. 1, 1862.
29. T. W. Montfort to his wife, Jan. 14, 1861, in "Letters from Confederate Soldiers," II, 13 (Georgia State Archives).
30. "Hanleiter Diary," July 8, 1862.
31. J. H. Jordan to his father, Feb. 14, 1863, in Jordan Papers (Georgia State Archives).
32. "Mercer Diary," Mar. 3, 1862.

..NOTES

33. Harden to his mother, Apr. 17, 1862, in Harden Papers.
34. "Mercer Diary," Aug. 19, 1862.
35. *Ibid.*, Aug. 23, 1862.
36. *Annual Cyclopaedia, 1863*, 208.
37. Sept. 24, 1862.
38. William M. Davis to Stephens, July 15, 1863, in Stephens Papers (Lib. of Cong.).
39. Augusta *Chronicle and Sentinel*, Jan. 7, 1864.
40. *Official Records*, Ser. IV, Vol. III, 344-349, 869, 870, 1102-1110.
41. The first Conscription Act provided that persons not liable for service might be received as substitutes for those who were. The system was abolished in 1864 after it had caused much resentment.
42. L. I. Chesnut to Alexander Chesnut, June 3, 1862, in Chesnut Papers.
43. Mollie Evans to John B. Evans, Mar. 8, 1863, in Evans Papers.
44. *Ibid.*, Apr. 4, 1863.
45. Dec. 23, 1863.
46. Quoted in Sandersville *Central Georgian*, Mar. 19, 1862.
47. Sarah S. Wright to Brown, May 27, 1861, in Brown Papers (Georgia State Archives).
48. "Adjutant-General Letter Books, 1861-1864, A. G. O.," Pt. I, 322, 323; *ibid.*, Pt. II, 324-326.
49. Quoted in Atlanta *Southern Confederacy*, Mar. 25, 1863.
50. Feb. 17, 1863.
51. Letter of C. H. Sutton, Feb. 17, 1863, published in Atlanta *Southern Confederacy*, Feb. 22, 1863.
52. Lee to Brown (telegram), June 12, 1863, in "Governor's Letter Books, 1861-1865," 491.
53. Brown to Lee, June 13, 1863, *ibid.*
54. "Adjutant-General Letter Books, 1861-1864, No. 21," 250; Vol. B, No. 44, Pt. II, 440.
55. Buckner to Brown, June 9, 1863, in Brown Papers (Georgia State Archives). The story that Dade County, the extreme northwestern county of Georgia, seceded from both the Union and from the state has never been verified to the extent of being placed in the official records of Georgia. Volunteers joined the state militia and 81 men were listed in the Lookout Dragoon Company of volunteers in Dade County. See letter of W. C. Brock, *et al.*, to Henry C. Wayne, Dec. 10, 1861 (Georgia State Archives); and an undated manuscript concerning Dade County volunteers in Georgia State Archives.
56. Augusta *Chronicle and Sentinel*, Dec. 4, 1863.
57. *Acts of the Gen. Assem. of Ga., 1863*, 61, 63.
58. *Official Records*, Ser. I, Vol. XXVI, Pt. II, 551-557; *ibid.*, Ser. IV, Vol. III, 396, 397.
59. Atlanta *Southern Confederacy*, July 15, 1862.
60. "Mercer Diary," Aug. 31, 1863.
61. Wilbur to "Mary," Aug. 31, 1862, in Wilbur Papers (Duke Univ. Lib.).
62. "Mercer Diary," Aug. 31, 1863.
63. Joseph E. Johnston to Jefferson Davis, Jan. 23, 1864, in Johnston Papers.
64. L. H. Briscoe to H. F. Price, Feb. 2, 1864, in "Adjutant-General Letter Books, 1864, No. 22," 1.
65. Huldah A. Briant to M. C. Briant, Mar. 4, May 8, 1864, in Huldah A. Briant Papers.
66. C. C. Norton to J. T. Nisbet, Apr. 20, 1864, in Nisbet Papers.
67. Henry L. Graves to his mother, Apr. 24, 1864, in "Confederate Diaries," VI, 316 (Georgia State Archives).
68. Savannah *Daily Morning News*, July 18, 1864.
69. *Ibid.*, Aug. 10, 1864.
70. Celathiel Helms to Mary Helms, July 6, 1864, in "Letters from Confederate Soldiers," II, 448 (Georgia State Archives).
71. Leggett to L. M. Dayton, Aug. 22, 1864, in William Tecumseh Sherman Papers.
72. A. J. Neal to Mrs. J. J. C. Neal, July 23, 1864, in Neal Papers.
73. Many soldiers on furloughs were not able to return to their commands and were unjustly called deserters.
74. B. H. Hill in Columbus *Daily Sun*, Oct. 11, 1864.

CONFEDERATE GEORGIA..

75. "Cumming Recollections," 65.
76. Jan. 22, 1864.
77. Kate Cumming, *A Journal of Hospital Life in the Confederate Army*, 121.
78. E. M. Briant to his sons, Apr. 15, 1864, in Briant Papers.
79. Mrs. H. A. Briant to M. C. Briant, May 8, 1864, *ibid*.
80. Andrew J. Hansell to Cobb, July 18, 1864, in Cobb Papers (private possession).
81. A. Murcheson to Brown, Nov. 21, 1864, in Brown Papers (Emory Univ. Lib.).
82. Official Records, Ser. I, Vol. XLV, 980, 990, 1192. Depredations were also widespread in Murray County, adjoining Tennessee.
83. Augusta *Chronicle and Sentinel*, Sept. 14, 1864.
84. Candler, ed., *Confederate Records*, II, 802-804; "Governor's Letter Books, 1861-1865," 736-739. Lawlessness was not limited to North Georgia. For example, renegades terrorized Morgan County in Middle Georgia.
85. Cobb to Davis, Jan. 6, 1865, in Cobb Papers (Duke Univ. Lib.).
86. J. R. Brown to A. J. Brown, Jan. 1, 1865, in J. R. Brown Papers.
87. H. A. Thomas to Cobb, Jan. 9, 1865, in Cobb Papers (private possession).
88. Andrew J. Hansell to Cobb, Jan. 10, 1865, *ibid*.
89. Cobb to his wife, Jan. 19, 1865, in Cobb Papers (Univ. of Georgia Lib.).
90. Alfred Prescott to P. Looney, Feb. 27, 1865, in "Confederate Bible Records," IX, 293-298 (Georgia State Archives).
91. Mrs. H. A. Briant to M. C. Briant, Jan. 25, 1865, in Briant Papers.
92. Findley to Brown, Jan. 26, 1865, in Brown Papers (Georgia State Archives).
93. Reynolds to Cobb, Jan. 22, 1865, in Cobb Papers (Univ. of Georgia Lib.).
94. Annie Briant to M. C. Briant, Mar. 1, 1865, in Briant Papers.
95. Henry Blackshear to J. William Blackshear, Mar. 27, 1865, in Blackshear Papers.
96. E. W. Brown to Joel Strickland, Apr. 7, 1865, in J. R. Brown Papers.

CHAPTER X

1. Johnston to Davis, Jan. 20, 1864, in Johnston Papers.
2. *Ibid.*; *Memoirs of Gen W. T. Sherman*, II, 23, 24; *Official Records*, Ser. I, Vol. XXXVIII, Pt. I, 59-61.
3. W. T. Sherman to John Sherman, May 26, 1864, in Sherman Papers.
4. A. J. Neal to John Neal, May 15, 1864, in Neal Papers.
5. A. J. Neal to Emma Neal, June 2, 1864, *ibid*.
6. W. T. Sherman to John Sherman, June 9, 1864, in Sherman Papers.
7. Z. J. Armistead to his brother, June 16, 1864, in "Confederate Diaries," VI, 354 (Georgia State Archives).
8. Candler, ed., *Confederate Records*, III, 574; Sherman, *Memoirs*, II, 70, 71. "If Grant had been at the head of this Army we would have whipped them but Sherman will not give us a chance. They outgeneral us in maneuvering by mere weight of numbers but we can fight them back at any point they wish to try." A. J. Neal to John Neal, June 20, 1864, in Neal Papers.
9. *Official Records*, Ser. I, Vol. LII, Pt. II, 702-709; *ibid.*, Ser. I, Vol. LII, Pt. III, 618.
10. Aug. 23, 1864.
11. Sandersville *Central Georgian*, July 27, 1864.
12. *Ibid.*, May 25, 1864.
13. June 6, 1864.
14. Quoted in Sandersville *Central Georgian*, May 25, 1864.
15. Mrs. Rebecca Hood, "Memories of the War between the States," in "Letters from Confederate Soldiers," II, 251-260 (Georgia State Archives).
16. Helena Jones Bell, "Reminiscences," in "Confederate Bible Records," IX, 155 (Georgia State Archives).
17. Candler, ed., *Confederate Records*, II, 710, *ff.*, 735-738.
18. Susan Dabney Smedes, *Memorials of a Southern Planter*, 217, 218.

..NOTES

19. George Stoneman to Mrs. Stoneman, Aug. 1, 1864, in Sherman Papers.
20. Jamie Frederick McKenzie, "When Sherman Marched Through Georgia," in "Reminiscences of Confederate Soldiers," III, 360 (Georgia State Archives).
21. Quoted in Savannah *Daily Morning News*, Aug. 11, 1864.
22. "Refugee," an unpublished story from the diary of a young Georgia girl of the sixties. Author unknown. (Typescript in Georgia State Archives).
23. Augusta *Chronicle and Sentinel*, Dec. 27, 1863.
24. "Reminiscences of Confederate Soldiers," I, 27, 28 (Georgia State Archives).
25. "Confederate Diaries," VII, 207, 208 (Georgia State Archives).
26. "Confederate Bible Records," IX, 167-170 (Georgia State Archives).
27. "Letters from Confederate Soldiers," II, 185 (Georgia State Archives).
28. "Confederate Bible Records," IX, 167-170 (Georgia State Archives).
29. "Confederate Diaries," VII, 192, 193 (Georgia State Archives).
30. *Official Records*, Ser. I, Vol. XXXVIII, Pt. III, 630, 632.
31. *Ibid.*, Ser. I, Vol. XXXVIII, Pt. III, 310, 633, 696, 697.
32. *Ibid.*, Ser. I, Vol. XXXVIII, Pt. III, 628-634.
33. Sherman, *Memoirs*, II, 118, 119. Many Atlanta inhabitants already had fled to Griffin, Macon, and other places.
34. Hood to Sherman, Sept. 12, 1864, in Sherman Papers.
35. *Official Records*, Ser. I, Vol. XXXIX, Pt. II, 417-422. Secretary of War Halleck approved Sherman's removal of the families. See letter of H. A. Halleck to Sherman, Sept. 28, 1864, in Sherman Papers.
36. *Official Records*, Ser. I, Vol. XXXIX, Pt. II, 381, 396.
37. Phillips, ed., *Correspondence of Toombs, Stephens, and Cobb*, 652-654.
38. Augusta *Constitutionalist*, Sept. 29, 1864. The statement that Georgia could negotiate treaties was not true.
39. "From the Autobiography of Herschel V. Johnson," *Amer. Hist. Rev.*, XXX, 2 (Jan., 1925), 334.
40. Sept. 27, Oct. 4, 1864.
41. Oct. 6, 1864.
42. George W. Nichols, *The Story of the Great March*, 38.
43. Henry Hitchcock, *Marching With Sherman*, 57.
44. Nichols, *The Story of the Great March*, 38.
45. *Official Records*, Ser. I, Vol. XXXIX, Pt. 3, 756; Sherman, *Memoirs*, II, 145-176.
46. Hitchcock, *Marching With Sherman*, 75.
47. Dolly Sumner Lunt [Burge], *A Woman's War-Time Journal*, 9, 10, 17, 18.
48. Letter of John H. Ash, of Effingham County, Nov. 16, 1864 (Georgia State Archives).
49. Conyngham, *Sherman's March*, 254.
50. "H. M." to his sister, Dec. 13, 1864, published in *The Countryman*, Jan. 10, 1865.
51. "M. A. N." to "Lou," Dec. 13, 1864, *ibid.*
52. Louisa Kenan White Sheehan, "Reminiscences of the Sixties," in "Confederate Bible Records," IX, 243 (Georgia State Archives).
53. "Governor's Letter Books, 1861-65," 730.
54. Candler, ed., *Confederate Records*, II, 790, 791, 799-802.
55. Macon became the temporary capital.
56. Milledgeville *Confederate Union*, Dec. 6, 1864, quoted in Columbus *Daily Times*, Dec. 16, 1864.
57. Thweatt to A. H. Stephens, Mar. 28, 1865, in Stephens Papers (Lib. of Cong.).
58. Macon *Telegraph and Confederate* (n. d.), quoted in Columbus *Daily Times*, Nov. 30, 1864.
59. Savannah *Daily Morning News*, Dec. 2, 1864.
60. "Miss Emma Manley's Experiences in the Sixties," in "Reminiscences of Confederate Soldiers," III, 305 (Georgia State Archives).
61. "A Paper Written . . . by Mrs. Cornwell . . . ," in "Confederate Dia-

CONFEDERATE GEORGIA..

ries," V, 255, 256 (Georgia State Archives).
62. Walker to Brown, Dec. 8, 1864, in Joseph E. Brown Papers (Duke Univ. Lib.).
63. Nov. 22, 1864.
64. Columbus *Daily Times,* Nov. 28, 1864.
65. *Ibid.,* Dec. 10, 1864.
66. Dec. 1, 1864.
67. Walker to Brown, Dec. 8, 1864, in Joseph E. Brown Papers (Duke Univ. Lib.). Wheeler's orders directed him to destroy everything from which the Federals might derive sustenance.
68. *Ibid.*
69. Brown to Pierre G. T. Beauregard, Apr. 8, 1865, in Joseph E. Brown Papers (Duke Univ. Lib.).
70. Roman to G. W. Grant, Jan. 22, 1865, in Roman Papers.
71. *Official Records,* Ser. I, Vol. XLIV, 95, 96, 110, 700-710, 955, 957.
72. Hardee to Charles C. Jones, May 14, 1866, in Hardee Papers.
73. Cobb to Reynolds, Jan. 15, 1865, in Cobb Papers (Duke Univ. Lib.).
74. Cobb to S. Cooper, Jan. 16, 1865, *ibid.*
75. Cobb to Brown, Apr. 9, 1865, *ibid.*
76. Wilson to Brown, May 3, 1865, in Joseph E. Brown Papers (Duke Univ. Lib.).

CHAPTER XI

1. Julia M. Conner to Alice E. Andrews, Nov. 1, 1862, in Niles Papers.
2. See Francis B. Simkins and James W. Patton, *The Women of the Confederacy,* 21-24; and "Confederate Reminiscences" in the Georgia State Archives (Unpublished letters, diaries, and reminiscences of the war, collected by the Georgia Division, United Daughters of the Confederacy, compiled between 1940 and 1942 by the Georgia Dept. of Archives and History, and bound by the Georgia Division, U. D. C.).
3. Fort, ed., *Memoirs of the Fort and Fannin Families,* 37, 70.
4. July 10, 1861.
5. Milledgeville *Southern Federal Union,* Aug. 6, 1861.
6. Americus *Sumter Republican,* Oct. 10, 1862.
7. From the Diary of Mrs. Mary Willis Cobb Johnson, in "Reminiscences of Confederate Soldiers," III, 95 (Georgia State Archives).
8. Mrs. Thomas Hardeman to her husband (n. d.), in "Confederate Diaries," IV, 192 (Georgia State Archives).
9. "Cook Journal," Nov. 19, 1861.
10. "Daily Journal for 1861 of Henrietta Eugenia Vickers Armstrong," Oct. 1, 1861, in "Confederate Diaries," V, 324 (Georgia State Archives).
11. Mary A. H. Gay, *Life in Dixie During the War,* 42.
12. Matthew Page Andrews, comp., *The Women of the South in War Times,* 296, 297.
13. Mrs. Thomas Hardeman to her husband (n.d.), in "Confederate Diaries," IV, 192 (Georgia State Archives).
14. Mrs. Sarah Davis Arnold, "Reminiscences of Confederate Women and War," in "Letters from Confederate Soldiers," II, 288 (Georgia State Archives).
15. Mrs. Willie W. Foreman, "Reminiscences," *ibid.,* II, 311.
16. Sarah Huff, "Reminiscences," *ibid.,* II, 335.
17. "Armstrong Journal," Apr. 23, May 23, June 19, 1861, in "Confederate Diaries," V, 296, 305, 312 (Georgia State Archives).
18. Americus *Sumter Republican,* Mar. 21, 1862.
19. Sept. 2, 1862.
20. Emma Tyler Blalock, "War Memories," in "Letters from Confederate Soldiers," II, 166-173 (Georgia State Archives).
21. Mrs. M. A. Swanson, "Reminiscences of the War," *ibid.,* II, 123-126.
22. Blalock, "War Memories," *ibid.,* II, 168.
23. Anna Harden to "Grandma," May 14, 1864, in Harden Papers.

NOTES

24. T. W. Montfort to his wife and children, Mar. 28, 1862, in "Letters from Confederate Soldiers," II, 91 (Georgia State Archives).
25. May 25, 1864.
26. Atlanta *Southern Confederacy*, Feb. 4, 1863.
27. Fannie A. Beers, *Memories*, 94, 95.
28. Apr. 27, 1861.
29. Milledgeville *Southern Federal Union*, Oct. 1, 1861.
30. Savannah *Republican*, Apr 28, 1862.
31. Shephard Green Pryor to his wife, Mar. 28, 1862, in "Reminiscences of Confederate Soldiers," III, 163, 164 (Georgia State Archives).
32. Penelope Tyson Pryor to her husband, Oct. 14, 1861, *ibid.*, III, 75.
33. *Ibid.*, Oct. 31, 1862, III, 242.
34. S. G. Pryor to his wife, Sept. 23, 1862, *ibid.*, III, 221.
35. *Ibid.*, Aug. 19, 1863.
36. R. L. Perkins to his wife, Oct. 31, 1863, in "Confederate Diaries," VI, 363, 364 (Georgia State Archives).
37. T. W. Montfort to his wife, Sept. 26, 1861, in "Letters from Confederate Soldiers," II, 20 (Georgia State Archives).
38. T. W. Montfort to his wife, Oct. 27, 1861, Jan. 22 and Feb. 8, 1862; *ibid.*, II, 23, 25, 46, 58.
39. M. F. Stephenson to Wier Boyd, May 10, 1863, in Boyd Papers.
40. M. E. Marshall to Irby H. Scott, July 27, 1862, in Scott Papers.
41. *Ibid.*
42. Mollie Evans to John B. Evans, Feb. 19, Mar. 9, 1863, in Evans Papers.
43. "Jennie" to her cousin, Mar. 8, 1864, in E. A. Davis Papers.
44. "Confederate Bible Records," IX, 80, 81 (Georgia State Archives).
45. Susan J. Howard to Brown, May 25, 1864, in Brown Papers (Georgia State Archives).
46. "Paper Written by Mrs. Annie Holloman Tropnell," in "Reminiscences of Confederate Soldiers," I, 133, 134 (Georgia State Archives).
47. G. W. S. Ware, "Reminiscences of the War," in "Confederate Bible Records," IX, 193, 194 (Georgia State Archives).
48. Berta T. Johnson, "Reminiscences of the Sixties," *ibid.*, IX, 231, 232.
49. Mrs. Marion Stone, "Reminiscences," *ibid.*, IX, 78.
50. Mrs. J. T. P. Austin, "Thrilling Capture and Escape During War," in "Reminiscences of Confederate Soldiers," I, 41-64 (Georgia State Archives).
51. Eunice Ginn, "The Twentieth of May," in "Letters from Confederate Soldiers," II, 145-150 (Georgia State Archives).
52. "Reminiscence," in "Confederate Bible Records," IX, 125, 126 (Georgia State Archives).
53. "From the Diary of Mary Willis Cobb Johnson," in "Reminiscences of Confederate Soldiers," III, 89 (Georgia State Archives).
54. "Emma Manley's Experiences in the Sixties," *ibid.*, III, 304.
55. Mary J. Green, "First Confederate Cemetery," in "Letters from Confederate Soldiers," II, 25-29 (Georgia State Archives).
56. *A History of the Origin of Memorial Day As Adopted by the Ladies' Memorial Association of Columbus, Georgia.*
57. "Mary" to John Iverson, July 20, 1863, in John L. Underwood, ed., *The Women of the Confederacy*, 62.
58. E. D. Graham to Laura Mann, Nov. 26, 1864, in "Letters from Confederate Soldiers," II, 318 (Georgia State Archives).
59. Donie Davis to James Davis, June 20, 1862, in E. A. Davis Papers.
60. Annie Briant to M. C. Briant, Mar. 1, 1865, in Briant Papers.
61. Bell I. Wiley, *The Plain People of the Confederacy*, 24, 25.
62. Oscar O. Winther, ed., *With Sherman to the Sea*, 119; *Official Records*, Ser. I, Vol. XXXVIII, Pt. III, 310.
63. Samuel Jarrett to Jefferson Hartman, Jan. 15, 1865, in Jefferson Hartman Papers.

CONFEDERATE GEORGIA..
CHAPTER XII

1. J. H. Hewitt, a music teacher in Augusta, was the author of several of these productions.
2. Oct. 15, 1864.
3. Augusta *Chronicle and Sentinel*, Sept. 23, Dec. 17, 1863; *Southern Field and Fireside*, Mar. 14, 1863; Bertram H. Flanders, *Early Georgia Magazines*, 129, 130.
4. Savannah *Daily Morning News*, Nov. 18, Dec. 23, 1862.
5. *Southern Field and Fireside*, Feb. 21, 1863.
6. Augusta *Chronicle and Sentinel*, June 16, 1864.
7. *Ibid.*, May 5, 1861.
8. Milledgeville *Daily Federal Union*, Nov. 10, 1861.
9. Atlanta *Daily Intelligencer*, June 27, 1862.
10. J. H. Graham to F. W. Graham, Jan. 16, 1862, in "Confederate Diaries," VIII, 195 (Georgia State Archives).
11. A member of the family of J. William Blackshear to his cousin, June 9, 1861, in Blackshear Papers.
12. Atlanta *Southern Confederacy*, Sept. 4, 1861.
13. Andrews, *Women of the South in War Times*, 292, 293.
14. When a Milledgeville girl invited a soldier to attend a dance, he replied that he had nothing suitable to wear. She offered to give him some woven jeans, but then asked him why he had no additional clothes. He replied that his valise was lost at Missionary Ridge. She retorted, "No man who runs from Missionary Ridge can wear Sue Woodall's jeans." He never did. "Reminiscences of Confederate Soldiers," III, 166 (Georgia State Archives).
15. "Letters from Confederate Soldiers," II, 46 (Georgia State Archives).
16. *Ibid*. Younger boys and girls had their parties too. An officer wrote from Savannah: "Little Georgia had a party the other Evening—some Six or eight *young ladies* and as many *young gentlemen*. . . . The candy and cake and custard cost 5$ and they were as happy as if they had a supper costing 500$." H. W. Mercer to his daughter, Mar. 20, 1863, in Walker-Mercer Papers.
17. Henry Graves to his mother, Nov. 18, 1863, in "Confederate Diaries," VI, 307 (Georgia State Archives).
18. Lou Burge was the stepdaughter of Mrs. Thomas Burge [Dolly Sumner Lunt], whose *A Woman's War-Time Journal* has been published. See the typed copy of the "Journal of Miss Lou Burge," in "Confederate Letters," X, 22-38 (Georgia State Archives).
19. *Ibid.*, X, 26, 27.
20. F. E. Miles to Joseph A. Miles, Nov. 15, 1861, in Miles Papers.
21. Matilda Harris to Alice E. Niles, Sept. 22, 1862, in Niles Papers.
22. N. F. Legg to John Miles, Jan. 30, 1863, in Miles Papers.
23. "Jewett" to Jefferson Howard DeVotie, Aug. 4, 1863, in Jefferson Howard DeVotie Papers.
24. Andrews, *War-Time Journal of a Georgia Girl*, 93.
25. Anna Niles to her cousin, Feb. 8, 1864, in Niles Papers.
26. E. D. Graham to Laura Mann, Nov. 26, 1864, in "Letters from Confederate Soldiers," II, 313 (Georgia State Archives).
27. Ellen Roberts to Ellora Reese, Dec. 4, 1864, in "Confederate Diaries," VIII, 209, 210 (Georgia State Archives).
28. S. W. Graves to Henry Graves, Jan. 4, 1863, *ibid.*, VI, 280.
29. Mollie Evans to John B. Evans, Feb. 9, 1863, in Evans Papers.
30. Kate Cumming, *Gleaning from the Southland*, 171.
31. A member of the family of William Blackshear to his cousin, Apr. 3, 1862, in Blackshear Papers.
32. P. T. Pryor to S. G. Pryor, Nov. 28, 1862, in "Reminiscences of Confederate Soldiers," III, 255 (Georgia State Archives).
33. William L. Tolbert to "Uncle Birdy,"

..NOTES

Nov. 5, 1861, in "Miscellaneous Soldiers' Letters, 1861-1865."
34. M. A. Miles to Joseph A. Miles, Dec. 20, 1861, in Miles Papers.
35. Sallie McGough to Mollie Evans, Jan. 22, 1864 in Evans Papers.
36. "Lou Burge Journal," in "Confederate Letters," X, 35 (Georgia State Archives).
37. "Cook Journal," Nov. 19, 1861.
38. John B. Evans to Mollie Evans, Sept. 6, 1863, in Evans Papers.
39. Andrews, *War-Time Journal of a Georgia Girl*, 69, 100.
40. F. E. Miles to Joseph A. Miles, Dec. 20, 1861, in Miles Papers.
41. Mat L. Jackson to her brother, Mar. 3, 1863, in Harden Papers.
42. Sallie McGough to Mollie Evans, May 22, 1864, in Evans Papers.
43. Beers, *Memories*, 89, 114.
44. Andrews, *War-Time Journal of a Georgia Girl*, 139.
45. "Diary of Josephine C. Habersham," July 13, 1864.
46. "Julia Ann Stanford Diary," June 30, July 4, 1861, in "Confederate Letters," X, 45, 46 (Georgia State Archives).
47. "Armstrong Journal," Apr. 30 to Sept. 29, 1861, in "Confederate Diaries," V, 298-339 (Georgia State Archives).
48. Emily Andrews to Alice E. (Niles) Andrews, June 19, 1864, in Niles Papers.
49. Henry Graves to his mother, Apr. 29, 1864, in "Confederate Diaries," VI, 319 (Georgia State Archives).
50. Henry Graves to Elizabeth, September, 1864, in Graves Papers.
51. Henry R. Jackson to Sarah Jackson, June 29, 1863, in Jackson-Prince Papers.
52. "Habersham Diary," July 19, 20, Aug. 29, 1863.
53. Henry Graves to Cora Graves, Aug. 3, 1863, in "Confederate Diaries," VI, 297 (Georgia State Archives).
54. "Lou Burge Journal," in "Confederate Letters," X, 35 (Georgia State Archives).
55. Kate Green to Joseph A. Miles, Jan. 31, 1862, in Miles Papers.
56. Lunt, *War-Time Journal*, 43-45.
57. Augusta *Chronicle and Sentinel*, Nov. 5, 1862, May 22, 1864.
58. Henry R. Jackson to Sarah Jackson, June 29, 1863, in Jackson-Prince Papers.
59. Andrews, *War-Time Journal of a Georgia Girl*, 67, 96.

CHAPTER XIII

1. Joel Chandler Harris to editors of *The Commonwealth*, June 2, 1863, in Joel Chandler Harris Papers.
2. Richard Barksdale Harwell, *Confederate Belles-Lettres*, 21.
3. A. S. Warrell to Stephens, May 15, 1861, in Stephens Papers (Lib. of Cong.).
4. Mar. 22, 1863.
5. U. S. Census Office, 7th Census, 1850, *Statistical View of the United States*, 157; U. S. Census Office, 8th Census, 1860, *Statistics of the United States*, 322.
6. The circulation of the Savannah *Daily Morning News* was 1,020 in 1850 and had increased rapidly during the 1850's.
7. Rabun Lee Brantley, *Georgia Journalism of the Civil War Period*, 16-47.
8. Columbus *Daily Sun*, Apr. 23, 1861.
9. W. Rice to Brown, Jan. 21, 1862, in Brown Papers (Georgia State Archives).
10. Columbus *Daily Sun* (n.d.), quoted in Augusta *Chronicle and Sentinel*, Jan. 27, 1863.
11. Augusta *Chronicle and Sentinel*, Apr. 12, 1865.
12. Apr. 13, 16, 1864.
13. Brantley, *Georgia Journalism, passim*.
14. *The Press Association of the Confederate States of America*, 30, 31, 57.
15. One possible exception may have been Morse's Augusta *Chronicle*, which in 1864-65 was accused of disloyalty by many Georgia newspapers.
16. Columbus *Daily Times*, Feb. 19, 1865.
17. *Ibid.*, Mar. 26, 1865.

CONFEDERATE GEORGIA..

18. Mar. 19, 1865.
19. Apr. 26, 1865.
20. Jan. 7, 1863.
21. Feb. 4, 1865.
22. Five literary periodicals were located in Athens; three each in Augusta, Macon, Savannah, and Atlanta; two in Eatonton; and one each in Penfield, Madison, Newnan, Turnwold, and Griffin.
23. The 1860 census gives twenty-two literary publications in Georgia. Thirteen were weeklies, eight were monthlies, and one was published quarterly. U. S. Census Office, 8th Census, 1860, *Preliminary Report*, 212.
24. Flanders, *Early Georgia Magazines*, 139-145, 152-156. *The Plantation* was distributed from Eatonton but was printed in New York.
25. *The Countryman*, May 6, 1862.
26. Mar. 11, 1862.
27. *The Countryman* was read all over the South and at one time had nearly 2,000 subscribers. It appeared weekly, three months comprising a volume, until the issue for Oct. 6, 1863, when, for twelve consecutive numbers, each volume consisted of only one issue. The last number of *The Countryman* was that of May 8, 1866.
28. The educational periodicials were: *Educational Journal* (Forsyth); *College Miscellany and Orphan's Advocate* (Covington); *Kennesaw Gem* (Marietta); *Educational Repository and Family Monthly* (Atlanta); and *Educational Monthly* (Lumpkin).
29. The book described the famous teacher, Dr. Moses Waddel, for many years president of the University of Georgia.
30. Sandersville *Central Georgian*, Feb. 19, 1862. The poem was written by Wesley P. Pledger of Sandersville.
31. Written by "Kate," Jasper, Ga., Sept. 10, 1861. Atlanta *Daily Intelligencer*, Sept. 18, 1861.
32. Richard Barksdale Harwell, "A Reputation by Reflection: John Hill Hewitt and Edgar Allan Poe," *The Emory University Quarterly*, III, 1 (1947), 109.
33. Richard Barksdale Harwell, ed., *King Linkum the First, a Musical Burletta*. Emory Sources and Reprints, Ser. IV, No. 1, pp. 3, 7, 8. Maria J. Westmoreland was another Georgia writer of drama during the war. Many of her plays were staged during the Reconstruction period.
34. U. S. Census Office, 8th Census, 1860, *Statistics of the United States*, 505.
35. U. S. Census Office, 7th Census, 1850, *A Statistical View of Each of the States*, 385.
36. After the war the libraries of Tefft and Smets were sold at sacrifice prices.
37. Savannah *Daily Herald*, Mar. 8, 1865.

CHAPTER XIV

1. Johnston to Stephens, May 2, 1861, in Stephens Papers (Lib. of Cong.).
2. Ben Mosely to Stephens, May 3, 1861, *ibid*.
3. Augusta *Chronicle and Sentinel*, July 29, 1864. A university student wrote to Stephens that the Phi Kappa Society was soliciting the aid of honorary members in defraying certain expenses upon their hall. Carlton Hillyer to Stephens, Feb. 11, 1862, in Stephens Papers. (Lib. of Cong.).
4. Atlanta *Southern Confederacy*, Apr. 2, 1862.
5. E. J. Black to Dr. R. C. Black, Columbus *Daily Sun*, Apr. 25, 1861.
6. Henry M. Bullock, *A History of Emory University*, 96-100, 149-151.
7. Louis Crawford to Capt. Edwin T. Davis, Feb. 26, 27, 1862, in "Letters from Confederate Soldiers," II, 545, 546 (Georgia State Archives).
8. J. H. Campbell, *Georgia Baptists*, 145, 146. Marshall College, a small Baptist college for men at Griffin, was suspended in 1862.
9. Henry R. Jackson to Mrs. M. J. Jackson, Nov. 12, 1863, in Jackson Papers.
10. Atlanta *Southern Confederacy*, June 21, 1862, June 25, 1863.

..NOTES

11. J. M. M. Caldwell to Brown, Feb. 5, 1863, in Brown Papers (Georgia State Archives).
12. Augusta *Chronicle and Sentinel*, July 22, 1862.
13. See photostat of a letter written on Dec. 28, 1863, by Dr. Joseph R. Wilson, father of President Woodrow Wilson, protesting the suspension of the college during the war. (Georgia State Archives).
14. Milledgeville *Daily Federal Union*, Nov. 20, 1861.
15. *Acts of the Gen. Assem. of Ga., 1858*, 49-51.
16. U. S. Census Office, 8th Census, 1860, *Statistics of the United States*, 508. These statistics do not include the Negroes. No figures are available for the slaves, but in 1860 there were 573 persons of "free color" classed as illiterate. *Ibid.*
17. U. S. Census Office, 7th Census, 1850, *A Statistical View of Each of the States*, lx; U. S. Census Office, 8th Census, 1860, *Statistics of the United States*, 506. Most sections of Middle Georgia had better schools than did the mountain and wire-grass regions.
18. U. S. Census Office, 7th Census, 1850, *A Statistical View of Each of the States*, lx; U. S. Census Office, 8th Census, 1860, *Statistics of the United States*, 506. The academies were listed by the Census Office as "academies and other schools."
19. Americus *Sumter Republican*, Apr. 18, 1862.
20. *Ibid.*, June 27, 1862.
21. Johnston to Stephens, July 8, 1862, in Stephens Papers (Lib. of Cong.).
22. Savannah *Daily Morning News*, Aug. 9, 1861.
23. Savannah *Republican*, Jan. 20, 1862.
24. LaGrange *Reporter*, Oct. 17, 1862.
25. W. H. H. Stewart to Stephens, Jan. 12, 1862, in Stephens Papers (Lib. of Cong.).
26. Emma Tyler Blalock, "War Memories," in "Letters from Confederate Soldiers," II, 169 (Georgia State Archives).
27. "Diary of Josephine C. Habersham," Sept. 9, 1863.
28. *Georgia House Journal, 1863*, 233.
29. "Julia A. Stanford Diary," Aug. 21, 30, Sept. 23, 1863, in "Confederate Letters," X, 55, 57, 63 (Georgia State Archives).
30. Kate Green to Joseph A. Miles, Jan. 31, 1862, in Miles Papers.
31. T. W. Montfort to his son, Nov. 14, 1861, in "Letters from Confederate Soldiers," II, 42 (Georgia State Archives).
32. A member of the J. William Blackshear family to another member (unsigned letter), Jan. 29, 1865, in Blackshear Papers.
33. Mary C. Thompson to Mr. and Mrs. Irby H. Scott, Jan. 30, 1863, in Scott Papers.
34. Columbus *Daily Sun*, Aug. 9, 1861.
35. Stephen B. Weeks, "Confederate Text-Books (1861-1865): a Preliminary Survey," *Report of the Commissioner of Education, 1898-1899*, 1140-1142, 1147, 1148.
36. Columbus *Daily Times*, Mar. 8, 1864.
37. Celathiel Helms to Mary Helms, Oct. 8, 1862, in "Letters from Confederate Soldiers," II, 421 (Georgia State Archives).
38. W. R. Stillwell to Mollie Stillwell, Dec. 11, 1862, in Stillwell Letters (Georgia State Archives).
39. T. W. Montfort to his son, Nov. 14, 1861, in "Letters from Confederate Soldiers," II, 42 (Georgia State Archives).
40. T. W. Montfort to his children, Nov. 3, 1861, *ibid.*, II, 31.
41. Mary Frances Brooks to Rhodom Maxie Brooks, Sept. 3, 1862, in "Confederate Diaries," VIII, 221, 222 (Georgia State Archives).
42. Fannie Boyd to Wier Boyd, May 25, 1862, Apr. 27, 1863, in Boyd Papers.
43. *Georgia Senate Journal, 1863*, 60, 70.
44. Orphans of deceased Masons received a gratuitous education at the Southern Masonic Female College in Covington.

45. The Union Society was founded in 1750 to educate orphans. The promoters represented several religious faiths.

CHAPTER XV

1. Union churches were churches located in sparsely populated areas and owned jointly by several denominations.
2. The number of each of the other denominations' churches in 1860 was: Union, 27; Christian, 15; Lutheran, 9; Catholic, 8; Universalist, 3; Jewish, 1. The one Jewish church was in Savannah. U. S. Census Office, 8th Census, 1860, *Statistics of the United States*, 365-370.
3. "Autobiography of George Gilman Smith," 68.
4. George H. Clark, *A Sermon Delivered in St. John's Church, Savannah, on Fast Day, Nov. 28, 1860.*
5. R. K. Porter, *Christian Duty in the Present Crisis*, 8, 20.
6. *The Church Intelligencer*, Jan. 24, 1861.
7. See Chapter XIV.
8. Stephen Elliott, *The Silver Trumpets of the Sanctuary*, 11, 12.
9. Stephen Elliott, *God's Presence With the Confederate States*, 4, 20, 21.
10. *A Discourse Delivered by Rev. J. Jones to the Rome Light Guards in the Presbyterian Church of Rome, Ga., on May 26, 1861*, 11.
11. *History of the Baptist Denomination in Georgia*, 225-230.
12. Savannah *Republican*, Dec. 10, 1861.
13. *Minutes of the Georgia Annual Conference of the Methodist Episcopal Church, South, Held at Macon, Georgia, Nov. 26-Dec. 4, 1862*, 39.
14. "The Presbyterian Church in Georgia on Secession and Slavery," *Georgia Historical Quarterly*, I, 3 (Sept., 1917), 263, 264.
15. *Minutes of the Synod of Georgia At their Seventeenth Annual Sessions, At Marietta, Georgia, With an Appendix, November, 1861*, 12, 13.
16. Of the three largest denominations in Georgia, the Presbyterian was the only one that had not experienced a sectional cleavage before the war began. None of the smaller denominations had divided.
17. *Address of the General Assembly of the Presbyterian Church in the Confederate States of America, to All the Churches of Jesus Christ.*
18. *Journal of the General Council of the Protestant Episcopal Church in the Confederate States*, 5-188.
19. Savannah *Daily Morning News*, June 11, 1861.
20. *The Church Intelligencer*, Aug. 23, 1861.
21. Columbus *Daily Sun*, July 22, 1861.
22. See letter of Henry C. Wayne to Brown, Sept. 19, 1861, in Telamon Cuyler Collection.
23. A minister presented a revolver to a soldier with the injunction, "If you get in a tight place and have to use it, ask God's blessing if you have time, but be sure and not let your enemy get the start of you. You can say amen after you shoot." Columbus *Weekly Times*, Dec. 30, 1861.
24. "Autobiography of George Gilman Smith," 66.
25. *Minutes of the Georgia Annual Conference of the Methodist Episcopal Church, South, Held in Columbus, Georgia, Nov. 25-Dec. 3, 1863*, 27.
26. Campbell to Stephens, July 16, 1862, in Stephens Papers (Lib. of Cong.).
27. "Alexander Means Diary for 1861," Nov. 6, 1861.
28. George G. Smith, Jr., *History of Georgia Methodism*, 326.
29. *Southern Christian Advocate*, Mar. 6, 1862.
30. Stephen Elliott to Rev. K. I. Stewart, Jan. 20, 1863, in "Stephen Elliott Letter Book," 17.
31. Elliott to Rev. A. F. Freeman, Dec. 6, 1862; Elliott to R. I. Maynard, Dec. 3, 1862, *ibid.*, 2-4.
32. Elliott to Rev. George Stickney, Dec. 11, 1862, *ibid.*, 11.
33. Elliott to Maynard, Mar. 23, 1863, *ibid.*, 39.

NOTES

34. Mary Randolph Harden to Edward R. Harden, Dec. 1, 1862, in Harden Papers.
35. "Diary of Julia A. Stanford," June 23, Sept. 20, 1861, in "Confederate Letters," X, 46, 47, 62 (Georgia State Archives).
36. C. W. Parker to Stephens, Feb. 15, 1862, in Stephens Papers (Lib. of Cong.).
37. *The Church Intelligencer*, Sept. 14, 1864.
38. Americus *Sumter Republican*, Sept. 12, 1862.
39. Wilbur to "Mary," Aug. 31, 1862, in Wilbur Papers (Duke Univ. Lib.).
40. "I did . . . intend to write immediately, but found it impossible amid the confusion attending the Baptist Carnival; indeed, I found the preachers so very entertaining that I did not even attempt it." Mary Hamilton to "Lucy", Oct. 10, 1864, in Cobb Papers (private possession).
41. Sandersville *Central Georgian*, Feb. 19, 1862.
42. *Ibid.*, Apr. 1, 1863. Writing from his headquarters at Dalton, General William J. Hardee asked an Episcopal minister, "What rules have you in our Church for fasting? I have kept this day, set apart for fasting, humiliation, and prayer. . . ." Hardee to John W. Beckwith, Dec. 10, 1863, in Beckwith Papers.
43. F. E. Miles to J. A. Miles, June 10, 1862, in Miles Papers.
44. Atlanta *Southern Confederacy*, June 15, 1861. Beebe also edited the *Southern Baptist Messenger* at Covington, a periodical published twice each month by the Old School, or Primitive, Baptists.
45. L. I. Chesnut to Alexander Chesnut, June 3, 1862, in Chesnut Papers.
46. S. W. Graves to Henry Graves, Jan. 4, 1863, in "Confederate Diaries," VI, 280 (Georgia State Archives).
47. George F. Pierce to "Bro," Oct. 21, 1861, in Hendrix Papers.
48. H. A. Tupper, *A Thanksgiving Discourse Delivered at Washington, Ga., on Thursday, September 18, 1862*, 4, 7.
49. *Sermon of Bishop George F. Pierce Before the General Assembly of Georgia, March 27, 1863*.
50. September, 1864.
51. *Minutes of the Synod of Georgia, At their Eighteenth Annual Sessions, At Macon, Georgia, With an Appendix. November, 1862*, 16, 17.
52. Lovick Pierce to "Brother Wightman," Aug. 19, 1863, in Hendrix Papers.
53. Columbus *Daily Times*, Feb. 1, 1864.
54. James Stacy, *A History of the Presbyterian Church in Georgia*, 182.
55. Linton Stephens to A. H. Stephens, Nov. 12, 1862, in Stephens Papers (Manhattanville College).
56. Jan. 31, 1865.
57. See "Miscellaneous Church Records" (Georgia State Archives).
58. Lunt, *War-Time Journal*, 406.
59. Preston B. Scott to Beckwith, June 10, 1864, in Beckwith Papers.
60. Beckwith to "Nellie," June 26, 1864, *ibid.*
61. S. P. Richardson, "Lights and Shadows of Itinerant Life," quoted in Heckman, *Northern Church Penetration of the South*, 70, 71.
62. Axson's daughter, Ellen Louise Axson, became the first Mrs. Woodrow Wilson.
63. Hitchcock, *Marching With Sherman*, 199.
64. C. C. Jones, *Religious Instruction of the Negroes*, 19-25.
65. Marshall J. Wellborn to Jesse M. L. Burnett, Mar. 6, 1863, quoted in Burnett, "Some Confederate Letters," *Georgia Historical Quarterly*, XXI, 2 (June, 1937), 198. ". . . if we believe the Bible sustains slavery, why object to the slave learning to read the Bible?" Columbus *Daily Sun*, Apr. 9, 1863.
66. *Acts of the Gen. Assem. of Ga., 1863 (extra sess.)*, 137.
67. *Sermon of Bishop Pierce Before the General Assembly of Georgia, March 27, 1863*.

68. *History of the Baptist Denomination in Georgia*, 260.
69. Columbus *Daily Times*, Mar. 17, 1865.
70. Elliott to I. K. Sapp of Charleston, S. C., Jan. 13, 1863, in "Stephen Elliott Letter Book," 8.
71. Elliott to Bishop Thomas Atkinson, Jan. 14, 1863, *ibid.*, 13.
72. Elliott to Thomas Atkinson and Richard Wilmer, May 14, 1863, *ibid.*, 42.
73. "Autobiography of George Gilman Smith," 90-97.
74. U. S. Census Office, 8th Census, 1860, *Statistics of the United States*, 365-370; U. S. Census Office, 9th Census, 1870, *The Statistics of the Population of the United States*, 506-525, 533, 534. No Union churches were listed in the Census of 1870, but there were ten Congregational churches whereas in 1860 no Congregational church was reported.

BIBLIOGRAPHY

I. PRIMARY SOURCES

A. MANUSCRIPT SOURCES

1. *Official Manuscripts*

Augusta Arsenal Records, 1863-1864, Duke University Library.

Confederate Archives, Adjutant-General's Office, The National Archives, Washington, D. C.
Atlanta Arsenal Letters.
Augusta Arsenal Letters.
Macon Arsenal Letters.
Medical Purveyors' Office, Macon, Ga., Letters and Telegrams.
Savannah Ordnance Letters.

Confederate Archives, County Militia Records of Georgia, 1861-1865. Duke University Library.

Georgia Archives, Georgia Department of Archives and History, Atlanta, Ga.
Adjutant-General Letter Books, 1862-1864, Nos. 12-22.
Adjutant-General Letter Books, 1861-1864, Vol. B-44, Adjutant-General's Orders, 2 parts.
Governor's Letter Books, 1861-1865.
Minutes of the Executive Department, 1860-1866.

2. *Other Manuscripts*

Alexander, Adam Leopole, Papers. Duke University Library.
Ash, John H., Papers. Georgia Department of Archives and History.
Barrow, David Crenshaw, Papers. University of North Carolina Library.
Beckwith, John W., Papers. University of North Carolina Library.
Blackshear, J. William, Papers. Duke University Library.
Boyd, Wier, Papers. Duke University Library.
Brent, George William, Papers. Duke University Library.
Briant, Huldah A. Fain, Papers. Duke University Library.

Brown, A. J., Papers. Duke University Library.
Brown, Bettie R., Papers. Duke University Library.
Brown, Joseph E., Papers. Duke University Library.
_____, Papers. Emory University Library.
_____, Papers. Georgia Department of Archives and History.
_____, Papers. Library of Congress.
Brown, J. R., Papers. Duke University Library.
Chesnut, Alexander, Papers. Duke University Library.
Cobb, Howell, Letter Books, 1863-1865. University of Georgia Library.
_____, Papers. Duke University Library.
_____, Papers. In private possession, Athens, Georgia. These papers belonged to the late Miss Mary Lamar Erwin and are in the custody of the University of Georgia.
_____, Papers. University of Georgia Library.
Comer, Laura B., Diary, 1862-1863. University of North Carolina Library.
Confederate Letters, Diaries, and Reminiscences. 15 vols. Georgia Department of Archives and History.
Cook, Anna Maria [Green], Journal. In possession of the Cook family in Milledgeville, Georgia.
Cumming, Joseph B., War Recollections. University of North Carolina Library.
Cuyler, Telamon, Collection. University of Georgia Library.
Davis, E. A., Papers. Duke University Library.
Davis, Jefferson, Papers. Duke University Library.
Davis, Jefferson, to Mrs. Howell Cobb, March 30, 1865. Letter was in possession of the late Miss Mary Lamar Erwin, Athens, Georgia.
De Bow, James D. B., Papers. Duke University Library.
De Votie, Jefferson Howard, Papers. Duke University Library.
Elliott, Stephen, Letter Book, 1862-1864. University of North Carolina Library.
Evans, John B., Papers. Duke University Library.
Georgia Methodist Conference Church Book, 1861-1877, Dahlonega, Georgia. Duke University Library.
Georgia Portfolio, vol. II. Duke University Library. A Georgia miscellany, compiled by Charles Colcock Jones, Jr.
Gibson, Samuel H., Papers. Georgia Department of Archives and History.
Graves Papers. University of North Carolina Library.
Habersham, Josephine C., Diary, June-October, 1863. University of North Carolina Library.
Hanleiter, C. R., Diary, 1861-1862. Atlanta Historical Society.
Hardee, William Joseph, Papers. Duke University Library.
Harden, Edward, Papers. Duke University Library.

BIBLIOGRAPHY

Harris, E. M., Papers. Duke University Library.
Harris, Joel Chandler, Papers. Emory University Library.
Hartman, Jefferson, Papers. Duke University Library.
Hendrix, Eugene Russell, Papers. Duke University Library.
Hill, Benjamin Harvey, Papers. Duke University Library.
Jackson, Henry Rootes, Papers. Georgia Department of Archives and History.
Jackson-Prince Papers. University of North Carolina Library.
Johnston, Joseph Eggleston, Papers. Duke University Library.
Jones, Charles Colcock, Jr., ed., Autograph Letters and Portraits of the Signers of the Constitution of the Confederate States. Duke University Library.
Jordan, J. H., Papers. Georgia Department of Archives and History.
Lamar, John B., Papers. Duke University Library.
Means, Alexander, Diary, 1861. Emory University Library.
Mercer, George A., Diary, 1862-1864. University of North Carolina Library.
Mercer-Walker Papers. Emory University Library.
Miles, Joseph A., Papers. Duke University Library.
Military Records, Depredations, 1865. Georgia Department of Archives and History.
Miscellaneous Church Records. Georgia Department of Archives and History.
Miscellaneous Georgia Poor Relief Papers, 1861-1865. Duke University Library.
Miscellaneous Confederate Papers. Georgia Department of Archives and History.
Miscellaneous Soldiers' Letters, 1861-1865. Duke University Library.
Neal, A. J., Papers. Emory University Library.
Niles, Alice E. Andrews, Papers. Duke University Library.
Nisbet, Eugenius Aristides, Papers. Duke University Library.
Petition of Lufborrow and Timmons to the Confederate Government, Richmond, Virginia, March, 1863. Georgia Department of Archives and History.
Petition of Lufborrow and Timmons to the Georgia Legislature, Richmond, Virginia, March, 1863. Georgia Department of Archives and History.
Pickens, Francis Wilkinson, Papers. Duke University Library.
Refugee. An unpublished story from the diary of a Georgia girl. Author unknown. Typescript in the Georgia Department of Archives and History.
Roman, Alfred, Papers. Library of Congress.
Scott, Irby H., Papers. Duke University Library.
Sherman, William Tecumseh, Papers. Library of Congress.

Smith, George Gilman, Autobiography. University of North Carolina Library.
Stephens, Alexander H., Papers. Manhattanville College of the Sacred Heart.
_____, Papers. Duke University Library.
_____, Papers. Emory University Library.
_____, Papers. Library of Congress.
Superintendents and Managers of a Group of Southern Railroads to the Secretatry of War, Augusta, Georgia. February, 1863. Georgia Department of Archives and History.
Thomas, James, Papers. Duke University Library.
Toombs, Robert, Papers. University of Georgia Library.
Warthen, Thomas J., Papers. Duke University Library.
Wayne, Henry C., Papers. Emory University Library.
Wilbur, Aaron, Papers. Duke University Library.
_____, Papers. Emory University Library.
Wilson, Joseph R., to Woodrow Wilson, December 28, 1863. Photostat of a letter. Georgia Department of Archives and History.

B. PRINTED SOURCES
1. *Newspapers and Periodicals*

Albany *Patriot.*
Americus *Sumter Republican.*
Army and Navy Herald, Macon.
Athens *Banner.*
Athens *Southern Watchman.*
Atlanta *Intelligencer.*
Atlanta *Southern Confederacy.*
Augusta *Chronicle and Sentinel.*
Augusta *Constitutionalist.*
Carrollton *Advocate.*
Child's Index, Macon.
Charleston *Daily Courier.*
The Church Intelligencer, Raleigh.
Columbus *Daily Enquirer.*
Columbus *Daily Sun.*
Columbus *Daily Times.*
The Countryman, Turnwold.
Gardener and Farmer, Columbus.
Georgia Literary and Temperance Crusader, Atlanta.
Harris County Enterprise, Hamilton.
The Independent South, Waynesville.
Knoxville (Tenn.) *Register.*

BIBLIOGRAPHY

LaGrange *Reporter.*
LaGrange *Daily Bulletin.*
Macon *Telegraph.*
Milledgeville *Federal Union.*
Milledgeville *Southern Recorder.*
The Plantation, Turnwold.
The Planters' Weekly, Greensboro.
Richmond (Va.) *Dispatch.*
Rome *Semi-Weekly True Flag.*
Sandersville *Central Georgian.*
Savannah *Daily Herald.*
Savannah *Daily Morning News.*
Savannah *Republican.*
Southern Baptist Messenger, Covington.
Southern Christian Advocate, Charleston and Augusta.
Southern Cultivator, Augusta and Athens.
Southern Field and Fireside, Augusta.
Southern Literary Companion, Newnan.

2. Official Publications

The Acts and Resolutions of the General Assembly of the State of Georgia, 1860-1865. Milledgeville, 1861-1866.
Clark, R. H., and T. R. R. Cobb and D. Irwin, *The Code of the State of Georgia, 1861.* Atlanta, 1861.
The Confederate Records of the State of Georgia. 6 vols. Compiled and published under authority of the legislature by Allen D. Candler. Atlanta, 1909-1911. Vols. I, II, III, IV, and VI have been published. Vol. V consists of unpublished manuscripts in the Georgia Department of Archives and History.
Congressional Globe. 46 vols. Washington, 1834-1873.
Georgia House Journals, 1860-1865. Milledgeville, 1861-1866.
Georgia Senate Journals, 1860-1865. Milledgeville, 1861-1866.
House of Representatives Executive Documents. Washington, 1847-1897.
Journal of the Congress of the Confederate States of America, 1861-1865. 8 vols. Washington, 1904-1905.
Journal of the Public and Secret Proceedings of the Convention of the People of Georgia Held in Milledgeville and Savannah, in 1861, Together with the Ordinances Adopted. Milledgevile, 1861.
Journal of the State Convention, Held in Milledgeville, in December, 1850. Milledgeville, 1850.
Knight, Lucian Lamar, comp. *Georgia's Official Register and Statistical Guide, 1923.* Atlanta, 1923.

Lamar, Lucius Q. C., *A Compilation of the Laws of Georgia.* Augusta, 1821.
Memminger, C. G., *Instructions for the Agents for Collecting . . . the Produce Loan.* Richmond, 1862.
―――――, *Regulations as to the Purchase of Produce.* Richmond, 1862.
Official Records of the Union and Confederate Navies in the War of the Rebellion. 30 vols. Washington, 1894-1922.
Poore, Benjamin Perley, ed., *The Federal and State Constitutions.* 2 vols. Washington, 1878.
Reports of the Comptroller-General of the State of Georgia, 1860-1866. Milledgeville, 1860-1866.
The Statutes at Large of the Confederate States, 1862-1864. Edited by James M. Matthews. 8 vols. Richmond, 1862-1864.
The Statutes at Large of the Provisional Government of the Confederate States of America . . . 1861 to 1862 . . . the Constitution of the Provisional Government and Permanent Constitution. . . . Edited by James M. Matthews. Richmond, 1864.
Thian, Raphael P., ed., *Correspondence of the Treasury Department of the Confederate States of America, 1861-1865.* Appendix, Part IV (1861-1865). Washington, 1879.
―――――, *Correspondence of the Treasury Department of the Confederate States of America, 1861-1865.* Appendix, Part V (1863-1865). Washington, 1880.
―――――, *Reports of the Confederate Treasury, 1861-1865.* Appendix, Part III (1861-1865). Washington, 1878.
United States Census:
  1850: *The Seventh Census of the United States.* 2 vols. Washington, 1853.
  1860: *The Eighth Census of the United States.* 4 vols. Washington, 1864-1866.
  1870: *The Ninth Census of the United States.* 3 vols. Washington, 1872.
The War of the Rebellion: A Compilation of the Official Records of the Union and Confederate Armies. 128 vols. Washington, 1880-1901.

3. Other Printed Sources

Address of the General Assembly of the Presbyterian Church in the Confederate States of America, to all the Churches of Jesus Christ. Augusta, 1861.
Andrews, Eliza Frances, *The War-Time Journal of a Georgia Girl. 1864-1865.* New York, 1908.
Annual Reports of the President of the Union Society, 1862-1865. Savannah, 1876.

BIBLIOGRAPHY

Armes, William D., ed., *The Autobiography of Joseph Le Conte.* New York, 1903.
Atlanta and West Point Railroad Company, Annual Report, 1866. Atlanta, 1866.
Autobiography of Colonel Richard Malcolm Johnston. Washington, 1900.
Barnwell, V. T., comp., *Barnwell's City Directory.* Atlanta, 1867.
Beers, Fannie A., *Memories. A Record of Personal Experiences and Adventure During Four Years of War.* Philadelphia, 1899.
Berry, Harrison, *Slavery and Abolitionism as Viewed by a Georgia Slave.* Atlanta, 1861.
Boggs, Marion Alexander, ed., *The Alexander Letters, 1787-1900.* Savannah, 1910.
Burnett, E. C. "Some Confederate Letters: Alabama, Georgia, and Tennessee," *Georgia Historical Quarterly,* XXI, 2 (June, 1937), 188-203.
Caldwell, John H., *The Thurstons of the Old Palmetto State, or Varieties of Southern Life, Illustrated in the Fortunes of a Distinguished Family in South Carolina.* New York, 1861.
Campbell, John A., *Reminiscences and Documents Relating to the Civil War During the Year 1865.* Baltimore, 1887.
Catalog of the Officers and Students of Mercer University, 1868-1869. Penfield, Georgia, 1869.
Clark, George H., *A Sermon Delivered in St. John's Church, Savannah, on Fast Day, Nov. 28, 1860.* Savannah, 1860.
Coffin, Charles C., *The Boys of '61; or Four Years of Fighting.* Boston, 1881.
Correspondence Between Governor Brown and President Davis on the Constitutionality of the Conscription Act. Atlanta, 1862.
Conyngham, David R., *Sherman's March Through the South. With Sketches and Incidents of the Campaign.* New York, 1865.
Crim, Matt, *Adventures of a Fair Rebel.* New York, 1891.
Cumming, Kate, *Gleanings from the Southland.* Birmingham, 1895.
————, *A Journal of Hospital Life in the Confederate Army of Tennessee, from the Battle of Shiloh to the End of the War.* Louisville, 1886.
Davis, Jefferson, *The Rise and Fall of the Confederate Government.* 2 vols. New York, 1881.
De Bow's Review. New Orleans and Charleston, 1846-1880.
De Leon, Thomas C., *Four Years in Rebel Capitals: an Inside View of Life in the Southern Confederacy.* Mobile, 1890.
A Digest of the Acts and Proceedings of the General Assembly of the Presbyterian Church in the United States, 1861-1944. Richmond, 1945.

A Discourse Delivered by Rev. J. Jones to the Rome Light Guards in the Presbyterian Church of Rome, Ga., on May 26, 1861. Rome, Georgia, 1861.

Elliott, Stephen, *God's Presence With the Confederate States.* Savannah, 1861.

――――――, *The Silver Trumpets of the Sanctuary.* Savannah, 1861.

English, Thomas H., ed., *Autobiography of "The Countryman," 1866, by Joseph Addison Turner.* Atlanta, 1943.

Folsom, James M., *Heroes and Martyrs of Georgia.* Macon, 1864.

Fort, Kate Haynes, ed., *Memoirs of the Fort and Fannin Families.* Chattanooga, 1903.

Fremantle, Arthur James Lyon, *Three Months in the Southern States: April-June, 1863.* New York, 1864.

Gay, Mary A. H., *Life in Dixie During the War.* Atlanta, 1897.

Grier's Almanac for the States of Georgia, South Carolina, Alabama and Tennessee for the Year 1862. Griffin, Georgia, 1861.

Harwell, Richard B., ed., *King Linkum the First, a Musical Burletta by John Hill Hewitt.* Emory Sources and Reprints, Ser. IV, No. 1. Atlanta, 1947.

Hedley, F. Y., *Marching Through Georgia.* Chicago, 1890.

Higginson, Thomas Wentworth, *Army Life in a Black Regiment.* Cambridge, Massachusetts, 1900.

Hines, James K., "Herschel V. Johnson," in *Report of the Forty-First Annual Session of the Georgia Bar Association, May 29-31, 1924* (Macon, 1924), 179-230. Consists largely of excerpts from Johnson's "Autobiography" and manuscripts.

Hood, John B., *Advance and Retreat. Personal Experiences in the United States and Confederate Armies.* New Orleans, 1880.

Hopley, Catherine C., *Life in the South; from the Commencement of the War.* 2 vols. London, 1863.

Howe, M. A. De Wolfe, ed., *Marching with Sherman; Passages from the Letters and Campaign Diaries of Henry Hitchcock, Major and Assistant Adjutant General of Volunteers, November 1864-May 1865.* New Haven, 1927.

Huse, Caleb, *The Supplies for the Confederate Army.* Boston, 1904.

Jackson, Henry W. R., *Confederate Monitor and Patriot's Friend.* Atlanta, 1862.

Johnson, Herschel V., "From the Autobiography of Herschel V. Johnson, 1856-1867," edited by Percy Scott Flippin, *American Historical Review,* XXX, 2 (Jan., 1925), 311-336.

Johnson, Robert Underwood, and Clarence Clough Buel, eds., *Battles and Leaders of the Civil War; Being for the Most Part Contributions by Union and Confederate Officers.* 4 vols. New York, 1887, 1888.

BIBLIOGRAPHY

Johnston, Joseph Eggleston, *Narrative of Military Operations, Directed During the Late War Between the States.* New York, 1874.

Johnston, Richard Malcolm, *Autobiography of Colonel Malcolm Johnston.* Washington, 1900.

────────, *Georgia Sketches . . . from the Recollections of an Old Man, by Philemon Perch.* Augusta, 1864.

Jones, C. C., *Religious Instruction of the Negroes.* Richmond, 1861.

Jones, Charles C., Jr., *Monumental Remains of Georgia.* Savannah, 1861.

Journal of the General Council of the Protestant Episcopal Church in the Confederate States. Augusta, 1863.

Le Conte, Joseph, *'Ware Sherman. A Journal of Three Months' Personal Experience in the Last Days of the Confederacy. With an Introductory Reminiscence by His Daughter, Caroline Le Conte.* Berkeley, California, 1937.

Le Louterel, Francois P., *Manual of Military Reconnaissances.* Atlanta, 1862.

Letter of Hon. Howell Cobb to the People of Georgia on the Present Condition of the Country. Washington, 1860.

Longstreet, Augustus Baldwin, *Master William Mitten.* Macon, 1864.

Lunt, Dolly Sumner [Mrs. Thomas Burge], *A Woman's War-Time Journal.* New York, 1918.

Mallett, J. W., "Work of the Ordnance Bureau." *Southern Historical Society Papers,* XXXVII (1909), 1-20.

Memorial of the Banks of Savannah to the Senate and House of Representatives of the Confederate States. Savannah, 1864.

Minutes of the Georgia Annual Conference of the Methodist Episcopal Church, South, Held at Macon, Georgia, Nov. 26-Dec. 4, 1862. Macon, 1863.

Minutes of the Georgia Annual Conference of the Methodist Episcopal Church, South, Held in Columbus, Georgia, Nov. 25-Dec. 3, 1863. Macon, 1864.

Minutes of the Synod of Georgia, At their Seventeenth Annual Sessions, At Marietta, Georgia, With an Appendix. November, 1861. Atlanta, 1862.

Minutes of the Synod of Georgia, At their Eighteenth Annual Sessions, At Macon, Georgia, With an Appendix. November, 1862. Atlanta, 1863.

Moore, Frank, ed., *The Rebellion Record; a Diary of American Events, with Documents, Narratives, Illustrative Incidents, Poetry, etc.* 11 vols. New York, 1861-1868.

Nichols, George W., *The Story of the Great March.* New York, 1865.

Olmstead, Charles H., "Fort Pulaski," *Georgia Historical Quarterly,* I, 2 (June, 1917), 98-105.

Olmstead, Frederick Law, *The Cotton Kingdom.* 2 vols. New York, 1861.
Phillips, Ulrich B., ed., *The Correspondence of Robert Toombs, Alexander H. Stephens, and Howell Cobb.* American Historical Association *Annual Report, 1911.* Vol. II. Washington, 1913.
——————, ed., *Plantation and Frontier Documents: 1649-1863.* Volumes I and II of *A Documentary History of American Industrial Society.* 10 vols. Cleveland, 1909.
Pittinger, William, *The Great Locomotive Chase.* Philadelphia, 1908.
Porter, David D., *The Naval History of the Civil War. Illustrated from Original Sketches Made by Rear-Admiral Walke and Others.* New York, 1886.
Porter, R. K., *Christian Duty in the Present Crisis.* Savannah, 1860.
Pratt, N. A., *Perils of a Dissolution of the Union.* Atlanta, 1856.
The Press Association of the Confederate States of America. Griffin, Georgia, 1863.
Proceedings of the Bible Convention of the Confederate States of America. Augusta, 1862.
Proceedings of the Convention of Railroad Presidents Association, Held at Chattanooga, Tenn., June 4, 5, 1861. Chattanooga, 1861.
Rains, George W., *History of the Confederate Powder Works.* Newburgh, New York, 1882.
Report of the Executive Committee of the Georgia Relief and Hospital Association to the Board of Superintendents, With the Proceedings of the Board Convened at Augusta, Ga., October 29, 1862. Augusta, 1862.
Reports of the Superintendent and Treasurer of the Western and Atlantic Railroad to Joseph E. Brown, Governor, September 30, 1861, October 1, 1864. Atlanta, 1861, 1864.
Richardson, James D., ed., *Messages and Papers of the Confederacy, 1861-1865.* 2 vols. Nashville, 1905.
Rowland, Dunbar, ed., *Jefferson Davis, Constitutionalist. His Letters, Papers and Speeches.* 10 vols. Jackson, Mississippi, 1923.
Russell, William Howard, *My Diary North and South.* New York, 1863.
Scharf, J. Thomas, *History of the Confederate States Navy.* Albany, New York, 1894.
Sermon of Bishop George F. Pierce Before the General Assembly of Georgia, March 27, 1863. Milledgeville, 1863.
Sherman, William T., *Memoirs of General William T. Sherman by Himself.* 2 vols. New York, 1876.
Shryock, Richard H., ed., "Letters of Richard D. Arnold, Mayor of Savannah, Georgia, M. D., 1808-1876." *Papers of the Trinity College Historical Society,* Double Series, XVIII, XIX. Durham, North Carolina, 1929.

..BIBLIOGRAPHY

Smedes, Mrs. Susan Dabney, *Memorials of a Southern Planter*. New York, 1890.
Stephens, Alexander Hamilton, *A Constitutional View of the Late War between the States: Its Causes, Character, Conduct, and Results*. 2 vols. Philadelphia and Chicago, 1868-1870.
Tupper, H. A., *A Thanksgiving Discourse Delivered at Washington, Ga., on Thursday, September 18, 1862*. Macon, 1862.
Warren, E. W., *Nellie Norton: or Southern Slavery and the Bible*. Macon, 1864.
Winther, Oscar O., ed., *With Sherman to the Sea. The Civil War Letters, Diaries, and Reminiscences of Theodore F. Upson*. Baton Rouge, 1943.

II. SECONDARY MATERIALS

The American Annual Cyclopaedia and Register of Important Events. 42 vols. New York, 1862-1903.
Andrews, Matthew Page, comp., *The Women of the South in War Times*. Baltimore, 1923.
Avery, Isaac W., *The History of the State of Georgia from 1850 to 1881*. New York, 1881.
Bass, James H., "Civil War Finance in Georgia," *Georgia Historical Quarterly*, XXVI, 3 and 4 (Sept.-Dec., 1942), 213-224.
————, "The Georgia Gubernatorial Elections of 1861 and 1863," *Georgia Historical Quarterly*, XVII, 3 (Sept. 1933), 167-188.
Battey, George M., Jr., *A History of Rome and Floyd County*. Atlanta, 1922.
Black, Robert C., "The Railroads of Georgia in the Confederate War Effort," *Journal of Southern History*, XIII, 4 (Nov. 1947), 511-534.
Boogher, Elbert W. G., *Secondary Education in Georgia, 1732-1858*. Philadelphia, 1933.
Bowden, Haygood S., *Two Hundred Years of Education*. Savannah, 1932.
Bowlby, Elizabeth Catherine, "The Role of Atlanta During the Civil War." M. A. Thesis (Emory University, 1939).
Brantley, Rabun Lee, *Georgia Journalism of the Civil War Period*. Nashville, 1929.
Brooks, Robert P., *The Agrarian Revolution in Georgia*. Madison, Wisconsin, 1914.
Bullock, Henry M., *A History of Emory University*. Nashville, 1936.
Butler, John C., *Historical Record of Macon and Central Georgia*. Macon, 1879.
Cain, Andrew W., *History of Lumpkin County, 1832-1932*. Atlanta, 1932.

Campbell, J. H., *Georgia Baptists*. Macon, 1874.
Candler, Allen D., and Clement A. Evans, eds., *Cyclopedia of Georgia*. 3 vols. Atlanta, 1906.
Carter, Adger McCrorey, "Public School Education in Georgia from 1850 to 1887." M. S. Thesis (University of Georgia, 1939).
Cheney, Sarah, "Francis Orray Ticknor," *Georgia Historical Quarterly*, XXII, 2 (June, 1938), 138-159.
Cheshire, Joseph B., *The Church in the Confederate States; A History of the Protestant Episcopal Church in the United States of America*. New York, 1914.
Christian, Rebecca, "Georgia and the Confederate Policy of Impressing Supplies," M. A. Thesis (Emory University, 1939).
Cleveland, Henry, *Alexander H. Stephens, in Public and Private. With Letters and Speeches, Before, During, and Since the War*. Philadelphia, 1866.
Cook, Anna Maria [Green], *History of Baldwin County*. Anderson, South Carolina, 1925.
Cooper, W. G., *Official History of Fulton County*. Atlanta, 1934.
Coulter, E. Merton, "A Century of a Georgia Plantation," *Mississippi Valley Historical Review*, XVI, 3 (Dec., 1929), 334-346.
——————, *College Life in the Old South*. New York, 1928.
——————, "Planters' Wants in the Days of the Confederacy," *Georgia Historical Quarterly*, XII, 1 (Mar., 1928), 38-52.
Cunyus, Lucy Josephine, *The History of Bartow County, Formerly Cass*. Cartersville, Georgia, 1933.
Derry, Joseph T., *Georgia*. Vol. VI in Clement A. Evans, *Confederate Military History*. 12 vols. Atlanta, 1899.
Eppes, Susan Bradford, *Through Some Eventful Years*. Macon, 1926.
Felton, Rebecca Latimer, *Country Life in Georgia in the Days of My Youth*. Atlanta, 1919.
——————, *My Memoirs of Georgia Politics*. Atlanta, 1911.
Fielder, Herbert, *A Sketch of the Life and Times and Speeches of Joseph E. Brown*. Springfield, Massachusetts, 1883.
Flanders, Bertram Holland, *Early Georgia Magazines: Literary Periodicals to 1865*. Athens, Georgia, 1944.
Flippin, Percy Scott, *Herschel V. Johnson of Georgia, State Rights Unionist*. Richmond, 1931.
Fox, W. F., *Regimental Losses in the American Civil War*. Albany, New York, 1898.
Griffith, Louis T. and John E. Talmadge, *Georgia Journalism, 1763-1950*. Athens, 1951.
Gray, Thomas S., Jr., "The March to the Sea," *Georgia Historical Quarterly*, XIV, 2 (June, 1930), 111-138.
Harper, Roland M., "Development of Agriculture in Lower Georgia

BIBLIOGRAPHY

from 1850 to 1880," *Georgia Historical Quarterly*, VI, 2 (June, 1922), 97-121.

————, "Development of Agriculture in Upper Georgia from 1850 to 1880," *Georgia Historical Quarterly*, VI, 1 (March, 1922), 3-27.

Harris, Joel Chandler, *On the Plantation*. New York, 1892.

Harris, Julia Collier, *Life and Letters of Joel Chandler Harris*. New York, 1918.

Hart, Bertha Sheppard, *Introduction to Georgia Writers*. Macon, 1929.

Harwell, Richard B., *Confederate Belles-Lettres*. Hattiesburg, Mississippi, 1941.

————, "A Reputation by Reflection: John Hill Hewitt and Edgar Allan Poe," *The Emory University Quarterly*, III, 1 (1947), 104-115.

Hay, Thomas Robson, "Davis, Bragg, and Johnston in the Atlanta Campaign," *Georgia Historical Quarterly*, VIII, 1 (Mar. 1924), 38-47.

Hays, Louise F., *History of Macon County, Georgia*. Atlanta, 1933.

Heard, George A., "St. Simons Island During the War Between the States," *Georgia Historical Quarterly*, XXII, 3 (Sept., 1938) 249-272.

Heathcote, Charles W., *The Lutheran Church and the Civil War*. New York, 1919.

Heckman, Oliver S., "Northern Church Penetration of the South, 1860 to 1880." Ph.D. Thesis (Duke University, 1939).

"Heroism of a Widow," *Southern Historical Society Papers*, XXIII (1895), 328-329.

Hesseltine, William B., *Civil War Prisons: A Study in War Psychology*. Columbus, Ohio, 1930.

Hill, Benjamin H., Jr., *Senator Benjamin H. Hill of Georgia*. Atlanta, 1893.

Hill, Louise Biles, *Joseph E. Brown and the Confederacy*. Chapel Hill, 1939.

Historical Sketch of Mercer University, 1833-1895. Macon, 1895.

History of the Baptist Denomination in Georgia: with Biographical Compendium and Portrait Gallery of Baptist Ministers and other Georgia Baptists. Atlanta, 1881.

A History of the Origin of Memorial Day As Adopted by the Ladies' Memorial Association of Columbus, Georgia. Columbus, Georgia, 1898.

Hull, Augustus L., *Annals of Athens, Georgia, 1801-1901*. Athens, Georgia, 1906.

————, *Historical Sketch of the University of Georgia*. Athens, 1894.

Huxford, Folks, "Early Methodism in South Georgia," *South Georgia Historical Collections*. Homerville, Georgia, 1947.

Irons, George V., "The Secession Movement in Georgia, 1850-61." Ph.D. Thesis (Duke University, 1936).

Johnson, Amanda, *Georgia As Colony and State*. Atlanta, 1938.
Johnston, Richard M. and William H. Browne, *Life of Alexander H. Stephens*. Philadelphia, 1878.
Jones, Charles C., Jr., *The Life and Services of Commodore Josiah Tattnall*. Savannah, 1878.
—————, and Salem Dutcher, *Memorial History of Augusta, Georgia*. Syracuse, 1890.
Jones, Charles E., *Education in Georgia*. United States Bureau of Education Contributions to American Educational History, edited by Herbert B. Adams. No. 5. Washington, 1889.
Knight, Lucian Lamar, *Georgia's Landmarks, Memorials, and Legends*. 2 vols. Atlanta, 1913.
—————, *A Standard History of Georgia and Georgians*. 6 vols. New York, 1917.
Lee, F. D., and J. L. Agnew, *Historical Record of the City of Savannah*. Savannah, 1869.
Little, Robert D., "General Hardee and the Atlanta Campaign," *Georgia Historical Quarterly*, XXIX, 1 (Mar., 1945), 1-22.
Lonn, Ella, *Desertion During the Civil War*. New York, 1928.
—————, *Foreigners in the Confederacy*. Chapel Hill, 1940.
—————, *Salt as a Factor in the Confederacy*. New York, 1933.
Marlin, Lloyd G., *The History of Cherokee County*. Atlanta, 1932.
Martin, John H., ed., *Columbus Geo., from its Selection as a "Trading Town" in 1827, to its Partial Destruction by Wilson's Raid, in 1865*. Columbus, Georgia, 1874.
McCallie, Elizabeth H., *The Atlanta Campaign*. Atlanta, 1939.
McElreath, Walter, *A Treatise on the Constitution of Georgia*. Atlanta, 1912.
McGuire, Peter S., "The Railroads of Georgia, 1860-1880," *Georgia Historical Quarterly*, XVI, 3 (Sept., 1932), 179-212.
McQueen, A. S., and Hamp Mizell, *History of Okefenokee Swamp*. Clinton, South Carolina, 1926.
Memoirs of Georgia. 2 vols. Atlanta, 1895.
Mitchell, Stephens, "Atlanta the Industrial Heart of the Confederacy," *Atlanta Historical Bulletin*, I, 3 (May, 1930), 20-32.
Moore, Albert B., *Conscription and Conflict in the Confederacy*. New York, 1924.
Northen, William J., *Men of Mark in Georgia*. 7 vols. Atlanta, 1907-1912.
Nottingham, Carolyn Walker and Evelyn Hannah, *History of Upson County, Georgia*. Macon, 1930.
Owsley, Frank L., *King Cotton Diplomacy; Foreign Relations of the Confederate States of America*. Chicago, 1931.
—————, *State Rights in the Confederacy*. Chicago, 1925.

BIBLIOGRAPHY

Pearce, Haywood J., Jr., *Benjamin H. Hill, Secession and Reconstruction*. Chicago, 1928.

Pendleton, Louis B., *Alexander H. Stephens*. Philadelphia, 1908.

Phillips, Ulrich B., *Georgia and State Rights. A Study of the Political History of Georgia from the Revolution to the Civil War, With Particular Regard to Federal Relations*. American Historical Association *Annual Report*, 1901. Vol. II. Washington, 1902.

——————, *The Life of Robert Toombs*. New York, 1913.

Pittman, Frances Harris, "Middle Georgia Life in the Fiction of Richard Malcolm Johnston." M. A. Thesis (Duke University, 1941).

"The Presbyterian Church on Secession and Slavery," *Georgia Historical Quarterly*, I, 3 (Sept., 1917), 263-265.

Ragsdale, B. D., *Story of Georgia Baptists*. 3 vols. Atlanta, 1932.

Ramsdell, Charles W., *Behind the Lines in the Southern Confederacy*. Baton Rouge, 1944.

——————, "Confederate Control of Manufacturing," *Mississippi Valley Historical Review*, VIII, 3 (Dec., 1921), 231-249.

Randall, James G., "The Newspaper Problem and Its Bearing Upon Military Secrecy During the Civil War," *American Historical Review*, XXII, 2 (Jan., 1918), 303-323.

Rosengarten, Joseph G., *The German Soldier in the Wars of the United States*. Philadelphia, 1886.

Roy, T. B., "General Hardee and the Military Operations Around Atlanta," *Southern Historical Society Papers*, VIII (1880), 337-387.

Sartain, James A., *History of Walker County, Georgia*. Dalton, Georgia, 1932.

Schwab, John C., *The Confederate States of America, 1861-1865; A Financial and Industrial History of the South During the Civil War*. New York, 1901.

Shryock, Richard H., *Georgia and the Union in 1850*. Durham, North Carolina, 1926.

Simkins, Francis B., and James W. Patton, *The Women of the Confederacy*. Richmond, 1936.

Smith, Ernest A., *The History of the Confederate Treasury*. Harrisburg, Pennsylvania, 1901.

Smith, George G., Jr., *The History of Georgia Methodism from 1786 to 1866*. Atlanta, 1913.

Stacy, James, *A History of the Presbyterian Church in Georgia*. Elberton, Georgia, 1912.

Stovall, Pleasant A., *Robert Toombs, Statesman, Speaker, Soldier, Sage*. New York, 1892.

Sumner, John O., ed., "Georgia and the Confederacy," *American Historical Review*, I, 1 (Oct., 1895), 97-102.

Tate, Luke E., *History of Pickens County*. Atlanta, 1935.

Tatum, Georgia Lee, *Disloyalty in the Confederacy.* Chapel Hill, 1934.
Telfair, Nancy, *A History of Columbus, Georgia, 1828-1928.* Columbus, Georgia, 1929.
Temple, Sarah B., *The First Hundred Years. A Short History of Cobb County, in Georgia.* Atlanta, 1935.
Thompson, C. Mildred, *Reconstruction in Georgia.* New York, 1915.
Underwood, John L., ed., *The Women of the Confederacy.* New York, 1906.
Von Abele, Rudolph, *Alexander H. Stephens.* New York, 1946.
Waddell, James D., *Biographical Sketch of Linton Stephens.* Atlanta, 1877.
Ware, Ethel K., *The Constitutional History of Georgia.* New York, 1946.
Weeks, Stephen B., "Confederate Text-Books (1861-1865): a Preliminary Survey," *Report of the Commissioner of Education, 1898-1899* (2 vols., Washington, 1900), I, 1139-1155.
Whitfield County History Commission. *Official History of Whitfield County, Georgia.* Dalton, Georgia, 1936.
Wiggins, Robert L., *Life of Joel Chandler Harris.* Nashville, Tenn., 1918.
Wiley, Bell I., *The Life of Johnny Reb, the Common Soldier of the Confederacy.* Indianapolis, 1943.
——————, *The Plain People of the Confederacy.* Baton Rouge, 1943.
——————, *Southern Negroes, 1861-1865.* New Haven, 1938.
Wood, Robert C., *Confederate Hand-Book; A Compilation of Important Data and Other Interesting and Valuable Matter Relating to the War Between the States, 1861-1865.* Washington, 1900.
Wyeth, John Allan, *Life of Lieutenant-General Nathan Bedford Forrest.* New York, 1908.

INDEX

Adair, George W., 43
Agriculture, affected by war, 119-122; diversification of, 122; scarcity of farm labor, 134; decline of, 136
Albany *Patriot*, 203
Americus, 31
Americus *Sumter Republican*, 156, 203
Amusements, *see* Social life
Anderson, George W., 74, 172
Anderson, Jeff, 144
Andersonville Prison, 159, 161-162
Andrews, Eliza Frances, 11, 196
Andrews, Garnett, opposes secession, 4, 11
Andrews, James J., raid of, 75, 76
Arms, problem of, 22-26
Army and Navy Herald, 211, 237
Arsenals, 23, 24, 83, 102, 103, 169, 248
Ash, John H., 167
Ashe, William S., 112
Athens, 58, 103, 175, 207
Atlanta, 58, 117, 144, 150, 248; and military industries, 28, 102; disloyalty in, 138; pillaged by Georgians, 150; Battle of, 162; fall of, 163; destruction of, 164, 165
Atlanta Arsenal, 24, 102
Atlanta *Daily Intelligencer*, 33, 203, 206
Atlanta Female Institute, 190
Atlanta *Southern Confederacy*, 203, 206
Atlanta and West Point Railroad, 110, 117
Atlantic and Gulf Railroad, 110, 111, 117
Augusta, 28, 29, 58, 223; seizure of arsenal at, 12; and military industries, 103; disloyalty in, 139
Augusta Arsenal, 12, 24, 83, 102, 103
Augusta *Chronicle and Sentinel*, 139, 203-206, 268
Augusta *Constitutionalist*, 201, 203, 209
Avery, Isaac W., 7, 19
Axson, Ellen Louise, 272
Axson, S. Edward, 242, 272

Bainbridge, 127
Banks, purchase of bonds by, 49, 58; liabilities of, 59; and change bills, 59; depreciation of capital of, 64
Baptists, 229, 230, 232, 234-240, 243, 245
Bartow, Francis S., 8, 12
Beauregard, P. G. T., 16, 88, 117, 168, 171
Beckwith, John W., 241
Beebe, William L., 238, 272
Beers, Fannie, 179, 196
Benjamin, Judah P., 84
Berry, Harrison, 128
Bibb County, 26
Bibles, supply of, 236, 237
Bill Arp (Charles H. Smith), 159, 212
Birch, E. P., 213
Blackmar and Brother, music publishers, 201
Blackshear, 154
Blind Tom, musician, 31, 190
Blockade, in diplomacy, 119
Blockade running, 148
Blome and Tehan, publishers, 201
Bonds, *see* Confederate securities, and State securities
Booker's Negro Minstrels, 189
Boughton, Nisbet, and Barnes, publishers, 201
Boykin, Samuel, 242, 243
Bragg, Braxton, 77-79, 95
Brent, George W., 116, 117
Bristow, G. F., 129
Brown, Joseph E., 12, 20, 21, 36, 37, 45-47, 58, 64, 94, 104, 111-113, 115, 119, 123, 128, 132, 133, 140, 142-144, 146, 148, 150, 152, 158, 159, 163, 164, 168-171, 210, 222, 249; advocates secession, 1, 3; seizes Fort Pulaski, 6; seizes Augusta Arsenal, 12; calls for volunteers, 18; organizes troops, 22; problem of arms, 22-26; problem of army clothing, 27, 28, 38, 104; third term election, 33-36; curbs liquor, 38-40; salt,

40, 41; fourth term election, 41-45; bonds, notes, and taxes, 48, 49, 55, 56, 58, 121-122; funding act, 54, 135, 136; speculation, 60; coastal defense, 66, 67, 69, 70, 72; state militia, 72, 87, 90, 163; controversy over state troops, 80-83; conflict over arms, 83, 84; opposes conscription, 86-90; exemption of state officers, 86, 143; Confederate reserves, 89; opposes impressment, 91-93; blockade runners, 94; seizure of state railroad, 95; habeas corpus and peace resolutions, 95-97
Brown, William G., 20
Browne, William M., 87
Brunswick and Florida Railroad, 112
Bryan, A. M., 116
Buckner, S. B., 147
Bugle-Horn of Liberty, 211
Burge, Dolly Sumner Lunt, 167
Burge, Lou, 191, 192, 267
Burke, Boykin and Company, publishers, 201, 227
Burke, J. W., 236
Byrd, William H., 261

Caldwell, John H., 212
Calhoun, James M., 43, 95, 163
Camp Davis, 22
Camp McDonald, 22, 81, 190
Camp Rough and Ready, 163
Camp Spaulding, 141
Camp Stephens, 22
Campbell, John A., 100
Campbell, J. H., 235
Capers, F. W., 26
Carrollton *Advocate*, 3
Cass County, 26
Cassville, 157
Catholics, 230, 233-235, 245, 271
Cazier, Mrs. M. C., 180
Central of Georgia Railroad, 40, 110, 111, 114, 116
Change bills, 59
Chattanooga, 77, 79
Chattanooga *Rebel*, 207
Cherokee Indians, 238, 244
Chickamauga, Battle of, 77, 79
Child's Index, The, 198, 211, 240
Chivers, Mrs. Harriet, 182
Christian Church, 230, 235, 271
Christian Index, 211, 243
Churches, 237, 238, 271; condition of, in 1860, 230; loyalty of, to Confederacy, 232-234; disruption of, 239, 241; interest of, in slaves, 242-245; losses of, 243, 244; growth of, 245; *see also* Clergy, and denominations
Clark, Josiah A., 83
Class feeling, and war, 144
Clergy, unionism among, 230, 231; support of secession by, 230, 231; loyalty of, 231-236, 240, 271; difficulties of, 239, 241, 244, 245; opposition to Federal authority, 242; welfare of slaves, 241-243
Cleveland, Henry, 99
Clinton, 169, 170
Clothing for troops, problem of, 26-29, 38
Coastal defenses, 253
Cobb, Howell, 7, 10, 12, 15, 21, 51, 53, 80, 90, 151, 152, 160, 168, 171-173; urges secession, 2; president of Montgomery convention, 13; considered for presidency of Confederacy, 13; enters military service, 19; and Confederate reserves, 88, 89; opposes enlisting slaves as Confederate troops, 133; opposes conscription, 153
Cobb, Mrs. Howell, 249
Cobb, John A., 259
Cobb, Thomas R. R., 12, 13, 19, 23; urges secession, 2, 5, 7, 8
Columbus, 31, 58, 72, 132, 147, 173; and military industries, 28, 102; and cotton and woolen mills, 104
Columbus *Daily Sun*, 203
Columbus *Enquirer*, 203, 206
Columbus Iron Works Company, 102
Columbus *Times*, 203, 206
Comer, Laura, 125, 126
Commissary Department, Confederate, 248
Commonwealth, The, 201
Confederate cemetery, 185, 186
Confederate debts, 54, 55; state support of, 49, 50, 52, 53; *see also* Confederate securities
Confederate Produce Loan, 50, 52
Confederate securities, note and bond issue of 1861, 49, 55, 251; produce loan, 50, 52; proposal for guarantee of, 53; depreciation of, 54; funding of, 54, 55, 108; counterfeiting, 59, 60; inflation

INDEX

of, 61, 62, 108, 109; repudiation of, 65, 219
Confederate States Bible Society, 236
Confederate States Railroad and Steamboat Guide, 202
Congregational Church, 273
Conscription, Act of April, 1862, opposition to, 85-87; press opinion of, 86, 87; Act of Sept., 1862, opposed by Brown and Stephenses, 87; opposed by Brown, 89; exemptions, 89, 142, 143; resistance to, 90, 138, 139, 142, 144-146, 148, 153-155; and purchase of substitutes, 143, 144, 262; Act of 1864, 250
Constitution, Confederate, 12, 13
Constitution, state, features of Constitution of 1861, 13, 14; ratification of, 14, 247
Conyngham, David R., 128
Cooper, Mark A., 106
Co-operationists, 5, 246
Cotton, proposals for government purchase of, 50-53; Confederate produce loan on, 50, 52; taxation of, 56; production of, 118, 258; embargo on, 118, 119, 258; limiting its production, 118-122, 259; trade of, through blockade 148
Cotton Planters Bank of Georgia, 120 258
Countryman, The, 210, 211, 269
Coweta County, 24, 63
Crawford, George W., 6, 246
Crawford, Martin J., 12, 21, 52
Crawford, N. M., 242
Crumbley, W. M., 120
Cumming, Joseph B., 150, 151, 254
Cumming, Kate, 151
Cummings, J. F., 91
Cunningham, G. W., 257
Cuyler, R. M., 24, 103

Dabney, Thomas, Jr., 160
Dade County, 139, 262
Dahlonega, 79, 140, 145, 182
Dallas, 157
Dalton, 79, 103, 106, 156, 157, 187, 236
Dana, Charles A., 78
Dances, 191, 198, 200
Davis, Jefferson, 20-22, 34, 86-89, 94, 100, 159, 231; elected President of Confederacy, 13; receives ovation in Georgia, 14; and controversy over state troops, 80-83; asks farmers to plant corn, 92; and habeas corpus and peace resolutions, 95-99; favors enrolling slaves as Confederate troops, 134; relieves Johnston of command, 158; visits Hood's army, 164; and exemption of students, 217
Davis, Moses W., 34, 66
Decatur, 176
DeRenne, George Wymberley Jones, 215
Desertion, action against, 137, 138, 144-148, 152-155; lawlessness of deserters, 140, 141; causes of, 140-143; terrorism of deserters, 144-146, 151-155; number of, 261; *see also* Disloyalty
Disloyalty, among Northerners and foreigners, 137-141; prevalence of, in North Georgia, 139, 140, 144-146, 151-154; causes of, 141; Peace Society, 147; increase of, 148-151
Draft, *see* Conscription
Dueling, 199
DuPont, S. F., 253

Eagle Manufacturing Company, 104, 106, 108, 223, 257
Eatonton, 168
Education, University of Georgia, 216, 217; church, 217-221; higher education of women, 219-221; medical, 221; grade school and academy, 222-229; textbook deficiency in, 226; orphan, 229, 270
Elections, 4, 5, 33-37, 41-47
Elliott, Stephen, 231, 233, 234, 237, 238, 240, 244
Elliott, Stephen, Jr., 20
Emory College, impact of war upon, 217-219
Enlistment, 248
Episcopalians, 230-235, 237, 241, 244, 245
Estill, J. H., 206
Etowah Iron Works, 106, 107, 117
Evans, Mollie, 143
Exemptions, from military service, 89, 90, 142, 143, *see also* Conscription
Ezra Church, Battle of, 162

Fannin County, 146, 152, 183
Finances, *see* Confederate securities, and State securities, and Taxation
Findley, James J., 154

293

Fingal, blockade-runner, 254
Flash, Henry Lynden, 213
Folsom, James M., 212
Foreign volunteers, 52, 53
Foreigners, 21, 138-140, 144, 148, 261
Forest City Foundry, 113, 114
Fort, Martha Low, 7, 174
Fort McAllister, 74, 172, 253
Fort Pulaski, 253, 254; seized by Georgia, 6; attacked and captured by Federals, 70-72
Forrest, Nathan Bedford, captures Streight's army, 77
Foster, Ira R., 28, 98
Fuller, William A., 76
Furlow, Timothy M., 43, 44

Gainesville, 139, 155
Gainesville Eagle, 203
Galt, E. M., 145
Gardner, James, 42, 203, 209
Gate City Guardian, 206
Gatewood, John, 152
Georgia Academy for the Blind, 221, 222
Georgia Forester, 204
Georgia Historical Society, 215
Georgia Literary and Temperance Crusader, 211
Georgia Military Institute, 143, 224
Georgia Platform, 2, 246
Georgia Railroad, 110, 111, 114-117, 165
Georgia Relief and Hospital Association, 29-31
Georgia Supreme Court, 91, 92, 255
Georgia Weekly, 209
Gibson, Samuel H., 261
Gillmore, Q. A., 254
Gilmer County, 152
Godon, S. W., 75
Grant, L. P., 117
Grant, Ulysses S., 79, 156
Graves, Henry, 195
Green, Anna Maria, 195
Green, Mary, 185
Grier's Almanac, 202
Griffin, J. R., 153

Habeas corpus, opposition to suspension of writ of, 95-99
Habersham County, 145
Haiman and Brother, manufacturers, 102
Halleck, H. A., 264
Hambleton, James B., 203

Hanleiter, C. R., 140, 141
Hardee, William J., 38, 158, 161-163, 172, 272
Harden, Edward R., 142
Harris, Joel Chandler, 201, 210, 211
Harris, W. L., 2
Harris County Enterprise, 204
Hazen, W. B., 172
Hearn Institute, 224
Hewitt, John Hill, 189, 214, 267
Higginson, Thomas Wentworth, 75
Hill, Benjamin H., 4, 7, 10-12, 50, 88, 96, 147; opposes secession, 2, 3, 8, 9; elected to Confederate Senate, 37; supports Confederate administration, 80, 87, 96
Hill, Joshua, 164; candidate for governor, 43-45
Hitchcock, Henry, 166
Holt, T. L., 108
Home guards, 31, 185
Hood, John B., 117, 158, 162, 163, 165, 166
Hopkins, T. S., 74
Horse races, 199
Hospital relief societies, 179
Hospitals, 29-31
Howard, Charles Wallace, 231, 235
Howard, Mrs. Charles Wallace, 183
Howard, O. O., 166, 167, 169, 170
Hudtwalcker, I. N., 139
Huff, James H., 106
Hughs, Richard, 18
Hussey, J. J., 51

Impressment of supplies, opposition to, 90-93, 142
Industry, *see* Manufacturing
Inflation, *see* Confederate securities
Irwin, David, 34
Iverson, Alfred, 37, 160

Jackson, Henry R., 15, 25, 26, 38, 68-70, 84, 85, 198
Jackson, Henry W. R., 212
Jasper County, 185
Jenkins, Charles J., 47, 246
Jewish church, 271
"Joe Brown Pikes," 26
Johnson, Andrew, 47
Johnson, George O., 38
Johnson, Herschel V., 45, 80, 95, 164, 246, 256; opposes secession, 2-4, 7-9,

..INDEX

11; opposes conscription, 85; opposes impressment, 91, 93; supports Davis, 96
Johnson, James, 47
Johnston, Albert Sidney, 25
Johnston, Joseph E., 79, 95, 106, 115, 148, 159, 186, 187; and Atlanta campaign, 156-158; removed from command, 158
Johnston, Richard Malcolm, 19, 32, 122, 212, 216, 217, 224
Jones, Charles C., 242
Jones, Charles C., Jr., 211
Jones, Seaborn, 81
Jones, William Louis, 211
Jonesboro, Battle of, 162, 163
Jordan, L. A., 121
"Jordan's Gang," 152
Judah, Henry M., 155

Kenan, Augustus H., 12, 20, 96
Kennesaw Mountain, Battle of, 157, 158
Kilpatrick, Judson, 166, 169
King, T. Butler, 75
King, William, 164
Kingston, 76, 127
Kingston Home Guards, 137
Knoxville *Register*, 207

Labor, in manufacturing, 104, 105, 109, 110; on railroads, 114; on plantations, 122-126, 135, 136
LaCoste, Marie, 213
Ladies' Gunboat Association, 178
Ladies' Memorial Association, 186
LaGrange, 27, 58, 185, 196, 199
LaGrange Female College, 220
LaGrange *Reporter*, 3
Lamar, Albert R., 6
Lamar, John B., 130
Lamar, Lucius Q. C., 96
Lathrop, Henry, 38
Lathrop and Company, manufacturers, 27
Lawrenceville, 103, 104
Lawton, Alexander R., 84, 85, 106; seizes Fort Pulaski, 6; at Savannah, 68-70, 73
LeConte, Joseph, 129
Lee, G. W., 146
Lee, Robert E., and coastal defense, 68-70, 84, 85
Leggett, M. D., 150
Lewis, John W., 37, 249

Libraries, 214, 215
Lincoln, Abraham, 1, 14-16, 164
Lipscomb, Andrew A., 119, 217
Liquor, suppression of distillation of, 38-40
Little Ada, blockade-runner, 94
Lloyd, Thomas E., 34
Logan, Joseph P., 7
Long, John, 152
Longstreet, Augustus Baldwin, 212
Lucy Cobb Institute, 221
Lufborrow and Timmons, manufacturers, 113, 114
Lumpkin, Joseph Henry, 246
Lumpkin, Wilson, 246
Lumpkin County, 145, 146
Lutherans, 230, 233, 238, 239, 245, 271
Lyon, Richard F., 132, 246

McBurney, James C., 150
"McCollum's Scouts," 152
McCoy, Thomas S., 116
McDonald, Charles J., 246
McIntosh, Lachlan H., 25, 26, 66, 67, 83
Macon, 18, 26, 58, 144, 160, 161; and military industries, 102, 103
McPeek, Allie, 184
McPherson, James B., 158
Macon Arsenal, 102, 103
Macon *Daily Telegraph*, 203, 204, 206, 207
Macon Manufacturers Company, 108
Macon and Western Railroad, 110, 111, 116, 117, 133
Madison, 168
Mallett, J. W., 133
Manufacturing, 101, 107, 110, 257; of munitions, 23-26; of clothing, 27, 28; military industries, 101-103; cotton mills, 103-105; woolen mills, 105; boot and shoe factories, 105, 106; iron industries, 106, 107; and profiteering, 108, 109
Marietta, 27, 75, 157, 158, 232
Marietta Paper Mill, 107
Marion County, 142
Marshall College, 269
Martin, William, 9
Maynard, R. I., 237
Means, Alexander, 8, 231, 235, 236
Memminger, Christopher G., 52, 53, 55, 234
Memorial of Savannah banks, 59

..295..

Memphis *Appeal*, 207
Mercer, George A., 74, 75, 138, 142, 147, 148
Mercer, Hugh W., 73, 132, 133, 267
Mercer University, impact of war upon, 218
Merchants and Planters Bank, 58
Methodists, 230-232, 234-239, 241-245
Military inventions, 60, 61
Milledgeville, 2, 10, 103, 168, 170, 174, 175, 191
Milledgeville *Confederate Union*, 206
Milledgeville *Federal Union*, 203
Milledgeville *Southern Recorder*, 203
Milledgeville Telegraph Company, 208
Millen, 161, 170
Money, and currency shortage, 50-53; depreciation of, 54; change bills, 59; counterfeiting of, 59, 60; inflation, 61, 65; *see also* Confederate securities, and State securities
Montfort, Theodorick W., 29
Montgomery, Confederate convention at, 12, 13
Morgan, Mrs. J. Brown, 185
Morgan County, 263
Morse, N. S., 206, 268
Murray County, 140, 142, 263

Naval engagements, 67, 68, 74
"Nancy Harts," 185
Neal, A. J., 79, 157, 263
Negroes, 10, 56, 117, 124, 125, 128-131, 133, 134, 168; in United States army, 75; crimes of, 126, 127; social life of, 131, 132; free Negroes, 131, 270; after emancipation, 135, 136; *see also* Slaves
Newnan, 10, 196, 241
Newspapers, attitude toward secession, 3, 4, 6; condition of, in 1860, 202-204; hardships of, in war, 204-207; changes of, 206, 207; employees of, go to war, 204; subscription and advertising rates of, 204, 205; newsgathering agencies 207, 208; censorship, 208; loyalty of editors of, 208, 209
Newton County, 18, 166
Newton Factory, 105
Nisbet, Eugenius A., 12; leader of secession convention, 7, 8; candidate for governor, 34-36
Nisbet, James A., 19, 256

Nonslaveholders, influenced by Brown, 10
North Georgia Citizen, 203, 206
Nurses, 179, 180

Oglethorpe University, impact of war upon, 219
Okefenokee Swamp, 146
Olmstead, Charles H., 70, 71
O'Reilly, Thomas, 165
Orphans, education of, 229
Orr, Gustavus J., 105
Orr, James L., 7
Ossabaw Island, 74
Overseers, difficulties of planters with, 122, 124; problems of, 123; exemption of, from military service, 123, 124
Oxford, 217, 218

Parks, W. J., 218
Peace movements, 96-99, 147, 153, 163, 164, 172
Peace Society, 147
Peachtree Creek, Battle of, 162
Phillips, William, 152
Pickens County, 139, 145, 152
Pierce, George F., 230, 231, 236, 239, 240, 243
Pike County, 146
Pillow, Gideon J., 147
Plantation, The, 210, 269
Planters, and produce loan, 50-52; and curtailment of cotton, 119, 122; and problems of overseers and slaves, 122-134; after the war, 135, 136
Pledger, Wesley P., 269
Porter, R. K., 231
Pratt, Nathaniel A., 230
Presbyterians, 230-234, 238, 242, 245, 271
Press Association of the Confederate States, 207, 208
Profiteering, 60, 62, 108, 109
Propaganda, newspaper, 6, 171, 208; religious, 240
Pye, Benier, 183

Quartermaster Department, Confederate, 248

Railroads, 114, 115; condition of, at outbreak of war, 110; impressment of rolling stock, 112; maintenance of, in wartime, 112-114; and conscription,

INDEX

114; and decreasing revenue of, 115
116; criticism of, 116; destruction of
116, 117; rehabilitation of, 117
Rains, George W., 103
Randolph, George W., 84, 86
Reese, Augustus, 8
Religion, in army, 236, 237; increase of, 237, 238; relapse of, 240, 241; *see also* Churches, and Clergy
Resaca, Battle of, 157
Reynolds, A. W., 53, 154
Reynolds, W. W., 173
Rhett, Robert Barnwell, 2, 7
Richardson, John M., 212
Richardson, S. P., 242
Riley, Harrison W., 140
Ringgold, 76, 156, 196, 241
Roberts, Hiram, 58, 66, 67
Roberts, Sam, 152
Rogers, Louise, 213
Roman, Alfred, 171, 172
Rome, 58, 77, 103, 151
Rome *Courier*, 203
Rome Female College, 221
Rosecrans, William S., 77-79
Roswell, 105
Rudler, A. F., 18
Ruffin, Edmund, 2
Russell, William Howard, 21
Rutherford, Mary Elizabeth, 186

St. Simons Island, 30, 68, 70, 75
Salt, efforts to obtain, 40, 41
Sandersville, 170
Sandersville *Central Georgian*, 203
Savannah, 10, 27, 58, 66, 67, 130, 153, 199, 223; defense of, 68-70, 72, 73; disloyalty in, 138, 139; capture of, by Federals, 172
Savannah Arsenal, 83, 103
Savannah and Augusta Railroad, 114
Savannah *Daily Herald*, 206
Savannah *Daily Morning News*, 202-206, 208, 268
Savannah *Republican*, 203, 206
Schreiner, Herman L., 214
Schreiner, J. C., 201
Scott, Irby H., 28, 135
Seago, A. K., 40
Secession, attitude toward, 3, 4; convention elections, 4, 5; convention of January, 1861, 6-9; Ordinance of, 8; opposition to, 8, 9; reasons for, 10;

reaction to, 10, 11; Convention of March, 1861, 13, 15
Secessionists, reasons for victory of, 5, 6
Seddon, James A., 89, 90, 93, 158
Seward, William H., 251
Sherman, T. W., 253
Sherman, William T., 116, 149, 150; Atlanta campaign, 156-159, 162, 163; destruction of Atlanta, 164, 165; peace negotiations of, 164; march to the sea, 166-172
Shorter, John G., 7
Sinclair, Carrie Belle, 213
Slaveholders, 5, 10; wartime problems of 122-126, 134, 135; exodus of, from state, 135
Slaves, impressment of, by Confederacy, 73, 133, 134; difficulty of controlling, 124-128; loyalty of, 128, 129; escape of, to Federals, 127, 128; problem of caring for, 129, 130; prices of, 130, 131; in army, 133, 134; religious care of, in war, 241-243; number of, 259; *see also* Negroes
Slocum, H. W., 166, 168
Smets, A. A., 215
Smith, Charles H., *see* Bill Arp
Smith, George G., 230, 235, 244, 245
Smith, Gustavus W., 159, 167
Smith, J. Henly, 50, 86
Smith, Norman W., 116
Sneed, James R., 250
Social life, theatrical performances, 188-190; at military camps, 190, 191; parties, 191, 196; love and romance, 191, 192, 194, 195; weddings, 193, 194; reading, 196, 197; dancing and music, 197; at Christmas, 198, 199
Soldiers' Aid Societies, 174-176
Soldiers' Friend, 211, 237
Soldiers' relief funds, 62, 63, 174-176, 253
Soldiers' Tract Association, 236
Southern Baptist Messenger, 204, 272
Southern Cultivator, 207, 211
Southern Female College, 225
Southern Field and Fireside, 201, 209, 210
Southern Literary Companion, 211
Southern Masonic Female College, 270
Southwestern Railroad, 110, 117
Speculation, 60-62, 148
Spencer, George, 170
Stafford, James B., 20

297 ..

Starr, Orr, and Stewart, manufacturers, 105
State debts, 48, 64, 65
State penitentiary, 25, 27, 169
State rights, 1-4, 7, 8, 36, 46, 53, 80-100; see also Brown, conscription, habeas corpus, impressment, H. V. Johnson, Stephens, Toombs
State securities, notes and bonds of, 48-50; treasury notes, 55, 56, 64; certificates of deposit, 64; depreciation of, 64; mortgage bonds of 1866, 65
Steadman, Enoch, 229
Steele, John H., 203
Stephens, Alexander H., 7, 12, 22, 23, 26, 30, 33, 34, 36, 37, 39, 44, 46, 49, 50, 54, 66, 80, 81, 125, 126, 246, 256; opposes secession, 2, 8, 10; elected Vice-President of Confederacy, 13; receives requests for military and civil appointments, 19, 20; opposes seizure of salt, 40; urges Brown to seek re-election, 41, 42; and purchase of cotton, 51-53; and Confederate financial acts, 54, 94; opposes conscription, 85, 86; opposes impressment, 92; and habeas corpus and peace, 95-100; refuses to confer with Sherman, 164
Stephens, Linton, 19, 41, 42, 46, 80, 241, 255; denounces Walker, 81; opposes conscription, 87; and habeas corpus and peace, 96-99; difficulties with slaves, 124, 125
Stewart County, 63
Stiles, Carey M., 68
Stockton and Company, publishers, 201
Stoneman, George, raid by, 159-161
Streight, Abel D., raid by, 76, 77

Tattnall, Josiah, 15; and coastal defense, 67, 68, 70
Taxation (Confederate), tax of 1861, 49; tax of 1863, 53, 54; tax in kind, unpopularity of, 53, 54; collection of taxes, 94, 142, 154; funding act, 134-136
Taxation (local), 26, 27, 63
Taxation (State), 48; collection of taxes, 53, 54, 64; ad valorem tax, 56; general property tax, 56; profit and income tax, 57, 58
Tefft, Israel K., 215
Textbooks, 227

Theatrical performances, 188-191
Thomas, George H., 78, 158, 166
Thomas, James R., 217, 218, 231
Thomas, Thomas W., 36, 98
Thompson, William T., 201, 202
Thrasher, J. J., 43
Thweatt, Peterson, 19, 26, 37, 64, 98; and gubernatorial election of 1863, 41, 42; and state bonds, 49, 50; and state taxes, 56-58; disapproves Brown's policy of mustering troops, 81, 82; urges limitation of cotton, 120; home wrecked by Federals, 169
Ticknor, Francis Orray, 212
Toombs, Robert, 12, 15, 80, 100, 159, 164, 247, 250, 255; secessionists, 2, 6, 8, 9; not elected President of Confederacy, 13; Secretary of State, 13; enters military service, 19; refuses senatorial position, 37; considered for governor, 41, 42; refuses to limit cotton acreage, 42, 92; not elected to Confederate Senate, 45; favors funding act, 53; opposes conscription, 85; opposes impressment, 91, 92, 142; opposes Confederate financial policies, 93, 94; opposes martial law, 95
Toon, J. J., and Company, publishers, 227
Trade with enemy, 147, 148
Trenholme, George A., 93
Troy Manufacturing Company, 107
Tucker, Henry H., 29, 30, 243
Tupper, H. A., 240
Turner, Joseph Addison, 27, 92, 134, 209-211, 215
Turner, William Wilberforce, 210
Tybee Island, 67, 68, 70, 71, 254

Union churches, 230, 271
Union Society, 229, 271
Unionists, 11, 43, 137-142, 147, 150, 152; see also Disloyalty
Universalist churches, 271
University of Georgia, impact of war upon, 216, 217
Upson County, 63
Upson Pilot, 204

Vickery, John, 127
Volunteers, call for, 18; number and character of, 18-22; mustering of, 80-82; transfer of, 82, 83

INDEX

Waddel, Moses, 269
Walker, Alexander C., 170, 171
Walker, L. P., 21-23, 66, 80, 81, 83
Walker, William H. T., 68, 69
Walker County, 139
Walsh, W. D., 217
Warren, E. W., 212
Washington, Ga., 27
Waters, H. H., 39
Watterson, Henry, 98
Wayne, Henry C., 24, 25, 28, 39, 68, 69, 72, 84, 85, 139, 145, 146, 159
Waynesboro *Independent South*, 205
Wayside Homes, 30, 178, 179, 235
Weddings, 193, 194
Wesleyan Christian Advocate, 211
Wesleyan Female College, 192, 220
Western and Atlantic Railroad, 48, 62, 75, 76, 110, 112-117, 222
Westmoreland, Maria J., 269
West Point, 175
Wheeler, Joseph, 79, 168, 170, 171
Whitaker, Jared I., 33, 203, 249

Wilbur, Aaron, 38, 94, 148
Wilson, J. H., 173
Wilson, James M., 117
Wilson, Joseph R., 270
Wirz, Henry, 162
Wofford, William T., 81, 154, 155
Women, engaged in making clothing, 27, 174-178; aid soldiers, 31, 174-177; styles of clothing of, 177, 178; raise gunboat funds, 178; establish wayside homes, 178, 179; in hospital service, 179, 180; problems of, 180, 181; bravery of, 182-185; loyalty of, 185-187; promiscuity of, 187; social life of, 190-199; education of, 220, 221, 223, 225, 228, 229
Woodrow, James, 232
Wright, A. R., 12, 41
Wright, R. K., 164
Wynnton Male Academy, 224

Yancey, William L., 7